MW00909774

Desserts	50 States Cookbook	Try

1. Connecticut Crullers pg. 14
2. Bluberry Pie pg. 19
3. Baked Apple Duplings pg. 19
4. Wellesley Fudge Cake & Icing pg. 26 _Not worth it_
5. Funnel Cakes pg. 73
6. Shoofly Pie pg. 73
7. Philadelphia Ice Cream pg. 74
8. Mobile Pecan Cake & Icing pg. 80
9. Georgian Pecan Cookies pg. 92
10. Pain Purdu pg. 103 (French Toast)
11. Black Bottom Pie pg. 110
12. Plantion Sour Cream Cookies pg. 110
13. Peachy Cornbread Shortcake pg. 145
14. Irish Scones pg. 151

The FIFTY STATES Cookbook

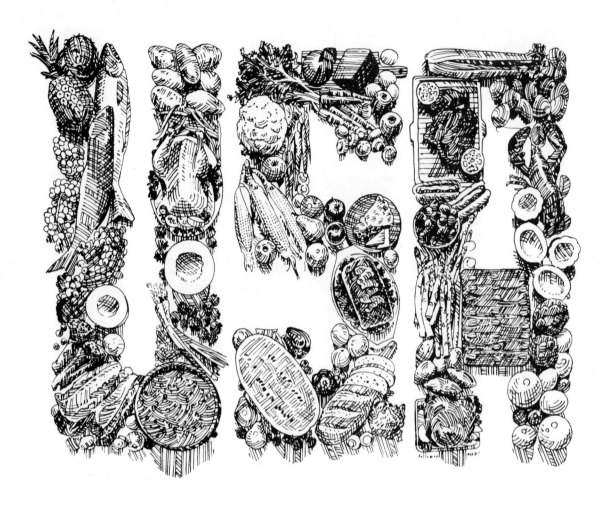

THE FIFTY STATES COOKBOOK

Barbara MacDonald, Carolyn Boisvert, and Peggy Miller:
Contributing Editors

The Culinary Arts Institute Staff:

Helen Geist: Director
Sherrill Corley: Editor • Helen Lehman: Assistant Editor
Edward Finnegan: Executive Editor • Charles Bozett: Art Director
Ethel La Roche: Editorial Assistant • Ivanka Simatic: Recipe Tester
Malinda Miller: Copy Editor • John Mahalek: Art Assembly

Book designed and coordinated by Charles Bozett and Laurel DiGangi

Illustrations by Dev Appleyard

Cover photograph by Zdenek Pivecka

The FIFTY STATES Cookbook

Culinary Arts Institute

1727 South Indiana Avenue, Chicago, Illinois 60616

Copyright © 1977

by

Consolidated Book Publishers

All rights reserved under the International and Pan-American Copyright
Conventions. Manufactured in the United States of America and published
simultaneously in Canada by Nelson, Foster & Scott, Ltd., Willowdale, Ontario.

Library of Congress Catalog Card Number: 76-53101
International Standard Book Number: 0-8326-0600-6

PHOTO ACKNOWLEDGMENTS

Adolph's Ltd.; Advisory Council for Jams, Jellies and Preserves;
American Dairy Association; American Lamb Council;
American Spice Trade Association; Bob Scott Studios;
California Apricot Advisory Board; California Avocado Advisory Board;
California Wine Institute; Florida Department of Citrus;
Fresh Bartlett Promotion Advisory Board; Glenn Embree; Halibut Association of North America;
Idaho Oregon Sweet Spanish Onion Promotion Committee; The McIlhenny Company (Tabasco);
National Fisheries Institute; Nectarine Administrative Committee;
The Quaker Oats Company; South African Rock Lobster Association;
Spanish Green Olive Commission; Washington State Apple Commission; Wheat Flour Institute

FOREWORD

How thirteen colonies became fifty states is a story that never fails to fascinate Americans. It unfolds like a drama, with scenes changing from frost-bitten New England to the Mid-Atlantic seaboard, down through the South, across the Midwest, Southwest, and West, and reaches its climax with the entry of Alaska and Hawaii.

As the settings changed, so did the ways of the people. The newcomers brought their old-world cooking styles with them, but as they moved, their recipes were adapted to suit the food at hand. The new land actually shaped the people as much as they shaped it.

The European arrivals found their new home already occupied by people with cooking methods different from their own. From the Indians and Mexicans they acquired new ways that eased their assimilation into the New World.

Those early Americans felt that they had a "manifest destiny" to claim the continent. Given a twentieth-century perspective, their push westward is taken for granted. But from their standpoint it must have seemed an enormous challenge, considering the difficulty of meeting everyday needs in unfamiliar surroundings.

Today's cook has it far easier. The land has been won, and so has the battle with Nature for food. The supermarket offers everything we need, often in a form ready to eat with no further effort.

But since less time is needed to find food, more is available to cook it in interesting ways. One of the techniques of creative cooks is to borrow from the culinary heritage of early America.

Another is to make the acquaintance of recipes from other regions. Today, space and time are no longer obstacles; modern travel accommodations make it possible to go from coast to coast—or to Hawaii—in just hours. Such mobility has introduced Americans to the foods of other states, and this has helped them to vary daily menus when back home. And modern transportation carries the specialty foods from one state to all the rest, making regional recipes easy to duplicate, given the appropriate recipes.

Realizing the need to update heirloom "receipts" into today's language and for use with today's food products, the CULINARY ARTS INSTITUTE has tested and compiled those most representative of the various regions. The biggest challenge to the editors was the selection and placement of the recipes. Some dishes, such as apple pie, belong as much to one state as another. In such cases, the recipe was placed to give balance, so that the chapter for each state provides the makings for a complete menu. To find a specific dish, look in the index.

The CULINARY ARTS INSTITUTE has discriminated carefully among possible recipes in making the selections for each state. Entries were selected to give as much variety as possible. Other recipes were well qualified to be included, but space limited the selection.

Since 1936, the CULINARY ARTS INSTITUTE has supplied American cooks with some of their best-known and most widely used cookbooks and booklets. CULINARY ARTS INSTITUTE recipes have all been prepared in its test kitchen and approved by a taste panel before publication.

Not only will *The Fifty States Cookbook* provide you with a broader perspective of American cooking; you will also find it a source of greater variety and enjoyment at mealtime.

CONTENTS

Connecticut, third smallest state in the United States, is also a favorite vacationland of contrasting beauty and great diversity. It is famous for both its picturesque rural towns and its huge urban centers. Most of its people live and work within the boundaries of the state, but there are many who commute miles each day into the metropolitan environs of New York City. Thus, today, the traditional New England modes of eating and living are being combined with those of a vast eastern megalopolis. For example, typical New England clam chowder never contains tomatoes. But in Connecticut, this chowder is prepared with tomatoes and is referred to as "Manhattan" clam chowder.

The first white settlers arrived in Connecticut in 1633 from the Netherlands. They built a small fort near Hartford, today's capital, but were never considered a permanent community. It was the English colonists from Massachusetts, led by Thomas Hooker, Roger Ludlow, and John Haynes in the 1600s, who, wanting to flee from the rigid authoritarianism of their former communities, built permanent homes along the Connecticut River. These hearty people brought their thrifty habits of food production and preparation with them. All early New Englanders were forced to use what the land and waters provided for them. Corn, beans, squash, and pumpkins came from their harvest, myriad seafoods from their coastal waters, and meat and poultry from their forests filled with wild game. Although typical New England puddings, stews, and pies are abundant in the state, Connecticut does have good reason to boast of a few indigenous dishes and variations of the so-called "traditional." Pumpkins of all shapes and sizes are made into the most delicious pies and moist brown breads. Pumpkin bread was supposedly a favorite among the Revolutionary War heroes two hundred years ago.

CONNECTICUT

Connecticut has often been referred to as the "Nutmeg State." However, even though Connecticut homemakers have always used nutmeg and other spices liberally in their cooking, the nickname originated from the days when shrewd Yankee peddlers sold wooden nutmegs in place of the scarce and valuable real thing, and not from the numerous spice-laden local recipes.

A very special election-day cake which originated in Hartford is a traditional New England favorite. Town meeting and election days were always great events, and people would gather for parties of punch and cake to celebrate victory or defeat. This special cake is prepared from flour, yeast, spices, nuts, and citron and is usually served with thick, rich cream, often whipped.

Onions were grown by the early settlers and some were even exported to the West Indies for profit. But these succulent vegetables also found their way into many a hearty midday stew or chowder. A regional stew of beef, bacon fat, onions, potatoes, and carrots, flavored with fresh garden-grown Connecticut herbs, is especially delicious when served over rosemary-flavored biscuits.

The mighty Connecticut River has always been a fisherman's haven. Broiled river shad is a local specialty. Oysters, flounders, lobsters, and clams are found near Long Island Sound. Clambakes and oyster roasts are popular pastimes. Seafood fanciers love to visit Mystic Seaport and Marine Museum, a restored whaling village in Mystic, Connecticut. It was built to recall the state's seafaring traditions of the 1800s.

New England and Connecticut cookery traditions are world famous. The first American printed cookbook was written by Amelia Simmons and published in Hartford in 1796. The Shaker establishment at Enfield is said to have distributed the first commercial seed in the United States. Their simple tastes in food meshed well with spartan Yankee fare. One of their successful recipes still with us today is Shaker Braised Steak, a delectable combination of vegetables, lemon juice, ketchup, and ordinary beef round steak.

Beef à la Mode

1½ **pounds beef for stew, cubed**
½ **cup flour**
1½ **teaspoons salt**
¼ **teaspoon pepper**
3 **tablespoons bacon fat**
4 **carrots, pared and sliced**
1 **large onion, sliced**
6 **potatoes, pared and quartered**
1 **can (29 ounces) tomatoes, drained (reserve juice)**
Herb mixture (1 tablespoon each basil, chervil, marjoram, and savory)
Rosemary Biscuits

1. Coat meat cubes with a mixture of flour, salt, and pepper, reserving remaining flour mixture.
2. Brown cubes in bacon fat.
3. Put meat into a deep casserole. Add carrots, onion, potatoes, and drained tomatoes.
4. Stir remaining seasoned flour into fat left in skillet. When mixture bubbles, gradually add reserved tomato juice, stirring constantly. Cook until slightly thickened.
5. Tie herb mixture in cheesecloth and add to casserole. Pour thickened liquid over meat and vegetables; add enough water to almost cover vegetables. Cover.
6. Bake at 325°F 3½ to 4 hours.
7. Serve over Rosemary Biscuits.

6 servings

Rosemary Biscuits: Prepare Baking Powder Biscuits (page 31), adding **1 teaspoon crushed rosemary** with the dry ingredients.

Shaker Braised Steak

3 pounds beef round steak
2 tablespoons flour
2 tablespoons butter
1 teaspoon salt
¼ teaspoon pepper
1 stalk celery, chopped
1 carrot, finely chopped
½ green pepper, finely
    chopped
2 medium onions, finely
    chopped
  Juice of ½ lemon
½ cup ketchup

1. Coat meat with flour.
2. Sauté in heated butter until well browned on both sides. Season with salt and pepper. Add chopped vegetables, lemon juice, and ketchup.
3. Cover tightly and simmer gently 2 to 2½ hours, or until steak is tender when tested with a fork.

About 6 servings

Baked Steak with Oyster Filling

1 beef round steak (2
    pounds), cut ½ inch
    thick
¼ teaspoon salt
¼ teaspoon paprika
3 tablespoons flour
¼ cup water
  Oyster Filling
6 potatoes, pared and
    cubed (optional)
6 onions, chopped
    (optional)
6 carrots, pared and sliced
    (optional)

1. Pound steak and sprinkle with seasonings; cut in half. Put 1 steak into a shallow 3-quart baking pan, cover with filling, and top with remaining steak. Sprinkle with flour. Add water and cover.
2. Bake at 350°F 1¼ hours. Baste occasionally, adding more water as necessary.
3. If desired, after the first half hour add potatoes, onions, and carrots to the baking pan to cook with the meat.

6 servings

Oyster Filling: Mix **1 cup chopped oysters, 2 cups soft bread crumbs, 1 tablespoon minced parsley, ¼ teaspoon celery seed, ¼ teaspoon minced onion,** and **¼ cup melted butter.** Use as directed.

Broiled Connecticut River Shad

1 shad (3 to 4 pounds)
  Melted butter
  Salt and pepper
  Parsley
¼ cup butter
1 tablespoon lemon juice

1. Have shad cleaned and split. Place skin side down on an oiled and preheated plank or broiler-proof platter. Brush with melted butter and sprinkle with salt and pepper.
2. Broil until tender, 15 to 20 minutes, depending upon size and thickness of fish. Remove to a serving platter and garnish with parsley.
3. Beat butter until softened; add lemon juice gradually, creaming until blended. Spread over fish. Serve at once.

6 to 8 servings

CONNECTICUT

Stuffed Clams

24 littleneck clams
3 fresh mushrooms,
    chopped fine
2 slices bacon, fried and
    finely crumbled
1 teaspoon minced parsley
  Salt and pepper
  Bread crumbs
  Butter or margarine

1. Cover bottom of a shallow baking pan with **rock salt**.
2. Scrub clams well and place in rock salt to hold clams in place and prevent liquor from running out when clams open.
3. Set in a 400°F oven until clams begin to open.
4. Remove from oven. Remove clams from shells; save liquor. Chop clams and combine with the clam liquor, mushrooms, bacon, parsley, salt, and pepper. Add enough bread crumbs to thicken, so that the mixture will hold its shape in shells; mix thoroughly.
5. Fill the clam shells. Sprinkle with bread crumbs and dot with butter.
6. Bake at 350°F about 12 minutes, or until brown on top.

4 servings

Oysters Baked in Shells

24 large oysters and shells
1 egg
½ teaspoon salt
⅛ teaspoon pepper
1 tablespoon cold water
1 cup bread crumbs
  Butter

1. Scrub the shells carefully to remove any sand or dirt.
2. Beat egg with salt, pepper, and water.
3. Dip oysters into the egg mixture, then into the crumbs. Place oysters back in shells; dot with butter.
4. Bake at 450°F 10 minutes.

4 servings

New England Baked Pumpkin

1 pumpkin or acorn
    squash (about 2
    pounds)
⅓ cup butter, melted
½ cup lightly packed
    brown sugar
1½ tablespoons chopped
    crystallized ginger
1 teaspoon cinnamon
¼ teaspoon salt

1. Cut pumpkin in quarters; remove seeds. Place pumpkin pieces in a greased shallow baking pan.
2. Combine remaining ingredients and spoon onto pumpkin.
3. Bake at 350°F about 1 hour, or until tender; baste occasionally during baking.

4 servings

Pumpkin Vegetable Skillet

4 cups pared diced
    pumpkin or 4 sweet
    potatoes, pared and
    diced
¼ cup bacon drippings
½ cup onion slices
1 clove garlic, minced
2 cups cut green beans
1 cup whole kernel corn
1 cup chopped tomatoes
½ cup chopped green
    pepper
1 teaspoon salt
½ teaspoon chili powder
¼ teaspoon pepper
½ cup chicken broth

1. Cook pumpkin in bacon drippings 5 minutes.
2. Add remaining ingredients; mix well. Cook covered over low heat 40 to 45 minutes, or until vegetables are tender.

6 servings

Pumpkin Bread

1 cup warm water
¾ cup sugar
1 package active dry yeast
3 tablespoons oil
2 teaspoons salt
1 cup canned pumpkin
½ cup instant nonfat dry
    milk
5 cups all-purpose flour
    (about)

1. Put water, sugar, and yeast into a large bowl; stir until sugar and a yeast are dissolved. Let stand 5 minutes.
2. Add oil, salt, pumpkin, and dry milk; beat well.
3. Gradually beat in enough flour to make a soft dough. Knead on a lightly floured surface until dough is smooth and elastic. Put into a greased bowl, cover, and let rise until double in bulk (about 1½ hours).
4. Punch down dough, turn over in bowl, cover, and let rise again until double in bulk (about 45 minutes).
5. Punch dough down and shape into two loaves. Put loaves into 2 greased 8×4×3-inch loaf pans. Cover; let rise until double in bulk (about 45 minutes).
6. Bake at 400°F 25 to 30 minutes.

2 loaves

Hasty Pudding

1 cup cornmeal
1½ teaspoons salt
½ cup cold water
2½ cups boiling water

1. Make a paste of the cornmeal, salt, and cold water, stirring until there are no lumps, and pour gradually into the boiling water, stirring constantly. Cook and stir until very thick.
2. Put into a double boiler, cover, and cook 30 minutes, stirring occasionally.
3. Serve hot with **sugar** and **milk,** or with plenty of **butter,** or as desired.

6 servings

CONNECTICUT

Election Day Yeast Cake

½ cup milk
2 packages active dry
yeast
½ cup warm water
1½ cups sifted all-purpose
flour
1¾ cups sifted all-purpose
flour
1 teaspoon salt
1½ teaspoons cinnamon
½ teaspoon mace
½ teaspoon nutmeg
¼ teaspoon cloves
½ cup butter
¾ cup sugar
3 eggs, well beaten
1 cup pecans, chopped
½ cup chopped candied
citron

1. Scald milk and cool to lukewarm.
2. Meanwhile, soften yeast in warm water in a bowl; set aside.
3. Add the lukewarm milk to softened yeast. Add 1½ cups flour gradually, beating well after each addition. Beat until mixture is smooth. Cover bowl with waxed paper and a clean towel and let rise in a warm place until very light and bubbly (about 45 minutes).
4. Meanwhile, blend remaining flour, salt, and spices.
5. Beat butter until softened. Add sugar gradually, creaming until fluffy after each addition. Add eggs in thirds, beating thoroughly after each addition.
6. Blend in yeast mixture. Gradually add dry ingredients, beating until smooth after addition. Add pecans and citron and mix well. Turn mixture into a greased (bottom only) 9-inch tube pan.
7. Cover with waxed paper and towel and let rise in a warm place until pan is almost full (about 2 hours).
8. Bake at 350°F 50 to 55 minutes. Remove from oven to wire rack and cool 10 minutes in pan. Cut around tube with paring knife to loosen cake. Loosen sides with spatula; invert on rack and lift off pan. Cool completely before slicing.

One 9-inch tube cake

Connecticut Crullers

2 tablespoons butter or
other shortening
1 cup sugar
2 eggs, well beaten
4 cups sifted all-purpose
flour
3½ teaspoons baking
powder
½ teaspoon grated nutmeg
½ teaspoon salt
1 cup cream
Fat for deep frying
heated to 360°F
Confectioners' sugar

1. Cream butter and sugar until thoroughly mixed. Add eggs and beat well.
2. Sift dry ingredients together and add alternately with cream to creamed mixture, mixing thoroughly.
3. Put dough on a well-floured surface and pat lightly until just thick enough to cut in thin strips ½ inch wide. Bring edges together to form a circle, leaving a hole in center, and press together.
4. Fry in hot fat until brown. Drain on absorbent paper. Dust with confectioners' sugar.

2 dozen crullers

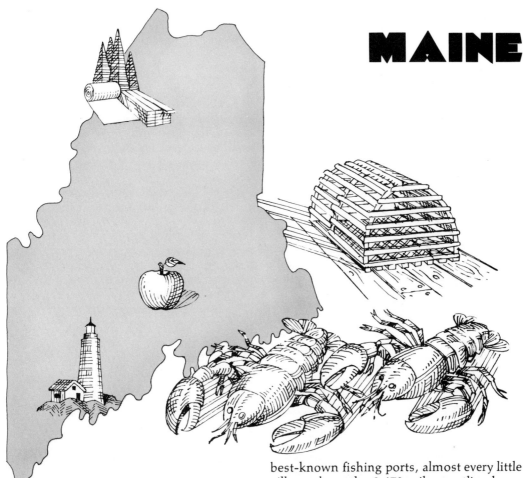

Maine, the "Pine Tree State," with its glorious crystal-clear lakes, towering trees, and rugged natural coastline, is the easternmost state in the United States. At one time most of its land was covered with virgin white pine. Even today forests cover 90 percent of the state. The production of lumber and paper is the leading industry; however, farming and fishing are also important. Most of the fertile farmland is located in the New England upland, a plateau covering the central and eastern part of the state. The White Mountain region in the west rises over five thousand feet and is filled with blue lakes, gorges, and spectacular scenery. The coastal lowlands near the Atlantic are in the southwestern section. Hundreds of islands are located in Maine's many bays and inlets.

Although Portland and Rockland are the best-known fishing ports, almost every little village along the 3,478 mile coastline has a small fleet of fishing boats. And the proud Maine fishermen will not let you forget that their lobster catch, along with clams, cod, pollack, scallops, flounder, and sardines, ranks among the nation's biggest. Down Easterners, as the people of Maine are called (early New Englanders used "down" for "north"), will tell you to come to Maine if you want real lobster. You will find lobster boiled, lobster broiled, lobster in salads, and lobster in soups. There are endless recipes for this local specialty, and they are all superb. Simplicity is the key to most of these dishes, for the people of Maine say that lobster is best when allowed to give you its own delicate flavor. Clams are also popular in the state, and a real treat is a regional cream of clam soup prepared very simply with shelled clams, milk, butter, flour, and seasonings.

English explorers arrived in Maine before the Pilgrims made it to Plymouth, but the

MAINE

first permanent English settlers built homes there in the middle 1620s. For almost a century they were subjected to the French and Indian Wars and were forced to adopt prudent and innovative methods of survival. This rugged pioneer background, combined with a cold and moist climate, helped many early Maine homemakers develop habits of thrift and ingenuity in managing their colonial kitchens. Foods from the forests were utilized, including the extraordinary wild roots and berries. Strawberries, blueberries, and raspberries are still abundant in Maine today and find their way into numerous delectable breads and desserts.

Potatoes are one of Maine's most important crops. Acadians from the eastern province of Canada brought the first potatoes to Aroostook County in the central plateau long before Maine became a state. Today, only Idaho grows more potatoes than Maine. Meat or fish and potatoes are the mainstay of the Down Easterners' diet. Potatoes, such as the Katahdins that come from north central Maine, are popular for thickening the typical New England stews and chowders. These regional soups are always the thick, meal-in-one varieties. Potato doughnuts and rolls, prepared from fresh or leftover mashed potatoes, are other Yankee-inspired ways of using this staple vegetable.

Delicious and McIntosh apples, Maine's chief fruit crop, are grown in the southern counties. New Englanders use apples in a variety of both main dish and dessert recipes. Apple Betty, prepared from leftover bread crumbs, brown sugar, and tart apples, is a good example of the conservative creativity of the region.

Livestock and poultry are also important to Maine's economy. Broilers are raised throughout the farm regions of the state. A favorite dish for many Down Easterners is fried chicken with a crispy crust.

Molasses and ginger, kitchen staples of old New England, are also used extensively in local cookery. Gingersnaps, gingerbreads, and pots of baked beans greet hungry families at many a Maine meal.

Grilled Lobster

1 live lobster (about 1½ pounds)
Tabasco Butter

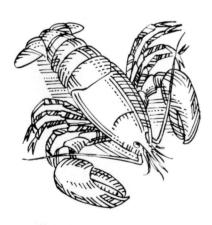

1. Purchase a lobster for each serving. Live lobsters may be killed and dressed for cooking at the market. If prepared at home, place the lobster on a cutting board with back or smooth shell up. Hold a towel firmly over the head and claws. Kill by quickly inserting the point of a sharp heavy knife into the center of the small cross showing on the back of the head. Without removing knife, quickly bear down heavily, cutting through entire length of the body and tail. Split the halves apart and remove the stomach, a small sac which lies in the head, and the spongy lungs which lie between meat and shell. Also remove the dark intestinal line running through the center of the body. Crack large claws with a nutcracker or mallet.
2. Brush meat with Tabasco Butter. Place shell side down on grill about 5 inches from coals. Grill about 20 minutes, or until shell is browned. Baste frequently with butter. Serve in shell with remaining butter.

Tabasco Butter: Melt ½ **cup butter** and stir in ½ **teaspoon Tabasco** and **1 tablespoon lime juice**.

Cream of Clam Soup

1 pint shelled clams
1 quart milk
3 tablespoons butter or
    margarine
1½ tablespoons flour
½ teaspoon salt
⅛ teaspoon paprika
⅛ teaspoon freshly ground
    pepper

1. Put clams through a meat grinder; put into a saucepan and add just enough **water** to cover. Simmer 3 minutes.
2. Heat milk. Blend butter with flour. Add a little of the milk to make a smooth paste. Pour paste into hot milk and stir until it thickens.
3. Add clams, salt, paprika, and pepper. Heat thoroughly.

6 servings

Yankee Pot Roast

1 beef chuck pot roast (3
    to 4 pounds)
⅓ cup flour
2 teaspoons salt
⅛ teaspoon pepper
¼ cup pork drippings
1½ cups water
1 bay leaf, crushed
8 to 10 small potatoes
8 to 10 small carrots
1 medium turnip
8 to 10 small onions
½ cup cold water
¼ cup flour

1. Set out a heavy saucepot or Dutch oven having a tight-fitting cover.
2. Coat pot roast with a mixture of flour, salt, and pepper.
3. Heat pork drippings in the saucepot. Brown meat slowly in the fat over medium heat, turning to brown on all sides.
4. When meat is well browned, add water and crushed bay leaf. Cover; reduce heat and cook over low heat 2 hours. If necessary, add more water during cooking period. Liquid surrounding meat should at all times be simmering, not boiling.
5. Meanwhile, wash and pare potatoes, carrots, turnip, and onions.
6. When meat has simmered 2 hours, slice the turnip and add with other vegetables to the saucepot. Continue to simmer 1 hour, or until meat and vegetables are tender.
7. Remove meat and vegetables from saucepot and arrange on a warm serving platter; keep warm. Strain liquid and add water, if necessary, to make 1½ cups liquid. Return to saucepot.
8. Pour cold water into a screw-top jar and sprinkle flour onto it. Cover jar tightly and shake until mixture is well blended. Slowly pour one half of mixture into pot roast liquid while stirring constantly. Bring to boiling. Gradually add only what is needed of remaining flour mixture for consistency desired. After final addition, cook 3 to 5 minutes.

About 8 servings

Corned Beef in Grapefruit Juice, 22;
Orange Soda Bread, 23

MAINE

Clam Pie

Hard-shelled clams (quahogs, as they're called in New England) or sea clams may be used for this pie. It is excellent company fare.

2 medium potatoes (about ⅔ pound)
1 to 1½ pints shucked clams
3 tablespoons butter or margarine
½ cup chopped onion
2 tablespoons flour
¼ teaspoon salt
Few grains pepper
¼ cup milk
Pastry for a 1-crust pie

1. Wash and cook potatoes about 25 to 35 minutes, or until potatoes are tender when pierced with a fork. Drain. Dry potatoes by shaking pan over low heat. Peel, dice, and set aside.
2. Drain clams, reserving clam liquid; finely chop and set aside.
3. Heat butter in a large skillet. Add onion and cook until onion is almost tender, stirring occasionally.
4. Blend in a mixture of flour, salt, and pepper. Heat until mixture bubbles.
5. Stirring constantly, add ¼ cup reserved clam liquid and milk. Bring to boiling; cook 1 to 2 minutes longer.
6. Remove from heat; add the diced cooked potatoes and chopped clams. Turn into an 8-inch pie pan.
7. Prepare pastry and roll into a round about 1 inch larger than pie pan. Cut a simple design near center of pastry to allow steam to escape during baking. Loosen one-half pastry and fold over other half. Moisten edge of pie pan with cold water. Lift pastry gently and place over hot mixture in pie pan; unfold. Trim edge so pastry extends about ¾ inch beyond edge of pie pan. Fold extra pastry under edge and gently press edges to seal to moistened rim of pie pan. Flute or press with a fork.
8. Bake at 450°F about 20 minutes, or until pastry is lightly browned.

4 to 6 servings

Maine Salad Bowls

Romaine or other salad greens
2 eggs
½ cup mayonnaise
3 tablespoons chili sauce
1 tablespoon minced onion
½ teaspoon prepared horseradish
2 cans (3¼ ounces each) sardines
¼ pound sharp Cheddar cheese

1. Rinse salad greens, drain, and pat dry. Tear into bite-size pieces; cover and chill in refrigerator at least 1 hour.
2. Meanwhile, hard-cook the eggs.
3. Combine mayonnaise, chili sauce, onion, and horseradish. Chill in refrigerator.
4. Drain sardines and set aside.
5. Cut Cheddar cheese into 8 strips or wedges, and slice the hard-cooked eggs.
6. Line 4 individual salad bowls with the greens. Arrange several sardines and egg slices in each bowl. Add two cheese strips to each bowl.
7. Serve with the salad dressing.

4 servings

Blueberry Pie

    6 cups fresh blueberries
      Pastry for a 2-crust
        9-inch pie
    1 cup plus 2 tablespoons
        sugar
    ⅓ cup flour
    ¾ teaspoon cinnamon
    ½ teaspoon nutmeg
    ¼ teaspoon salt
    2 tablespoons lemon juice
    2 tablespoons butter or
        margarine

1. Wash and sort blueberries; drain.
2. Prepare pastry. Roll out enough pastry to line a 9-inch pie pan; line pie pan. Roll out remaining pastry for top crust and slit pastry with knife in several places to allow steam to escape during baking.
3. Add sugar, flour, cinnamon, nutmeg, and salt to blueberries and toss gently together.
4. Pour filling into pastry-lined pan, heaping slightly in center. Sprinkle with lemon juice and dot with butter, cover with top crust and flute edge.
5. Bake at 425°F 10 minutes. Turn oven control to 350°F and bake 40 to 45 minutes longer, or until crust is light golden brown.
6. Cool on rack.

One 9-inch pie

Baked Apple Dumplings

    2 cups sifted cake flour
    1 teaspoon baking powder
    ½ teaspoon salt
    6 tablespoons shortening
    1 egg yolk, beaten
    ⅓ cup milk
    6 to 8 apples, pared and
        cored
      Sugar
      Cinnamon
      Butter or margarine
      Juice of ½ lemon
    1½ cups sugar
    ¾ cup water
    ¼ cup corn syrup
    1 tablespoon butter
    ½ teaspoon vanilla extract

1. Sift flour, baking powder, and salt together. Add shortening and mix lightly with a fork.
2. Combine beaten egg yolk and milk; add to the first mixture.
3. Place dough on a floured surface and roll about ¼ inch thick. Cut into 6-inch squares. Place an apple in the center of each square; fill center of apple with sugar, sprinkle with cinnamon, and add a small piece of butter. Pinch edges of dough together on top. Place in a well-greased baking pan. Sprinkle with lemon juice.
4. Bake at 450°F 10 minutes.
5. Combine sugar, water, corn syrup, butter and vanilla extract and bring to boiling; cook 5 minutes. When dumplings have baked for 10 minutes, pour syrup over them and turn oven control to 350°F; bake 25 minutes longer, basting occasionally with syrup.
6. Serve with warm **cream.**

6 to 8 servings

Mince Pie

    3½ cups mincemeat
        (page 20)
    1 teaspoon grated lemon
        peel
    1 tablespoon lemon juice
      Pastry for a 2-crust pie

1. Blend mincemeat and lemon peel and juice in a saucepan; heat thoroughly. Cool slightly.
2. Prepare a 9-inch pie shell; roll out remaining pastry for top crust. Set aside.
3. Turn filling into unbaked pie shell. Cover with top crust and flute edge.
4. Bake at 450°F 10 minutes. Turn oven control to 350°F and bake 40 minutes longer, or until crust is light golden brown. Cool on wire rack.

One 9-inch pie

MAINE

Mincemeat

½ cup (about 4 ounces)
   ground suet
1½ cups ground cooked
   beef
 4 medium-sized apples
 1 cup packed brown sugar
 1 cup apple cider
 ½ cup fruit jelly
 ½ cup seedless raisins,
   chopped
 ½ cup currants
 2 tablespoons molasses
 1 teaspoon salt
 1 teaspoon ground
   cinnamon
 ½ teaspoon ground cloves
 ½ teaspoon ground
   nutmeg
 ¼ teaspoon ground mace
 1 tablespoon grated
   lemon peel
 1 tablespoon lemon juice

1. Mix suet and beef in a large, heavy skillet and set aside.
2. Wash, core, pare, and chop apples (about 3 cups, chopped).
3. Combine apples with meat in skillet with the brown sugar, cider, jelly, raisins, currants, and molasses. Stir in a mixture of the salt and spices.
4. Cook slowly, uncovered, about 1 hour, or until most of the liquid has been absorbed; stir occasionally to prevent sticking to bottom of skillet.
5. Stir in lemon peel and juice.
6. If not used immediately, pack hot mincemeat into sterilized jars, cover, and refrigerate.

About 3½ cups mincemeat

Fisherman's Swizzle

12 lemons
36 oranges
 2 pounds confectioners'
   sugar
 2 cups cognac
 2 cups peach brandy
 3 cups Jamaica rum
 4 quarts carbonated water
   Ice

1. Squeeze juice from lemons and oranges and pour into a punch bowl. Add confectioners' sugar and stir until it dissolves.
2. Add cognac, peach brandy, and rum. Pour in carbonated water; add ice.
3. Serve in glasses with swizzle sticks for final stirring.

About 2½ gallons

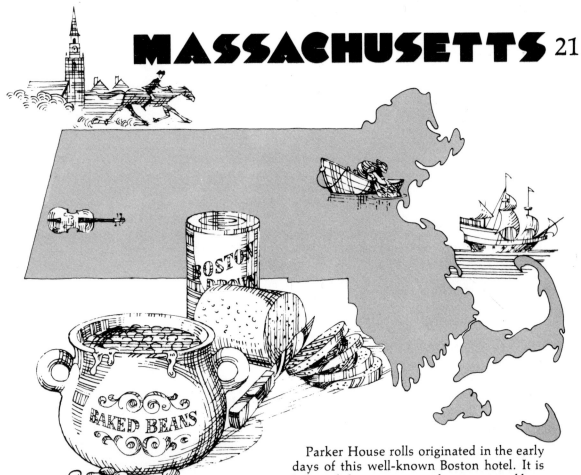

The cookery of Massachusetts began in the kitchens of the Pilgrims and the Puritans. It was born to the tune of hardship, cooperative effort, and thankful praise. The first Thanksgiving celebrated a bountiful harvest of corn and beans which the Indians had taught the new residents to cultivate.

Later, wheat was grown and New England bread making began to flourish. Cornmeal was made into johnny cakes, griddlecakes, biscuits, bread, and shortcakes. Famous Boston brown bread was developed from cornmeal, wheat flour, raisins, and the ever-popular molasses. Light and airy popovers became a must at many meals. The legendary anadama bread was supposedly created by a husband who was angry because his lazy wife served him only cornmeal mush. One day he seized the cornmeal, threw in some yeast, flour, and molasses, and muttered while he mixed, "Anna dam'er, Anna dam'er."

Parker House rolls originated in the early days of this well-known Boston hotel. It is believed that a pastry cook, exasperated by a hotel crisis, grabbed pieces of dough, squeezed them in his fists and flung them into the oven. The result was the creased and celebrated Parker House roll.

Boston baked beans were developed in the early colonies when it was against the local custom to work on the Sabbath. Innovative women began their meal preparations on Saturday by soaking and slowly baking the dried beans overnight in readiness for the Sunday meal. Most Massachusetts family recipes that have been handed down through several generations call for mustard, molasses, brown sugar, vinegar, and salt pork to be added to the baking beans.

The Concord grape was produced in the town of Concord as early as the middle 1800s and later became a well-known commercial product. Cranberry sauce, the traditional Thanksgiving accompaniment to turkey, is an old "Bay State" favorite. Cranberries are also used in regional breads, salads, and desserts.

Early English settlers combined their pudding-making abilities with the foods provided by their new land and came up with numerous hearty desserts. We still have favorite local recipes for suet, bird's nest, Indian, cracker, mincemeat, and rice-raisin puddings.

Other renowned Massachusetts desserts are Boston Cream Pie, which is actually a rich cake topped by a creamy vanilla sauce, and Marlborough Pie, a glorified apple pastry prepared from tart applesauce, lemon juice, sugar, and plenty of eggs.

Harvard beets, a sweet-and-sour dish, and succotash, a mixture of corn and lima beans, are favorite Massachussets vegetables. Corn pudding, which dates back to Puritan days, is also popular.

Seafood is a prominent Bay State staple. Cape Cod is distinguished for its fishing prowess. Codfish, baked, boiled, or in the form of cakes, is part of its heritage. Clams or quahogs, as they are called in this region, are found along the Atlantic coast. Other fish caught and processed in the state are flounder, mackerel, lobster, tuna, and swordfish.

The New England clambake is a ritual along the coast during hot summer evenings. Well-scrubbed clams are smothered in layers of seaweed and baked in shallow pits over hot stones. When served steaming, with plenty of melted butter, this seafood is unequaled.

Although Massachusetts cuisine is often associated with that of the early English colonists, the influence of the Irish is evident in such dishes as Irish stews, robust soups, and "genuine" corned beef and cabbage.

Corned Beef in Grapefruit Juice

1 **corned brisket of beef (about 4 to 5 pounds) Water**
1½ **quarts grapefruit juice**
1 **large onion studded with 12 whole cloves**
8 **peppercorns**
1 **celery stalk with leaves, cut in thirds**
1 **bay leaf**
1 **tablespoon caraway seed**
1 **green pepper, sliced**
10 **carrots, pared and halved**
8 **small white onions**
4 **baking potatoes, pared and halved**
1 **green cabbage, cut in quarters**

1. Put corned beef into a heavy kettle. Add water to cover. Bring to boiling and cover tightly. Reduce heat and simmer 1 hour.
2. Pour off water and add grapefruit juice and water to cover. Add onion studded with cloves, peppercorns, celery, bay leaf, caraway seed, and green pepper. Bring to boiling; reduce heat and simmer, covered, 2 hours.
3. Add carrots, onions, and potatoes; cook 30 minutes.
4. Add cabbage and cook 30 minutes.
5. Serve meat and vegetables on a platter.

8 servings

Harvard Beets

5 **medium beets (about 1 pound)**
2 **tablespoons sugar**
1 **tablespoon cornstarch**
½ **teaspoon salt**

1. Leaving on 1- to 2-inch stem and the root end (this helps beets to retain red color), cut off leaves from beets. Wash and cook covered in boiling salted water to cover in a 2-quart saucepan having a tight-fitting cover 30 to 45 minutes, or until just tender.

Cold water
3 tablespoons cider vinegar
2 tablespoons butter or
   margarine

2. When beets are tender, drain if necessary, and reserve liquid in a measuring cup. Set aside.
3. Plunge beets into running cold water. Peel off and discard skin, stems, and root ends. Dice or slice beets and set aside.
4. Mix sugar, cornstarch, and salt in saucepan. Pour enough cold water into beet liquid to make ¾ cup.
5. Add liquid to mixture in saucepan along with vinegar, stirring constantly. Bring rapidly to boiling, stirring constantly; add the beets and butter. Keep mixture moving with a spoon, bring again to boiling; cover and simmer 8 to 10 minutes. Serve immediately.

4 servings

Boston Baked Beans

2 pounds dried navy beans,
   rinsed
¾ pound fat bacon or salt
   pork
3 tablespoons sugar
   (optional)
1 tablespoon salt
½ teaspoon dry mustard
⅓ cup molasses (less, if
   preferred)
1 cup boiling water

1. Soak beans in cold water overnight.
2. In the morning, drain, and cover with 2 quarts water in a saucepan. Heat to simmering and cook slowly 1 to 1½ hours, or until skins burst readily when a bean is removed from the pan and blown upon. Drain.
3. Prepare the pork by scalding and scraping. Cut off one slice and score through the rind in squares. Place the slice of pork in the bottom of a bean pot, add the beans, and bury the larger piece of pork in the top portion of the beans, having only the scored rind exposed.
4. Mix the salt, sugar, mustard, molasses, and boiling water and pour over beans.
5. Cover the pot and bake at 250°F 6 to 8 hours. If beans appear dry, add hot water as needed.
6. Uncover during the last half hour of baking.

12 servings

Orange Soda Bread

3½ cups all-purpose flour
 1 teaspoon salt
 1 teaspoon sugar
 1 teaspoon baking soda
 1 cup buttermilk
 ½ cup fresh orange juice
 1 egg
 1 cup raisins
 1 tablespoon grated
   orange peel

1. Combine flour, salt, sugar, and baking soda in a bowl. Make a well in the center and pour in buttermilk and orange juice; mix well.
2. Add egg, raisins, and orange peel; beat until smooth (dough will be sticky).
3. Knead lightly on a well-floured surface. Shape into a round loaf and put into a well-greased 9-inch round layer cake pan. Cut an X across the top of loaf.
4. Bake at 350°F 40 minutes, or until a cake tester inserted in center comes out clean. Serve warm.

1 loaf

MASSACHUSETTS

Steamed Boston Brown Bread

1 cup rye flour
1 cup whole wheat flour
1 cup yellow cornmeal
1½ teaspoons baking
powder
¾ teaspoon baking soda
1 teaspoon salt
2 cups buttermilk
¾ cup dark molasses
1 cup dark or golden
raisins

1. Mix flours, cornmeal, baking powder, baking soda, and salt in a large bowl.
2. Combine buttermilk, molasses, and raisins. Add liquid mixture to flour mixture; stir only enough to moisten flour.
3. Spoon batter into 3 well-greased 16-ounce fruit or vegetable cans, filling each about two-thirds full. Cover cans tightly with aluminum foil.
4. Place filled cans on a trivet in a steamer or saucepot with a tight-fitting cover. Pour boiling water into the steamer to no more than one half the height of the cans. Tightly cover steamer. Steam 3 hours. Keep water boiling gently at all times. If necessary, add more boiling water during steaming.
5. Remove cans from steamer; remove foil. Run a knife around inside of cans to loosen loaves and unmold onto wire rack. Serve warm. Or cool, wrap, and store loaves; resteam to serve.

3 loaves

Anadama Bread

½ cup yellow cornmeal
2 cups boiling water
2 tablespoons shortening
½ cup molasses
1½ teaspoons salt
1 package active dry yeast
½ cup warm water
6 cups all-purpose flour
Melted butter or
margarine

1. Stirring constantly, add the cornmeal to the boiling water in a large bowl. Stir in the shortening, molasses, and salt. Set aside to cool to lukewarm.
2. Meanwhile, dissolve yeast in warm water.
3. Blend 1 cup of the flour into lukewarm cornmeal mixture; beat until very smooth. Mix in yeast. Add about half of the remaining flour and beat until very smooth. Then mix in enough of the remaining flour to make a soft dough.
4. Turn onto a lightly floured surface. Cover and let rest 5 to 10 minutes.
5. Knead dough until satiny and smooth. Form into a ball and put into a greased deep bowl. Turn dough to bring greased surface to top. Cover; let rise in a warm place until double in bulk (about 1 hour).
6. Punch down dough and turn onto a lightly floured surface. Divide into halves and form into smooth balls. Shape into loaves. Place in 2 greased 9×5×3-inch loaf pans. Cover; let rise again until double in bulk (about 1 hour).
7. Bake at 375°F 40 to 45 minutes, or until bread tests done. Remove from pans, brush tops with melted butter, and cool on wire racks.

2 loaves

Boston Cream Pie

1 cup sifted cake flour
1 teaspoon baking powder
¼ teaspoon salt
1 cup sugar
3 eggs, well beaten
2 or 3 teaspoons lemon
    juice
6 tablespoons hot milk (do
    not boil)
    Creamy Vanilla Filling

1. Sift flour, baking powder, and salt together.
2. Add sugar gradually to the beaten eggs, beating until very thick and piled softly. Mix in lemon juice.
3. Sprinkle dry ingredients over egg mixture about one fourth at a time; gently fold in until just blended after each addition.
4. Add hot milk all at one time and quickly mix just until smooth. Turn batter into 2 greased 9-inch round layer cake pans.
5. Bake at 375°F 15 to 25 minutes, or until cake tests done.
6. Cool 8 to 10 minutes in pan on wire rack. Remove cake from pan and cool completely on rack.
7. Prepare Creamy Vanilla Filling.
8. Place one cake layer on serving plate and spread with chilled filling. Cover with second layer.
9. Sift ¼ cup confectioners' sugar over top of cake. For a lacy design, sift confectioners' sugar over a lace paper doily on top of cake; carefully remove doily.

One 9-inch layer cake

Creamy Vanilla Filling

⅓ cup sugar
2½ tablespoons flour
¼ teaspoon salt
1½ cups cream
3 egg yolks, slightly
    beaten
1 tablespoon butter or
    margarine
2 teaspoons vanilla extract
¼ teaspoon almond extract

1. Mix sugar, flour, and salt in a heavy saucepan. Stir constantly while gradually adding cream. Bring to boiling; stir and cook 3 minutes.
2. Vigorously stir about 3 tablespoons of the hot mixture into the egg yolks; immediately blend into cream mixture. Stir and cook about 1 minute.
3. Remove from heat and blend in remaining ingredients. Press a circle of waxed paper onto top (this prevents a crust from forming). Cool slightly, then chill.

Marlborough Pie

1½ cups applesauce
¾ cup firmly packed
    brown sugar
4 eggs, slightly beaten
¼ cup butter, melted
1 teaspoon grated lemon
    peel
3 tablespoons lemon juice
½ teaspoon salt
¼ teaspoon nutmeg
1 unbaked 9-inch pastry
    shell

1. Combine applesauce, brown sugar, eggs, butter, lemon peel and juice, salt, and nutmeg; mix well. Turn into pastry shell.
2. Bake at 450°F 15 minutes. Turn oven control to 300°F and bake 45 to 55 minutes, or until a knife comes out clean when inserted in filling halfway between center and edge. Cool on a wire rack.

One 9-inch pie

MASSACHUSETTS

Wellesley Fudge Cake

4 ounces (4 squares)
  unsweetened
  chocolate
½ cup hot water
½ cup sugar
2 cups sifted cake flour
1½ teaspoons baking
  powder
½ teaspoon baking soda
½ teaspoon salt
½ cup butter or margarine
2 teaspoons vanilla extract
1¼ cups sugar
4 eggs, well beaten
⅔ cup milk
  Fudge Frosting

1. Combine chocolate and water in a heavy saucepan. Place over very low heat, stirring constantly, until chocolate is melted. Add the ½ cup sugar and stir until dissolved. Set aside to cool.
2. Sift flour, baking powder, baking soda, and salt together; set aside.
3. Cream butter with vanilla extract; gradually add the 1¼ cups sugar, creaming until fluffy. Add eggs one at a time, beating thoroughly after each addition. Blend in chocolate mixture.
4. Beating only until smooth after each addition, alternately add dry ingredients in fourths and milk in thirds to creamed mixture. Turn batter into 2 greased 8×8×2-inch baking pans and spread evenly to edges.
5. Bake at 350°F 25 to 30 minutes, or until cake tests done.
6. Cool and remove from pans. Fill and frost with Fudge Frosting.

One 8-inch square layer cake

Fudge Frosting

4 ounces (4 squares)
  unsweetened chocolate,
  cut in pieces
3 cups sugar
1 cup milk
½ cup butter or margarine
2 tablespoons light corn
  syrup
1 tablespoon vanilla extract

1. Combine all ingredients except extract in a heavy 3-quart saucepan. Heat slowly until mixture boils rapidly, stirring constantly.
2. Set candy thermometer in place. Cook to 234°F (soft-ball stage; remove from heat while testing). Using a pastry brush dipped in water, wash down the crystals from sides of saucepan from time to time during cooking.
3. Remove from heat and cool to 110°F without stirring or jarring.
4. Mix in vanilla extract. Beat to spreading consistency.

NEW HAMPSHIRE

New Hampshire's hundreds of lakes and ponds are scattered throughout the rolling valleys, New England uplands, and sharp ridges of the White Mountains. Wild flowers, shrubs, and vines cover abandoned fields and slopes, transforming the "Granite State" into a countryside of picture-postcard beauty.

The manufacture of leather goods and wood products accounts for most of New Hampshire's income, for the terrain, soil, and severe winter climate are not friendly to agriculture. Most of the farms are devoted to producing dairy products and poultry. Chicken, cheese, and egg dishes, prepared in the old English fashion, are popular. Thus, pies and pastries in this region are often made with meat or poultry. The prudent and conservative Yankee homemaker's recipe repertoire holds numerous ideas for using leftover foods. Besides chicken-cheese and zesty meat pot pies, several stews and soups are New Hampshire favorites of long standing.

Lamb has always been prevalent in New England. Minted stuffed lamb, roast leg of lamb, and savory lamb stew adorn the local dining tables during many cold winter evenings.

Apples are plentiful in the Granite State; farmers also produce blueberries and strawberries, and a few vegetables, such as potatoes, sweet corn, squash, and pumpkins. Harvest time means pumpkin, squash, and apple pie to many New Hampshirites. Pumpkin rolls and breads are also enjoyed during the crisp autumn days. The summer fruits often find their way into delicious deep-dish pies covered with ample amounts of thick, rich cream.

Long before the first English white settlers arrived in the region in the early 1620s, the Indians fished, hunted, and cultivated their own fields of corn. The colonists learned methods of forest survival and the cultivation of native grains from the friendly tribes. Although the majority of the original colonists came to New Hampshire directly from

England, a few were Puritans and members of other religious groups fleeing the rigid rules of the Massachusetts Bay colony. For many years, New Hampshire was under the jurisdiction of Massachusetts and shared the same governor. Thus, the culinary customs of the New World Puritans fused with the late arrivals from England to form traditional northeast cookery. A familiar English steamed pudding became an Indian pudding, a tasty yet nutritious mixture of milk, cornmeal, molasses, and spices. The average New England soup and pudding is hearty enough to satisfy almost any hungry family member.

Molasses has continued to be a customary ingredient in several local New Hampshire recipes. Baked beans, brown bread, gingerbread, and cake recipes call for this addition. Molasses, along with apples, currants, wine, and a variety of spices, was used in the region's earliest pumpkin pies. It was also added to stout New England rum.

Salt-water fish, although found in some indigenous recipes, is not the mainstay of a New Hampshirite's diet. The state's Atlantic coastline measures a mere thirteen miles. However, lobster, clams, haddock, and cod are caught near the shore. And a very enjoyable fish chowder is available in the colorful cafés of the chief salt-water fishing center of Portsmouth.

New Hampshire claims fame as the birthplace of four important Americans of very diverse professions. Franklin Pierce, fourteenth president of the United States; Daniel Webster, a leading nineteenth-century statesman and orator; Mary Baker Eddy, founder of the Christian Science religion; and Alan Shephard, the first American in space, were all born in the state. Whether the wholesome, nourishing New England foods early in their lives had anything to do with their later success and contributions to the nation is only conjecture, but surely it cannot be ignored!

Baked Bean and Tomato Soup

1½ cups baked beans
 1 stalk celery, diced
 1 tablespoon diced onion
 3 cups water
 2 cups cooked tomatoes
 1 tablespoon melted
    butter or other fat
 1 tablespoon flour
 1 teaspoon salt
   Dash pepper

1. Combine beans, celery, onion, and water in a saucepan and let simmer 30 minutes, or until the vegetables are soft.
2. Add the tomatoes and rub through a sieve. Return to saucepan.
3. Heat butter and stir in flour; slowly add to the puréed vegetables, stirring constantly. Season with salt and pepper. Heat to boiling and serve.

6 servings

Roast Leg of Lamb

 1 lamb leg (5 to 6 pounds)
 2 teaspoons salt
¼ teaspoon pepper
   Parsley or mint leaves

1. Place lamb skin side down on rack in a shallow roasting pan with rack. Insert roast meat thermometer in center of thickest part of meat, being sure that bulb does not rest on bone or in fat.
2. Roast lamb uncovered at 300°–325°F about 3 hours, allowing 25 to 35 minutes per pound. Meat is medium

done when thermometer reaches 160°F and well done at 170°–180°F.

3. If desired, place paper frill around edge of leg bone. Serve on warm platter. Garnish with parsley or mint leaves.

About 10 servings

Minted Stuffed Lamb: Heat ⅓ **cup butter** in a large skillet. Add **2 tablespoons finely chopped celery** and **2 tablespoons finely minced onion.** Cook over low heat until onion is almost tender. Add ½ **cup finely chopped mint leaves** and ½ **cup water.** Simmer about 5 minutes. Mix in **2 cups soft bread crumbs, 1 teaspoon salt,** and ¼ **teaspoon pepper.** Follow recipe for Roast Leg of Lamb, substituting 4- to 5-pound lamb shoulder cushion roast for lamb leg. Lightly fill pocket with stuffing; sew or skewer opening to hold stuffing inside. Roast at 300°F about 2½ hours, allowing 30 to 35 minutes per pound. Remove skewers or thread and serve.

Meat Pies

1 **onion, diced**
2 **tablespoons butter or other fat**
2 **cups cubed cooked meat**
1½ **tablespoons flour**
1¼ **cups milk or gravy**
1 **tablespoon Worcestershire sauce**
1 **cup cooked peas**
1 **cup sliced cooked carrots**
1 **cup diced boiled potatoes**
Baking Powder Biscuits (page 31)

1. Brown onion in butter in a skillet. Add meat and brown well.
2. Remove meat and onion from skillet and add flour, milk, and Worcestershire sauce. Blend well. Turn into a buttered baking dish. Mix in vegetables.
3. Prepare biscuits and place them on meat and vegetable mixture.
4. Bake at 425°F 15 to 20 minutes, or until thoroughly heated and biscuits are a delicate brown.

6 servings

Variations: Instead of rounds, cut dough with a sharp knife diagonally across dough, first one way and then the other, forming diamond-shaped biscuits.

Increase milk in biscuits to ⅞ cup and drop dough from a teaspoon onto meat and vegetable mixture.

Omit potatoes. Add **1 cup of any cooked vegetable.** Omit baking powder biscuit crust. Cover meat and vegetable mixture with **2 cups hot mashed potatoes;** bake as for Meat Pies.

Beefsteak Pie: Follow recipe for Meat Pies. Use **2 pounds beef round steak** and uncooked vegetables. Brown onion and meat. Add **3 cups water** instead of milk, add vegetables, salt, and pepper; cover and simmer 1 hour. Turn into baking dish, cover with baking powder biscuit crust, and bake as directed.

NEW HAMPSHIRE

Chicken-Cheese Saucer Pies

Pastry for a 2-crust pie
¼ **cup butter**
¼ **cup chopped onion**
3 **tablespoons flour**
¼ **teaspoon salt**
¼ **teaspoon garlic salt**
¼ **teaspoon pepper**
½ **cup strong chicken broth
   (1 chicken bouillon
   cube dissolved in ½
   cup boiling water)**
1 **cup cream**
½ **teaspoon Worcestershire
   sauce**
2 **cups diced cooked
   chicken**
1 **can (4 ounces) sliced
   mushrooms, drained**
¼ **cup shredded sharp
   Cheddar cheese**

1. Prepare pastry. Make one pastry ball slightly larger than the other. Roll out larger ball and cut into four 8½-inch rounds. Fit into 4 small individual pie pans. Roll out remaining ball for top crusts and cut into four 6½-inch rounds. Cover with waxed paper and set aside.
2. Heat butter in a skillet over medium heat. Add onion and cook until almost tender, stirring occasionally. Blend in a mixture of flour, salt, garlic salt, and pepper. Heat until mixture bubbles. Add chicken broth and cream gradually while stirring constantly. Stir in Worcestershire sauce.
3. Bring to boiling, stirring constantly until thickened and thoroughly blended. Add chicken and mushrooms and mix gently. Set aside to cool.
4. Put one fourth of the cooled filling into each pastry shell. Sprinkle cheese over the filling. Cover with pastry rounds; seal and flute edges.
5. Bake at 450°F 15 to 20 minutes, or until pastry is delicately browned.

4 chicken pies

New England Bacon and Hominy

3 **cups cooked whole
   hominy**
2 **tablespoons butter or
   other fat**
1 **small onion, chopped**
1 **green pepper, chopped**
2 **cups cooked tomatoes**
1 **tablespoon sugar**
1 **teaspoon salt**
½ **pound sliced bacon**

1. Put hominy into a well-buttered shallow baking dish.
2. Melt butter and sauté onion and pepper until light brown. Add tomatoes, sugar, and salt and simmer 10 minutes.
3. Pour mixture over hominy, and cover with bacon slices, arranged in a basket-weave pattern.
4. Bake at 325°F about 30 minutes, until bacon is cooked.

6 to 8 servings

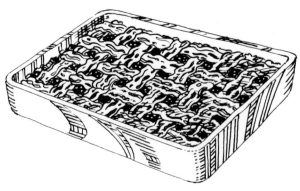

Baking Powder Biscuits

2 cups sifted all-purpose
    flour
1 tablespoon baking
    powder
½ teaspoon salt
¼ cup butter or other
    shortening
¾ cup milk (about)

1. Sift dry ingredients together. Add butter and cut in with pastry blender or two knives. Add milk to make a soft dough.
2. Put on a floured surface and knead lightly with fingertips. Roll out ½ inch thick and cut with floured biscuit cutter.
3. Place on an ungreased baking sheet.
4. Bake at 450°F about 12 minutes.

About 14 (2-inch) biscuits

Baptist Cakes

1 tablespoon butter or
    margarine
1 tablespoon sugar
1 teaspoon salt
½ cup scalded milk
¼ cup boiling water
½ cake compressed yeast
¼ cup lukewarm water
3 cups sifted all-purpose
    flour
    Fat for deep frying
    heated to 365°F

1. Combine butter, sugar, and salt in a large bowl. Add hot liquid; stir. Cool to lukewarm.
2. Meanwhile, soften yeast in lukewarm water.
3. Add half of flour to milk mixture; mix thoroughly with a spoon, then add another cup of flour. Continue to mix, adding remaining flour gradually.
4. Turn out on a floured surface and knead until smooth and elastic. Return to bowl, cover, and let rise until double in bulk.
5. Turn out on floured surface and roll to ⅛-inch thickness. Cut in strips 2½ inches wide and cut across to make squares or diamonds. Cover and let stand 10 to 15 minutes.
6. Fry in hot fat about 4 minutes, or until delicately brown. Drain on absorbent paper.
7. Serve hot with **maple syrup.**

About 20 cakes

Hasty Pudding Biscuits

4 cups Hasty Pudding
    (page 13)
1 cake compressed yeast
½ cup lukewarm water
1 egg, well beaten
1 tablespoon melted butter
    or other shortening
½ teaspoon cinnamon
½ teaspoon ginger
½ cup molasses
4 to 5 cups sifted
    all-purpose flour

1. Cool the Hasty Pudding until lukewarm.
2. Meanwhile, soften yeast in lukewarm water.
3. Add yeast to pudding and mix well. Stir in egg, butter, spices, and molasses. Add enough flour to make a stiff dough. Knead well.
4. Put dough into a bowl, cover, and let rise overnight.
5. Shape dough into biscuits, put on baking sheets, and let rise until light.
6. Bake at 400°F about 20 minutes, or until lightly browned.

About 3 dozen biscuits

Twin Mountain Muffins

More than fifty years ago, Fannie Farmer printed a recipe for Twin Mountain Muffins which became a basic New England recipe.

¼ cup butter
¼ cup sugar
1 egg, well beaten
2 cups all-purpose flour
4 teaspoons baking powder
½ teaspoon salt
1 cup milk

1. Cream butter and sugar, add egg, and mix well.
2. Mix flour with baking powder and salt. Add to creamed mixture alternately with milk, beating well after each addition.
3. Fill greased muffin-pan wells about half full.
4. Bake at 350°F 25 minutes, or until done.

About 1½ dozen

Indian Pudding

3 cups milk
½ cup yellow cornmeal
¼ cup sugar
1 teaspoon salt
1 teaspoon cinnamon
½ teaspoon ginger
1 egg, well beaten
½ cup molasses
2 tablespoons butter or margarine
1 cup cold milk

1. Scald milk in top of double boiler. Remove from heat. Stirring constantly, slowly blend in a mixture of cornmeal, sugar, salt, cinnamon, and ginger. Stir in a blend of the egg and molasses.
2. Cook and stir over boiling water 10 minutes, or until very thick. Beat in the butter.
3. Turn into a well-buttered 1½-quart casserole. Pour cold milk over top.
4. Bake at 300°F 2 hours, or until browned.

About 6 servings

New Hampshire Fruit Cookies

1 cup butter
1½ cups sugar
3 eggs, well beaten
1½ tablespoons water
3¼ cups sifted all-purpose flour
1 teaspoon baking soda
¼ teaspoon salt
½ teaspoon cinnamon
½ cup raisins, chopped
½ cup currants, chopped
1 cup walnuts, chopped

1. Cream butter and sugar until light and fluffy. Add eggs and water; beat thoroughly.
2. Blend flour, baking soda, salt, and cinnamon. Add to creamed mixture; mix well. Mix in fruit and nuts.
3. Drop by teaspoonfuls on greased cookie sheet.
4. Bake at 350°F 15 minutes.

About 4 dozen cookies

Mincemeat Goodies: Follow recipe for New Hampshire Fruit Cookies. Omit water, raisins, currants, and cinnamon. Add **1 cup mincemeat** and **1 teaspoon each of cloves and nutmeg.** Use only ½ cup walnuts.

African Rock Lobster en Casserole, 59

Often called "Little Rhody," Rhode Island is no wider than thirty-seven miles at any point, nor longer than forty-eight miles. However, this smallest state in the Union has the longest official title: "The State of Rhode Island and Providence Plantations." This originally referred to the islands in Narragansett Bay and the plantations on the mainland. Almost 13 percent of Rhode Island's surface area is water. With this vast amount of inland sea, fish of all kinds are important to Rhode Islanders. Hard-shelled clams, called quahogs, are its most valuable shellfish. Lobsters, clams, and scallops are also caught by the local fishermen. Other deep-sea fish found near the coast are bluefish, swordfish, sea bass, tuna, flounder, pickerel, and mackerel. These seafoods, prepared in a variety of ways, are enjoyed almost daily by the local population.

The Rhode Island Red, a famous breed of chicken, was developed in the town of Little Compton. A romantic tale of its beginning tells of a sea captain from the area who was so fascinated with the exotic red-and-black-plumaged birds in the Orient that he brought several home to be cross-bred with his own domestic chickens. The result was the Rhode Island Red. Poultry prepared in any fashion is served in Rhode Island; however, a few specialties, such as chicken fricassee, chicken potpie, and chicken and oyster casserole are the most popular.

"Greenings," or shiny green Rhode Island apples, are used to make the most delicious pies and pandowdies. In the early days of the state, an enterprising merchant discovered these tart apples growing in the Far East. He promptly returned with cuttings and the Rhode Island apple was born.

An old indigenous recipe for apple slump calls for these green apples, sugar, water, and cinnamon to be poured, while still hot, over freshly baked biscuits, and then topped with very rich cream.

There is nothing that equals Rhode Island's white cornmeal. It is smooth and silky, like talcum powder, instead of gritty and grainy like most meals. And it is this fine white cornmeal that is used to make the famous Rhode Island jonny cake. The local people prefer to drop the "h" from the regular New England "johnny" cake. The name is a shortened version of "journey," which recalls Colonial times when little cakes of cornmeal were prepared for the traveler's knapsack. Rhode Islanders eat their jonny cakes for breakfast, lunch, or dinner. They are superb when served hot, dripping with melted butter and maple syr-

up. Thrift is a tradition in New England and Rhode Island housewives continue to honor this virtue. Leftover jonny cakes are never wasted, but creatively turned into new treats, such as jonny cake cream toast, which is served piping hot from an oven casserole.

No discussion of Rhode Island and food would be complete without mentioning the exquisite cuisine and lavish dinner parties of Newport society at the turn of the century. The entertainment budget of some of the more extravagant hostesses for a single season would run into hundreds of thousands of dollars. Multicourse menus, rare wines, gold serving plates, and French *haute cuisine* were the order of the day. There is still elegance in Newport today, but it is a subdued elegance within a memorable and very historic setting.

New England Clam Chowder

¼ **pound salt pork, cubed**
2 **small onions, minced**
1 **quart shucked clams**
6 to 8 **medium potatoes, pared and sliced**
Cold water
Salt
½ **teaspoon pepper**
1 or 2 (13 ounces each) **cans evaporated milk**
6 or 8 **soda crackers, split**
Cold milk

1. Fry salt pork in a saucepot until golden brown. Add onion and cook 2 or 3 minutes.
2. Remove stomach from clams; chop hard parts and leave soft parts whole or chop them, as preferred.
3. Arrange potatoes and hard parts of clams in layers over onion; cover with water. Bring to boiling and simmer until potatoes are soft.
4. Add soft part of clams, salt to taste, pepper, and desired amount of evaporated milk. Heat to boiling and add crackers which have been soaked in cold milk. Heat thoroughly.

6 to 8 servings

Baked Swordfish

1 **swordfish steak, about 2 inches thick***
Salt and pepper
Juice of 1 lemon
2 **onions, sliced**
1 **green pepper, minced**
2 **tablespoons butter or other fat**
½ **cup water**

1. Rinse swordfish and place in a well-greased baking pan. Sprinkle with salt and pepper, and pour lemon juice over fish.
2. Place slices of onion on top of fish and then add green pepper. Dot with butter and add water to pan.
3. Bake at 400°F about 40 minutes, basting frequently.
4. Serve garnished with **lemon quarters** and **parsley.**
*Allow about ⅓ pound fish per serving.

Chicken Fricassee

1 **stewing chicken, (4 to 5 pounds), cut up**
1 **large onion, quartered**
6 **stalks celery with leaves, cut in pieces**
½ **bunch parsley**
1 **bay leaf**
2 **teaspoons salt**
3 **peppercorns**
¼ **cup flour**
1 **cup cream**
2 **teaspoons lemon juice**

1. Put chicken, gizzard, heart, and neck into a kettle. Refrigerate liver. (If desired, brown chicken pieces in a skillet with hot fat; pieces may be coated with seasoned flour before frying.)
2. Add hot water to kettle to barely cover; add onion, celery, parsley, bay leaf, salt, and peppercorns. Bring water to boiling; remove foam.
3. Cover kettle tightly and simmer 2 to 3 hours, or until thickest pieces of chicken are tender when pierced with a fork. Add liver last 15 minutes of cooking.
4. Remove chicken and giblets from broth. Strain broth and cool slightly; skim off fat.
5. Heat 4 tablespoons of chicken fat in the kettle; blend in flour and heat until bubbly, stirring constantly.
6. Continue stirring and gradually add 2 cups of the chicken broth and the cream. Bring to boiling; cook and stir 1 to 2 minutes. Mix in lemon juice and chicken pieces; heat thoroughly.
7. Serve chicken and gravy in a warm serving dish and garnish with **parsley.**

About 6 servings

Chicken Potpie

1 **stewing chicken (about 5 pounds)**
2 **stalks celery, diced**
1 **carrot, pared and diced**
1 **onion, chopped**
½ **teaspoon salt**
⅛ **teaspoon pepper**
⅓ **cup flour**
1 **cup cooked broad noodles or cooked potato balls**
1 **hard-cooked egg, sliced Pastry for a 2-crust pie**

1. Put chicken into a kettle and cover with **boiling water.** Add celery, carrot, onion, salt, and pepper. Cover and simmer 2 to 3 hours, or until chicken is tender.
2. Cool chicken and broth. Remove skin and bones from chicken and cut chicken into pieces.
3. Remove fat from broth, put into a large skillet, and heat fat. Stir in flour. Gradually add broth, stirring constantly. Cook and stir until thickened. Add chicken to gravy; mix in noodles and sliced egg.
4. Roll out pastry; line a casserole with one pastry round. Turn chicken mixture into lined casserole and top with second pastry round. Make several slits in pastry to allow for escape of steam. Flute pastry edges.
5. Bake at 450°F 20 to 25 minutes, or until pastry is browned.

6 to 8 servings

Chicken and Oyster Casserole

1 broiler-fryer chicken, quartered
¼ cup flour
½ teaspoon salt
Few grains pepper
1 cup boiling water
1 cup cream
2 tablespoons butter
2 cups oysters

1. Coat chicken quarters with a mixture of flour, salt, and pepper. Put into a shallow casserole, pour boiling water over it, and cover casserole.
2. Bake at 350°F about 1 hour, or until chicken is tender.
3. Remove from oven, add cream, butter, and oysters. Cover, return to oven, and cook about 10 minutes, or until edges of oysters begin to curl.
4. Serve with hot **biscuits.**

4 servings

Scalloped Oysters and Scallops

½ cup melted butter or other fat
2 cups bread crumbs or cracker crumbs
1 quart oysters, drained
1 tablespoon celery seed
Salt and pepper
1 cup half-and-half
1 pint scallops

1. Mix the melted butter or other fat and bread crumbs together and put a thin layer in the bottom of a buttered baking dish. Cover with oysters and seasonings; add some of the half-and-half. Add a layer of scallops, seasonings, and a layer of crumbs.
2. Add another layer of oysters and the remainder of the half-and-half. Top with the remaining scallops and buttered crumbs.
3. Bake at 400°F 30 minutes.

8 servings

Sailor's Omelet

6 eggs, separated
¼ teaspoon salt
1 teaspoon minced parsley
1 teaspoon anchovy paste
1 tablespoon butter
Paprika

1. Beat yolks of the eggs until light.
2. Add salt, parsley, and anchovy paste.
3. Fold in stiffly beaten whites.
4. Melt butter in heavy skillet and pour in mixture. Cook until bottom is brown, then place in oven.
5. Bake at 350°F until top is brown. Sprinkle with paprika and serve at once.

6 servings

Potatoes in Sauce

1 tablespoon butter or other fat
1 onion, sliced
1 teaspoon chopped green pepper
5 cold boiled potatoes
1 teaspoon parsley
Salt and pepper
1 cup gravy or thick broth

1. Melt butter in a heavy saucepan and sauté the onion and green pepper. Do not brown.
2. Slice the potatoes in thick slices and add to the onion. Add parsley, seasonings to taste, and gravy.
3. Cover pan and simmer until heated.

4 servings

Fried Tomatoes

4 firm ripe or green
    tomatoes
½ cup cornmeal
1 teaspoon salt
⅛ teaspoon pepper
¼ cup butter or margarine

1. Cut out stem ends of tomatoes and slice ½ inch thick.
2. Mix cornmeal, salt, and pepper in a shallow dish. Coat both sides of tomato slices with the mixture.
3. Heat butter in a skillet. Add as many tomato slices at one time as will life flat in skillet. Lightly brown both sides, turning once; cook only until tender. Add more butter as needed.

About 4 servings

Molded Cucumber Salad

1 cucumber, pared and
    diced
½ teaspoon salt
½ canned pimento, diced
½ teaspoon lemon juice
2 teaspoons unflavored
    gelatin
¼ cup cold water
1 cup whipping cream,
    whipped

1. Combine cucumber, salt, pimento, and lemon juice.
2. Soften gelatin in cold water 5 minutes; then dissolve over hot water and beat into whipped cream.
3. Mix in cucumber mixture and pour into individual molds which have been rinsed in cold water or oiled with salad oil. Chill until firm.

4 servings

Rhode Island Jonny Cake

2 cups white cornmeal
2 tablespoons sugar
2¼ teaspoons salt
2 cups milk

1. Mix cornmeal, sugar, and salt in a bowl. Make a well in center of dry ingredients and add milk all at one time. Beat until smooth and thoroughly mixed.
2. Heat a griddle or skillet; it is hot enough for baking when drops of water sprinkled on surface dance in small beads. Lightly grease griddle.
3. For each jonny cake, spoon 1 tablespoon of batter onto the heated griddle. Cook until browned on one side. Using a spatula, carefully turn and brown second side. Repeat procedure for the remaining batter.
4. Serve hot with **butter** and **maple syrup.**

About 4 dozen jonny cakes

Rhode Island Griddlecakes

2 cups water-ground
white cornmeal
1 cup all-purpose flour
1 teaspoon salt
⅛ teaspoon ginger
2½ cups buttermilk
1 tablespoon molasses
2 tablespoons warm water
1 teaspoon baking soda
3 tablespoons butter
1 cup confectioners' sugar
¼ teaspoon cinnamon

1. Mix cornmeal, flour, salt, and ginger in a bowl.
2. Gradually stir in buttermilk to make a stiff batter.
3. Mix 1 tablespoon of molasses into warm water; add soda and stir until it foams up. Mix into batter.
4. Bake on a hot griddle.
5. Cream butter with confectioners' sugar and add cinnamon. Serve with hot griddlecakes.

About 2½ dozen griddlecakes

Rhode Island Apple Slump

Baking Powder Biscuits
(page 31)
1½ quarts pared and cored
apple quarters
1 cup sugar
½ cup water
2 teaspoons cinnamon

1. Prepare Baking Powder Biscuits.
2. Combine apples, sugar, water, and cinnamon in a saucepan, cover tightly, and bring to boiling over low heat. When boiling, put biscuits on top, cover tightly, and continue to cook over low heat about 25 minutes.
3. Remove biscuits to individual serving dishes and spoon cooked applesauce over them. Serve with **cream.**

8 to 10 servings

Rhode Island Cob Pie

This is a version of pandowdy that is sweetened with molasses instead of sugar.

4 tart apples
¾ cup light molasses
½ teaspoon cinnamon
2 tablespoons butter
Baking Powder Biscuits
(see page 31)

1. Pare and slice apples; arrange in a well-buttered shallow baking dish. Pour molasses over apples, sprinkle with cinnamon, and dot with butter.
2. Prepare biscuit dough and roll on a lightly floured surface to ½-inch thickness and the size of baking dish. Set dough on apples. Slit top to allow steam to escape.
3. Bake at 350°F 30 to 35 minutes, or until apples are tender.
4. To serve, cut out squares of biscuit, turn pieces upside down, and spoon apples over biscuits. Serve hot with **nutmeg-flavored whipping cream.**

6 servings

White pine, sugar maple, and hemlock cover the wooded hillsides of the "Green Mountain State," known for its natural beauty, excellent skiing facilities, and abundance of maple syrup. Centuries before the first white settlers arrived in Vermont, the Indians were tapping the mature maple trees to collect the syrup in birchbark buckets. At first the early colonists made just enough syrup and sugar for their own sweetening uses, but later they saw the advantage of commercializing their enviable product. Today Vermont's maple trees produce almost a half million gallons of syrup every year.

"Sugaring is fun," say the sugar-makers of Vermont. A revealing picture of the past is the early spring tapping of the sugar trees. Although oil burners often replace wood fires for boiling the sap, the process has changed very little over the years. Obtaining the syrup is slow work, for it takes forty gallons of maple sap to produce just one gallon of pure maple syrup. Thus, although the product may be plentiful in one's back yard, it is still very dear, even to the Vermont homemaker.

Vermont's numerous maple sugar and syrup recipes are traditional treasures, for Vermonters love their syrup on anything from cereal and grapefruit to pancakes and custard pie. The delicate, sweet syrup is used on ham, in baked bean and sweet potato casseroles, and in eggnogs. Maple cakes and cookies are also popular. Several excellent authentic Shaker (religious group) recipes of this region, call for maple sugar or syrup. "Sugar on Snow" parties are traditional in Vermont after a light, fresh snowfall. The syrup is heated to the appropriate temperature so that the liquid becomes a soft waxy taffy when poured over ice or snow.

Agriculture is more important in Vermont than in the other New England states. Dairy farming accounts for most of the farm income. Simple specialties of egg and cheese are common Green Mountain supper dish-

VERMONT

es. Vermont is said to have more cattle than people. This plentiful supply of beef has inspired many recipes. A traditional winter dish is Red Flannel Hash, a pungent concoction of beets, beef, and potatoes served hot with butter and cream.

Farmers also grow potatoes and apples. Baked apples, Vermont style, and other tasty desserts are familiar favorites. Mincemeat used in a variety of ways is especially prevalent in holiday recipes.

The earliest explorers in Vermont were probably the French, but the first permanent white settlers were of English origin from Massachusetts. During the Revolutionary War, Vermont's Green Mountain Boys, led by Ethan Allen, gained fame when they captured British-held lands.

This individualistic Yankee spirit is still strong in Vermont. The early New England pioneers were courageous, conservative, and thrifty. They were careful to use what the land provided for them. Wild game was abundant in their forests. Deer were common, and turkeys ran wild. This brown-feathered bird was one of the wonders of the New World and provided the newcomers with a daily supply of fresh meat. Even now, Vermont turkeys spell excellence on any menu. Roast Vermont turkey with oyster dressing, cranberry sauce, and stuffed acorn squash can provide a Thanksgiving feast any day of the week. Broiled Green Mountain venison steaks or chops are exceptional when served with a sauce of melted butter, lemon juice, and a little sherry.

Beef Stock

3 pounds lean beef (chuck or plate), cut in 1-inch pieces
1 soup bone, cracked
3 quarts cold water
1½ tablespoons salt
2 large onions
2 whole cloves
5 carrots, pared and cut in large pieces
2 turnips, pared and cut in large pieces
3 stalks celery with leaves, sliced
4 leeks, washed and sliced
1 bay leaf
2 sprigs parsley
3 sprigs thyme

1. Put meat and soup bone into a large saucepot; add water and salt. Cover and bring to boiling. Remove foam. Cover saucepot and simmer about 4 hours, removing foam as necessary.

2. Slice 1 onion; insert the cloves into second onion. Add onions, remaining vegetables, and herbs to saucepot. Cover and bring to boiling. Reduce heat and simmer about 1½ hours.

3. Remove from heat; remove soup bone and strain stock through a fine sieve. Allow to cool. (The meat and vegetables strained from stock may be served as desired.)

4. Remove fat that rises to surface (reserve for use in other food preparation). Store stock in a covered container in refrigerator for future use, or reheat and serve with slices of crisp **toast.**

About 2½ quarts stock

Brown Stock: Follow recipe for Beef Stock. Cut any meat from soup bone and brown the meat along with beef pieces in ¼ **cup fat** in saucepot before cooking. Proceed as directed.

Vegetable Soup

1 tablespoon bacon fat
1 pound lean soup meat
1 large onion, chopped
1 green pepper, chopped
1 cup sliced potato
1 cup diced carrot
½ turnip, pared and
    chopped
2 quarts water
⅓ cup chopped celery
1 tablespoon chopped
    parsley
¼ teaspoon thyme leaves
1 bay leaf
1 teaspoon salt
¼ teaspoon pepper
2 cups fresh corn cut from
    cob or 1 can (16
    ounces) whole kernel
    corn, drained
1 cup chopped tomatoes

1. Heat bacon fat in a saucepot. Add meat, onion, and green pepper and sauté until onion is golden.
2. Add potato, carrot, and turnip; cook 2 minutes longer, then add water and remaining ingredients, except corn and tomatoes.
3. Cover and simmer 4 hours. Add corn and cook 1 hour. Remove bay leaf and meat, if desired; let cool and skim off all fat.
4. Add and stir in tomatoes; simmer 5 minutes before serving.

6 servings

Cider Roast Ham

1 smoked ham, whole
    (about 10 pounds)
¾ cup firmly packed brown
    sugar
2 tablespoons maple syrup
½ teaspoon dry mustard
    Whole cloves
¾ cup apple cider

1. Follow directions on wrapper for roasting or place ham fat side up on rack in roasting pan. Insert roast meat thermometer in center of thickest part of lean; bulb should not rest on bone or in fat.
2. Roast uncovered at 300°F 2½ hours.
3. Meanwhile, prepare glaze.
4. For glaze, blend brown sugar, maple syrup, and dry mustard.
5. When ham has roasted 2½ hours, remove from oven. Remove rind (if any), being careful not to remove fat. Cut fat surface into diamond pattern, or use a scalloped cutter to make a flower design. Insert whole cloves in center of patterns.
6. Spread the glaze over ham. Return ham to oven and continue roasting about 45 minutes, or until internal temperature reaches 160°F. (Total roasting time is about 3 hours, allowing 18 to 20 minutes per pound.) During roasting, occasionally baste ham with apple cider. Garnish as desired.

About 20 servings

VERMONT

VERMONT

Red Flannel Hash

6 medium beets, cooked
4 medium potatoes, cooked
1 cup cooked beef, chopped
1 teaspoon salt
¼ teaspoon pepper
3 tablespoons butter or
    other fat
1 tablespoon cream

1. Chop beets and potatoes, mix with chopped beef, and season with salt and pepper.
2. Put 2 tablespoons of butter in a heavy skillet. Add the beef mixture and moisten with a little hot water. Cover and cook slowly until meat is heated through and browned.
3. Shortly before serving, add cream and remaining butter. Stir, heat, and serve.

4 servings

Roast Turkey

1 ready-to-cook turkey (10
    to 12 pounds)
Oyster Stuffing
Salt
Melted fat
Gravy (favorite recipe)

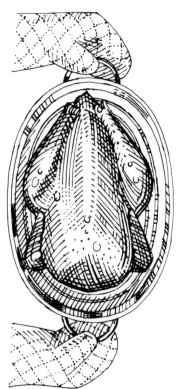

1. Rinse bird with cold water. Drain and pat dry with absorbent paper or soft cloth.
2. Prepare oyster stuffing.
3. Rub body and neck cavities with salt. Fill lightly with stuffing. (Extra stuffing may be put into a greased covered baking dish or wrapped in aluminum foil and baked with turkey the last hour of roasting time.)
4. Fasten neck skin to back with skewer and bring wing tips onto back. Push drumsticks under band of skin at tail, or tie with cord. Set, breast up, on rack in shallow roasting pan. Brush with melted fat.
5. If meat thermometer is used, insert it in center of inside thigh muscle or thickest part of breast meat. Be sure that tip does not touch bone. If desired, cover top and sides of turkey with cheesecloth moistened with melted fat. Keep cloth moist during roasting by brushing occasionally with fat from bottom of pan.
6. Roast, uncovered, at 325°F 4 to 4½ hours. When turkey is two-thirds done, cut band of skin or cord at drumsticks. Continue roasting until turkey tests done (the thickest part of the drumstick feels soft when pressed with fingers and meat thermometer registers 180° to 185°F).
7. For easier carving, let turkey stand 20 to 30 minutes, keeping it warm. Meanwhile, prepare gravy from drippings.
8. Remove cord and skewers from turkey and place on heated platter. Garnish platter as desired.

About 16 servings

Oyster Stuffing: Combine **3 quarts soft bread crumbs, 4 teaspoons salt,** ½ **teaspoon pepper, 1 pint to 1 quart small oysters,** whole or cut in small pieces, ¾ **cup oyster liquor** (use turkey stock or milk if needed), ½ **cup butter** or **turkey fat,** melted, mixing well.

VERMONT

Eggs Fairlee

3 tablespoons butter or
    other fat
4 onions, sliced
8 hard-cooked eggs, sliced
½ teaspoon salt
    Dash paprika
    Medium White Sauce
    Cracker crumbs, buttered

1. Melt butter and brown onion. Cover bottom of a buttered casserole with half the onion, add eggs, season, and cover with remaining onion.
2. Pour white sauce over all; sprinkle top with buttered crumbs.
3. Bake at 400°F until crumbs are brown (about 20 minutes).

6 servings

Medium White Sauce: Melt **2 tablespoons butter or margarine** in a saucepan. Blend in **2 tablespoons flour**, **½ teaspoon salt**, and **⅛ teaspoon pepper**. Cook and stir until bubbly. Gradually add **1 cup milk**, stirring until smooth. Bring to boiling; cook and stir 1 to 2 minutes.

Maple Baked Beans

1 pound dried navy beans
¼ pound lean salt pork
1 medium onion, chopped
1 teaspoon salt
1 teaspoon dry mustard
1 cup maple syrup
3 cups water

1. Soak beans in 1½ quarts water overnight.
2. Cook beans until skins start to break (about 40 minutes). Drain. Put into a bean pot.
3. Put salt pork, onion, salt, dry mustard, maple syrup, and water into bean pot with beans. Cover.
4. Bake at 300°-325°F about 3 hours. Add water as necessary during baking to keep beans moist.
5. Just before serving, toss beans with additional maple syrup.

About 6 servings

Cheese Muff

8 slices buttered white
    bread
4 ounces pasteurized
    process American
    cheese, thinly sliced
    Salt and pepper
4 eggs, beaten
1 quart milk

1. Put 4 slices of bread on bottom of a square baking dish; cut bread if necessary to fit neatly. Cover bread with thin slices of cheese, sprinkle with salt and pepper. Cover with remaining buttered bread, cutting to fit. Add a second layer of sliced cheese and sprinkle with salt and pepper.
2. Combine eggs and milk; pour over bread and cheese.
3. Bake at 325°F 40 minutes, or until the top is lightly browned.

6 servings

VERMONT

Baked Kidney Beans

1 pound dried red kidney
    beans, rinsed
¼ pound salt pork or bacon
1 cup maple syrup
¼ cup ketchup
1 teaspoon salt
½ teaspoon dry mustard
⅛ teaspoon pepper
1 small onion
    Boiling water

1. Put beans into a saucepan, pour in 1½ quarts **water,** and mix in ⅛ teaspoon **baking soda.** Bring to boiling, reduce heat, and simmer 5 to 10 minutes. Drain and rinse beans.

2. Put half of beans in a bean pot.

3. Score salt pork and add to beans. Add remaining beans. Mix maple syrup and remaining ingredients; pour onto beans. Cover beans with boiling water. Cover bean pot.

4. Bake at 300°F 4 hours, or until beans are soft. (Add water during baking if necessary to keep beans moist.) Remove cover for the last half hour and allow top to brown.

About 6 servings

Maple Fruit Bread

2 tablespoons shortening,
    melted
1 cup maple syrup
1 egg, well beaten
    Grated peel of 1 orange
2½ cups all-purpose flour
1 tablespoon baking
    powder
½ teaspoon baking soda
½ teaspoon salt
¾ cup nuts, chopped
¾ cup orange juice

1. Blend shortening, maple syrup, egg, and peel thoroughly.

2. Mix flour, baking powder, baking soda, and salt; stir in nuts. Add dry ingredients alternately with orange juice to creamed mixture, mixing well after each addition. Turn into a greased 9×5×3-inch loaf pan.

3. Bake at 350°F about 1 hour, or until done.

1 loaf

Maple-Cheese Spoon Dessert

3 apples
1½ cups maple syrup
2 cups all-purpose flour
1 tablespoon baking
    powder
½ teaspoon salt
½ cup finely diced
    pasteurized process
    sharp American
    cheese
1½ cups milk

1. Pare apples and slice thinly. Arrange in an even layer in a buttered 13×9×2-inch baking pan. Pour maple syrup over apples.

2. Mix flour with baking powder and salt; add cheese. Add milk and stir just until mixed. Drop by spoonfuls onto apples.

3. Bake at 425°F 30 to 35 minutes. Serve warm. If desired, serve with nutmeg-flavored sweetened whipped cream.

About 8 servings

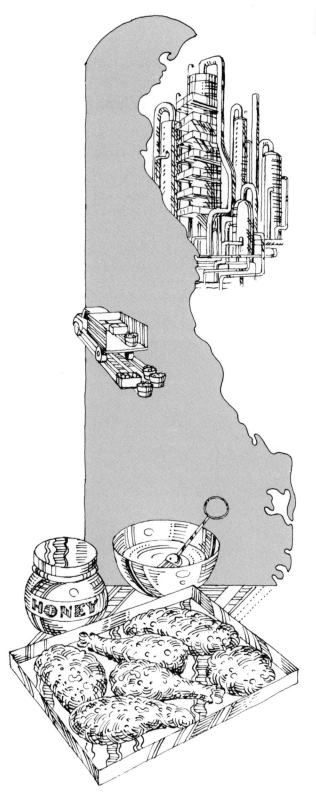

Delaware, the second smallest state, was the first of the thirteen colonies to ratify the Constitution. From the pastured valleys and wooded slopes of the north, through the Atlantic coastal plains, marshes, and sandy beaches to the great cypress swamp along the southern Maryland border, there is a lot of history, charm, agriculture, and industry packed into the 2,000-plus square miles that comprise Delaware.

Colonial New Sweden was first settled by Swedes and Finns in 1638. Later the Dutch took possession, and Delaware-Dutch history is commemorated in the Zwaanendael Museum in Lewes.

Other remnants of the culture of the early colonists linger, but the strongest influence was, and remains, Anglo-Saxon. The English took control of the area when the land was granted to William Penn in 1682. Their impact has been particularly strong in Kent and Sussex, the southernmost of Delaware's three counties.

This largely rural area is populated by farmers who moved from Maryland's Eastern Shore. Many towns' names speak of their British beginnings: Dover (the capital), Kent, Canterbury, Georgetown, Milton, and Milford.

Northern New Castle County is more urbanized and industrialized than downstate, and has attracted greater ethnic diversity. The Wilmington area remains culturally close to southeastern Pennsylvania.

Situated on the western shores of the Delaware River and Delaware Bay, Delaware also has a small Atlantic coastline plus numerous freshwater ponds and streams. This proximity to large bodies of water moderates the climate, making the growing season over six months long.

Countless bays, coves, and inlets provide a haven for recreational boating, fishing, and swimming. The waterways also allow for commercial fishing, transportation, and commercial and industrial uses.

Important food resources from the water include oysters, clams, crabs, and turtles. Among the more plentiful fish are flounder, shad, sturgeon, pike, trout, and catfish.

Corn and wheat were early cash crops, and grist mills were built on the banks of many streams. By the end of the eighteenth century the flour mills along Brandywine Creek were the most famous in America.

Truck farming became important and retains its significance today, due to good transportation to nearby markets. From the mid-nineteenth century until about 1900, peaches were cultivated on a large scale. Some of today's crops and agricultural products are soybeans, potatoes, mushrooms, beans, tomatoes, berries, hogs, eggs, and dairy products.

By far the most important agricultural development of the twentieth century has been the poultry industry. Broiler-fryers are the chief agricultural commodity of the Delmarva Peninsula, where several hundred million of the tender young chickens are raised annually.

Delaware shares the Delmarva Peninsula with parts of Maryland and Virginia. Together these states sponsor the National Chicken Festival and Chicken Cooking Contest, with the site alternating each year. The days are filled with parades and pageants; a Poultry Princess is crowned; contestants whip up their chicken specialties, and tons of fried chicken are consumed by thousands of visitors.

Delawareans enjoy many food preferences in common with the South, including a passion for chicken in all its forms. They also share the culinary inclinations that come down from Philadelphia's English Quaker background. Added to these legacies, the bounty from the sea and other local factors uniquely flavor the cookery of the proud First State.

Hot Mushroom Appetizers

1 **pound large fresh
   mushrooms**
½ **pound chicken livers**
½ **teaspoon fresh onion
   juice**
3 **tablespoons butter or
   margarine**
1 **cup crushed wheat wafers**
1 **chicken bouillon cube**
½ **cup boiling water**
½ **teaspoon salt**
⅛ **teaspoon tarragon leaves,
   crushed**
   Garlic Butter

1. Wash mushrooms; remove stems and set caps aside.
2. Chop stems and combine with chicken livers and onion juice. Cook in heated butter in a skillet 10 minutes, stirring occasionally to cook evenly. Remove livers and chop.
3. Return chopped livers to skillet with wafer crumbs, bouillon cube dissolved in water, the salt, and tarragon. Blend thoroughly.
4. Generously brush mushroom caps, inside and out, with Garlic Butter; fill with the chicken liver mixture. Place in a shallow baking pan.
5. Bake at 375°F about 20 minutes. Garnish with **sieved hard-cooked egg yolk.** Serve hot.

About 2 dozen appetizers

Garlic Butter: Mix thoroughly ½ **cup softened butter or margarine** and **1 minced garlic clove.**

Oyster-Potato Fries

Crisp little cakes of oysters with French-fried potato coating, delectably seasoned.

¼ cup dairy sour cream
¼ cup all-purpose flour
½ teaspoon salt
½ teaspoon seasoned salt
1 egg, beaten
2 cups finely shredded
    potatoes, drained
1 pint oysters, well drained
    Fat for deep frying
    heated to 365°F

1. Stir sour cream and a mixture of flour, salt, and seasoned salt into the beaten egg. Combine with potatoes and blend thoroughly. Add 4 or 5 oysters at a time to potato mixture.

2. Drop mixture by tablespoonfuls with an oyster in each spoonful into the hot fat. Do not crowd the oysters; they should be free to float one layer deep. Fry 2 to 3 minutes, or until golden brown.

3. Remove with slotted spoon and drain over fat before removing to absorbent paper.

About 30 cakes

Flounder Stuffed with Crab Meat

1 pound lump crab meat,
    bony membrane
    removed
1 slice white bread, crusts
    trimmed and bread cut
    in ¼-inch cubes
3 tablespoons lemon juice
1 tablespoon dry sherry
¾ teaspoon salt
¾ teaspoon dry mustard
⅛ teaspoon seasoned salt
¾ teaspoon Worcestershire
    sauce
¼ teaspoon Tabasco
1 cup Medium White Sauce
    (page 43)
1 egg yolk
    Butter or margarine
4 fresh flounder fillets
    (about 2 pounds) with
    pockets cut in sides

1. Combine crab meat (do not break up lumps) with bread cubes, lemon juice, sherry, salt, dry mustard, seasoned salt, Worcestershire sauce, and Tabasco. Mix gently; add a mixture of the white sauce and egg yolk. Continue tossing lightly.

2. Butter flounder and fill pockets with the crab meat stuffing. Put into a shallow broiler-resistant baking dish. Sprinkle generously with **paprika**.

3. Bake at 350°F 10 to 12 minutes and brown under broiler before serving.

4 servings

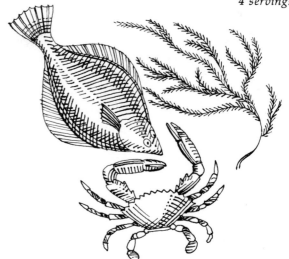

DELAWARE

Finnish Meatballs

Dill-flavored meat-vegetable morsels are served with a sour cream-tomato sauce.

1½ pounds ground beef
    round steak
1 egg, slightly beaten
2 teaspoons salt
½ teaspoon pepper
½ teaspoon dill weed
2 cups grated raw potato
½ cup finely chopped
    onion
½ cup finely chopped
    green pepper
1 to 2 tablespoons butter
    or margarine
1 can (8 ounces) tomato
    sauce
⅓ cup cold water
1 tablespoon flour
1 cup dairy sour cream

1. Combine in a bowl ground meat, egg, salt, pepper, and dill, then the vegetables; toss to mix. Lightly shape into 1-inch balls.
2. Brown meatballs evenly on all sides in hot butter in a large skillet. When thoroughly cooked, remove meatballs to a warm serving dish; keep hot.
3. Add tomato sauce to the drippings in skillet and stir in a blend of water and flour. Bring rapidly to boiling, stirring mixture constantly; cook 1 to 2 minutes.
4. Reduce heat. Stirring gravy vigorously with a French whip or spoon, add sour cream in very small amounts. Heat thoroughly, about 3 minutes (do not boil). Pour gravy over meatballs and serve.

About 6 dozen meatballs

Delmarva Broiled Chicken

Delmarva's famous broiler-fryers broiled to a turn, with a basting of seasoned honey glaze.

1 broiler-fryer chicken
    (about 3 pounds), cut
    in pieces
½ cup honey
⅓ cup soy sauce
6 tablespoons lemon juice
2 teaspoons dry mustard
2 cloves garlic, minced

1. Spread chicken pieces generously with a mixture of remaining ingredients.
2. Arrange chicken, skin side down, in a shallow baking pan or broiler pan without rack. Broil 6 to 9 inches from source of heat 25 to 30 minutes, brushing occasionally with butter or remaining honey mixture. Turn and broil, continuing to brush, 20 minutes longer, or until tender.

4 servings

Shirred Eggs with Sausage and Cheese

¼ pound salami or bologna,
    thinly sliced
2 tablespoons butter or
    margarine
¼ pound Swiss or Cheddar
    cheese, thinly sliced
6 eggs
¾ teaspoon salt
    Few grains pepper
    Dash Worcestershire
    sauce

1. Brown salami lightly in butter in a skillet; reserve drippings in skillet.
2. Line a 9-inch pie plate with salami and add an even layer of cheese.
3. Break and slip eggs, one at a time, onto the cheese. Pour drippings over all. Season with salt and pepper and drizzle with Worcestershire sauce.
4. Bake at 325°F about 22 minutes, or until done as desired. Serve immediately with **buttered toast.**

6 servings

Nectarine Lemon Pie, 74

Crab-Stuffed Eggs

12 hard-cooked eggs, cut in
   halves lengthwise
1 can (6½ ounces) crab
   meat, drained and
   flaked
2 tablespoons melted
   butter or margarine
¼ cup dairy sour cream
2 to 3 tablespoons
   mayonnaise
4 teaspoons grated onion
½ teaspoon Worcestershire
   sauce
½ teaspoon salt
⅛ teaspoon white pepper

1. Remove egg yolks from whites. Sieve yolks, toss
with crab meat.
2. Blend in a mixture of the remaining ingredients.
Stuff egg whites. Garnish each with **pimento** or **parsley**.

24 stuffed egg halves

Herb-Buttered Green Beans

1½ pounds green beans
3 tablespoons melted
   butter or margarine
½ teaspoon salt
¼ teaspoon lemon juice
¼ teaspoon rosemary or
   savory

1. Wash, break off ends, and cut green beans into
pieces.
2. Cook beans 15 to 20 minutes, or until tender. (Or
use two 9-ounce packages frozen cut green beans; cook
following directions on package.)
3. Drain beans immediately and add butter, salt,
lemon juice, and rosemary and toss gently.

4 or 5 servings

Savory Limas

4 slices bacon
½ cup chopped onion
½ clove garlic, minced
1 can (about 10 ounces)
   condensed tomato soup
1 tablespoon sugar
2 teaspoons prepared
   mustard
4 cups (two 16-ounce cans)
   lima beans or 2
   packages (10 ounces
   each) frozen lima
   beans, cooked
   following package
   directions
½ teaspoon Worcestershire
   sauce

1. Fry bacon until crisp in a large, heavy skillet with a
tight-fitting cover. Remove bacon and crumble; reserve.
2. Pour off all but 2 tablespoons fat, add onion and
garlic, and sauté until tender, stirring occasionally.
3. Remove from heat and blend in a mixture of tomato
soup, sugar, and mustard. Stir in bacon, lima beans,
and Worcestershire sauce.
4. Cover and heat over low heat 10 to 12 minutes, or
until flavors are well blended.

About 6 servings

Rock Lobster Bouillabaisse, 76

Dutch Apple Pie

This one-crust pie has a luscious apple-custard filling and a crunchy walnut-cheese topping.

DELAWARE

3 to 4 (about 1 pound) tart
    cooking apples
1 unbaked 9-inch pie
    shell
1 egg, slightly beaten
1 cup whipping cream
1½ teaspoons vanilla extract
1 cup sugar
3 tablespoons flour
½ teaspoon cinnamon
¼ teaspoon nutmeg
⅛ teaspoon salt
4 teaspoons butter or
    margarine
½ cup walnuts, coarsely
    chopped
¾ cup shredded sharp
    Cheddar cheese

1. Wash, quarter, core, pare, and thinly slice apples. Turn slices into unbaked pie shell.
2. Blend the egg, cream, and vanilla extract. Gradually add a mixture of sugar, flour, nutmeg, cinnamon, and salt, mixing well. Pour over apples in pie shell. Dot with butter, Sprinkle walnuts over top.
3. Bake at 450°F 10 minutes; turn oven control to 350°F and bake 35 to 40 minutes, or until apples are tender and top is lightly browned.
4. Remove from oven and sprinkle cheese over top. Serve warm.

One 9-inch pie

Spicy Peach Cobbler

1 can (29 ounces) peach
    slices, drained (reserve
    1 cup syrup)
½ cup firmly packed brown
    sugar
2 tablespoons cornstarch
⅛ teaspoon salt
⅛ teaspoon cinnamon
⅛ teaspoon cloves
2 tablespoons cider vinegar
1 tablespoon butter or
    margarine
1 cup all-purpose biscuit
    mix
½ cup shredded sharp
    Cheddar cheese
2 tablespoons butter or
    margarine, melted
¼ cup milk

1. Place drained peaches in a 1-quart shallow baking dish; set aside.
2. Combine brown sugar, cornstarch, salt, cinnamon, and cloves in a saucepan; stir in the reserved peach syrup, vinegar, and 1 tablespoon butter. Bring mixture to boiling, stirring frequently; cook until clear and thickened. Pour over peaches and set in a 400°F oven.
3. Combine biscuit mix and cheese and mix thoroughly. Stir in melted butter and milk to form a soft dough. Remove baking dish from oven and drop by heaping tablespoonfuls onto peaches.
4. Return to oven and bake 20 minutes, or until crust is golden brown. Serve warm.

6 servings

Maryland cooks have a great respect for tradition, and take pride in their time-honored recipes. They appreciate fine-quality foods, particularly those locally grown or produced.

Many food customs are rooted in English origins. George Calvert, first Lord Baltimore, was granted the land in 1632. The manorial life style of the landed gentry led to elegant traditions like hunt breakfasts, many of which persist in some areas today. Southern Maryland and the Eastern Shore remain largely British in background, while Baltimore and the Washington, D.C. area are now quite cosmopolitan.

Maryland is divided roughly in half by Chesapeake Bay. The flat, low plains of the Eastern Shore have made it ideal for truck farming. The Eastern Shore shares the Delmarva Peninsula with Delaware and Virginia, and is famous for its poultry industry.

Across the Bay, the five southernmost counties of the western shore are known as southern Maryland, a place where tradition runs deep. One of the state's most famous

dishes, Stuffed Ham, has been prized here since early colonial days. Beaten biscuits and Maryland-style fried chicken also add luster to the area's sparkling reputation for good cooking.

It is the Chesapeake itself, however, that stamps Maryland's food with its most indelible characteristics. The bay and the tidal rivers that pour into it yield a great variety of fish and shellfish; Chesapeake crabs and oysters are probably the best known.

Crab cookery reaches its pinnacle in Maryland, from soups to salads, from simple steamed or boiled crabs to glamorous preparations like Crab Imperial. A seasonal delight is soft-shelled crabs, caught in the spring after the old hard shells are shed, but before new ones are formed. Their arrival signals a rite of spring, the soft-shell crab festival. Great quantities of the unshelled crustaceans are consumed, along with copious amounts of beer or ale. Soft-shelled crabs are usually fried, either sautéed in

MARYLAND

butter, or breaded and deep-fried.

Crab feasts are to Maryland what corn roasts are to the Midwest and clambakes to New England. The public suppers are frequently fund-raising affairs sponsored by churches, schools, or volunteer fire departments.

The menu stars crab, of course, often in the form of that Maryland specialty, crab cakes. Fried chicken and ham are offered, too, along with mashed potatoes and gravy or potato salad, depending on the season. Other vegetables are string beans, coleslaw, and a special Maryland favorite, kale, seasoned with a bit of bacon or salt pork. The typical breads are hot biscuits and corn bread. Dessert time brings a big selection of tempting homemade pies and handsome cakes.

Marylanders have a long-standing fondness for the fabled diamondback terrapins from the salt marshes. Today terrapin stew is not served as often as in the past because of the expense and the time-consuming preparation.

Also historically important is the canvasback duck. The wild ducks which feed on the grasses and grains of the marshes are delicately flavored. They were especially prized by the gourmets of the nineteenth and early twentieth centuries.

Kitchen gardens bordered with herbs are common, and one of the characteristics of Maryland cookery is the abundance of vegetables. Often several different varieties are served at a meal. Turnips and sweet potatoes are popular, and sauerkraut is served locally with roast turkey.

Fried Soft-Shelled Crabs

12 **soft-shelled crabs**
½ **cup all-purpose flour**
½ **teaspoon salt**
¼ **teaspoon pepper**
½ **cup butter**

1. Kill crabs by inserting a sharp-pointed, narrow-bladed knife into the body between the eyes.
2. Wash, cut off the pointed apron on underside, and cut off spongy material beneath points at each end of shell. Turn the crab and cut off the face.
3. Coat crabs evenly with a mixture of the flour, salt, and pepper. Shake off excess flour. Set crabs aside.
4. Heat butter in a skillet over low heat. Fry only as many crabs at one time as will lie flat in the pan. Cook until crabs are browned and crisp on the edges. Turn and brown second side.
5. Serve crabs hot with **brown butter.**

4 to 6 servings

Maryland Crab Cakes

3 tablespoons butter or
    margarine
¾ cup finely chopped onion
1 cup soft bread crumbs
1 pound crab meat, flaked
    and bony tissue
    removed
3 eggs, beaten
¾ teaspoon salt
1 teaspoon dry mustard
⅛ teaspoon paprika
1 teaspoon Worcestershire
    sauce
3 tablespoons chopped
    parsley
1 to 2 tablespoons cream
½ cup all-purpose flour
    (about)
   Butter, margarine, or
    cooking oil

1. Heat butter in a skillet. Add onion and cook about 3 minutes, stirring occasionally. Remove from heat and stir in bread crumbs and then flaked crab meat.
2. Mix together eggs, salt, dry mustard, paprika, Worcestershire sauce, and parsley. Combine with crab meat mixture and add enough cream to hold together. Shape into about twelve 2½-inch cakes. Coat with flour.
3. Heat a ¼-inch layer of butter in a large skillet. Add cakes and fry until golden brown (about 3 minutes per side).
4. Serve with **lemon wedges.**

4 to 6 servings

Diamondback Terrapin Stew (Chesapeake Bay Style)

3 large terrapins
6 hard-cooked eggs
3 tablespoons flour
½ teaspoon nutmeg
3 tablespoons lemon juice
1 tablespoon grated lemon
    peel
   Soup stock
1 onion, sliced
2 stalks celery, diced
1 tablespoon
    Worcestershire sauce
   Salt and red pepper
½ cup cream
2 cups sherry
   Hot milk, if necessary

1. Drop live terrapin into boiling water and let stand 5 minutes. Remove from water, rub skin off feet, tail, and head with a towel, drawing head out with a skewer. Clip off claws. Scrub shell, using boiling water. Break shell apart with sharp ax. Remove meat and liver. Discard gall bladder (being careful not to break it as it is bitter), heart, sandbag, and entrails. Cut the liver in thin slices. Take out eggs, remove film, and set eggs aside in cold water.
2. Mash yolks of hard-cooked eggs; add flour, nutmeg, lemon juice and peel. Put into a large, heavy saucepan. Stir in 1 cup soup stock, add onion, celery, terrapin, terrapin eggs, and enough more stock to cover meat. Cook covered until meat falls from bones.
3. Remove bones; add Worcestershire sauce, salt, red pepper, chopped egg whites, cream, sherry, and if necessary a little hot milk. Heat thoroughly, stirring occasionally, and serve with **toast.**

6 servings

MARYLAND

Maryland Stuffed Ham

1 fully cooked smoked
    ham (about 12 pounds)
1 package (10 ounces)
    fresh spinach
1 bunch green onions
1 bunch parsley
1 cup dry red wine
¾ cup honey
3 tablespoons water
4 teaspoons cornstarch
2 tablespoons cider vinegar

1. Trim thick skin, if necessary, from ham. Make 3-inch-deep cuts with a sharp knife at 1-inch intervals all over fat side.
2. Trim off stems from spinach and cut out any coarse ribs. Trim onions and parsley and wash along with spinach; dry thoroughly, finely chop, and mix well.
3. Pack greens mixture into cuts to fill openings.
4. Place ham, fat side up, in a large, shallow baking pan. Brush with some of the wine.
5. Bake at 325°F 2½ hours, brushing several times with wine.
6. Stir honey into remaining wine; brush some of the mixture over ham. Continue baking and brushing with mixture 30 minutes, or until well glazed. Remove from oven and allow to stand about 20 minutes for easier carving.
7. Pour mixture from baking pan into a 1-quart measuring cup. Skim off fat. Add water to measuring cup to make 3 cups liquid. Pour into roasting pan and heat to boiling.
8. Blend water with cornstarch; stir into boiling liquid. Cook and stir, scraping brown residue from bottom and sides of pan, until sauce boils; boil 3 minutes. Remove from heat; stir in vinegar.
9. Put ham on a warm platter and accompany with the sauce in a bowl.

About 24 servings

Fried Chicken à la Maryland

Flour-coated chicken pieces are slowly fried, then served with cream gravy. Also popular is batter-coated, deep-fried chicken.

2 broiler-fryer chickens,
    cut in halves or
    quarters*
¾ cup all-purpose flour
1 teaspoon salt
¼ teaspoon pepper
½ cup butter
¼ cup water
    Cream Gravy

1. Rinse chicken and pat dry. Shake pieces in a bag with flour, salt, and pepper.
2. Heat butter in a heavy skillet and when hot, drop in pieces of chicken and brown quickly on all sides. Reduce heat, add water, cover, and cook over low heat until tender (about 30 minutes).
3. Serve chicken with Cream Gravy. Garnish with small **corn fritters** and cooked **bacon.**
*Allow ¾ pound chicken per serving.

Cream Gravy: Blend **2 tablespoons chicken drippings** with **2 tablespoons flour.** Season with **salt** and **pepper.** Add **1 cup milk or cream** and **1 cup chicken broth** or **stock** gradually, stirring constantly. Heat to boiling; stir and cook 2 minutes.

Country Style Kale

2 pounds fresh kale
6 slices bacon
1 teaspoon butter or bacon
   fat
1 teaspoon salt
¼ teaspoon pepper
3 hard-cooked eggs, halved
   Paprika
   Vinegar

1. Wash kale and cut out middle rib portion. Cook in a small amount of water about 15 minutes, or until tender.
2. Fry bacon until crisp; drain.
3. Mix butter, salt, and pepper with kale. Turn into a serving bowl. Crumble bacon over kale. Top with eggs, sprinkle with paprika, and if desired, drizzle with vinegar.

About 6 servings

Creamed Tomatoes

4 firm ripe or green
   tomatoes
½ cup cornmeal
1 teaspoon salt
½ teaspoon sugar
⅛ teaspoon pepper
¼ cup butter or margarine
2 tablespoons cream

1. Cut out stem ends of tomatoes and slice ½ inch thick.
2. Mix cornmeal, salt, sugar, and pepper in a shallow dish. Coat both sides of tomato slices with the mixture.
3. Heat butter in a skillet. Add as many tomato slices at one time as will lie flat in skillet. Lightly brown both sides, turning once; add butter as needed. Stir browned tomatoes to break up; cook 5 minutes.
4. Just before serving, stir in cream.

About 4 servings

Hominy Grits Soufflé

1 cup warm cooked
   hominy grits (prepared
   following package
   directions)
3 tablespoons hot milk
2 tablespoons finely
   chopped onion
½ teaspoon salt
3 egg yolks, beaten
½ cup shredded Cheddar
   cheese
3 egg whites, beaten to
   stiff, not dry, peaks

1. Combine warm grits, milk, onion, and salt in a bowl. Beat egg yolks until thick and lemon colored. Stir egg yolks and cheese into grits mixture. Fold in egg whites.
2. Turn mixture into an ungreased 1-quart casserole or soufflé dish. Set in a baking pan. Pour boiling water around casserole to a depth of 1 inch.
3. Bake at 350°F about 1 hour. Serve immediately.

4 to 6 servings

Lord Baltimore Cake

While feathery white Lady Baltimore Cake rightfully belongs to South Carolina, we have claimed its counterpart for Maryland. The golden butter cake layers are richly endowed with fluffy white frosting and a filling flavored with macaroons, cherries, and nuts.

2½ cups sifted cake flour
½ teaspoon salt
1 tablespoon baking powder
¾ cup butter or margarine
1 teaspoon vanilla extract
½ teaspoon lemon extract
1¼ cups sugar
⅔ cup egg yolks (7 or 8)
¾ cup milk
Lord Baltimore Frosting

1. Blend the flour, salt, and baking powder together. Set aside.
2. Cream the butter and extracts. Gradually add sugar, creaming together until light and fluffy.
3. Beat egg yolks until thick and lemon colored. Add to creamed mixture and beat until light and fluffy.
4. Add dry ingredients in fourths and milk in thirds, beating well after each addition. Pour batter into three greased and waxed-paper-lined 9-inch round layer cake pans.
5. Bake at 375°F 20 to 25 minutes, or until cake tests done. Remove from oven to cooling racks. Peel off paper.
6. When cool fill and frost layers with Lord Baltimore Frosting.

One 3-layer 9-inch cake

Lord Baltimore Frosting

3 cups sugar
¾ cup water
¼ teaspoon cream of tartar
4 egg whites
2 teaspoons vanilla extract
½ cup dry macaroon crumbs
¼ cup chopped pecans
¼ cup chopped blanched almonds
12 candied cherries, quartered
2 teaspoons lemon juice
¼ teaspoon orange extract

1. Combine sugar, water, and cream of tartar in a heavy 3-quart saucepan. Cook without stirring to 238°F (soft-ball stage).
2. Beat the egg whites until stiff, but not dry, peaks are formed. Pour one-half of the syrup in a fine stream into beaten egg whites while beating constantly. Cook remainder of syrup to 248°F (firm-ball stage).
3. Remove from heat and pour all the remaining syrup in a fine stream into the frosting, beating thoroughly. Add flavoring and beat mixture until thick enough to spread.
4. Divide in half. To one half, add the remaining ingredients and mix carefully. Spread between layers of Lord Baltimore Cake. Frost sides and top with remaining half of frosting.

NEW JERSEY

New Jersey, despite being an industrial giant and ranking in the top ten states in population, is relatively unknown to many outsiders. However, one spot familiar to most Americans is Atlantic City.

The Boardwalk, Steel Pier, and Convention Hall rival the sea, sun, and sand for attention. But for one weekend each year the Miss America Pageant steals the scene from them all. Atlantic City is the largest in a string of seaside resorts stretching from Sandy Hook to Cape May.

While the resorts are great for vacations, most of the people actually live in the industrial heart of the state, along the route between New York and Philadelphia. New Jersey is as highly urbanized as industrialized, being the most densely populated of the fifty states.

New Jersey's peninsular position between the Hudson and Delaware rivers has influenced its settlement and history. The rivers brought Dutch, Scandinavian, and British colonists into the country, then provided transportation to nearby markets for the products of agriculture and industry.

In the nineteenth century German, Italian, Polish, Slovak, Jewish, Hungarian, Russian, and other immigrant groups found opportunities in flourishing factories, trades, and financial institutions.

Each group brought with them cherished food customs, many of which are retained today in New Jersey's cosmopolitan array. For example, the Italians contributed their wonderful ways with veal, Mediterranean vegetables, and of course, pasta. From eastern Europe came the Slavic talents for incorporating seeds and nuts in all manner of breads, cakes, and pastries.

Visitors motoring through New Jersey might be surprised to learn that there are numerous farms tucked away throughout the state, particularly in the southern half.

On some of the highest-priced farmland in the nation, highly specialized farmers grow food for the surrounding megalopolis. They concentrate on producing, processing,

NEW JERSEY

and marketing eggs, dairy products, and garden vegetables such as asparagus, beets, eggplant, potatoes, and tomatoes. Fruits, including apples, peaches, cranberries, and other berries have also helped New Jersey earn its nickname of the "Garden State." However, fresh produce is disappearing from the markets as more and more goes to the canneries and frozen food plants.

Apples were a staple food of eastern colonists, and apple cider was the common beverage of the day. Most of the colonial cider was hard, or fermented. It was produced by allowing sweet cider to stand until the natural sugar fermented and turned into alcohol.

Hard cider may be distilled to produce apple brandy, commonly known as applejack. The powerful potion is sometimes known, too, as "Jersey lightning," because a great percentage of the apple brandy distilled in the United States is turned out in New Jersey.

As in all coastal states, seafood such as oysters, clams, and crabs is popular. Fisheries, chiefly around Cape May, also produce fluke, porgy, sea bass, whiting, and cod.

A popular New Jersey festivity is the shad bake, a cousin of the New England clambake. The shad is a member of the herring family, caught in eastern rivers in the spring when they swim upriver to spawn.

For the community dinners, long beds of charcoal are first prepared. The fillets of shad are salted and peppered, then nailed skin side down to greased hardwood boards. Strips of bacon crisscrossed over the top add flavor and keep the fish moist and tender. The planks are placed upright alongside the radiating coals at a slight outward angle to facilitate even cooking, much in the old Indian method of open-fire cooking. At home, shad is frequently basted with butter and broiled.

Broiled Shad

For a real springtime treat, serve with Lemon Chive Potatoes, Asparagus Polonaise, and Deep Dish Strawberry-Rhubarb Pie.

1 shad (3 to 4 pounds)
Melted butter
Salt and pepper
¼ cup butter
1 tablespoon lemon juice
Parsley

1. Clean and split shad. Place fish skin side down on an oiled and preheated wooden plank or broiler-proof platter. Brush with melted butter and sprinkle with salt and pepper.
2. Broil until tender (15 to 20 minutes, depending upon size and thickness of fish).
3. Beat butter until softened. Gradually add lemon juice, beating until smooth. Spread butter over fish. Garnish with parsley. Serve hot.

6 to 8 servings

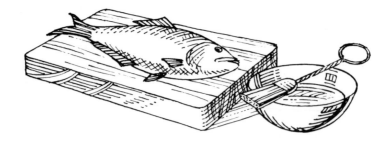

African Rock Lobster en Casserole

6 (3 ounces each) frozen
South African rock
lobster tails
¼ cup butter or margarine
¼ cup flour
2 cups chicken broth
2 egg yolks, fork beaten
⅓ cup half-and-half
2 to 3 teaspoons
Worcestershire sauce
1 teaspoon dry mustard
blended with about 1
tablespoon cold water
1 or 2 packages (10 ounces
each) frozen asparagus
spears, cooked
following package
directions
1 package (8 ounces)
spaghetti, cooked and
drained
Parmesan-Romano
cheese
¼ cup toasted slivered
almonds

1. Drop frozen lobster tails into boiling salted water. Return to boiling and simmer 3 minutes.
2. Remove cooked lobster tails and place under running cold water until cool enough to handle. With scissors, cut along each edge of bony membrane on the underside of shell; remove meat.
3. Dice half of the meat and cut remainder into chunks; set aside.
4. Heat butter in a heavy saucepan; stir in flour. Cook until bubbly. Add broth gradually while blending thoroughly. Stirring constantly, bring rapidly to boiling and cook 1 to 2 minutes. Immediately blend about 3 tablesponfuls into egg yolks and stir into the hot sauce. Cook 3 to 5 minutes, stirring constantly.
5. Blend in half-and-half, Worcestershire sauce, mustard, and diced lobster. Heat thoroughly.
6. Divide cooked asparagus equally among 6 individual casseroles. Spoon over spaghetti and hot lobster sauce. Generously shake cheese over all. Top with lobster chunks and almonds.

6 servings

Veal Marsala

¼ cup olive oil
1 clove garlic, thinly
sliced
1½ to 2 pounds veal cutlets,
cut about ½ inch thick
¼ cup flour
½ teaspoon salt
⅛ teaspoon pepper
¼ cup Marsala
¼ cup water
¼ teaspoon chopped
parsley
⅛ teaspoon salt
⅛ teaspoon pepper

1. Heat olive oil in a large, heavy skillet; add garlic and lightly brown.
2. Pound cutlets on a wooden board and cut into six pieces.
3. Coat veal with a mixture of flour, ½ teaspoon salt, and ⅛ teaspoon pepper.
4. Add veal to garlic and olive oil and slowly brown on both sides.
5. While veal is browning, combine Marsala, water, chopped parsley, and remaining salt and pepper. Slowly add Marsala mixture to browned veal.
6. Cover skillet and simmer over low heat about 20 minutes, or until veal is tender. If sauce tends to become too thick, add a small amount of water.

6 servings

White Clam Sauce for Linguine

2 cups water
2 dozen washed
    cherrystone clams*
½ cup chopped onion
¼ cup snipped parsley
3 cloves garlic, minced
¼ cup olive oil
2 tablespoons flour
¼ to ½ teaspoon salt
    Few grains pepper
8 ounces linguine, cooked

1. Bring water to boiling in a large saucepot or Dutch oven. Add clams. Cover and steam until shells are partially opened.
2. Drain, reserving 1½ cups of the cooking liquid. Remove clams from shells; coarsely chop clams and set aside.
3. Add onion, parsley, and garlic to hot olive oil in a large skillet; cook about 3 minutes, stirring occasionally.
4. Mix in flour, salt, and a few grains pepper; cook until bubbly. Add reserved clam liquid gradually, while blending thoroughly. Bring rapidly to boiling, stirring constantly, and boil 1 to 2 minutes. Mix in the chopped clams and heat (do not boil).
5. Serve clam sauce on cooked linguine.

4 servings

*Canned minced clams (three 7½-ounce cans) and the drained liquid (about 1½ cups) may be substituted for the whole clams and the reserved liquid.

Eggs Florentine

Layers of spinach, hard-cooked eggs, and savory cheese sauce are topped with buttery bread crumbs, baked hot and lightly browned.

2 packages (10 ounces
    each) frozen spinach
1 teaspoon seasoned salt
    Nutmeg
½ cup shredded Swiss
    cheese
1 tablespoon butter or
    margarine
1 tablespoon flour
¼ teaspoon garlic salt
⅛ teaspoon white pepper
¾ cup milk
1 tablespoon butter or
    margarine
4 eggs
1 tablespoon butter or
    margarine, melted
2 tablespoons shredded
    Swiss cheese
2 tablespoons fine dry
    bread crumbs

1. Cook spinach according to package directions, using seasoned salt instead of salt. Drain thoroughly.
2. Put one half the spinach into a greased shallow 5-cup baking dish. Sprinkle lightly with nutmeg and then with the ½ cup cheese. Top evenly with the remaining spinach.
3. Set in a 325°F oven and heat 15 minutes. Remove from oven.
4. Meanwhile, heat 1 tablespoon butter in a saucepan. Blend in flour, garlic salt, and pepper. Heat until bubbly. Add the milk gradually, stirring until blended. Bring to boiling, stirring constantly, and cook 1 to 2 minutes. Set aside and keep warm.
5. Heat 1 tablespoon butter in a skillet until hot. Break eggs, one at a time, into a saucer and slip into skillet. Reduce heat, cover, and cook slowly until eggs are just set (about 4 minutes).
6. Arrange eggs on the hot spinach in a lengthwise row, overlapping the edges slightly. Spoon sauce around egg yolks. Sprinkle mixture of the remaining ingredients over sauce. Serve immediately.

4 servings

NEW JERSEY

Lemon-Chive Potatoes

12 small new potatoes
(about 1½ pounds)
⅓ cup butter or margarine
2 tablespoons minced
chives
2 teaspoons grated lemon
peel
1 tablespoon lemon juice
½ teaspoon salt
⅛ teaspoon pepper

1. Wash potatoes; cook covered in boiling salted water about 20 minutes, or until potatoes are tender when pierced with a fork.
2. Meanwhile, melt butter in a small saucepan. Stir in chives, lemon juice, salt, lemon peel, and pepper. Keep mixture warm.
3. Drain potatoes. To dry them, shake pan over low heat. Peel potatoes immediately and place in warm serving dish. Pour butter mixture over potatoes and turn them to coat well. Serve immediately.

4 servings

Asparagus Polonaise

Polonaise (French for Polish), when referring to vegetables, means a garnish of bread crumbs lightly browned in butter.

2 pounds fresh asparagus,
washed
⅓ cup butter
2 tablespoons
herb-seasoned stuffing
mix, finely crushed
Few drops lemon juice

1. Put asparagus into a small amount of boiling salted water in a skillet; bring to boiling, reduce heat, and cook 5 minutes, uncovered. Cover and cook 10 minutes, or until just tender.
2. Meanwhile, brown butter lightly in a saucepan; add the crushed stuffing mix and brown lightly. Sprinkle with lemon juice; pour over cooked asparagus spears. (Finely chopped hard-cooked eggs are sometimes sprinkled over Asparagus Polonaise.)

4 servings

Parmesan-Eggplant Slims

In this recipe sliced eggplant is coated with a mixture of crumbs, Parmesan cheese, and Italian salad dressing mix. Crisply fried in olive oil, these slices are irresistible.

32 round scalloped crackers,
finely crushed (1⅓
cups)
2 tablespoons shredded
Parmesan cheese
2 teaspoons Italian salad
dressing mix
½ cup olive oil
1 clove garlic, cut in half
1 medium eggplant, cut
crosswise in ¼-inch
slices
1 egg, slightly beaten

1. Blend crumbs, cheese, and salad dressing mix.
2. Heat olive oil and garlic in a large skillet over low heat about 10 minutes; remove garlic.
3. Dip eggplant into crumb mixture, then into egg and again into crumbs. Pour off and reserve all but a few tablespoons of oil. Add enough slices to lie flat in skillet; fry about 3 minutes on each side, or until browned. Repeat with remaining slices, adding oil as needed.
4. To serve, overlap two rows of eggplant slices on a heated platter; garnish with **parsley**.

About 8 servings

NEW JERSEY

Kulich

The mosquelike shape of this traditional Easter bread is attained by baking the loaves in coffee cans.

1 package active dry yeast
¼ cup warm water
¼ cup butter or margarine, softened
¼ cup sugar
1 teaspoon salt
¼ cup milk, scalded
2¼ cups all-purpose flour
1 egg, slightly beaten
½ teaspoon vanilla extract
¼ teaspoon ground cardamom
¼ cup chopped candied red cherries
¼ cup chopped candied green cherries
2 tablespoons chopped toasted almonds
¾ cup confectioners' sugar
4 teaspoons milk

1. Dissolve yeast in warm water.
2. Put butter, sugar, and salt into a bowl; add the scalded milk and stir until butter is melted. Cool to lukewarm.
3. Beat ½ cup of the flour into milk mixture. Stir in the yeast, then beat in egg, vanilla extract, and cardamom. Add remaining flour gradually, beating thoroughly after each addition. Cover; let rise in a warm place until double in bulk (1½ to 2 hours).
4. Punch down dough; let rise again until almost double in bulk (30 to 45 minutes).
5. Turn dough onto a lightly floured surface. Distribute cherries and almonds evenly over dough; knead about 15 times. Shape dough into a ball and put into a well-greased 1-pound coffee can. Cover; let rise again until double in bulk (30 to 45 minutes). Place can on a baking sheet, if desired.
6. Bake at 350°F 45 minutes, or until bread is well browned. Cool in can 10 to 15 minutes, then turn out onto a wire rack to cool completely.
7. Blend the confectioners' sugar and milk until smooth. Spoon icing over Kulich and allow it to drip down sides. Garnish top with a whole candied red cherry.

1 loaf Kulich

Deep Dish Strawberry-Rhubarb Pie

2 cups strawberries
3 cups rhubarb pieces
1½ cups sugar
2 tablespoons cornstarch
½ cup fine dry bread crumbs
Pastry for a 1-crust pie

1. Wash, hull, and cut large strawberries in half; wash and cut rhubarb into 1-inch pieces.
2. Toss strawberries and rhubarb with a mixture of the sugar and cornstarch.
3. Put bread crumbs into a deep pie dish. Cover with fruit mixture; top with pastry and seal at edges. Cut gashes in pastry for escape of steam.
4. Bake at 425°F 40 to 50 minutes, or until pastry is lightly browned.

1 deep dish pie

NEW YORK 63

Four elements have influenced the development of New York's cookery: the varied ethnic groups; the bounty of the Long Island seacoast; the produce of farms, orchards, and vineyards; and the menus of its opulent restaurants and hotels.

The state, and in particular New York City, most nearly characterizes the American melting pot. The Dutch first settled Manhattan at the present site of Albany in the 1620s, and their influence remained strong even after the English took over.

In cooking the Dutch made use of spices, wines, and rum and molasses imported by the Dutch West India Company. They are credited with contributing many recipes to our American heritage, such as doughnuts, waffles, and coleslaw.

From the American Revolution until about 1830 restless New Englanders poured into New York, and much upstate cooking still reflects this Yankee heritage. It is substantial, unadorned farm fare.

The early English and Irish immigrants brought their ingrained preference for oatmeal and potatoes. Germans introduced their sausages, pretzels, cheeses, rye breads, and other specialties. Later, Polish, Hungarian, Austrian, and Russian Jews settled east of Manhattan's Bowery. Italians, Slavs, and Greeks further enriched the culture toward the end of the nineteenth century, and Chinatown took form.

Most recent newcomers are Puerto Ricans who have settled in Spanish Harlem and other areas. Markets feature foods imported from the Caribbean, such as tropical tubers and roots, plantains, and canned vegetables. More commonplace items like beans, rice, dried salt cod, pumpkin, and coconut are also Puerto Rican staples.

Strictly American in background, however, is maple syrup. The sugar maple is found in many upstate counties, and some of the country's finest maple syrup is produced here.

West of the Catskills is New York's dairy country, with its wide valleys and rich grazing lands. Dairy products provide roughly half the state's farm income; also important are livestock, eggs, poultry, apples, potatoes, corn, and wheat.

West central New York is punctuated by the Finger Lakes. Along with the Hudson Valley and the Lake Erie shoreline, this region is the site of extensive vineyards. To date, most eastern wines have been made from native American grapes of the species *Vitis labrusca.* Hardy grapes like Concord, Delaware, and Catawba resist diseases and withstand cold winters when grown near moderating large bodies of water. Wines made from these grapes have a somewhat wild taste, described as "foxy."

Some eastern vintners have been experimenting with grafting French hybrid and European vines of the *vinifera* species onto American rootstock. Wines from these vines (Pinot Chardonnay, Pinot Noir, and Johannisberg Riesling) compare favorably with European and California wines from the same grapes. New York produces popular champagnes, red and white table wines, sparkling wines, sherry, and port.

A second important agricultural area is Long Island. The soils are well suited to market farming; fruits and vegetables such as berries, cabbage, onions, cauliflower, corn, beans, and beets are grown here.

A different type of Long Island crop is the tender, succulent domestic duckling. Long Island ducklings are descended from white Peking ducks brought from China in the nineteenth century, and about half the United States supply now comes from Long Island.

Another Long Island product is seafood that abounds in the surrounding waters. Among the shellfish are clams, scallops, oysters, lobsters, and mussels. Nearly half the country's hard-shell clams come from these bays. The tiny bay scallops are more highly prized than the larger sea scallops.

For well over a century New York City has enjoyed the reputation of housing some of the finest restaurants and hotels, and many culinary classics have been created in their kitchens. Eating in such places was not merely dining; it was a total experience in opulence and elegance.

Dawn's Hutspot

    2 cups water
    1 teaspoon salt
    1 beef chuck roast,
        boneless (about 1½
        pounds)
    6 large carrots, pared and
        quartered
    6 medium potatoes, pared
        and diced
    6 onions, chopped
 1½ teaspoons salt
    ¼ teaspoon pepper

1. Put water and 1 teaspoon salt into a large saucepot. Bring to boiling. Add beef; cover and cook over low heat 2 hours.
2. Add carrots to meat and cook 20 minutes.
3. Add potatoes and onions; cook about 30 minutes, or until liquid is absorbed and vegetables are soft.
4. Keep meat hot. Season vegetables with remaining salt and the pepper; mash thoroughly.
5. Cut meat into thick slices or chunks. Spoon mashed vegetables onto center of a warm platter; surround with meat pieces.

About 6 servings

Lime Chiffon Pie, 85

Old Drovers Inn Cheese Soup

New York's sharp Cheddar cheese, especially that of Herkimer County, is world famous.

¼ cup butter or margarine
½ cup diced carrot
½ cup diced green pepper
½ cup minced onion
½ cup diced celery
2 tablespoons flour
1 quart well-seasoned
    chicken stock
6 ounces mild Cheddar
    cheese, finely shredded
6 ounces sharp Cheddar
    cheese, finely shredded
  Milk
  Salt and pepper

1. Heat butter in the top of a double boiler over direct heat. Add carrot, green pepper, onion, and celery; cook until tender but not brown. Blend in the flour; cook and stir 1 minute.
2. Pour in stock, cooking and stirring until thickened.
3. Set over boiling water. Add cheeses and stir until melted. Thin to cream consistency with milk.
4. Strain the soup and season to taste with salt and pepper. Serve hot or chilled.

About 2 quarts soup

Manhattan Clam Chowder

Manhattan's chowder is more highly seasoned than the New England version, and is richly flavored with green pepper, celery, and tomatoes.

¼ pound salt pork, cubed
2 small onions, minced
½ green pepper, chopped
½ cup chopped celery
1 quart shucked clams
6 to 8 medium potatoes
  Cold water
  Salt (if needed)
½ teaspoon pepper
5 cups water
  Dash each cayenne
    pepper, sage, and
    thyme
6 to 8 saltine crackers, split
  Cold milk
3 cups tomato juice

1. Fry salt pork in a deep kettle until golden brown. Add onion, green pepper, and celery and cook together 2 to 3 minutes.
2. Remove stomach from clams; chop hard parts and leave soft parts whole or chop them, as preferred.
3. Arrange potatoes and hard parts of clams in layers over onion mixture; cover with cold water, bring to boiling, and simmer until potatoes are soft. Add soft part of clams, seasonings, and 5 cups water. Season with cayenne, sage, and thyme. Heat to boiling.
4. Meanwhile, soak crackers in milk.
5. Just before serving, add tomato juice and soaked crackers. Heat thoroughly.

6 to 8 servings

NEW YORK

Frankfurter Kabobs, 120; Vegetable Kabobs, 120;
Shrimp Kabobs, 120;
Basic Molasses Barbecue Sauce, 120

NEW YORK

Mrs. Schwager's Stuffed Cabbage

1 head cabbage (3 pounds)
1 pound ground beef chuck
1 egg
1 teaspoon salt
¼ teaspoon pepper
1 large onion, sliced
2 or 3 stalks celery, sliced
⅓ cup ketchup
3 tablespoons lemon juice
1 tablespoon sugar
1 tablespoon brown sugar
1 teaspoon salt
½ bay leaf
1 clove

1. Separate 8 cabbage leaves; put into a saucepot and cover with water. Bring to boiling and cook 10 minutes. Drain; cool leaves.
2. Coarsely shred remaining cabbage.
3. Mix meat, egg, 1 teaspoon salt, and ¼ teaspoon pepper. Shape into 8 meatballs. Roll each meatball in a cabbage leaf. Put rolls into saucepot. Add shredded cabbage, the onion, and celery. Add enough water to half cover cabbage rolls. Cover and cook over low heat 1 hour.
4. Add ketchup, lemon juice, sugars, remaining salt, bay leaf, and clove. Cook covered 45 to 60 minutes.

8 servings

Roast Duckling with Orange Sauce

2 ducklings (4 to 5 pounds each)
2 teaspoons salt
½ teaspoon pepper
1 clove garlic, peeled and cut crosswise into halves
½ cup dry white wine
½ cup orange marmalade

Sauce:
2 tablespoons butter or margarine
1 can (13¾ ounces) condensed chicken broth
½ cup orange marmalade
¼ cup dry white wine
¼ cup orange juice
2 teaspoons cornstarch
2 teaspoons lemon juice
2 tablespoons slivered orange peel

1. If frozen, let ducklings thaw according to package directions. Remove giblets, necks, and livers from ducklings. Reserve livers for sauce; if desired, reserve giblets and necks for soup stock. Remove and discard excess fat. Wash, drain, and pat dry with paper toweling. Rub cavities with salt, pepper, and garlic. Fasten neck skin of each to back with a skewer. Tuck tail ends into cavities. Tie legs together and tuck wing tips under ducklings. Prick skin generously so during roasting fat is released. Place ducklings, breast side up, on a rack in a large, shallow roasting pan.
2. Roast at 350°F 2 to 2½ hours, or until legs can be moved easily, basting several times during roasting and removing accumulated drippings about every 30 minutes. Remove ducklings from oven and spread surface with mixture of wine and marmalade. Return to oven and continue roasting 10 minutes.
3. For sauce, melt butter in a skillet. Add duckling livers and sauté until lightly browned. Remove and chop livers. Add chicken broth, marmalade, wine, orange juice, and cornstarch blended with lemon juice. Cook, stirring constantly, over low heat 10 minutes, or until sauce bubbles and thickens. Stir in chopped livers and orange peel.
4. Transfer ducklings to a heated platter. Remove skewers and twine. Garnish, if desired, with watercress and orange slices. Reheat sauce if necessary and serve with duckling.

8 servings

Peas in Rice Ring

1 package (6 or 6¾ ounces)
    seasoned wild and
    white rice mix
3 pounds fresh peas
    Butter

1. Cook rice mix according to package directions.
2. Meanwhile, rinse and shell peas just before cooking to retain their delicate flavor. Cook covered in boiling salted water to cover for 15 to 20 minutes, or until peas are tender. Drain and add just enough butter so peas glisten.
3. Butter a 1-quart ring mold. When rice is done, turn into mold, packing down gently with spoon. Invert onto a warm serving platter and lift off mold.
4. Spoon hot peas into rice ring just before serving.

About 6 servings

Cheese Blintzes

This Jewish specialty has gained national renown. Serve for brunch, luncheon, or as a dessert.

1½ cups creamed cottage
    cheese, drained
¼ cup dairy sour cream
1½ tablespoons sugar
½ teaspoon salt
2 tablespoons butter or
    margarine
1½ cups all-purpose flour
3 tablespoons sugar
½ teaspoon salt
1¼ cups milk
2 eggs, well beaten
1 tablespoon butter or
    margarine

1. Combine cottage cheese, sour cream, 1½ tablespoons sugar, and salt in a bowl; refrigerate.
2. To prepare pancakes, heat 2 tablespoons butter until melted; set aside to cool.
3. Combine flour, 3 tablespoons sugar, and ½ teaspoon salt in a bowl.
4. Beat melted butter and milk into beaten eggs. Combine with dry ingredients and beat until smooth.
5. Heat a 6-inch skillet (it is hot enough when drops of water dance in small beads). Grease lightly with **butter** or **margarine.**
6. Pour into skillet only enough batter to coat skillet thinly; immediately tilt back and forth to spread evenly. Cook over medium heat about 2 minutes, or until lightly browned on bottom and firm to touch on top. With spatula, remove pancake to a plate, brown side up.
7. Repeat with remaining batter. (It should not be necessary to grease skillet for each pancake.) Stack pancakes as they are baked.
8. For blintzes, spoon about 1½ tablespoons filling into center of brown side of one pancake. Fold two opposite sides to center. Roll up. Press edges to seal. Repeat for each pancake.
9. Heat remaining butter in a large skillet. Arrange several blintzes in skillet, sealed sides down. Brown on all sides over medium heat, turning carefully with tongs.
10. Remove blintzes to a serving platter. Serve hot with **sour cream** and **blueberries, currant jelly,** or **blueberry** or **blackberry jam.**

About 12 blintzes

NEW YORK

Waldorf Salad

This popular apple salad is said to have been the creation of Oscar of the Waldorf, maitre d' of the famous hotel for half a century.

2 medium red apples, rinsed, cored, and diced
1 cup diced celery
½ cup coarsely chopped walnuts
¼ cup mayonnaise
4 crisp cup-shaped lettuce leaves

1. Combine the apples, celery, and walnuts in a bowl; add mayonnaise and toss to mix thoroughly. Chill in refrigerator.
2. To serve, place lettuce leaves on individual salad plates, and spoon a portion of the salad mixture into each.

4 servings

Cheesecake Van Buren

This creamy dessert is a gourmet's delight, named for a New York native, President Martin Van Buren.

1½ cups crushed zwieback
2 tablespoons brown sugar
¼ cup melted butter
2 packages (8 ounces each) cream cheese, softened
1 cup sugar
6 eggs, separated
2 tablespoons flour
Pinch salt
1 teaspoon grated lemon peel
1 tablespoon lemon juice
New York Glaze

New York Glaze
1 can (17 ounces) pitted dark sweet cherries in heavy syrup
2 tablespoons sugar
1½ teaspoons cornstarch
⅛ teaspoon salt
½ cup water
1 teaspoon brandy
1 teaspoon Madeira
Red food coloring (optional)

1. Blend zwieback crumbs, brown sugar, and butter. Line the bottom and sides of a generously buttered 10-inch springform pan with a thin layer of crumb mixture; press firmly.
2. Beat cream cheese and sugar until fluffy. Beat in egg yolks, one at a time. Stir in flour, salt, lemon peel, and juice.
3. Beat egg whites until stiff, not dry, peaks are formed. Fold into cheese mixture. Turn into pan.
4. Bake at 350°F until center tests done (about 1 to 1½ hours). Remove to wire rack to cool completely. When cooled, pour glaze over cheesecake and refrigerate until glaze is set.

One 10-inch cheesecake

1. Drain cherries, reserving ¼ cup syrup.
2. Combine sugar, cornstarch, and salt in a small saucepan. Add reserved syrup and water gradually, stirring constantly. Bring rapidly to boiling, stirring constantly; cook about 3 minutes, or until mixture is thickened and clear. Remove from heat; stir in brandy, Madeira, and, if desired, a few drops of red food coloring.
3. Add cherries and pour over cooled cheesecake.

Ask almost anyone to name the dominant influence in Pennsylvania's food, and the answer would surely be "Pennsylvania Dutch." This is a cookery so distinctive, richly varied, and comprehensive that entire books have been written about it.

The original Pennsylvania Dutch were German and Swiss Protestants. The term "Dutch" evolved from the Americanization of the word "Deutsch," meaning German.

Both "plain" and "fancy" Dutch settled in the green, rolling agricultural district of southeastern Pennsylvania. The "plain" life style of the soberly clad Amish has changed little since colonial times. Farmers then and farmers still, they work hard and enjoy simple pleasures. Their prosperous farms and rich harvests attest to the fact that this austerity is a matter of choice, not necessity.

The "fancy" Dutch are more liberal, and in outward appearance are very much like their non-Dutch neighbors. Their barns are decorated with bright geometric patterns called "hex signs."

The "plain" and "fancy" Dutch share two common bonds. The first one is their language—the old German dialect of their forefathers liberally laced with quaint English idioms. The second is their collectively hearty appetite and love of good food.

Pennsylvania Dutch is among the most enduring and distinctive styles of regional cooking. Many dishes closely resemble those left behind in Germany, though in the New World some recipes were adapted to use available foods. The cookery has remained surprisingly intact, not only in Pennsylvania, but in Ohio, Indiana, Illinois, and other areas where the "plain people" migrated.

Pennsylvania Dutch food is practical, good, wholesome, and memorable. The German influence is evident in the emphasis on pork, cabbage, traditional coffee cakes, and Christmas cookies, potatoes, noodles, and dumplings.

Foods made from the locally grown corn and buckwheat are standard fare, as is chicken—usually simmered in broth. There is almost always pie for dessert—in the past as often as three times a day! Also ever

PENNSYLVANIA

present are apples—fresh, dried, in spicy apple butter and cider.

Apple cider vinegar is widely used for preserving, especially the items that make up the famous "Seven Sweets and Seven Sours." By tradition, Dutch cooks set their tables with piquant condiments to add variety and interest to the meal, and to spark appetites. They choose from jams, jellies, bread and butter pickles, chowchow, spiced peaches, pickled beets, tomato relish, mustard pickles, corn relish, and a host of others, all made from home-grown produce.

This wonderful heritage is celebrated each summer at the Pennsylvania Dutch Folk Festival in Kutztown. Dutch food specialties are available for sampling, while area residents demonstrate old-fashioned skills like quilting, drying fruits, shelling corn, and barn raising.

A second important influence in Pennsylvania cooking is less well known outside the state. Colonial Philadephia developed a lavish style of dining that had an English base, yet made generous use of imports from Europe and the Indies. The food was rich, with emphasis on luxurious preparations of capon, squab, terrapin, oysters, and the creamiest of desserts. The affluent also enjoyed the finest wines and spirits.

The cooking of the mother country prevailed through the eighteenth and nineteenth centuries, and many typically English dishes are still popular. However, many dishes often associated with Philadelphia today are simpler specialties with a Pennsylvania Dutch accent. Some of these, like scrapple, sticky buns, and pepper pot, were adopted by Philadelphians—the question of origin has been blurred by time.

Snapper Soup

3½ pounds veal knuckle
1 cup chicken fat or other fat
3 onions, finely chopped
2 stalks celery, chopped
2 carrots, diced
¼ teaspoon thyme
½ teaspoon marjoram
3 whole cloves
1 bay leaf
1 tablespoon salt
½ teaspoon pepper
1 cup all-purpose flour
3 or 4 quarts beef broth
2 cups strained tomatoes
Canned or frozen meat from 1 snapper turtle, cut into pieces
2 cups sherry
Dash Tabasco
3 slices lemon
1 hard-cooked egg, chopped

1. Have knuckles broken into pieces. Put into roasting pan with chicken fat, onions, celery, carrots, thyme, marjoram, cloves, bay leaf, salt, and pepper.
2. Bake at 400°F until brown.
3. Remove from oven; add flour, mix well, and cook 30 minutes longer. Pour browned mixture into a large soup kettle; add broth and tomatoes and simmer 3½ hours.
4. Combine snapper meat with 1 cup sherry, salt, Tabasco, and lemon in a saucepan and simmer 10 minutes.
5. Strain soup and combine the two mixtures. Add egg, remaining sherry, and serve.

12 servings

Philadelphia Pepper Pot

2 pounds honeycomb tripe
2 pounds plain tripe
1 veal knuckle
1 large onion
1 bay leaf
4 medium potatoes, pared and cubed
1 bunch parsley or pot herbs
1 tablespoon salt
Dash cayenne pepper
Suet Dumplings
1 tablespoon chopped parsley

1. Cook tripe the day before using. Wash thoroughly, place in a kettle, and cover with water. Cook 8 hours. Drain and cool. Cut into pieces about ½ inch square.
2. The next day, wash veal knuckle, put into a kettle, cover with 3 quarts cold water, and simmer about 3 hours.
3. Remove meat from bones and cut into small pieces. Strain broth and return to kettle.
4. Add onion and bay leaf and simmer about 1 hour. Then add potatoes and parsley. Add meat and tripe and season with salt and cayenne.
5. Prepare dumplings, flour well to prevent sticking, and drop into hot soup. Cook about 10 minutes. Add chopped parsley and serve at once.

About 10 servings

Suet Dumplings: Combine **1 cup finely chopped suet, 2 cups sifted all-purpose flour, ¼ teaspoon salt,** and enough **water** to make a stiff dough. Roll into dumplings about the size of marbles. Cook as described.

Schnitz un Knepp (Apples and Buttons)

Schnitz means "cut" and to the Pennsylvania Dutch the word has come to mean cut dried apples, which when soaked and cooked, are used as stewed fruit, for pie fillings, or in this meat dish.

1 quart dried apples (about an 8-ounce package)
1 smoked pork shoulder roll (3 pounds)
2 tablespoons brown sugar

Dumplings:
2 cups sifted all-purpose flour
4 teaspoons baking powder
1 teaspoon salt
¼ teaspoon pepper
1 egg, well beaten
3 tablespoons butter or margarine, melted
½ cup milk

1. Cover the dried apples with **water;** soak overnight.
2. The next day, cover smoked pork roll with water in a large Dutch oven or kettle, cover loosely, and simmer about 30 minutes. Add the apples and water in which they have been soaked and continue to simmer about 1 hour. Stir in the brown sugar.
3. To prepare the dumplings, mix flour, baking powder, salt, and pepper in a bowl. Add all at one time a mixture of the beaten egg, melted butter, and milk; mix only until dry ingredients are moistened. Drop by tablespoonfuls onto simmering mixture. Tightly cover the Dutch oven and cook 20 minutes; do not remove cover during cooking.

8 to 10 servings

PENNSYLVANIA

Sausage Scrapple

Scrapple or ponhaws is a dish probably of Pennsylvania Dutch origin.

Cornmeal mush
1 pound bulk pork sausage

1. Prepare cornmeal mush following package directions.
2. Fry sausage until thoroughly cooked; drain and stir into the mush. Turn into a loaf pan. Cool, cover, and chill thoroughly.
3. Cut mush into ½-inch slices. Fry slowly in a greased skillet until golden brown on each side.

About 6 servings

Booky Baked Crab

Baked crab is featured at Bookbinder's Sea Food House, Philadelphia, Pennsylvania.

½ cup butter
¾ cup all-purpose flour
1 cup milk
3 egg yolks, beaten
Few grains salt
Few grains pepper
Pinch dry mustard
1 teaspoon Worcestershire sauce
3 pounds large lump crab meat

1. Melt butter in a saucepan; stir in flour to make a paste. Remove from heat and stir in the milk.
2. Cook and stir until very thick and smooth. Blend a little sauce into egg yolks and return to sauce; mix well. Mix in the salt, pepper, dry mustard, Worcestershire sauce, and the crab meat.
3. Form into 6 patties and place in a shallow baking dish.
4. Bake at 350°F 15 to 20 minutes.

6 servings

Mennonite Pod Peas

¼ pound bacon, diced
2 quarts sugar peas in pods
2 teaspoons salt
½ teaspoon pepper

Brown bacon in a saucepan. Add peas, salt, and water to cover; cook 1 hour. Drain; mix in pepper.

6 servings

Fastnachts

1 package active dry yeast
¼ cup warm water
3 cups sifted all-purpose flour
1 teaspoon sugar
2 cups milk, scalded and cooled to lukewarm
3 eggs, well beaten

1. Dissolve yeast in warm water. Add 3 cups of the flour and 1 teaspoon sugar to the milk; beat until smooth. Blend in the yeast.
2. Cover; let rise in a warm place until double in bulk.
3. Beat in eggs, butter, remaining sugar, salt, nutmeg, and enough remaining flour to make a soft dough.
4. Cover; let rise until double in bulk. Punch down dough and divide into two portions. Roll each portion

¼ cup melted butter or
 margarine
1 cup sugar
1½ teaspoons salt
½ teaspoon nutmeg
3½ to 4 cups sifted
 all-purpose flour
Fat for deep frying
 heated to 370°F

on a lightly floured surface into a round about ½ inch thick. Cut dough with a doughnut cutter; cover the cutouts with waxed paper and a clean towel; let rise in a warm place until double in bulk.

5. Fry in hot fat 3 to 4 minutes, or until lightly browned, turning them to brown evenly. Remove from fat; drain.

About 4 dozen doughnuts

Funnel Cakes

1¼ cups all-purpose flour
2 tablespoons sugar
1 teaspoon baking powder
¼ teaspoon salt
1 egg, beaten
⅔ cup milk
Fat for deep frying
 heated to 375°F

1. Mix flour, sugar, baking powder, and salt in a bowl. Add a mixture of egg and milk, beating until batter is smooth.
2. Holding finger over bottom of a funnel having a ⅜- to ½-inch hole, fill funnel with batter. Hold funnel as near surface of heated fat as possible; remove finger and drop batter into hot fat, using a circular movement from center outward to form a spiral cake about 3 inches in diameter. Immediately replace finger on bottom of funnel; then form other cakes (as many as will float uncrowded).
3. Fry until cakes are puffy and golden brown, turning once. Lift from fat with a slotted spoon and drain for a few seconds before removing to absorbent paper.
4. Sift **confectioners' sugar** lightly over cakes and serve warm.

2 to 2½ dozen cakes

Note: A candy patty funnel with its regulating stick is very helpful to use when making funnel cakes.

Shoofly Pie

Pennsylvania Dutch in origin, this old-fashioned pie has found favor in other sections of our country.

1 cup all-purpose flour
⅔ cup firmly packed dark
 brown sugar
¼ teaspoon salt
5 tablespoons butter or
 margarine
⅔ cup very hot water
5 tablespoons molasses
1 tablespoon dark brown
 sugar
½ teaspoon baking soda
1 unbaked 8-inch pie shell

1. Combine flour, ⅔ cup brown sugar, and salt in a bowl. Cut in butter until particles resemble rice kernels; set aside.
2. Blend hot water with the molasses, 1 tablespoon brown sugar, and baking soda.
3. Reserving 3 tablespoons crumb mixture for topping, stir molasses mixture into remaining crumb mixture. Pour into unbaked pie shell. Sprinkle reserved crumbs over filling.
4. Bake at 350°F 35 to 40 minutes, or until top springs back when touched lightly.

One 8-inch pie

PENNSYLVANIA

Nectarine Lemon Pie

1¼ cups sugar
⅓ cup cornstarch
¼ teaspoon salt
1½ cups hot water
2 tablespoons butter
3 egg yolks, beaten
1 teaspoon grated lemon peel
⅓ cup lemon juice
2 cups thinly sliced nectarines
1 baked 9-inch pastry shell
Mallow Meringue

1. Blend sugar, cornstarch, and salt in a saucepan. Stir in hot water and add butter. Cook over medium heat, stirring constantly, until mixture boils and is thickened.
2. Stir a small amount of hot mixture into egg yolks. Blend into mixture in saucepan. Cook and stir 2 or 3 minutes; do not boil.
3. Remove from heat and stir in lemon peel and juice. Cool slightly, then fold in sliced nectarines. Turn into baked pastry shell.
4. Top with Mallow Meringue and spread meringue evenly to pastry edge so filling is completely covered.
5. Bake at 450°F 1 to 2 minutes, or just until lightly tinged with brown.
6. Cool thoroughly before cutting. Decorate top with a few nectarine slices, if desired.

One 9-inch pie

Mallow Meringue: Beat **3 egg whites** with a **few grains salt** until stiff. Beat in **1 cup marshmallow cream**, a heaping tablespoonful at a time, continuing to beat until mixture forms peaks that curve over slightly. Fold in **1 teaspoon vanilla extract**.

Philadelphia Ice Cream

¾ cup sugar
⅛ teaspoon salt
2 cups light cream, scalded
1 teaspoon vanilla extract
2 cups heavy cream, whipped

1. Stir sugar and salt into scalded cream; set aside to cool. Blend in vanilla extract.
2. Pour mixture into refrigerator trays and freeze until mushy.
3. Remove from freezer and turn into a chilled large bowl. Beat with a rotary beater just until smooth. Fold in the whipped cream. Return to trays and freeze until firm (about 2 hours).

About 2 quarts ice cream

Strawberry Ice Cream: Follow directions for Philadelphia Ice Cream through step 2, omitting vanilla extract. Force **3 cups fresh strawberries** through a food mill; add **¾ cup sugar** to pulp and let stand about 20 minutes. Stir into beaten mixture before final freezing.

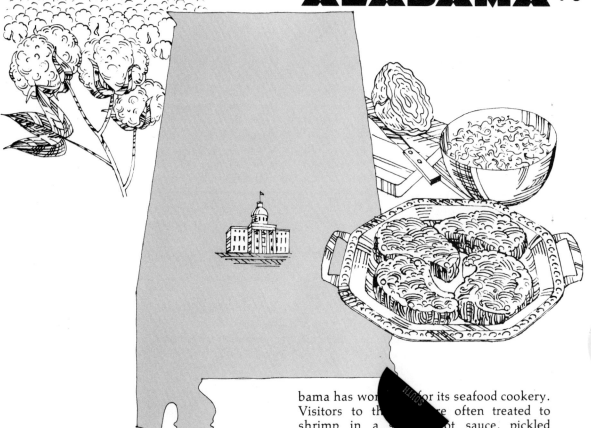

Alabama is often referred to as the "Cotton State" or the "Heart of Dixie." Its name is of Choctaw Indian origin and means "thicket-clearers" or "vegetation gatherers."

There are lush forests of pine, oak, and gum trees, and thickets of moss, ferns, and vines. A thick and tasty Pine Bark Stew is thought to have originated along the river banks in these densely forested parts of Alabama. Wild game and birds find excellent breeding grounds in the many forests and swamps. Several indigenous recipes are available for preparing wild duck and other game birds. They are frequently popular holiday treats.

Fresh-water fish, such as catfish and buffalofish, are found in its streams, and salt-water red snapper, mullet, flounder, shrimp, shad, crabs, and oysters are plentiful along the Gulf of Mexico. Southern coastal Alabama has won for its seafood cookery. Visitors to the area are often treated to shrimp in a spicy hot sauce, pickled shrimp, crab soup, or oysters prepared in a dozen different ways.

Almost one fourth of Alabama's population is engaged in agriculture. Although cotton is the chief income crop, Alabama is also a leading producer of peanuts and pecans. Most of the peanuts are grown in the more tropical southeastern area. Strawberries are grown in Cullman County and blackberries in Chilton County. Many farmers also produce peaches, oranges, apples, pears, and plums. Other popular fruits are cantaloupe and watermelon. Field crops such as corn, wheat, and soybeans are also plentiful. Vegetables include potatoes, turnips, sweet corn, peas, peppers, tomatoes, okra, cucumbers, and green beans. An exceptional southern herb salad dressing is a local specialty and is served over many of the fresh raw vegetables.

Livestock production is very important to the economy of Alabama. Hogs are raised in

ALABAMA

all parts of the state. Thus, one may be introduced to stuffed pork chops or boiled spareribs, southern style, throughout the area. Pork and beef with barbecue sauce are also regional favorites. Much of the central valley is devoted to dairy farming and cattle grazing. Alabama also ranks high in its production of broilers. This availability of poultry has resulted in countless methods for preparing chicken. Besides the old stand-bys of broiled chicken, chicken and dumplings, and southern fried chicken, there are gourmet selections of baked spring chicken with crab apples and variations of chicken royale. Other special dishes in the dairy and poultry-raising regions are delicate light soufflés and omelettes.

The raising of bees is an important livelihood for many people in Alabama. Thousands of bees are shipped out of the state; however, an abundance of honey is produced for local usage and delicious Alabama honey recipes are numerous.

Superb desserts are typical of the Deep South, and Alabama is no exception. There are pecan pies and cakes, sweet potato pones and pies, blackberry and strawberry desserts, plus a very special and celebrated white fruit cake.

It is no surprise to find in the Heart of Dixie delectable recipes for black-eye peas, cornmeal sticks, grits, and sweet potato biscuits. Gourmet delights abound during Mardi Gras week in Mobile, not only in the grandest homes and elegant hotels, but also in the humblest hearths and out-of-the-way cafés.

Southern traditions continue to flourish in this state which held the first capital and first White House of the Confederacy, Montgomery. But in addition to these deep historic roots, we also find the contempory Twentieth Century Space Orientation Center at Huntsville. These modern installations have no doubt brought a fusing together of all the regions of the country, thereby creating a composite of interesting cuisine. A northern sauce on a southern salad, or southern grits in a northern soufflé may no longer be uncommon.

Rock Lobster Bouillabaisse

¼ cup olive oil
1 cup chopped celery
1 onion, chopped
1 clove garlic, chopped
½ teaspoon thyme
1 bay leaf
1 can (28 ounces) tomatoes (undrained)
1 bottle (8 ounces) clam juice
1 cup dry white wine
¼ cup chopped parsley
1½ pounds fish fillets (turbot, flounder, cod, or halibut), cut in 2-inch pieces
1 pound frozen South African rock lobster tails
Salt and pepper

1. Heat olive oil in a saucepot and sauté celery, onion, and garlic until tender but not brown. Add thyme, bay leaf, tomatoes, clam juice, wine, and parsley. Cover and simmer 15 minutes.
2. Add fish to saucepot. Cut each frozen rock lobster tail into 3 pieces, crosswise through hard shell, and add to stew. Simmer 10 minutes.
3. Season to taste with salt and pepper. Remove bay leaf.
4. Ladle into large bowls and serve with slices of **French bread.**

6 servings

Mobile Oyster Soup

1 quart oysters
1 quart milk
2 tablespoons butter
1 tablespoon minced
    parsley
    Dash onion salt or 1
    teaspoon onion juice
1½ teaspoons salt
⅛ teaspoon pepper

1. Drain oysters, reserving liquor in a saucepan. Remove any shell particles. Heat oyster liquor; do not boil.
2. Heat milk in a double boiler; stir in hot oyster liquor. Add butter, seasonings, and oysters. Cook until oysters are plump and edges begin to curl. Serve at once.

About 6 servings

Stuffed Pork Chops

2 teaspoons lemon juice
1 apple, quartered, cored,
    pared, and diced
2 cups soft bread crumbs
1 teaspoon salt
1 teaspoon celery seed
⅛ teaspoon black pepper
½ cup chopped onion
¼ cup butter or margarine
¼ cup apple cider
8 pork chops, cut 1 to 1¼
    inches thick (have
    meat dealer cut a
    pocket for stuffing)
2 teaspoons fat

1. Sprinkle lemon juice over apple in a bowl. Mix with bread crumbs, salt, celery seed, and pepper.
2. Cook onion in hot butter in a large skillet until soft. Turn the contents of the skillet into apple mixture; toss lightly with enough of the apple cider to just barely moisten. Fill pocket of each chop with stuffing.
3. Brown chops on both sides in hot fat in the skillet. Remove to a large, shallow baking dish. Cover tightly with aluminum foil.
4. Bake at 350°F 1 hour, or until chops are tender and thoroughly cooked.

8 servings

Pine Bark Stew

Pine Bark Stew is so named because of its having been prepared on the bank of the river where the fish were caught and pine bark used to build a quick fire. Moreover, it is known to have been served on large, smooth pieces of pine bark.

½ pound sliced bacon
5 pounds white potatoes,
    pared and cut in pieces
4 cups cooked tomatoes
2 pounds onions, peeled
    and cut in pieces
2 quarts water
3 pounds skinned catfish
    fillets
1 cup ketchup
    Salt and pepper

1. Fry bacon until crisp in a large kettle.
2. Force vegetables through a food chopper and add with water to bacon. Simmer for 3 hours, stirring frequently.
3. Cut catfish into pieces and add to stew; continue simmering 15 minutes, or until fish is done.
4. Before serving, stir in ketchup and salt and pepper to taste.

10 to 12 servings

ALABAMA

Country Captain

1 broiler-fryer chicken (3 to 3½ pounds), cut in serving-size pieces
¼ cup all-purpose flour
½ teaspoon salt
Pinch ground white pepper
3 to 4 tablespoons lard
2 onions, finely chopped
2 medium green peppers, chopped
1 clove garlic, minced
1½ teaspoons salt
½ teaspoon ground white pepper
1½ teaspoons curry powder
½ teaspoon ground thyme
½ teaspoon snipped parsley
5 cups undrained canned tomatoes
2 cups hot cooked rice
¼ cup dried currants
¾ cup roasted blanched almonds
Parsley sprigs

1. Remove skin from chicken. Mix flour, ½ teaspoon salt, and pinch white pepper. Coat chicken pieces.
2. Melt lard in a large, heavy skillet; add chicken and brown on all sides. Remove from skillet; keep hot.
3. Cook onions, peppers, and garlic in the same skillet, stirring occasionally until onion is lightly browned. Blend 1½ teaspoons salt, ½ teaspoon white pepper, curry powder, and thyme. Mix into skillet along with parsley and tomatoes.
4. Arrange chicken in a shallow roasting pan and pour tomato mixture over it. (If it does not cover chicken, add a small amount of water to the skillet in which mixture was cooked and pour liquid over chicken.) Place a cover on pan or cover with aluminum foil.
5. Cook in a 350°F oven about 45 minutes, or until chicken is tender.
6. Arrange chicken in center of a large heated platter and pile the hot rice around it. Stir currants into sauce remaining in the pan and pour over the rice. Scatter almonds over top. Garnish with parsley.

About 6 servings

Wild Duck with Pecan Stuffing

4 cups soft bread crumbs
1 cup finely chopped celery
1 cup finely chopped onion
1 cup seedless raisins
1 cup pecans, chopped
½ teaspoon salt
½ cup milk, heated
2 eggs, beaten
2 wild ducks (about 2½ pounds each), dressed
6 slices bacon
1 cup ketchup
½ cup chili sauce
¼ cup Worcestershire sauce
¼ cup steak sauce

1. Mix bread crumbs, celery, onion, raisins, pecans, and salt thoroughly. Add hot milk to the beaten eggs and toss with crumb mixture.
2. Rub cavities of birds with **salt.** Fill with stuffing (leave cavity open).
3. Place, breast up, on rack in shallow roasting pan. Lay 3 strips bacon over breast of each bird.
4. Roast uncovered at 450°F 15 minutes for very rare, 20 minutes for medium rare, and 25 minutes for medium well. Baste ducks with a mixture of the remaining ingredients while roasting.
5. To serve, place ducks on heated platter and garnish with **parsley** and **orange slices.**
6. Skim the fat from the liquid left in roasting pan and serve liquid with ducks.

4 or 5 servings

ALABAMA

Creamed Oyster Loaf

1 loaf Vienna bread
  Melted butter or
    margarine
1 quart oysters
½ cup butter or margarine
½ cup cream
2 tablespoons minced
    celery
2 teaspoons salt
⅛ teaspoon white pepper
2 drops Tabasco

1. Cut a thin lengthwise slice from top of bread.
2. With a small, sharp knife, cut down around edge of loaf, ¾ inch from edges, keeping shell intact. Pull out soft center.
3. Prepare ½ cup soft bread crumbs; reserve remaining bread for use in other food preparation.
4. Brush inside of bread shell and cut side of top slice, and toss bread crumbs, with melted butter.
5. Place bread shell, top slice buttered side up, and bread crumbs on a baking sheet.
6. Bake at 350°F 12 to 15 minutes, or until lightly browned, turning bread crumbs once or twice.
7. Meanwhile, drain oysters, reserving liquor.
8. Pick over oysters to remove any shell particles.
9. Heat butter in a saucepan over low heat. Add oysters with reserved oyster liquor. Simmer 3 minutes, or until oysters are plump and edges curl.
10. Remove from heat and stir in bread crumbs, cream, celery, salt, white pepper, and Tabasco. Turn the mixture into bread shell and cover with top slice.
11. Return loaf to oven and bake about 15 minutes.

About 6 servings

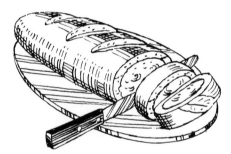

Soybeans, Southern Style

2 cups cooked soybeans
2 cups whole kernel corn
¼ cup shredded Cheddar
    cheese
2 cups cooked tomatoes,
    drained (reserve liquid)
2 teaspoons salt
1 cup buttered crumbs

1. Arrange alternate layers of beans, corn, cheese, and drained tomatoes in a buttered casserole. Mix salt with juice drained from tomatoes and pour over mixture.
2. Cover with buttered crumbs. Bake at 350°F about 30 minutes, or until crumbs are browned.

6 servings

Creamy Cole Slaw

½ cup dairy sour cream
½ cup mayonnaise
1 tablespoon lemon juice
2 teaspoons celery seed
1 teaspoon sugar
¼ teaspoon salt
  Few grains cayenne
    pepper
4 cups (about 1 pound)
    shredded cabbage

1. Blend sour cream, mayonnaise, lemon juice, celery seed, sugar, salt, and pepper thoroughly. Set in refrigerator to chill.
2. Put shredded cabbage into a bowl and set in refrigerator to chill.
3. Before serving, pour chilled dressing over cabbage; toss lightly until cabbage is well coated. Serve immediately.

6 to 8 servings

Sweet Potato Biscuits

2½ cups sifted all-purpose
    flour
  2 tablespoons baking
    powder
  ¾ teaspoon salt
  ½ cup cold shortening
  1 egg, well beaten
  ¾ cup milk
1½ cups mashed sweet
    potatoes
   Milk for brushing

1. Sift flour, baking powder, and salt together into a bowl. Cut in shortening with a pastry blender or two knives.
2. Combine egg, milk, and sweet potatoes; add to flour mixture and mix well. Chill.
3. Knead dough lightly on a floured surface. Roll out to ½-inch thickness. Cut with a floured biscuit cutter. Put on a greased baking sheet. Brush tops with milk.
4. Bake at 400°F 15 minutes.

30 biscuits

Mobile Pecan Cake

1 cup shortening
2 cups sugar
6 eggs, separated
4 cups sifted cake flour
1 teaspoon baking powder
¼ teaspoon salt
½ teaspoon baking soda
1 teaspoon grated nutmeg
1 cup orange juice
3 cups pecans, chopped
1 pound seeded raisins
  Orange Seven-Minute
    Frosting
  Whole pecans

1. Beat shortening until softened, add sugar gradually, creaming until light and fluffy and sugar is complete dissolved.
2. Add egg yolks and beat thoroughly.
3. Sift flour with baking powder, nutmeg, soda, and salt; fold into creamed mixture alternately with orange juice. Add chopped nuts and raisins.
4. Beat egg whites; fold into batter. Turn into a waxed-paper-lined 10-inch tube pan.
5. Bake at 325°F about 3½ hours. Frost and garnish with whole pecans.

One 10-inch tube cake

Orange Seven-Minute Frosting

2 egg whites
1½ cups sugar
¼ cup water
  Few grains salt
¼ teaspoon cream of tartar
   or 1½ teaspoons corn
   syrup
  Juice and grated peel of
   ½ orange

1. Combine all ingredients except orange juice and peel in the top of a double boiler. Cook over boiling water, beating constantly with a rotary beater, 7 minutes, or until mixture holds a point when beater is lifted.
2. Remove from heat, add orange juice and peel, and continue beating until cool enough to spread.

*Enough frosting for
a 10-inch tube cake,
or two 9-inch layers*

Blue Cheese Sour Cream Dressing, 128

Florida, our southernmost state except for Hawaii, boasts of having more continuous sunshine and more water surface than any other state in the Union. In fact, over 7 percent of its total area is water! Lake Okeechobee, in south central Florida, covers seven hundred square miles and is the second largest body of fresh water in the United States.

A great tourist and retirement haven, Florida has earned the nicknames of "Sunshine" and "Peninsula" State. There is no point in Florida which is more than seventy miles from either the Atlantic Ocean or the Gulf of Mexico.

The vast amount of sunshine, water, and mild climate is responsible for Florida's ample supplies of fruit and fish. Even though the soils of Florida vary from the highly fertile muck and peat of the Everglades to the poor sandy soil of the coastline dunes, it still manages to produce almost two thirds of the entire nation's supply of citrus fruits. In contrast to most states, agriculture is expanding in Florida. Besides oranges, grapefruit, tangerines, and lemons, more than sixty varieties of vegetables are grown commercially in the state. Modern methods of refrigeration and freezing have contributed to the importance of the food industry.

With this lavish fruit bounty at their doorstep, Florida homemakers have created any number of superb fruit salads and desserts. Favorites are Kumquat-Avocado Mold and a very special Lime Pie.

Catfish, lobsters, mullet, oysters, shrimp, crabs, and red snappers are all important to Florida's fishing industry. Seafood specialties are prevalent in the state. Red snapper, baked, boiled, or fried, is a diet mainstay in the coastal areas. But some believe the greatest of all Florida fish is the pompano, highly prized for its rich and delicate flavor. There are several methods of preparing this valuable fish, but all of them include a rare

FLORIDA

blending of herbs and seasonings.

Although both the French and English settled in the Florida territory during the colonizing period, no extensive or consistent patterns of food habits from these groups appear to have carried over into the present. It is the Spanish influence that is the most noticeable in Florida. The oldest European settlement in the United States was founded by the Spaniards at St. Augustine in 1565, forty-two years before the establishment of Jamestown in Virginia, and fifty-five years before the arrival of the Pilgrims.

This Latin influence, especially in southern Florida, continues to expand because of the great Cuban influx during the latter half of this century. Cuban-style pot roast, chick-en with saffron rice, roast beef stuffed with hard-cooked eggs, Spanish bean soup, and strong sweet coffee are all fun to sample, especially in the Latin-style cafés with the atmosphere of both old and new Spain.

Pecans and peanuts are produced in northern and western Florida. The tropical climate of the southern areas is conducive to the growing of coconut palms. Coconut pralines, pies, and cookies are common local treats.

Guava, a small pear-shaped red or yellow fruit with a grainy texture and rather musky odor, is used in making Florida's popular guava jams and jellies. This fleshy fruit, often consumed fresh, is also a nutritious food because of its high vitamin C content.

Papaya Cocktail

2 cups papaya balls
4 sprigs mint
   Lemon French Dressing

Spoon papaya into cocktail glasses. Garnish each with a sprig of mint. Serve with Lemon French Dressing.

4 servings

Lemon French Dressing

½ cup lemon juice
½ cup salad oil
1 teaspoon salt
1 teaspoon paprika
2 tablespoons sugar or
   honey

Combine ingredients in the order listed. Mix well before serving.

1 cup dressing

Shrimp and Avocado Cocktail

1½ pounds shrimp, cooked,
      peeled, and deveined
   Peppy Cocktail Sauce
      (page 83)
1 small avocado
   Lettuce or curly endive
   Lemon wedges

1. Chill shrimp in refrigerator until ready to serve.
2. Prepare sauce and chill in refrigerator.
3. Rinse, peel, and cut avocado into halves, remove and discard pit; dice and mix with the shrimp.
4. Arrange lettuce in 6 chilled sherbet glasses and spoon shrimp and avocado into glasses.
5. Top each serving with some of the Peppy Cocktail Sauce and serve with lemon wedges.

6 servings

Peppy Cocktail Sauce

1 cup ketchup
1 tablespoon lemon juice
1 tablespoon prepared
   horseradish
1 tablespoon sugar
1 teaspoon onion juice
½ teaspoon salt
¼ teaspoon Worcestershire
   sauce
   Few drops Tabasco

Combine all ingredients in a small bowl. Cover; chill in refrigerator.

About 1 cup sauce

Conch Chowder

4 raw conchs
¼ pound salt pork, cut in
   small cubes
2 tablespoons butter
2 cups finely chopped
   onion
1 large green pepper,
   peeled, seeded, and
   cored
1 can (16 ounces) Italian
   plum tomatoes
4 large potatoes, pared and
   cut in cubes
2 quarts water
   Salt and freshly ground
   black pepper

1. Wash and scrub conch shells. Remove the meat from the shell. Skin the flesh and remove the intestinal vein. Clean well. Grind the meat.
2. Cook salt pork in butter until almost crisp. Add onion and green pepper and cook, stirring, until onion is wilted. Add the tomatoes, ground conch, potatoes, and water. Season with salt and pepper to taste. Simmer covered until potatoes are mushy (about 1 hour). Serve hot.

4 to 6 servings

Cuban Pot Roast

1 beef round eye round
   roast (3 pounds)
¼ pound smoked ham
¼ pound bacon
1 cup finely chopped onion
2 tablespoons finely
   chopped capers
1 clove garlic, minced
¼ cup chopped green olives
   Salt and pepper
¼ cup lard
1 cup beef broth
½ cup tomato sauce
1 tablespoon vinegar

1. Using a long, sharp, thin-bladed knife, make an incision 1½ to 2 inches deep through center of roast.
2. Grind ham and bacon; add onion, capers, garlic, and olives; mix well. Stuff roast with mixture. Sprinkle roast with salt and pepper.
3. Heat lard in a Dutch oven; brown roast on all sides.
4. Pour a mixture of broth, tomato sauce, and vinegar over meat.
5. Bake, uncovered, 2½ to 3 hours, or until meat is tender; baste occasionally. Add water if needed.

About 8 servings

FLORIDA

Crab-Flake Timbales

1 cup Medium White
    Sauce (page 43)
¼ teaspoon paprika
1½ cups flaked crab meat
2 egg yolks, beaten
2 egg whites, beaten to
    stiff, not dry, peaks
1 cup whipping cream,
    whipped

1. Prepare white sauce; add paprika and crab meat and cook a few minutes.
2. Cool. Fold in beaten egg yolks and whipped cream, then beaten egg whites.
3. Pour into well-buttered timbale forms or custard cups. Set in hot water in a shallow pan.
4. Bake at 300°F about 40 minutes, or until a knife inserted in center comes out clean.

6 servings

Red Snapper with Tomato Sauce

3 pounds red snapper
    Salt and pepper
2 onions, sliced
1 carrot, diced
¼ cup sliced celery
2 tablespoons minced
    parsley
1 quart cold water
2 tablespoons butter or
    margarine
1 cup tomato sauce
1 tablespoon flour
1 cup half-and-half

1. Clean fish, sprinkle with salt and pepper, and refrigerate several hours.
2. Put onion, carrot, celery, and parsley into a saucepot, add cold water, and bring to boiling. Add fish, butter, and tomato sauce and simmer covered until fish separates easily from the bones.
3. Arrange fish carefully on a hot platter.
4. Strain broth. Blend flour with half-and-half and add to hot broth. Cook until thickened, stirring constantly. Pour over fish.

6 to 8 servings

Royal Poinciana Pompano with Shrimp Stuffing

2 cups cooked shrimp
2 eggs
1 cup half-and-half
½ cup chopped mushrooms
¼ cup sherry
1 teaspoon salt
⅛ teaspoon pepper
    Few grains paprika
6 pounds boned pompano

1. Grind shrimp.
2. Beat eggs and ½ cup half-and-half together.
3. Mix shrimp, mushrooms, wine, and seasonings; stir in egg mixture.
4. Spread mixture on ½ of pompano. Fasten the two halves of each fish together and place in baking dish. Pour remaining cream over fish.
5. Bake at 350°F 45 minutes. Serve garnished with sliced **cucumbers** marinated in **French dressing.**

6 to 8 servings

Kumquat-Avocado Mold

¾ cup boiling water
1 package (3 ounces) lemon-flavored gelatin
¼ teaspoon salt
1¼ cups chilled ginger ale
1 pint fresh kumquats, rinsed and thinly sliced
2 ripe avocados, peeled and diced

1. Pour boiling water over gelatin in a bowl and stir until gelatin is dissolved. Mix in salt and ginger ale.
2. Chill until slightly thicker than consistency of thick, unbeaten egg white.
3. Mix in kumquats and avocados. Turn into a 1-quart mold. Chill until firm.
4. Unmold onto a chilled serving plate. Garnish as desired.

6 servings

Orange Nut Bread

2 cups sifted all-purpose flour
1 teaspoon baking soda
¾ teaspoon salt
½ cup sugar
1 egg, well beaten
¾ cup strained orange juice
2 tablespoons lemon juice
1 teaspoon grated orange peel
¼ teaspoon grated lemon peel
¼ cup shortening, melted
¾ cup pecan pieces

1. Sift flour with baking soda, salt, and sugar.
2. Combine egg, orange juice, lemon juice, grated peel, and melted shortening; add dry ingredients, stirring only until well mixed.
3. Add pecans and turn into an 8×4×2-inch loaf pan, lined with greased waxed paper.
4. Cover and let stand 20 minutes. Remove cover.
5. Bake at 350°F 1 hour.

Lime Chiffon Pie

1 envelope unflavored gelatin
¼ cup cold water
4 egg yolks, slightly beaten
⅔ cup sugar
2 teaspoons grated lime peel
½ cup lime juice
¼ teaspoon salt
2 to 3 drops green food coloring
4 egg whites
½ cup sugar
1 baked 9-inch pastry shell

1. Soften gelatin in cold water; set aside.
2. Mix egg yolks, sugar, lime peel and juice, and salt in top of a double boiler. Cook over simmering water, stirring constantly, until mixture is slightly thickened.
3. Remove from water and blend in gelatin, stirring until gelatin is dissolved. Mix in the food coloring. Cool. Chill until mixture is partially set.
4. Beat egg whites until frothy; gradually add ½ cup sugar, beating constantly until stiff peaks are formed. Spread over gelatin mixture and fold together. Turn into pastry shell. Chill until firm.

One 9-inch pie

FLORIDA

Palm Beach Poinciana Cake

2 cups butter
2 cups sugar
9 egg yolks, well beaten
3 tablespoons lemon juice
1 tablespoon grated
   lemon peel
¼ teaspoon salt
3¼ cups sifted cake flour
9 egg whites, beaten to
   stiff, not dry, peaks
½ pound citron, chopped
½ pound raisins, chopped
2 cups chopped blanched
   almonds
   Poinciana Cake Filling
   Seven Minute Frosting

1. Cream butter with sugar until light and fluffy, add egg yolks, lemon juice, peel, and salt; beat well.
2. Add half of flour alternately with beaten egg whites.
3. Dredge fruit and nuts with remaining flour and add to batter; mix well. Divide equally in four 9-inch round layer cake pans lined with waxed paper.
4. Bake at 300°F 40 to 50 minutes, or until firm to the touch.
5. Spread filling between layers, and frosting on sides and top.

One 4-layer 9-inch cake

Poinciana Cake Filling

2 cups sugar
1 cup boiling water
2 tablespoons grated lemon
   peel
⅓ cup lemon juice
1 tablespoon cornstarch
   Cold water
2 cups grated coconut

1. Heat sugar, boiling water, and lemon peel and juice to boiling in a saucepan. Stir in cornstarch mixed with a little cold water.
2. Boil until syrup spins a thread (234°F). Remove from heat; beat until creamy. Mix in coconut.

Enough filling for a 4-layer cake

Seven Minute Frosting

2 egg whites
1½ cups sugar
⅓ cup water
   Few grains salt
¼ teaspoon cream of tartar
   or 1½ teaspoons corn
   syrup
1 teaspoon vanilla extract

1. Combine all ingredients except vanilla extract in the top of a double boiler. Cook over boiling water, beating constantly with a rotary beater, 7 minutes or until mixture holds a point when beater is lifted.
2. Remove from heat, add vanilla extract, and continue beating until cool enough to spread.

About 5 cups frosting

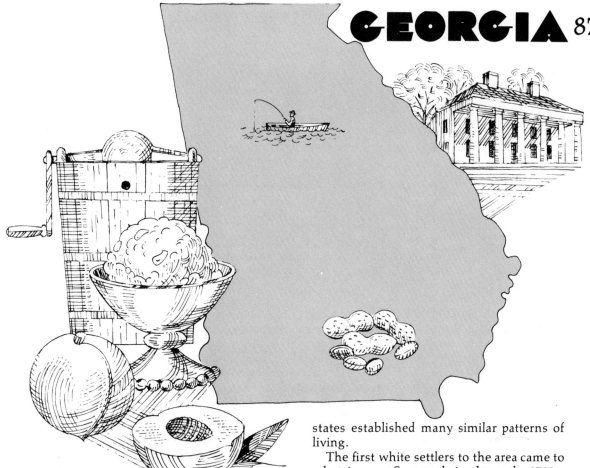

The "Empire State of the South," as Georgia is often called, is one of the country's leading manufacturing states. Its capital city, Atlanta, is a large, modern, industrial and cultural center. Before the twentieth century most Georgians lived in rural areas, but today the majority of the population live in metropolitan communities.

This change has influenced food habits in the region. What was once leisurely "plantation living" has turned into a more hurried industrial existence. However, southern hospitality and southern cooking have not been lost. Georgia is still the magnificent land of natural beauty, mild climate, exquisite flowers, moss-draped trees, and delicious Deep South cuisine.

Until the early nineteenth century, Georgia also comprised most of Mississippi and Alabama. Thus, the early residents of these states established many similar patterns of living.

The first white settlers to the area came to what is now Savannah in the early 1700s. Most of them were English, German Lutherans, Scottish Highlanders, Portuguese Jews, Piedmontese, and Swiss. After 1750 myriads of permanent residents, including many Negro slaves, arrived from Virginia and the Carolinas. As was true in most of the early colonies, the foods and methods of preparing them derived from what was available, what could easily be produced on the local land, and from the ethnic backgrounds and traditions the settlers brought with them.

Georgia is sometimes called the "Peach State," for it is one of the most important peach-producing states in the country. William Bartram, great eighteenth-century naturalist, during one of his many celebrated travels in this area, wrote: "I came upon peach and fig trees loaded with fruit . . . affording a very acceptable dessert after the heats and toil of the Day." Bartram also recorded his fondness for fish, "stewed in the juice of Oranges . . ." And today many fine peach and other fruit recipes are an integral part of Georgia cookery. Peach fritters, pies, ice creams, and pickles are only a few choice examples.

Throughout the South, corn is an important crop. Georgia cornmeal is the basis for several tasty southern breadstuffs. The region's cornmeal muffins, waffles, battercakes, fritters, or grits swimming in butter and syrup are unsurpassed as a breakfast treat. Corn dumplings boiled in turnip and mustard greens, and corn pone, ham, and buttermilk make a hearty supper for even the hungriest guest.

Peanuts, or goobers, as they are known in the South, are grown extensively in the southern part of the state. The ingenious Georgians have been unusually creative in their use of these versatile and nutritious nuts. Cream of peanut butter soup, peanut stuffing, and peanut cookies, cakes, pies, and puddings are a few of the more common concoctions.

Pecans are also important to the Georgian economy. Each southern state claims to have its own version of the famed pecan pie, and Georgia is no exception. A pudding containing pecans and raisins is usually served at Christmastime. Another holiday treat from an old English recipe is syllabub, prepared from thick cream, confectioners' sugar, and rum.

Watermelons and sweet potatoes, old favorites of the South, are also plentiful in Georgia. Chilled watermelon, ripened on the vine, is a true summer delicacy.

The Okefenokee Swamp region and the Savannah and Altamaha rivers provide the east central areas of the state with freshwater fish. Georgia's Atlantic coastline supplies shrimp, clams, crabs, oysters, and shad. Georgian deviled crab is especially appetizing.

Livestock farmers in the area raise both beef and hogs. Roast pork is believed to have been prepared and served in the Georgia territory as early as the mid 1500s. Even today it is a staple main dish in many Georgia homes.

Okra Gumbo

1 **small chicken, cut in pieces**
2 **tablespoons oil**
½ **pound cooked ham, diced**
1 **bunch green onions, sliced**
¼ **cup chopped parsley**
2 **small hot red peppers, seeded and cut in thin strips**
1 **teaspoon paprika**
¼ **teaspoon marjoram**
1 **bay leaf**
8 **fresh tomatoes, peeled and cut in pieces**
2 **pounds okra, sliced**
2 **quarts boiling water**
1 **teaspoon salt**
⅛ **teaspoon pepper**
 Cooked rice

1. Brown chicken pieces in oil in a saucepot. Add ham, onion, parsley, peppers, paprika, marjoram, bay leaf, and tomatoes. Cook 20 minutes, stirring frequently.
2. Add okra to chicken mixture and cook until okra is tender (about 10 minutes). Add water and simmer about 45 minutes. Stir in salt and pepper.
3. Serve over hot cooked rice.

About 10 servings

Peanut Butter Soup

½ cup finely chopped
   onion
⅔ cup finely chopped
   celery
¼ cup butter or margarine
2 tablespoons flour
1 quart milk
1½ cups chicken broth
   (dissolve 2 chicken
   bouillon cubes in 1½
   cups boiling water)
1 cup smooth peanut
   butter
½ teaspoon salt

1. Cook onion and celery in hot butter in a large saucepan about 5 minutes, stirring occasionally. Blend in the flour and heat until mixture bubbles, stirring constantly.
2. Add milk and broth gradually, stirring constantly. Bring rapidly to boiling, stirring constantly. Cook 1 to 2 minutes.
3. Gradually stir white sauce into peanut butter until mixture is smooth. Return to saucepan. Stir in the salt and heat thoroughly.

About 1½ quarts soup

Roast Suckling Pig

1 suckling pig, about 25
   to 30 pounds
   Salt and pepper
1½ pounds dry bread, diced
1½ cups milk
2 eggs
2 apples, sliced
2 onions, diced
⅓ cup chopped parsley
1 potato
   Melted lard or salad oil
1 small whole apple

1. Wipe pig, inside and out, with a clean damp cloth. Sprinkle entire cavity with salt and pepper. If necessary to make pig fit into pan (and oven) cut crosswise in half just behind shoulders.
2. Put bread into a large mixing bowl. Add milk and let soak 20 minutes. Add eggs, sliced apples, onion, and parsley; mix well.
3. Spoon stuffing into cavity of pig. (There will not be enough stuffing to entirely fill cavity.)
4. Use metal skewers to hold cavity closed and lace with string.
5. Set pig belly side down in roasting pan. Tuck feet under body. Cover tail, snout, and ears with foil. Place whole potato in mouth.
6. Roast at 375°F 8 to 10 hours. Baste frequently with melted lard. When pig is done, juices run golden and skin is a crackling, translucent, golden-chocolate brown.
7. Set pig on platter. Remove potato from mouth; replace with apple. If desired, make a wreath of parsley sprigs for neck or to cover joint behind shoulders.

About 25 servings

GEORGIA

GEORGIA

Scrapple

4 large pig knuckles
½ pound lean pork
1 tablespoon salt
3 quarts water
2 tablespoons finely
    chopped onion
½ teaspoon pepper
1 teaspoon crushed sage
2⅔ cups cornmeal

1. Put pig knuckles, pork, and salt into a large, heavy saucepot; add water. Simmer about 2½ hours, or until meat is very tender and comes away from the bones.
2. Remove meat from liquid; discard the bones and finely grind the meat.
3. Strain the liquid and put 8 cups of it into the saucepot; cool remaining liquid. Return the meat to liquid and add onion, pepper, and sage. Bring to boiling.
4. Meanwhile, mix cornmeal with 4 cups of cooled broth; add gradually to boiling mixture, stirring and cooking until thickened. Cook over very low heat, stirring frequently, about 30 minutes.
5. Turn mixture into loaf pans, cool, cover, and chill thoroughly.
6. To serve, slice ½ inch thick and fry in hot fat until golden brown on both sides.

Roast Fresh Ham

1 pork leg (fresh ham),
    whole (12 to 14 pounds)
1 tablespoon coarse salt
4 teaspoons ginger
  Bay leaves

1. Score rind of pork, spacing slits ½ inch apart, and rub with a mixture of salt and ginger. Put bay leaves in several of the slits. Insert a meat thermometer so tip is slightly beyond center of thickest part of meat, being sure that tip does not rest in fat or on bone.
2. Place on a rack in a shallow roasting pan.
3. Roast, uncovered, at 325°F to 350°F until internal temperature registers 170°F. (Allow 22 to 26 minutes per pound.) Remove thermometer and transfer roast to carving board or heated serving platter. Let roast stand 20 to 30 minutes before carving to allow meat to absorb juices and become easier to carve.

18 to 20 servings

Planked Shad

3 to 4 pounds dressed shad
  Salt and pepper
  Melted butter or
    margarine (about ½
    cup)
2 cups hot mashed potatoes
  Parsley and lemon slices

1. Broil shad 10 minutes.
2. Meanwhile, oil a plank and preheat in hot oven.
3. Place shad on plank, skin side down. Season with salt and pepper.
4. Bake at 400°F 15 minutes.
5. Remove from oven and force mashed potatoes through a pastry bag and tube around the fish. Return to oven until potatoes are brown and fish tests done. Garnish with parsley and lemon.

6 to 8 servings

Oyster Roast (Back-to-Nature Method)

This method of preparing oysters is ideal for a campfire or for the open fireplace indoors. Salt, pepper, and vinegar are the only accompaniments necessary.

Oysters in the shell*
Salt and pepper
Vinegar

1. Wash shells of oysters; then place shell oysters on raked out red-hot coals. Allow to remain for a few minutes; remove and let shells cool sufficiently to allow handling.
2. Remove the upper shell of each oyster quickly by inserting a strong, thin knife between the shells near the thick end and running it around until muscle holding the shell is cut.
3. Serve with seasonings.
*Allow 9 to 10 small, 6 to 7 medium, 5 to 6 large oysters per person.

Fried Okra

1 pound small okra pods
Boiling water
Salt and pepper
1 egg, slightly beaten
Cracker crumbs or corn
 meal
Fat for deep frying heated
 to 370°F

1. Wash pods and remove stems, leaving pods unopened.
2. Put okra into a saucepan and pour in 1 inch of boiling water. Cover and cook until tender (about 10 minutes). Drain.
3. Sprinkle okra with salt and pepper; roll first in egg and then in cracker crumbs.
4. Fry in hot fat until brown.

6 servings

Georgian Sweet Potatoes

4 large sweet potatoes
¼ cup butter
¼ cup molasses
1 teaspoon salt
Butter

1. Cook sweet potatoes until tender; peel and mash. Add ¼ cup butter, molasses, and salt; beat well.
2. Turn mixture into a buttered casserole. Dot with bits of butter.
3. Bake at 350°F 30 to 40 minutes, or until top is browned.

6 servings

Good Old Southern Popovers

1½ cups sifted all-purpose
 flour
½ teaspoon salt
3 eggs
1½ cups milk

1. Sift flour and salt into a bowl.
2. Beat eggs, add milk, and stir gradually into flour to make a smooth batter. Beat thoroughly with egg beater.
3. Fill greased custard cups or sizzling hot heavy metal popover or muffin-pan wells two thirds full.
4. Bake at 450°F 15 minutes, then turn control to 350°F and continue baking 20 minutes, or until firm.

12 large popovers

GEORGIA

Georgia Pecan Cookies

2 egg whites
1 cup brown sugar
½ teaspoon maple flavoring
1 cup pecans, chopped
1 cup fine dry bread
    crumbs
⅛ teaspoon salt

1. Beat egg whites until stiff, not dry, peaks are formed. Beat in brown sugar and flavoring.
2. Combine nuts, crumbs, and salt and fold into egg whites.
3. Shape into small balls and place on a greased cookie sheet.
4. Bake at 325°F about 20 minutes.

About 3 dozen cookies

Georgia Peach Ice Cream

4 cups peach pulp
2 cups sugar
1 tablespoon lemon juice
3½ cups undiluted
    evaporated milk
½ cup water
2 egg yolks, slightly
    beaten
¼ teaspoon salt
2 egg whites, beaten stiff,
    but not dry
½ teaspoon vanilla extract
½ teaspoon almond extract

1. Select peaches which are ripe and juicy. Peel and mash enough to make the required amount of pulp. Add 1 cup sugar and the lemon juice. Let stand 30 minutes.
2. Force through a food mill or sieve.
3. Blend 2 cups evaporated milk with water and bring to scalding point in double boiler.
4. Combine egg yolks, remaining sugar, and salt. Pour hot milk slowly over egg mixture, blending well. Return to double boiler. Cook, stirring constantly, until mixture coats spoon. Remove from heat and cool.
5. Add remaining milk, egg whites, and extracts to cooled mixture. Combine with fruit and freeze.

12 servings

Note: If desired, add 4 drops red coloring before freezing.

KENTUCKY 93

Kentucky's once forested central wilderness, explored and tamed by courageous frontiersmen such as Daniel Boone and James Herrod in the mid-eighteenth century, is now a lush land of Bluegrass horse farms, fields of tobacco and corn, and sophisticated cities. Extensive coal fields and the Mississippi River in the western part of the state, the Appalachian Mountains in the east, and the rocky ridges, bluffs, and famous Mammoth Cave in the south all add to Kentucky's rich and diverse heritage.

Many of the earliest permanent white settlers in the state were of French or English origin and arrived in Kentucky from previous established homes in Pennsylvania and Virginia. Thus, both North and South meet in this border state. Southern specialties of fried chicken, hominy grits, chitlins, hush puppies, and sweet potatoes, along with more all-American chicken hash and

hot potato salad, are part of the everyday fare. On world-famous Derby Day, Kentucky tradition calls for the serving of mint juleps prepared with freshly crushed mint, and other typical dishes, such as country ham cured with sugar and special spices, red gravy, corn pudding, Kentucky Bibb lettuce salad, locally grown fruit, and one of the many delicious fruit or cream pies or cakes.

The eastern mountainous regions favor such foods as dried beans, yellow tomatoes, and summer squash. The beans are usually boiled with salt pork and served plain or in soups, stews, and salads. Along the Ohio and Mississippi rivers one might find catfish or carp featured on the local menu.

Shakertown, called Pleasant Hill, located near Lexington in central Kentucky, was settled in 1805 by the Shakers, a religious group. They are remembered today, not only for their creative arts and crafts and fine furniture, but also for their excellent cuisine prepared from simple foods, such as corn, beans, spinach, and livestock produced on their efficient farms.

Variations of the famous Kentucky stew,

called burgoo, can be found throughout the state. There are almost as many tales about the origin of this hearty meal-in-one as it has ingredients. Some say it dates back to Biblical times; others say it was the mainstay of shipboard menus on French sailing vessels in the mid-eighteenth century and was brought by the first settlers to Kentucky. Still others claim that it originated as a pioneer dish prepared from wild herbs, squirrels, rabbits, and game birds. One story relates that during the Civil War, when rations were short, General Morgan's aide created the stew out of wild game to feed the hungry troops. In 1932, the horse who won the Kentucky Derby was even named Burgoo King. Traditionally, this stew was prepared in enormous quantities, cooked in huge kettles over open fires, and served out-of-doors for large public gatherings, especially on Derby Day or at horse sales or political rallies. A typical recipe called for over a ton of potatoes, eight hundred pounds of meat and poultry, plus large portions of tomatoes, corn, cabbage, and onions. However, today many average standard recipes have been developed for this hearty dish.

Of course, no discussion of Kentucky foods could be complete without mentioning the varied uses made of bourbon whiskey of which Kentucky is a leading producer. There seems to be no end to the list of delicate bourbon desserts and confections that have been developed over the years by ingenious homemakers.

Black Bean Soup

2 cups black beans
12 cups water
¼ pound salt pork
½ pound lean beef, cut in
   small pieces
1 carrot, diced
3 small onions, minced
3 cloves
¼ teaspoon mace
   Dash red pepper
3 hard-cooked eggs, sliced
1 lemon, sliced
¼ cup sherry wine

1. Wash beans, pick them over, and soak overnight.
2. In the morning, drain and add water listed, salt pork, beef, carrot, onion, and seasonings. Cover and cook slowly for 3 hours, or until beans have become very soft.
3. Remove meat and rub beans through a sieve. Place in a tureen, add sliced eggs, lemon, cooked meat, and sherry wine.   *8 to 10 servings*

Note: A ham bone or any other salt meat may be used instead of salt pork.

Batter-Fried Chicken

1 frying chicken, 2 to 3 pounds, ready-to-cook weight
1 cup flour
1 tablespoon paprika
1 teaspoon salt
¼ teaspoon pepper
1 egg, beaten
½ cup water
2 tablespoons melted butter or margarine
1 cup fine, dry bread crumbs
Fat for deep frying

1. Clean chicken, disjoint, and cut into serving-sized pieces. Rinse and pat dry with absorbent paper.
2. Sift together flour, paprika, salt, and pepper.
3. Combine egg, water, and melted butter; add to dry mixture; beat until smooth.
4. Dip pieces of chicken into batter, letting excess drain off. Roll in crumbs. Let stand 10 minutes to "seal" coating.
5. Heat deep fat to 350°F. Place pieces of chicken in hot fat, one at a time, and avoid crowding. Deep fry about 2 minutes, or until lightly browned. Turn pieces several times during cooking.
6. Remove with tongs or slotted spoon; drain over the fat a few seconds. Place pieces one layer deep in shallow baking pan.
7. Bake at 325°F 45 to 60 minutes, or until thickest pieces are fork-tender. Turn pieces several times while in oven. If chicken seems dry, drizzle a mixture of 2 tablespoons melted butter and 2 tablespoons milk over it.

3 or 4 servings

Chicken Hash

A southern Sunday breakfast dish.

2 tablespoons butter or chicken fat
1½ tablespoons flour
1 cup chicken stock
2 cups chopped cooked chicken

1. Melt butter, blend in flour, add chicken stock gradually, stirring constantly until the boiling point is reached, then add chicken.
2. Place in a buttered casserole and bake at 350°F 20 minutes. Garnish with **toast**.

4 to 6 servings

Chitterlings (Chitlins)

Chitterlings (the smaller intestines of swine) are obtainable at some butcher shops.

2 pounds chitterlings
1 tablespoon whole cloves
1 red pepper, chopped
1 egg, slightly beaten
1 tablespoon water
Cracker crumbs

1. Wash chitterlings thoroughly and cover with boiling salted water. Add cloves and red pepper.
2. Cook until tender. Drain. Cut in pieces the size of oysters. Dip each piece in egg beaten with water, then in cracker crumbs.
3. Fry in hot deep fat (370°F) until brown.

4 to 6 servings

KENTUCKY

KENTUCKY

Burgoo

- 1 pound boneless beef (chuck or rump), cut in pieces
- ¼ pound boneless lamb shoulder, cut in pieces
- 1 beef soup bone, cracked
- 1 pound chicken breasts, thighs, or legs
- 4 teaspoons salt
- ¾ teaspoon black pepper
- ¼ teaspoon cayenne pepper
- 2 quarts water
- 1½ cups whole kernel corn
- 1⅓ cups lima beans
- 1 cup diced potato
- 1 cup chopped onion
- ½ cup chopped green pepper
- ½ cup diced carrot
- 1 cup sliced okra
- 2½ cups canned tomatoes with liquid
- 1 clove garlic, crushed or minced
- ½ cup chopped parsley

1. Put the meat, soup bone, chicken, salt, peppers, and water into a saucepot; cover and bring to boiling. Reduce heat and simmer about 2 hours, skimming off foam during first part of cooking.

2. Add corn, lima beans, potato, onion, green pepper, and carrot; cover and simmer 1 hour. Remove cover and cook 1 hour longer, stirring occasionally to prevent sticking on bottom of pot.

3. Add the okra, tomatoes, and garlic; cover and simmer 1 to 1½ hours longer. About 10 minutes before end of cooking period, remove bones and any pieces of fat, then stir constantly for remaining time. (Stew will thicken rapidly and may scorch if not carefully watched at this point.)

4. Remove from heat and stir in the parsley.

About 3 quarts

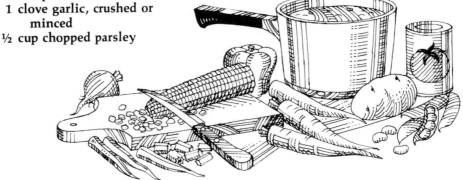

Fried Kentucky Country Ham (With Red Gravy)

- 1 medium thick slice country ham (such as Smithfield)
- ½ cup cold water

1. Place ham slice in frying pan without shortening; do not cook too fast; turn several times to avoid burning.

2. When evenly browned on both sides, remove from the frying pan; add ½ cup of cold water to ham gravy and let cook until gravy turns red.

Variation: There are many ways to make Red Ham Gravy—with water or coffee. One way is to add a cup of strong black coffee to the pan drippings. Let boil down until there is a layer of reddish brown sauce on bottom with layer of clear ham grease on top. When blended this makes a wonderful gravy.

Basic White Bread, 168

Cheese Hominy Casserole

1 large can whole hominy
2 cups medium white sauce
½ teaspoon celery salt
1 teaspoon paprika
¼ teaspoon pepper
¼ pound grated American cheese
½ teaspoon nutmeg

1. Mix drained hominy with white sauce. Add seasonings.
2. Place in casserole. Sprinkle with grated cheese and nutmeg.
3. Bake at 400°F 20 to 30 minutes.

4 to 6 servings

Hush Puppies

These morsels, according to southern colonial folklore, were originally made at fish fries and on hunting trips to feed to the hungry, howling hounds to quiet them—hence the name "hush puppy."

2 cups yellow cornmeal
1 tablespoon flour
1 tablespoon sugar
1 teaspoon baking powder
¾ teaspoon baking soda
¼ cup finely chopped onion
1¼ cups buttermilk
1 egg, well beaten
   Fat for deep frying heated to 375°F

1. Mix the cornmeal, flour, sugar, baking powder, and baking soda in a bowl. Add the onion and a mixture of the buttermilk and egg; mix until well blended. Using about a heaping tablespoon for each, form into small cakes.
2. Put into the hot fat only as many cakes at one time as will float uncrowded one layer deep. Fry 3 to 4 minutes, or until well browned. Turn cakes with tongs or a fork as they rise to the surface and several times during cooking (do not pierce). Lift cakes from fat with slotted spoon and drain before removing to absorbent paper. Serve hot.

About 1½ dozen

Hot Potato Salad

6 potatoes, boiled in jackets
½ pound bacon, diced
½ cup cooked celery, diced
1 onion, chopped fine
¼ cup vinegar
1 tablespoon sugar
½ teaspoon salt
½ teaspoon celery seed
¼ teaspoon paprika
¼ teaspoon pepper
¼ teaspoon mustard
1 tablespoon chopped parsley

1. Peel and dice potatoes.
2. Cook bacon until crisp. Remove from pan and drain. Add potatoes, celery, onion, vinegar, and dry seasonings to bacon drippings. Sprinkle with crumbled bacon and chopped parsley.

6 servings

Picnic Pear Nut Bread, 175;
Honey-Glazed Filbert Roast Chicken, 173

Southern Corn Pudding

3 eggs
2 cups canned cream style
  corn
2 tablespoons melted butter
  or other fat
2 cups milk
1 teaspoon salt
⅛ teaspoon pepper
½ teaspoon sugar
1 cup cracker crumbs
¼ cup butter

1. In mixing bowl beat eggs well.
2. Combine with corn, melted butter and milk. Stir well. Add seasoning and sugar.
3. Pour into well-buttered casserole; sprinkle with cracker crumbs, then dot with butter.
4. Bake at 350°F 40 minutes.

6 servings

Kentucky Bourbon Cake

¾ pound (3 sticks) butter
2¼ cups firmly packed light
  brown sugar
2 cups sugar
6 eggs
5½ cups sifted all-purpose
  flour
1 teaspoon mace
¼ teaspoon salt
2 cups bourbon whiskey
3½ cups (1 pound) pecans

1. Cream butter until soft in a large mixing bowl. Combine brown and white sugar thoroughly. Gradually work half the sugar into butter, keeping it as smooth as possible.
2. In a separate bowl beat eggs until light and fluffy. Then gradually beat in remaining sugar until it is a smooth, creamy mixture. Stir into butter mixture thoroughly.
3. Sift flour, mace, and salt together. Add flour combination and whiskey to batter, alternating them and beginning and ending with flour. Break pecans into pieces and stir into batter.
4. Pour into a well-greased 10-inch tube pan (batter should almost fill the pan) and bake at 300°F 1½ to 1¾ hours, or until cake shrinks slightly from pan. Allow cake to cool in the pan about 15 minutes, then turn out onto cake rack, and cool completely. Bourbon Cake improves with age. It should be well-wrapped in foil and stored in the refrigerator. Do not freeze.

1 cake

Kentucky Mint Julep

1 lump sugar
  Crushed ice
  Bourbon
  Fresh mint sprigs

1. Chill silver mug, heavy cut-crystal tumbler, or goblet in the refrigerator.
2. Dissolve sugar in a little water; reserve.
3. Fill mug with finely crushed ice, add enough bourbon to cover the ice, and stir until the outside of the mug is heavily frosted.
4. Stir in the sugar syrup to taste. Tuck 4 or 5 mint sprigs into the ice so that they protrude above the mug.

1 serving

Louisiana, Creole, and New Orleans are all synonymous with the finest of quality cuisine. From the exciting romanticism of southern Louisiana, where the Mississippi River joins the Gulf of Mexico, to the central underground salt domes capped by vast marshes, to the peaceful, gently rolling western prairies, the "Bayou State" is to the gourmet what Colorado is to the skier.

It has been said that a French chef and a Spanish cook wed in the heart of New Orleans, the home of Creole cookery. The Indians also played a role in its birth, the result being an exquisite combination of herbs and seasonings. Even the most ordinary meats and vegetables prepared in Creole fashion are pleasing to the palate.

The Creole population of southern Louisiana are descendants of the original French and Spanish settlers. The ancestors of the southern Cajuns were French colonists from the Acadia region of eastern Canada. The name "Cajun" is derived from "Acadian." French is still spoken in many parts of the state. Most of the people living in northern Louisiana have Anglo-Saxon roots. About a third of the population are Negroes. The state was ruled by Spanish governors until Napoleon managed to acquire the territory from Spain in 1800. The United States government then made the famous Louisiana Purchase in 1803. This very rich history and mixture of backgrounds adds to the distinction of Louisiana cookery.

Agriculture plays a significant role in the economy of the Bayou State. Its mild climate and ample rainfall are important natural assets. Cotton is the chief crop, but rice and sugar cane are also grown in abundant quantities. Louisiana is the country's leading producer of sweet potatoes. Farmers also grow white potatoes, beans, cauliflower, okra, cabbage, tomatoes, and a variety of other vegetables. Thus, the culinary tastes of many Louisianians are similar to those of the rest of the Deep South: varieties of

LOUISIANA

sweet potato dishes, soups of okra and beans, cornmeal mixtures, hot biscuits, and desserts like pecan pie. Strawberries are also raised locally, and many fine Louisiana recipes exist for shortcakes and pastries.

Seafood is very popular in this southern state. Oysters and shrimp are found along the coast. The inland waters provide freshwater fish such as crayfish and catfish. Red beans and rice are distinctive foods of the Cajuns. Molasses is used extensively in cooking and baking throughout the state.

Two of the better-known typical Creole dishes are the gumbos and jambalaya. Gumbo, a savory soup or stew of various seafoods, tomatoes, and usually okra for thickening, is a meal in itself. Its unusual name is derived from a regional patois or French dialect spoken by some of the Negroes and Creoles. Jambalaya, an old standby in Creole cookery, usually contains shrimp or oysters, ham or bacon, tomatoes, several seasonings, and plenty of Louisiana rice.

New Orleans, a city no connoisseur of fine food could live without visiting, boasts of being the mecca for excellent dining. World-famous dishes, usually printed in French on the menu, include Huitres en Coquille à la Rockefeller (oysters baked with spinach sauce), Pompano en Papillote (pompano fish with seafood sauce baked in paper), and Bouillabaisse (a spicy fish stew with wine, tomatoes, and numerous seasonings).

Creole Bouillabaisse

Frenchmen use the fish and shellfish of the Mediterranean for their fish stew. The Creoles have a similar method of cooking fish, using red snapper and redfish from the Gulf waters.

1 pound red snapper fillets
1 pound redfish fillets
2 teaspoons minced parsley
1 teaspoon salt
¾ teaspoon thyme
½ teaspoon allspice
⅛ teaspoon pepper
2 bay leaves, finely crushed
1 clove garlic, finely minced or crushed in a garlic press
2 tablespoons olive oil
1 large onion, chopped
1 cup white wine
3 large ripe tomatoes, peeled and cut in ¼-inch slices
3 or 4 lemon slices
1 cup hot Fish Stock (see below) or hot water
¾ teaspoon salt
⅛ teaspoon pepper
Dash cayenne pepper
Pinch of saffron
6 slices buttered, toasted bread

1. Thoroughly rub into fish fillets a mixture of parsley, salt, thyme, allspice, pepper, bay leaf, and garlic. Set fillets aside.
2. Heat olive oil in a large skillet over low heat; add onion and fillets. Cover and cook over low heat 10 minutes, turning fillets once.
3. Remove fish fillets from skillet; set aside and keep warm. Pour wine into skillet, stirring well; add tomato slices and bring to boiling. Add lemon slices, hot fish stock, salt, pepper, and cayenne pepper. Simmer about 25 minutes, or until liquid is reduced by almost one half.
4. Add fish fillets to skillet and continue cooking 5 minutes longer
5. Meanwhile, blend several tablespoons of the liquid in which the fish is cooking with saffron. When fish has cooked 5 minutes, spread saffron mixture over fillets. Remove fillets from liquid and place on buttered toast. Pour liquid over fish. Serve at once.

6 servings

Fish Stock: Combine **1 quart water, 1 tablespoon salt**, and **1 pound fish trimmings** (head, bones, skin, and tail) in a large saucepan. Cover and simmer 30 minutes. Strain liquid and use as directed.

About 1 quart stock

LOUISIANA

Pompano en Papillote

½ cup coarsely chopped
   cooked shrimp
½ cup coarsely chopped
   cooked lobster meat
1 cup Thick White Sauce
   (see Medium White
   Sauce, page 43;
   increase butter and
   flour to 3 to 4
   tablespoons each and
   substitute cream for
   milk)
¼ cup white wine
4 fresh pompano fillets
   (about 6 ounces each)
1 teaspoon salt
⅛ teaspoon pepper

1. Add shrimp and lobster to white sauce; stir in wine. Chill in refrigerator.
2. To make papillotes, fold four 12×9-inch pieces of parchment paper into halves crosswise. From other paper, make a pattern of a half heart that is as wide and long as the folded parchment paper. Place straight edge of pattern on folded edge of parchment paper, trace and cut out heart shapes. Set papillotes aside.
3. To fill papillotes, cut each pompano fillet in half crosswise, keeping halves of the same fillet together (If frozen, thaw fillets completely.)
4. Brush inside of each paper heart with **vegetable oil**. On one half of each paper heart lay fillet half, skin side down. Sprinkle the four halves with one half of salt and pepper.
5. Remove filling from refrigerator and divide into fourths. Place one fourth on each fillet half; pat with back of spoon over fish. Place matching fillet half over filling, skin side up. Sprinkle all four with remaining salt and pepper. Fold top half of paper heart over fillet. (Top half will not meet edge of bottom paper half.)
6. To seal papillotes and complete, starting at top end of paper heart, fold small portion of bottom edge over top and crease; hold folded portion down with one hand while folding and creasing next portion, overlapping it on folded portion. Repeat, following outline of heart, folding and creasing. At end, twist paper. Repeat with remaining papillotes. Place papillotes in a shallow baking dish.
7. Bake at 375°F about 30 minutes, or until papers are puffed and golden brown.
8. Serve papillotes on warm dinner plates. Cut a cross in top of paper with scissors just before serving.

4 servings

Rice Pilau

6 slices bacon
1 large onion, chopped
1 stalk celery, chopped
2 tablespoons bacon
   drippings
2 cups sieved cooked
   tomatoes
1½ cups hot water
2 teaspoons salt
⅛ teaspoon pepper
1 cup uncooked rice

1. Cut bacon into small pieces and fry in a saucepan. Remove bacon from fat and drain on absorbent paper.
2. Add onion and celery to bacon fat. Cook over medium heat, stirring occasionally, until onion is tender. Combine tomatoes, hot water, salt, and pepper with onion and celery; mix thoroughly.
3. Cover and bring mixture to boiling. Gradually add rice to mixture so boiling will not stop. Simmer covered, 20 minutes, or until a rice kernel is entirely soft when pressed between fingers and nearly all the liquid is absorbed.
4. Blend in reserved bacon pieces and serve hot.

4 to 6 servings

Creole Pot-au-Feu

Pot-au-Feu is often called the Stock Pot. This stock is used in a variety of Creole soups.

3 pounds lean beef (chuck or plate), cut in 1-inch pieces
1 beef soup bone, cracked
3 quarts water
1½ tablespoons salt
1 teaspoon crushed red pepper
5 carrots
2 turnips
1 parsnip
4 leeks (white part only)
3 stalks celery with leaves
1 large onion
2 ripe tomatoes
  Herb bouquet*
2 whole cloves
1 medium onion

1. Put beef, soup bone, water, salt, and red pepper into a large saucepot. Cover and bring to boiling. Remove foam and continue to simmer 4 hours, removing foam as necessary.
2. Meanwhile, wash, pare or scrape carrots, turnips, and parsnip; cut in large pieces and set aside.
3. Clean leeks, celery, and large onion; slice and set aside. Chop tomatoes.
4. Add all vegetables to saucepot with herb bouquet. Insert cloves in medium onion and add to saucepot. Cover and simmer 1½ hours longer. Remove saucepot from heat.
5. Strain liquid through a fine sieve and allow to cool. (The meat and vegetables strained from broth may be served as desired.) When cool, put into refrigerator to chill. Remove hardened layer of fat; use for other food preparation.
6. Store stock in covered container in refrigerator for future use. If broth is to be used immediately, skim fat from cooled broth; reheat and serve with **toast**.

About 2½ quarts stock

*Herb bouquet: Tie 3 to 4 sprigs parsley, 1 sprig thyme, and ½ bay leaf in cheesecloth.

Oysters Rockefeller

1 egg, well beaten
2 cups Medium White Sauce (page 43)
2 dozen shell oysters
2 tablespoons sherry
2 tablespoons butter or margarine
1 tablespoon finely chopped onion
1 pound fresh spinach, cooked, drained, and finely chopped
1 tablespoon minced parsley
⅛ teaspoon cayenne pepper
¼ teaspoon salt
  Few grains ground nutmeg
¼ cup shredded Parmesan cheese

1. Stir egg into white sauce; set aside.
2. Pour coarse salt into a 15×10×1-inch jelly roll pan to a ¼-inch depth. Open oysters and arrange the oysters-in-the-shells on the salt; sprinkle ¼ teaspoon sherry over each.
3. Heat butter in a heavy skillet. Add onion and cook until partially tender. Add chopped spinach, 2 table-spoons of the white sauce, parsley, and cayenne to the skillet along with salt and nutmeg; mix thoroughly. Heat 2 to 3 minutes.
4. Spoon spinach mixture over all of the oysters. Spoon remaining white sauce over spinach. Sprinkle each oyster with cheese.
5. Bake at 375°F 15 to 20 minutes, or until tops are lightly browned.

4 to 6 servings

Pain Perdu (*Lost Bread*)

Creoles relish this crisp-crusted treat as a breakfast bread. This delicacy has much in common with French toast.

   2 eggs
   1 cup milk or cream
   ¼ cup sugar
   ½ teaspoon salt
   ¼ teaspoon vanilla extract
  12 slices bread (slightly dry
       bread produces firmer
       Pain Perdu)
       Fat or oil for deep
         frying, heated to 375°F
   ¼ cup confectioners' sugar
   ½ teaspoon nutmeg

1. Beat eggs, milk, sugar, salt, and vanilla extract slightly in a shallow bowl. Set mixture aside.
2. Arrange 12 slices bread in three stacks on flat work surface. If desired, trim off crusts with a sharp knife. Cut stacks of slices into strips or diagonally into halves. Or, spread out a few slices at a time over the working surface and cut them individually into rounds with a large cookie cutter or a knife.
3. Dip bread pieces one at a time into the egg mixture. Coat each side well. Allow any excess coating to drip off before lowering slice into the heated fat.
4. Add only as many pieces at one time as will float uncrowded one layer deep in the fat. Fry 1 to 2 minutes, or until golden brown. Turn pieces with a fork as necessary. Drain.
5. Mix confectioners' sugar and nutmeg; sift over pieces.
6. Serve immediately.

6 servings

Note: Orange-flower water and brandy are often used as part of the liquid when Pain Perdu is made.

Quick Calas

Until recent years, the old woman selling calas was a daily early morning figure on the streets of New Orleans. Upon hearing her cry "Belle cala, tout chaud!" the Creole cooks would rush out to get fresh, hot calas to serve to their masters and mistresses with their morning coffee. Calas of old New Orleans were leavened with yeast, but here is a modern adaptation of a favorite Creole specialty.

   ⅔ cup all-purpose flour
   ½ cup sugar
   1 tablespoon baking
       powder
   ½ teaspoon salt
   ½ teaspoon nutmeg
   3 eggs
   2 cups cooked rice
   ¼ teaspoon vanilla extract
       Fat or oil for deep
         frying, heated to 360°
         (hydrogenated
         vegetable shortening,
         all-purpose shortening,
         or lard)
       Confectioners' sugar

1. Mix flour, sugar, baking powder, salt, and nutmeg; set aside.
2. Beat eggs until thick and piled softly. Thoroughly blend in cooked rice and vanilla extract. Add dry ingredients and mix until well blended.
3. Drop batter by tablespoonfuls into heated fat; add only as many calas at one time as will float uncrowded one layer deep in the fat. Fry about 2 minutes, or until golden brown. Turn calas with a fork as they rise to the surface and several times during cooking (do not pierce). Remove with a slotted spoon; drain over fat a few seconds before removing to absorbent paper.
4. Sprinkle calas with confectioners' sugar. Serve hot.

About 20 calas

LOUISIANA

Blancmange

⅓ cup sugar
3 tablespoons cornstarch
⅛ teaspoon salt
½ cup cold milk
1½ cups milk, scalded
1 teaspoon vanilla extract
4 egg whites

1. Blend sugar, cornstarch, and salt in a saucepan. Stir in cold milk.
2. Gradually add scalded milk, stirring constantly. Stirring gently and constantly, bring mixture to boiling. Cook 1 minute.
3. Remove cornstarch mixture from heat. Stir in vanilla extract.
4. Beat egg whites until rounded peaks are formed; spread beaten egg whites over mixture and fold together.
5. Turn into a 1-quart mold and chill in refrigerator until firm.
6. When ready to serve, unmold and serve with **fruit** or **sweetened whipped cream.**

About 6 servings

Coupe St. Jacques

2 cups fresh pineapple wedges
1 cup orange pieces
1 cup fresh peach pieces
½ cup white seedless grapes, halved
¼ cup fresh blueberries
1 cup confectioners' or granulated sugar
⅓ cup kirsch
¼ cup fresh raspberries
Lime, orange, and raspberry sherbet (1 pint or more each)

1. Prepare the fresh fruits and combine all fruits (except raspberries) in a bowl; toss gently with the sugar and pour the kirsch over all. Refrigerate to chill thoroughly.
2. Before serving, gently mix in the raspberries. Spoon mixture into chilled serving dishes, spooning some of the juice over fruit.
3. Top each serving with one scoop of lime, orange, and raspberry sherbet. Serve at once.

12 to 14 servings

The "Magnolia State," as Mississippi is often called, was first explored by such Spanish adventurers as Hernando de Soto in the mid-sixteenth century. However, it was about 150 years later when white settlers, led by Pierre le Moyne, built a fort near Mobile and the colonization of the territory began in earnest. Mississippi belongs to the traditional Deep South. It was the second state to pass the ordinance of secession from the Union in 1861. When times were hard during the Civil War and food was scarce in besieged Vicksburg, it has been said that women were dressing and cooking rats to nourish the troops and local population. However, no recipes for these indelicate concoctions appear to have reached the printed page.

Most of the typical Mississippi cookery is similar to that found in the other states below the Mason-Dixon line. Sweet potato pone, buttermilk biscuits, chicken bread, and corn sticks are everyday dishes to Mississippi homemakers.

Much of the state's terrain is lowland and is divided into two main regions, the Mississippi Alluvial Plain and the East Gulf Coastal Plain. Although cotton is the state's chief crop and is grown primarily on the Mississippi Plain, many foods are also important to the area's economy. These include soybeans, potatoes, corn, other grains, and grain sorghums. Sugar cane and sweet sorghum are grown locally and used in making refined sugar and syrup.

Mississippi is a leading producer of edible nuts. Pecans are grown predominantly in the southeastern part of the state. Pecan pies and cakes are common desserts to the average Mississippian.

This southern state also ranks high in the raising of poultry and livestock. The typical homemaker uses chicken in a wide variety of ways. Recipes such as chicken hash, and a special cornmeal bread baked in chicken drippings much like the English Yorkshire pudding, have been handed down by word of mouth through several generations.

Mississippi fruits include cantaloupes, figs, peaches, pears, plums, strawberries, and watermelon. The early French settlers were delighted with this enormous medley of fresh produce. Assorted fruit salads, pies, and, of course, watermelon pickles quickly became old favorites.

Beans, cowpeas, cabbage, sweet potatoes, cucumbers, mustard greens, turnips, tomatoes, and okra are typical vegetables of the state. There are several traditional southern ways of preparing okra, pea soups, cold vegetable salads, turnips, and sweet potatoes in the kitchens of Mississippi. One of the most savory soups is called Mississippi Court Bouillon and is probably the result of early French influence. Among its ingredients are redfish, green peppers, herbs, garlic, and onion added to a base of shortening and flour.

It is believed tomatoes were introduced into Mississippi in the 1870s and that they were first added to what had been a prerevolutionary stew of carrots, celery, cabbage, onions, green beans, peas, turnips, okra, and parsley.

Seafoods and fish comprise a good share of the average Mississippian's diet, especially in the coastal regions and along the inland rivers. Mississippi is often called "catfish country." This fish is a staple in many a southerner's diet. Outdoor oyster bakes have always been popular events, plus festivals which usually feature a Shrimp Queen.

A traditional breakfast, "Ole Miss' style," in the luxurious plantation manor houses might include as many as three kinds of meat, eggs, buttermilk biscuits, hominy grits, and even waffles.

Corn pone and pot liquor was a dish at first only eaten by the servants, but later, as its food value became recognized, many of the more affluent southerners introduced it into their own diets.

Shrimp Fritters

1 pound uncooked shrimp
1 cup all-purpose flour
1 teaspoon baking powder
½ teaspoon salt
  Few grains pepper
2 eggs, beaten
  Milk (about ½ cup)
⅓ cup minced onion
1 tablespoon minced
  parsley
  Dash Tabasco
  Fat for deep frying
    heated to 375°F

1. Peel, devein, and mince shrimp.
2. Mix flour, baking powder, salt, and pepper in a bowl. Add eggs and enough milk to make a thick batter. Add onion, parsley, Tabasco, and shrimp; mix well.
3. Drop batter by tablespoonfuls into heated fat. Fry until golden brown (about 2 minutes).
4. Serve hot accompanied with cocktail sauce, if desired.

About 2½ dozen fritters

Mississippi Court Bouillon

1 tablespoon oil
2 tablespoons flour
1 cup finely chopped onion
3 cloves garlic, minced
3 sprigs parsley

1. Heat oil in a deep skillet. Blend in 2 tablespoons flour. Add onion, garlic, parsley, basil, thyme, bay leaves, and Worcestershire sauce. Cook until lightly browned. Add water and tomatoes; simmer 15 minutes.

¼ teaspoon basil
¼ teaspoon thyme
2 bay leaves
1 tablespoon
   Worcestershire sauce
1 quart water
1 can (16 ounces) tomatoes
   (undrained)
3 pounds thick boneless
   fish fillets
1 cup white wine
2 teaspoons salt
¼ teaspoon pepper
   Flour

2. Dip fish in wine, season with salt and pepper, and coat with flour. Put slices side by side in skillet. Cover skillet and simmer 30 minutes, or until fish is tender when tested with a fork. Remove bay leaves.
3. Serve fish and gravy over **hot cooked rice.**

8 to 10 servings

Almond-Chicken Soup

½ cup blanched almonds,
   finely chopped
3 cups chicken broth
1 teaspoon onion juice
1 bay leaf, finely crushed
3 tablespoons flour
3 tablespoons butter or
   other fat, melted
2 cups milk
1 cup half-and-half or
   evaporated milk
   Salt and pepper

1. Put almonds into a saucepan.
2. Add chicken broth, onion juice, and bay leaf. Simmer 15 minutes.
3. Combine flour and butter; add to broth, stirring constantly until boiling point is reached.
4. Add milk and half-and-half; season to taste.

6 servings

Ham Roll-Ups

2 medium sweet potatoes
3 tablespoons melted
   butter or other fat
½ cup crushed pineapple
¼ cup chopped pecans
½ cup cracker crumbs
3 tablespoons brown sugar
2 (¼ inch thick) slices
   uncooked smoked ham
   or boiled ham (1½ to 2
   pounds)
¾ cup pineapple juice

1. Cook sweet potatoes in boiling salted water until tender; drain, peel, and mash. Add butter, pineapple, pecans, cracker crumbs, and brown sugar; mix well.
2. Spread thick layer of filling on each slice of ham, roll as for jelly roll, fasten with wooden picks or tie into shape. Put rolls into a baking dish. Pour pineapple juice over them.
3. Bake at 350°F 1 hour for smoked ham and 20 minutes for boiled ham. Baste frequently with liquid in pan. Cut each roll in thirds.

6 servings

MISSISSIPPI

Red Snapper Marguery

2 pounds red snapper
½ pound Cheddar cheese, shredded
3 hard-cooked eggs, chopped
2 pounds cooked shrimp, chopped
1 cup canned mushrooms
1 tablespoon chopped truffles or oysters
Salt and pepper
1 cup Medium White Sauce (page 43)

1. Steam or boil fish and remove skin and bones. Separate fish into large pieces.
2. Arrange half of fish pieces in a buttered casserole. Cover with layers of half of cheese, eggs, shrimp, mushrooms, and truffles. Season layers with salt and pepper. Repeat layers and pour white sauce over all.
3. Bake at 350°F about 30 minutes.

6 to 8 servings

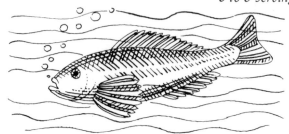

Baked Fish Steaks

2 pounds fish steaks or fillets, such as cod, haddock, halibut, or salmon, 1 inch thick
1½ teaspoons curry powder or tarragon
½ teaspoon salt
⅛ teaspoon pepper
4 bacon slices

1. Wash, coarsely chop, and mix together equal amounts of **parsley, celery leaves,** and **onion** (enough to line a shallow baking dish).
2. Sprinkle both sides of fish steaks with a mixture of the curry powder, salt, and pepper. Arrange on parsley mixture. Place a bacon slice on each steak.
3. Bake uncovered at 350°F 25 to 30 minutes, or until fish flakes easily.
4. Serve with a **lemon-butter sauce.**

4 servings

Hominy and Shrimp Baked in Tomato Sauce

1 can (15 ounces) hominy, drained
1 cup shrimp, cooked
4 tablespoons butter or margarine
1½ tablespoons flour
¼ teaspoon salt
1½ cups tomato juice
1 teaspoon grated onion
1 cup soft bread crumbs

1. Spread two thirds of hominy in bottom of buttered shallow baking dish; cover with layer of shrimp, then remaining hominy.
2. Melt 2 tablespoons butter in a saucepan; add flour and salt, blending well. Add tomato juice. Cook until mixture thickens, stirring constantly.
3. Remove from heat, add onion; pour over hominy and shrimp. Cover with bread crumbs mixed with remaining 2 tablespoons of melted butter.
4. Bake at 350°F 20 minutes, or until browned and crisp.

6 servings

Dixie Chicken Shortcake

2 cups chicken stock
2 tablespoons flour
1 pound mushrooms,
    cleaned and sliced
2 tablespoons butter
4 cups diced cooked chicken
    Salt and pepper
    Southern Cornbread

1. Mix a small amount of chicken stock with flour in a saucepan. Stir in remaining stock. Bring to boiling; stir and cook until slightly thickened.
2. Sauté mushrooms in butter. Add chicken and mushrooms to sauce. Season to taste with salt and pepper.
3. Cut cornbread into 8 pieces and split. Cover the lower halves with some of the chicken mixture. Cover with the top crusts and spoon chicken mixture over cornbread.

8 servings

Southern Cornbread

1 cup white cornmeal
½ teaspoon baking soda
½ teaspoon salt
1 egg, beaten
1 cup buttermilk
1 tablespoon melted
    shortening

1. Combine cornmeal, baking soda, and salt in a bowl.
2. Mix egg, buttermilk, and shortening; add to dry ingredients; mix well. Pour into a greased shallow pan.
3. Bake at 450°F 18 minutes.

8 servings

Old-Fashioned Green Beans and Bacon

¾ pound fresh green beans,
    cut
8 slices bacon, diced
2 medium potatoes, pared
    and cut in ½-inch
    pieces
1 small onion, sliced
¼ cup water
½ teaspoon salt

1. Put beans into ½ inch of boiling salted water in a saucepan. Cover and cook 15 minutes. Drain.
2. Meanwhile, fry bacon until crisp in a saucepan.
3. Add potatoes, green beans, onion, water, and salt to bacon and fat. Cook covered about 15 minutes, or until potatoes are tender.

About 4 servings

Peach Fritters

1 cup all-purpose flour
2 tablespoons sugar
¼ teaspoon salt
⅔ cup milk
2 eggs, separated
2 tablespoons butter,
    melted
6 large ripe peaches,
    peeled and pits
    removed
3 tablespoons lemon juice
    Fat for deep frying
    heated to 365°F

1. Combine flour, sugar, and salt in a bowl. Add a mixture of milk, egg yolks, and melted butter; beat with electric or hand rotary beater until smooth.
2. Beat egg whites until stiff, not dry, peaks are formed and fold into batter.
3. Cut peaches into ½-inch slices; toss with the lemon juice. Coat each slice with batter.
4. Fry in heated fat until nicely browned. Drain. Sprinkle generously with **confectioners' sugar** or serve with a favorite **pudding sauce.**

About 8 servings

Black Bottom Pie

½ cup sugar
4 teaspoons cornstarch
½ cup cold milk
1½ cups milk, scalded
4 egg yolks, slightly
   beaten
1 envelope unflavored
   gelatin
¼ cup cold water
1 tablespoon rum extract
1½ ounces (1½ squares)
   unsweetened
   chocolate, melted and
   cooled
2 teaspoons vanilla extract
1 baked 10-inch pie shell
4 egg whites
¼ teaspoon salt
¼ teaspoon cream of tartar
½ cup sugar
1 cup whipping cream,
   whipped
½ ounce (½ square)
   unsweetened
   chocolate

1. Blend ½ cup sugar and cornstarch in a saucepan. Stir in the cold milk, then the scalded milk, adding gradually. Bring rapidly to boiling, stirring constantly. Cook 3 minutes.
2. Turn mixture into a double-boiler top and set over boiling water. Vigorously stir about 3 tablespoons of hot mixture into egg yolks. Immediately blend into mixture in double boiler. Cook over simmering water, stirring constantly, 3 to 5 minutes, or until mixture coats a metal spoon. Remove double-boiler top from hot water immediately.
3. Soften gelatin in the cold water. Remove 1 cup of the cooked filling and set aside. Immediately stir softened gelatin into mixture in double boiler until completely dissolved. Cool until mixture sets slightly. Blend in rum extract.
4. Blend the melted chocolate and vanilla extract into the 1 cup reserved filling. Cool completely; turn into the baked pie shell, spreading evenly over bottom. Chill until set.
5. Beat egg whites and salt until frothy. Add cream of tartar and beat slightly. Gradually add remaining ½ cup sugar, beating well after each addition; continue beating until stiff peaks are formed. Spread over gelatin mixture and gently fold together. Turn onto chocolate filling in pie shell. Chill until firm.
6. Spread whipped cream over pie, swirling for a decorative effect. Top with chocolate curls shaved from the ½ ounce unsweetened chocolate. Chill until ready to serve.

One 10-inch pie

Plantation Sour Cream Cookies

1 cup butter or other
   shortening
2 cups firmly packed brown
   sugar
1 cup dairy sour cream
3 eggs, beaten
1 teaspoon vanilla extract
4 cups sifted all-purpose
   flour
2 teaspoons baking soda
1 teaspoon nutmeg
½ teaspoon salt

1. Cream butter and brown sugar in a large bowl. Add sour cream, eggs, and vanilla extract; mix well.
2. Blend dry ingredients; add gradually to first mixture, mixing until blended.
3. Drop by spoonfuls onto well-greased cookie sheet.
4. Bake at 350°F 12 minutes, or until browned

About 8 dozen cookies

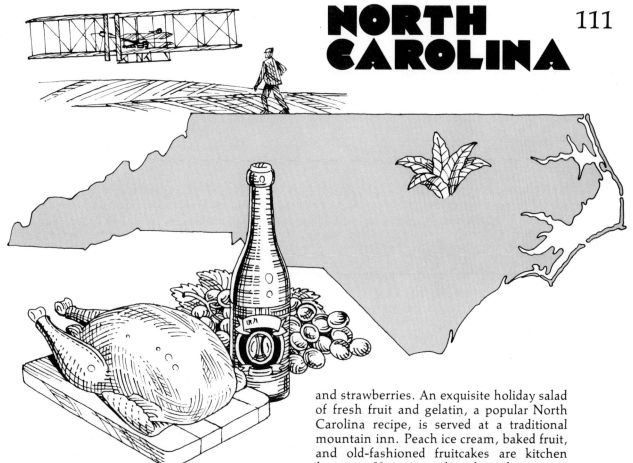

North Carolina, the "Tar Heel State," was one of the thirteen original colonies. The name Carolina was used in honor of Charles I, king of England in the early seventeenth century. The geography of North Carolina varies from the eastern Appalachian Mountains, with an elevation of over six thousand feet, to the central Piedmont Plateau, to the low and swampy southeastern coastal plain. Because of this diversity in altitude and climate, North Carolina has the greatest variety of plant life of any state in the eastern United States.

Most of the farms in the Tar Heel State are small by western standards, averaging only eighty acres. Tobacco, corn, cotton, peanuts, hay, and potatoes are the chief crops, but there is also a great variety of other vegetables and fruits. Important fruits are apples, melons, peaches, dewberries, and strawberries. An exquisite holiday salad of fresh fruit and gelatin, a popular North Carolina recipe, is served at a traditional mountain inn. Peach ice cream, baked fruit, and old-fashioned fruitcakes are kitchen favorites. Variations of a palate-pleasing applesauce cake are featured on many menus throughout the state.

Scuppernong, a kind of grape that is grown on the coastal plain, is consumed locally and also shipped to other sections of the country. A delicious iced beverage prepared from this grape is often served in the summertime. Scuppernongs are used in jellies and pies and in making a delicate wine preferred by many local wine connoisseurs.

Cabbages, cucumbers, and green peppers are the greatest income producers grown by the local truck farmers. North Carolina homemakers prepare casseroles of them, stuff them, and also make crisp salads of all three. Onions, lima beans, string beans, sweet corn, and tomatoes are also grown in large quantities. Green and lima beans seasoned by southern cooks can delight even a gourmet.

In 1585, Sir Walter Raleigh of England

sent an expedition to Roanoke Island that became the first English colony of settlers to colonize this area. However, hard times caused this colony to return to England and be replaced by another; but misfortune again struck and this colony perished. It went down in history as the Lost Colony. The first permanent white settlers arrived in North Carolina from Virginia. Many of these were also of English origin. A few were French Huguenots, others were from Switzerland and Germany. They all brought with them their own traditional customs and methods of food preparation, which had to be adapted to their new pioneer environment. In the mideighteenth century a band of Moravians, originally from a province of the Austria-Hungary empire, moved to the Winston-Salem area of North Carolina. Their food legacies include superb cream and sugar cakes.

In 1776, when North Carolina finally became an independent state, approximately one third of its population were of English origin, nearly one third Scottish or Scotch-Irish, one fifth Negro and about one tenth German. This amalgamation of nationalities and races provides the basis for an interesting and varied cuisine. Unlikely dishes found in North Carolina today are Irish potato soufflé and glazed carrots, probably a carry-over from the early Scotch-Irish settlers.

In the mountain regions of the state it is not unusual to find roast partridge served with a hot sauce, baked ham, and a creamy cheese-custard dish. White cornmeal has traditionally replaced the yellow variety in the North Carolina hoecakes and dodgers.

Hopping John, a choice concoction of bacon or salt pork, black-eye peas, rice, and seasonings was originally from South Carolina, but is now relished extensively in North Carolina and throughout the South. Other North Carolina foods that merit praise are seafoods and savory recipes prepared from such favorites as shrimp, oysters, and sea bass.

Sausage, Cabbage, and Apples en Casserole

1 **pound bulk pork sausage**
1 **medium cabbage,
    shredded**
3 **apples, sliced
    Salt**
1 **tablespoon vinegar**

1. Mold sausage into flat cakes and fry in a skillet until crisp.
2. In a greased baking dish, arrange layers of cabbage and apples, lightly salting each layer and ending with a layer of apples. Place sausage cakes on top.
3. Rinse skillet with vinegar and pour over sausages. Cover.
4. Bake at 350°F until tender (about 45 minutes).

6 servings

Molded Shrimp Salad

1⅔ **cups boiling water**
1 **package (3 ounces)
    lemon-flavored gelatin**
1 **cup cooked shrimp**
½ **cup chopped celery**
¼ **cup chopped stuffed
    olives**
¼ **cup chopped sweet
    pickles**
¼ **teaspoon salt**

1. Add boiling water to gelatin and stir until dissolved. Cool.
2. Add remaining ingredients and pour into a large mold or into individual molds. Chill until firm. Unmold on **crisp salad greens** and garnish with **mayonnaise.**

6 servings

Southern Jugged Soup

6 potatoes, sliced
1 onion, sliced
6 tomatoes or 2 cups
    cooked tomatoes
1 turnip, diced
2½ cups peas
1 carrot, grated
¼ cup uncooked rice
1 tablespoon salt
1 tablespoon sugar
½ teaspoon pepper
    Dash allspice
2 quarts soup stock

1. Arrange vegetables, rice, and seasonings in alternate layers in a casserole or crock.
2. Pour broth over vegetables. Cover tightly.
3. Set casserole in a pan of hot water.
4. Cook in a 300°F oven 4 to 6 hours.

8 to 10 servings

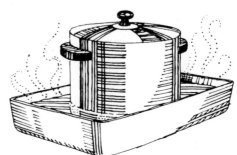

Roast Partridge

4 partridges
4 strips bacon
    Salt and pepper
1 cup sour cream*
    Toast

1. Clean partridges thoroughly inside and out. Fasten long strips of bacon over breasts. Rub inside and out with salt and pepper and put in uncovered roasting pan.
2. Roast at 350°F 30 minutes.
3. When partridges are rich brown, pour sour cream over them. Let cream bubble up in pan for a minute. Place partridges on slices of **hot toast.** Pour sauce from pan over birds. Garnish with **orange slices.**

4 to 6 servings

*Pour **1½ teaspoons lemon juice** or **vinegar** into a measuring cup. Add **cream** or **half-and-half** to fill cup to 1-cup line; stir.

Baked Hen in Scuppernong Wine

1 roasting hen or capon (5
    to 6 pounds)
1 cup wine such as
    scuppernong or sauterne
    Freshly ground nutmeg
    Gravy

1. Prepare hen for roasting, using stuffing, or roast plain.
2. Bake at 325°F about 2½ hours, or until chicken is tender. About one-half hour before serving, pour wine over hen and sprinkle generously with nutmeg. Baste with pan drippings until serving time.
3. If desired, make gravy with the drippings and chopped giblets (if available). (This chicken has a wonderful flavor; the leftover meat makes piquant creamed chicken.)

6 servings

NORTH CAROLINA

Hopping John

¼ pound piece bacon or
    salt pork
1½ quarts cold water
 1 cup dried black-eye peas
 1 cup uncooked rice
 ½ teaspoon salt
 ¼ teaspoon pepper

1. Put bacon into a large saucepan; add water and bring to boiling. Reduce heat; cover and simmer 45 minutes.
2. Meanwhile, sort and wash black-eye peas thoroughly. Add peas gradually to water so boiling will not stop. Cover pan and simmer about 1½ hours, or until peas are almost tender; stir occasionally.
3. Add rice, salt, and pepper gradually so boiling will not stop. Cover and simmer about 30 minutes, stirring occasionally, or until a rice kernel is soft when pressed between fingers. If necessary, add more boiling water during cooking.
4. Remove bacon and drain pea-rice mixture thoroughly in a colander or sieve. Cover colander with a clean cloth and set over hot water until ready to serve.
5. Meanwhile, slice the bacon and keep warm.
6. To serve, turn the pea-rice mixture into a warm serving bowl and garnish with **parsley.** Accompany with the sliced bacon.

6 to 8 servings

Vegetable Scrapple

3½ cups boiling water
1¼ cups yellow cornmeal
 1 tablespoon salt
 ½ teaspoon pepper
 ½ cup finely chopped
    onion
 ⅓ cup finely chopped
    carrot
 ¼ cup finely chopped
    green pepper
 2 tablespoons finely
    chopped pimento
 1 cup (about 5 ounces)
    peanuts, coarsely
    chopped
 2 tablespoons fat

1. Pour boiling water into top of double boiler; add cornmeal, salt, and pepper slowly, stirring constantly. Cook over direct heat until thickened, stirring constantly.
2. Add the chopped onion, carrot, green pepper, and pimento; set over simmering water and cook 1 hour.
3. Stir peanuts into cooked cornmeal mixture. Pour into a greased 9×5×3-inch loaf pan, spreading to edges. Chill in refrigerator about 4 hours.
4. Cut chilled scrapple into slices 1 inch thick.
5. Heat fat in a skillet over medium heat. Arrange slices in skillet. Cook at one time only as many slices as will lie flat in skillet. When lightly browned on one side, turn and brown other side. Serve warm.

6 to 8 servings

Aspic with Vegetables

4 envelopes unflavored
    gelatin
5½ cups chicken broth
 1 tablespoon tomato paste
 2 egg whites, slightly
    beaten

1. Soften gelatin in 1 cup cooled chicken broth.
2. Pour remaining chicken broth into a large saucepan. Add tomato paste, egg whites, egg shells, and softened gelatin. Bring to boiling over low heat, stirring constantly with a wire whisk. Remove from heat and set aside 10 minutes.

2 egg shells, crushed
¼ cup red wine
2 cups cooked green peas
2 cups sliced cooked
    carrots
½ cup mayonnaise

3. Set a strainer lined with a damp clean tea towel over a large bowl. Pour aspic mixture into strainer and allow it to drip; do not squeeze out liquid. Stir wine into clear liquid. Reserve 1 cup liquid.

4. Divide peas and carrots equally into individual molds, arranging vegetables in layers. Mix reserved liquid with mayonnaise. Chill until thickened. Spoon mixture over partially set vegetable aspic. Chill until firm.

5. Unmold on **lettuce.**

10 to 12 servings

Shrimp Potato Salad

6 medium potatoes
3 tablespoons salad oil
2 tablespoons wine vinegar
¾ cup mayonnaise
½ cup prepared mustard
1 clove garlic, minced
½ teaspoon salt
¼ to ½ teaspoon cayenne
    pepper
1 pound cooked shrimp,
    cut in halves
3 hard-cooked eggs,
    chopped
1 cup chopped celery

1. Cook potatoes until tender; peel and cut into cubes while still warm. Put into a large bowl. Drizzle oil and vinegar over potatoes and toss lightly.

2. Mix mayonnaise, mustard, garlic, salt, and cayenne. Add mayonnaise mixture, shrimp, eggs, and celery to potatoes; toss until well mixed.

3. Turn into a salad bowl and, if desired, garnish with sliced pimento-stuffed olives and lettuce.

About 10 servings

Cranberry-Orange Mold

1 cup fresh cranberries,
    ground
1 cup sugar
½ cup boiling water
1 package (3 ounces)
    lemon-flavored gelatin
1 cup orange juice
2 teaspoons grated orange
    peel
1 can (about 8 ounces)
    crushed pineapple,
    drained
1 cup chopped celery
½ cup coarsely chopped
    pecans

1. Mix cranberries and sugar; set aside about 2 hours.

2. Meanwhile, pour boiling water over gelatin in a bowl; stir until dissolved. Stir in orange juice. Chill until slightly thickened.

3. Stir cranberry mixture, orange peel, drained pineapple, celery, and nuts into gelatin mixture. Turn into a 1-quart mold.

4. Chill until firm.

5. Unmold on lettuce-lined plate and serve with **mayonnaise.**

About 8 servings

Hoe Cake

This is a simple bread which country people used to bake on their hoes when working in the fields.

1 cup white cornmeal
½ teaspoon salt
½ cup milk or water
    Salt pork drippings
    Butter

1. Mix cornmeal, salt, and enough boiling milk or water to make a batter which will not spread when dropped on a griddle.
2. Grease griddle with salt pork drippings and drop the batter on the hot griddle. Each cake should be about ½ inch thick. Cook slowly and when browned, place ¼ teaspoon butter on top of each cake, turn and brown other side.

4 servings

Note: Sometimes the batter is placed on griddle in 1 large cake and as soon as it is browned on one side is turned onto a freshly greased griddle to brown other side. The thin, crisp crust is peeled off with a knife, placed on a hot plate, and spread with butter. When another brown crust has formed, the cake is turned again, the crust removed and buttered, and the process continued until the cake is all browned. These crisp buttered crusts are served piled together and cut in sections.

Raisin-Nut Chess Pie

⅓ cup butter
1 teaspoon vanilla extract
1 cup sugar
2 eggs
¼ cup cream
1 cup chopped raisins
1 cup chopped pecans
1 unbaked 8-inch pastry
    shell

1. Cream butter with vanilla extract and sugar. Add eggs, one at a time, beating well after each addition. Mix in cream, raisins, and pecans. Pour into unbaked pastry shell.
2. Bake at 450°F 10 minutes. Turn oven control to 350°F and bake 30 minutes.

One 8-inch pie

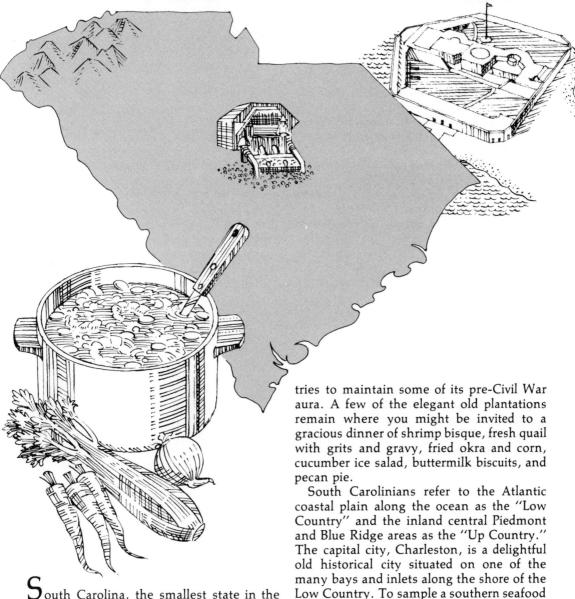

South Carolina, the smallest state in the Deep South, is not only important in manufacturing, especially textiles, but also in agriculture. It claims to grow more peaches than any state except California. About half of its people live in rural areas, and almost one third live in the three main metropolitan centers: Charleston, Columbia, and Greensville.

This deeply traditional southern state was the first to secede from the Union, and still tries to maintain some of its pre-Civil War aura. A few of the elegant old plantations remain where you might be invited to a gracious dinner of shrimp bisque, fresh quail with grits and gravy, fried okra and corn, cucumber ice salad, buttermilk biscuits, and pecan pie.

South Carolinians refer to the Atlantic coastal plain along the ocean as the "Low Country" and the inland central Piedmont and Blue Ridge areas as the "Up Country." The capital city, Charleston, is a delightful old historical city situated on one of the many bays and inlets along the shore of the Low Country. To sample a southern seafood specialty in one of its hospitable homes or quaint cafés is a savory certainty. Shrimp dipped in egg and crumbs and fried, baked shrimp paste, she-crab soup, oyster bisque, and broiled oysters are all a treat for a seafood fancier.

The hearty mountain people, many of them descendants of the early English and Scotch-Irish settlers, enjoy variations of bean soup and stew, hominy and bean cakes, potatoes, chicken, and even possum.

Typical South Carolina cookery is predominately an amalgamation of the many ideas and customs brought by the early Spanish, French, and English settlers. The slave trade flourished in the state before the Civil War, and now about 35 percent of the population is Negro. Thus, local foods range from the Deep South dishes to the more epicurean.

Although tobacco and cotton are the chief crops in South Carolina's economy, several important foods are also grown. Soybeans and corn are used mainly for feeding animals; however, the corn is also made into meal, syrup, oil, and grits. The vegetables and fruits are similar to those produced in other southern states, mainly cabbage, cucumbers, green beans, sweet potatoes, tomatoes, watermelons, and peaches. Peach desserts, watermelon preserves, sweet pota-

to delicacies, and crisp southern salads are plentiful.

Pork, chicken, and egg dishes are popular throughout the state because of the large quantity of hogs and chickens produced. There are recipes available that have been handed down from great-great-grandmothers for southern bean soup, chicken salad, and chicken bog (a chicken and rice mixture usually simmered in a deep casserole).

Pork, bacon, and ham are very traditional in the state, not only as "extras" in soups and stews, but also as main dishes.

In early years most of the plantations in the Low Country geared their economy to rice, but in later years they shifted to the many popular crops of today. However, rice is often found on South Carolina menus, either as an accompaniment or as an ingredient in one of the fine main dishes or luncheon casseroles.

Creamy Shrimp Mold

1 envelope unflavored
    gelatin
¼ cup water
3 tablespoons lemon juice
2½ cups cooked shrimp,
    finely chopped
1 cup finely chopped
    celery
2 hard-cooked eggs,
    chopped
2 canned pimentos, finely
    chopped
1 bottle (2 ounces)
    pimento-stuffed
    olives, drained and
    finely chopped
2 tablespoons grated
    onion
1 cup mayonnaise
¼ teaspoon salt
¼ teaspoon pepper

1. Soften gelatin in water and lemon juice in a small saucepan. Stir over low heat until gelatin is dissolved.
2. Combine shrimp, celery, eggs, pimento, olives, onion, mayonnaise, salt, and pepper in a bowl. Add dissolved gelatin gradually, mixing well.
3. Turn into a fancy 1-quart mold. Chill until firm.
4. Serve as an appetizer mold with **crackers.**

One 1-quart mold

Southern Bean Soup

- 3 cups water
- 1 cup dried navy beans, rinsed
- 1½ quarts water
- 1 ham bone
- 1 cup chopped celery
- 1 small onion, minced
- 3 tablespoons butter
- 3 tablespoons flour
- Salt and pepper
- Lemon slices
- Hard-cooked egg, sliced

1. Heat water to boiling in a saucepan. Add beans gradually to water so that boiling continues. Boil 2 minutes. Remove from heat and set aside 1 hour.
2. Drain beans and add to ham bone and 1½ quarts water in a large saucepan. Add celery and onion; cover and cook slowly until beans become soft (about 3 hours).
3. Remove bone. Strain soup, pressing beans through a sieve. If necessary, add more water to make 5 cups of soup. Return to saucepan and heat.
4. Blend butter, flour, salt, and pepper; stir into hot bean broth slowly and simmer until thickened.
5. Serve hot topped with lemon and egg slices.

4 to 6 servings

Note: Black-eye peas may be used instead of beans.

Shrimp Bisque

- 2 quarts water
- 1 small white onion, halved
- 1 tablespoon salt
- 1 bay leaf
- 2 whole cloves
- 1 tablespoon wine vinegar
- ½ cup finely chopped celery with tops
- 2 pounds raw medium shrimp (unshelled)
- ¼ cup uncooked rice
- ¼ cup butter
- 1 cup grated carrot
- ¼ cup minced onion
- 1 tablespoon minced scallion with top
- 1 tablespoon minced fresh parsley
- ¼ teaspoon thyme
- 2 teaspoons salt
- ½ teaspoon freshly ground black pepper
- ½ cup cream
- ½ cup dry white wine

1. Pour water into a saucepot. Add onion halves, salt, bay leaf, cloves, wine vinegar, and celery. Bring to a rolling boil and cook 10 minutes. Add shrimp and simmer 5 minutes.
2. Drain shrimp; strain and reserve 4 cups broth. Cool, then shell shrimp. Mince all but one dozen cooked shrimp and set aside.
3. In a small saucepan with cover, cook rice until tender in 2 cups of reserved broth. Do not drain and keep warm.
4. Melt butter in a large skillet. Add carrot, onion, scallion, and parsley; sauté, stirring often until vegetables are lightly browned. Add remaining 2 cups of broth together with thyme, salt, and pepper; simmer covered 30 minutes. Then add the minced shrimp and the rice together with its shrimp stock. Simmer covered 10 minutes. Blend in cream and wine and heat thoroughly; do not boil.
5. Serve hot garnished with whole shrimp.

About 6 servings

SOUTH CAROLINA

Frankfurter Kabobs

12 frankfurters, each cut in
    3 or 4 pieces
12 whole mushrooms,
    cleaned
3 medium tomatoes, cut in
    quarters or eighths
1 cup Basic Molasses
    Barbecue Sauce
1 tablespoon prepared
    mustard
1 to 2 tablespoons
    pineapple syrup
    (optional)

1. Thread franks, mushrooms, and tomato pieces onto 8- to 10-inch skewers.
2. Combine sauce, mustard, and pineapple syrup, if used. Mix well and brush generously over kabobs.
3. Cook 5 to 6 inches above the hot coals, 3 to 4 minutes on each side; brush with the sauce several times during cooking.

6 kabobs

Vegetable Kabobs. Follow recipe for Frankfurter Kabobs except: Insert on 6 skewers the following:
    ½-inch thick slices yellow squash or 1-inch thick
      slices zucchini
12 cherry tomatoes
  1-inch strips green pepper (using 2 peppers)
  1-inch cubes unpared eggplant (using 1 small eggplant)
    Small cooked white onions (16-ounce can, drained)
12 whole mushrooms, cleaned
Omit prepared mustard and add ½ cup **chili sauce.** Increase grilling time to 5 minutes on each side.

Shrimp Kabobs. Follow recipe for Frankfurter Kabobs except: Insert on 6 skewers the following:
    Raw shrimp (about 2 pounds), shelled (leaving on tails) and deveined
  1-inch strips green pepper (using 2 peppers)
    Small cooked white onions (16-ounce can, drained)
12 whole mushrooms, cleaned
12 large pimento-stuffed olives
12 large pitted ripe olives
Omit prepared mustard, Add **1 tablespoon prepared horseradish.** Grill kabobs 5 minutes on each side.

Basic Molasses Barbecue Sauce

¼ cup cornstarch
4 cups lemon juice (about 2
    dozen lemons)
2 cups cooking oil
1 jar (12 ounces) light or
    dark molasses
¼ cup salt
1 tablespoon black pepper
6 bay leaves, broken in
    pieces
3 cloves garlic, minced

1. Combine cornstarch and lemon juice in a saucepan. Cook and stir over low heat until mixture bubbles and thickens. Cool.
2. Using rotary or electric beater, beat in remaining ingredients until thoroughly blended and thickened.
3. Store in refrigerator until needed.

About 2 quarts sauce

Deep-fried Shrimp

2 pounds fresh shrimp
    with shells
1 cup fine dry bread
    crumbs
2 eggs, slightly beaten
2 tablespoons milk
2 tablespoons paprika
1 teaspoon salt
¼ teaspoon pepper
⅛ teaspoon cayenne pepper
    Fat for deep frying
    heated to 350°F

1. Peel and devein shrimp.
2. Put bread crumbs into a shallow pan or dish. Mix eggs, milk, and seasonings in a bowl.
3. Dip shrimp into egg mixture then coat with bread crumbs.
4. Add only as many shrimp at one time to fat as will float uncrowded one layer deep. Fry 2 to 3 minutes, or until golden brown. Turn shrimp several times during frying. Drain.
5. Serve hot with desired sauce.

6 to 8 servings

Chicken Terrapin

2 pairs sweetbreads
5 cups chopped chicken,
    cooked
1 quart half-and-half
1 tablespoon cornstarch
    Milk
2 egg yolks, slightly
    beaten
1 tablespoon butter
    Salt and pepper
¼ cup sherry

1. Cover sweetbreads with boiling water (to which **1 teaspoon salt** and **1 tablespoon vinegar** have been added to each quart of water), cover, and simmer 20 minutes.
2. Drain and cover with cold water until cool enough to handle. Remove all the membrane; cut sweetbreads into small pieces. Combine with chicken.
3. Pour half-and-half into a heavy saucepan and stir in cornstarch which has been mixed with a little cold milk. Bring to boiling, stirring constantly; cook until thickened. Add a small amount of sauce to egg yolks; stir into sauce in pan. Cook until thickened. Add butter, salt and pepper to taste, chicken, and sweetbreads. Heat thoroughly.
4. Just before serving, mix in sherry. Serve either on **toast** or in **patty shells.**

10 to 12 servings

Okra and Corn

4 slices bacon
1 onion, sliced
1 package (10 ounces)
    frozen okra, thawed
    and cut into ¼-inch
    thick slices
1 package (10 ounces)
    frozen corn, thawed
1½ cups (about 2 medium)
    peeled and diced
    tomatoes
¼ cup diced green pepper
½ teaspoon salt
⅛ teaspoon pepper

1. Fry bacon in a skillet; reserve fat. Drain and crumble bacon; set aside.
2. Put 2 tablespoons fat in skillet and add onion, okra, and corn. Cook, stirring constantly, 10 minutes.
3. Mix in tomatoes, green pepper, salt, and pepper. Cook over low heat about 20 minutes.
4. Turn into warm serving dish and sprinkle the bacon over top.

About 8 servings

Cucumber Ice Salad

16 (¼ pound)
     marshmallows, cut
⅓ cup lemon juice
 2 medium cucumbers
 1 teaspoon grated onion
½ teaspoon salt
 3 drops green food
     coloring
    Few grains cayenne
     pepper
 2 egg whites
 1 tablespoon sugar
 8 medium tomatoes

1. Chill a bowl in refrigerator.
2. Heat together marshmallows and lemon juice in top of a double boiler, stirring occasionally, until marshmallows are melted.
3. Meanwhile, rinse, pare, and cut cucumbers into halves lengthwise and remove seed. Grate (enough to yield 2 cups pulp) and mix with onion, salt, food coloring, and cayenne pepper.
4. Remove marshmallow mixture from simmering water; blend in cucumber mixture. Pour into a refrigerator tray. Place in freezer and freeze until mixture is mush-like in consistency.
5. Beat egg whites until frothy. Add sugar and beat until rounded peaks are formed.
6. Turn frozen mixture into the chilled bowl and beat with rotary beater. Spread egg whites over cucumber mixture and fold together. Immediately return mixture to refrigerator tray and freeze until firm (about 4 hours).
7. To complete salad, rinse and cut ½-inch slices from tops of tomatoes. Remove pulp with a spoon. Invert the shells and place in refrigerator to drain and chill while cucumber mixture is freezing.
8. To serve, fill the tomato shells with cucumber ice and serve at once on chilled salad plates.

8 servings

Buttermilk Biscuits

 2 cups sifted all-purpose
    flour
2½ teaspoons baking
    powder
 1 teaspoon salt
¼ teaspoon baking soda
⅓ cup lard or vegetable
    shortening
¾ cup buttermilk
   Milk

1. Blend flour, baking powder, salt, and baking soda in a bowl. Cut in lard with pastry blender or two knives until particles are the size of rice kernels. Add buttermilk and stir with a fork only until dough follows fork.
2. Gently form dough into a ball and put on a lightly floured surface. Knead lightly with fingertips 10 to 15 times. Gently roll dough ½ inch thick.
3. Cut with a floured biscuit cutter or knife, using an even pressure to keep sides of biscuits straight. Place on ungreased baking sheet, close together for soft-sided biscuits or 1 inch apart for crusty ones. Brush tops lightly with milk.
4. Bake at 450°F 10 to 15 minutes, or until biscuits are golden brown.

About 2 dozen biscuits

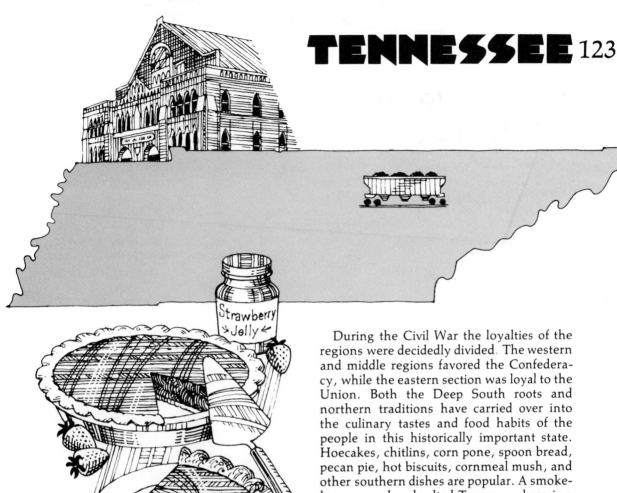

Strawberry Jelly

Tennessee, originally a county of North Carolina and the political base of three United States presidents (Andrew Jackson, James K. Polk, and Andrew Johnson) was believed to have derived its name from an ancient Cherokee Indian capital. The state is divided into three geographic sections: the Blue Ridge and Appalachian Ridge and Valley in the east, the Nashville Basin and Highland Rim adjacent to the Cumberland and Tennessee rivers in the middle, and the Gulf Coastal Plain along the Mississippi River in the west.

During the Civil War the loyalties of the regions were decidedly divided. The western and middle regions favored the Confederacy, while the eastern section was loyal to the Union. Both the Deep South roots and northern traditions have carried over into the culinary tastes and food habits of the people in this historically important state. Hoecakes, chitlins, corn pone, spoon bread, pecan pie, hot biscuits, cornmeal mush, and other southern dishes are popular. A smokehouse cured and salted Tennessee ham is a favorite among many gourmet cooks. A thick red gravy should be served over biscuits, spoon bread, or potatoes with this special ham. Select methods of preparing and stuffing chicken and pork are also prevalent among local homemakers.

Most Tennesseans are American-born, descendants of settlers who came from England, Scotland, Ireland, France, Germany, and Africa. Although the many generations of living in this country have fused the numerous backgrounds together, ethnic traditions are probably responsible for popular egg bread and fried apple pie, along with the locally grown black walnuts which are sometimes served pickled. Jams, jellies, and other preserves are not only prepared and served as condiments with hot breads and biscuits, but are often used as ingredients in cakes and pies. Jelly pie and blackberry jam cake are savory examples. Delicious local

TENNESSEE

soups and stews trace their origins from pioneer days. Possum, squirrel, and wild onions were some of the earliest ingredients. Today, beans, chicken, beef, and turkey are more frequently used. Methods of preparing venison and other wild meats have been handed down for generations in many parts of Tennessee. The early settlers would prepare their wild game over open-pit fires; savory sauces were derived from ordinary seasonings to accompany these everyday meats.

Favorite Tennessee-grown vegetables include spinach, turnips, tomatoes, green beans, zucchini, corn, and sweet potatoes. Several varieties of sweet potato casseroles and pies are daily fare in many homes. Corn pudding, soups, and breads are popular. A spicy corn relish is often served with the main dish. A salad of Tennessee-grown crisp turnip greens, fresh green beans, or

tender sweet corn can be a summer delight.

Apples, strawberries, and peaches are grown in the western and central parts of the state. Tennessee ranks among the leading producers of strawberries. A strawberry festival is held every year at Humboldt in the western region. Their famous strawberry preserves and deep dish strawberry pie, along with other unusual berry delights, are featured at this annual event.

Nashville has become world famous as the capital for country music, and the eastern mountain region is known for its many folk tunes. Several of the old-country and folk favorites sung in these parts have food in their titles. Songs and supper would appear to go together if one analyzes any of the well-known tunes, such as "Jimmy Crack Corn," "When Its Chitlin Time in Cheatham County," "Chicken in the Bread-Tray," and "Red, Red Wine."

Cream of Corn Soup

2½ cups cream-style corn
1 slice onion
2 cups cold milk
3 tablespoons butter or
   margarine
3 tablespoons flour
½ teaspoon salt
   Dash pepper
3 cups hot milk

1. Heat corn, onion, and cold milk in a heavy saucepan until scalding.
2. Melt butter in a saucepan. Blend in flour, salt, and pepper. Add hot milk gradually, stirring constantly. Bring to boiling and cook 3 minutes.
3. Force corn through a sieve; mix with white sauce. Serve hot.

6 to 8 servings

Possum and Sweet Taters

1 opossum
  Salt
1 quart water
4 slices bacon
  Bread Stuffing
8 small sweet potatoes

1. Scald opossum in lye water and scrape off the hair, taking care not to break skin. Dress whole, leaving head and tail. Rinse thoroughly. Rub inside and out with salt; let stand in cool place overnight.
2. Place breast up in a roaster and add water. Place bacon across breast; cover roaster.
3. Bake at 350°F 45 minutes.
4. Fill opossum with Bread Stuffing moistened with juices from roaster; surround with sweet potatoes.
5. Bake uncovered until opossum is very tender and

well browned (about 1 hour). Allow ⅓ pound per person.

Bread Stuffing: Soak **4 slices white bread** in **cold water** and squeeze dry. Using a fork, lightly toss with a mixture of **1 teaspoon salt**, **⅛ teaspoon black pepper**, and **¼ teaspoon poultry seasoning**. Mix in **1 teaspoon chopped parsley** and **1 teaspoon grated onion**. Add **2 tablespoons melted butter** and **1 slightly beaten egg** and toss lightly until thoroughly mixed.

Memphis Sweetbreads and Mushrooms

1 pound sweetbreads
2 tablespoons butter
2 tablespoons flour
1 teaspoon salt
   Dash pepper
2 cups milk
1 pound fresh mushrooms
½ teaspoon salt
¼ cup fine bread crumbs
2 tablespoons butter

1. Simmer sweetbreads 20 minutes in water to cover (adding **1 teaspoon salt** and **1 tablespoon vinegar** per quart of water); drain, cover with cold water or chipped ice until firm.
2. When firm enough to handle, remove all loose membranes. Sauté in 1 tablespoon butter.
3. Blend in 1 tablespoon of flour; add salt and pepper and 1 cup of milk. Simmer until thickened.
4. Wash mushrooms, sauté in remaining butter, blend in remaining flour, and add salt and remaining milk.
5. When thickened, combine with sweetbread mixture and turn into casserole. Cover with bread crumbs and dot with butter.
6. Brown in a 400°F oven 5 to 8 minutes.

6 servings

Mushroom-Stuffed Chicken Breasts

5 large whole chicken
   breasts, boned and
   halved
   Salt and pepper
½ pound mushrooms,
   cleaned
3 tablespoons lemon juice
¼ cup butter
2 tablespoons chopped
   fresh chives
   Paprika
½ cup boiling chicken broth
1 tablespoon cornstarch
2 tablespoons water

1. Split each piece of chicken part way through the center to make a pocket. Sprinkle cavity lightly with salt and pepper.
2. Slice mushrooms and drizzle with lemon juice to prevent discoloration.
3. Put half of butter into a skillet, add mushrooms, and cook until mushrooms are limp. Spoon some of the mushrooms and chives into pockets in chicken.
4. Arrange chicken, skin side up, in a buttered baking dish and season with salt and pepper. Sprinkle with paprika. Dot with remaining butter. Cover tightly with aluminum foil.
5. Bake at 350°F 25 minutes. Remove cover and pour boiling broth over chicken. Continue cooking 20 minutes.
6. Combine cornstarch with water; stir into liquid in baking dish. Continue baking about 10 minutes, basting twice.

10 servings

TENNESSEE

Chicken Pie with Sweet Potato Crust

3 cups cooked chicken
   pieces
1 cup diced cooked carrots
6 cooked small white
   onions
1 tablespoon chopped
   parsley
2 tablespoons flour
1 teaspoon salt
⅛ teaspoon ground black
   pepper
1 cup undiluted evaporated
   milk
1 cup chicken broth
   Sweet Potato Crust

1. Put chicken into a shallow 1½-quart baking dish; top with carrots, onions, and parsley.
2. Mix flour, salt, and pepper in a saucepan. Add evaporated milk and broth gradually, stirring constantly. Bring to boiling and boil 1 to 2 minutes. Pour over chicken mixture.
3. Top with Sweet Potato Crust; flute edges.
4. Bake at 350°F about 40 minutes, or until crust is lightly browned.

About 6 servings

Sweet Potato Crust: Blend **1 cup sifted all-purpose flour, 1 teaspoon baking powder,** and **½ teaspoon salt** together. Mix in **1 cup cool mashed sweet potato, ⅓ cup melted butter,** and **1 well-beaten egg.** Chill thoroughly. On a lightly floured surface, roll out dough ¼ inch thick and a little larger than baking dish. Proceed as directed in recipe.

Brunswick Stew

1 frying chicken (2 to 2½
   pounds), cut in pieces
1 teaspoon salt
¼ teaspoon pepper
2 onions, sliced
2 tablespoons bacon fat
3 cups water
3 tomatoes, peeled and
   quartered
½ cup sherry
2 teaspoons Worcestershire
   sauce
1 pound fresh lima beans
½ cup okra, sliced
3 ears green corn, kernels
   cut from cobs
2 tablespoons butter
½ cup bread crumbs

1. Sprinkle chicken pieces with salt and pepper.
2. Lightly brown onion in bacon fat in a skillet. Add seasoned chicken pieces and brown on all sides.
3. Put chicken and onion into a Dutch oven.
4. Add water, tomatoes, sherry, and Worcestershire sauce. Cook covered over low heat 30 minutes. Add lima beans, okra, and corn; simmer 1 hour.
5. Add butter and bread crumbs; mix well and cook 30 minutes.

6 to 8 servings

Roast Spareribs with Apple Stuffing

2 matching pork sparerib
   racks*
¼ cup diced salt pork or
   bacon
1 onion

1. Have spareribs cracked through the center to make carving easier.
2. Fry salt pork until crisp.
3. Chop onion, parsley, and celery and fry a few minutes. Add apple and sugar and cook until apples are

TENNESSEE

1 sprig parsley
2 or 3 stalks celery
5 or 6 tart apples, chopped
¼ to ½ cup sugar
1 cup bread crumbs
1 teaspoon salt
⅛ teaspoon pepper
Flour

tender and somewhat candied. Mix in crumbs.
4. Place one section of ribs, meaty side down, in a shallow roasting pan and spread with hot stuffing. Cover with other section and sew edges together. Sprinkle with salt, pepper, and flour.
5. Bake uncovered at 350°F until tender (about 1½ hours).
*Allow ¾ pound person.

Sweet Potato Casserole

6 cups hot cooked sweet potato
1 cup sugar
¼ cup butter or margarine
½ teaspoon vanilla extract
⅛ teaspoon nutmeg
3 eggs

1. Put sweet potato, sugar, butter, vanilla extract, and nutmeg into a large mixer bowl; beat until blended. Add eggs, one at a time, beating well after each addition.
2. Turn mixture into a 1½-quart soufflé dish.
3. Bake at 400°F 30 minutes.
4. Serve immediately.

10 to 12 servings

Okra and Tomatoes

2 cups sliced okra
2 cups sliced tomatoes
3 tablespoons butter
1 small onion, finely chopped
1 teaspoon salt
¼ teaspoon pepper

1. Combine okra and tomatoes in pan without water.
2. Add butter, onion, salt, and pepper.
3. Simmer 1 hour.

4 servings

Vegetable Salad

Crisp salad greens
1 small onion, sliced
1 cup sliced raw cauliflower
1 can (16 ounces) cut green beans, chilled and drained
1 can (about 15 ounces) green asparagus spears, chilled and drained
Blue Cheese Sour Cream Dressing (page 128)

1. Half-fill six individual salad bowls with the greens. Arrange vegetables on greens.
2. Accompany with a bowl of the dressing garnished with **snipped parsley.**

6 servings

Blue Cheese Sour Cream Dressing

1 package blue cheese salad
  dressing mix
1 package (3 ounces) cream
  cheese, softened
1 cup dairy sour cream

1. Prepare salad dressing following package directions.
2. Blend dressing with cream cheese in a bowl. Stir in sour cream until dressing is of desired consistency.
3. Serve dressing with **fruit and vegetable salad.**

About 1½ cups dressing

Batter Bread

3 eggs
1 cup milk
1 cup buttermilk
⅓ cup white cornmeal
2 teaspoons baking powder
¼ teaspoon baking soda
½ teaspoon salt
2 tablespoons butter,
  melted

1. Set an 8-inch square baking pan in oven to heat.
2. Beat eggs; add milk and buttermilk and beat well.
3. Mix cornmeal, baking powder, baking soda, and salt. Add to liquid mixture and mix well. Blend in butter.
4. Grease heated pan and pour in batter.
5. Bake at 400°F until set in center (about 1 hour). Serve at once.

6 servings

Strawberry Jam Cake

1 cup butter or other
  shortening
½ cup sugar
1 cup strawberry jam
½ cup strong black coffee
1 teaspoon cinnamon
¼ teaspoon cloves
3 eggs, separated
2½ cups sifted cake flour
¼ cup buttermilk
1 teaspoon baking soda

1. Cream butter and sugar, beating until light and fluffy. Add jam, coffee, and spices.
2. Beat egg yolks and blend with jam mixture. Add flour alternately with buttermilk combined with baking soda, mixing well after each addition.
3. Beat egg whites until stiff, not dry, peaks are formed. Fold into batter. Divide into layer pans which have been lined with waxed paper.
4. Bake at 350°F about 30 minutes. Spread with favorite frosting.

Two 9-inch layers

Jelly Pie

½ cup butter
⅛ teaspoon salt
1 cup sugar
4 egg yolks, beaten
½ cup strawberry jelly
1 teaspoon lemon juice
4 egg whites, beaten until
  stiff, but not dry
1 unbaked 9-inch pastry
  shell

1. Cream butter, salt, and sugar until fluffy. Add beaten egg yolks and jelly and combine thoroughly. Add lemon juice and fold in beaten egg whites. Pour into unbaked pastry shell.
2. Bake at 425°F 10 minutes; turn oven control to 350°F and continue baking 20 to 25 minutes, or until set.

One 9-inch pie

Planked Fish Fillet Dinner, 178

Virginia, the "Old Dominion State," has the unsurpassed distinction of being the home of eight United States presidents. The third, the extremely versatile Thomas Jefferson, was perhaps our first great gourmet. His home at Monticello was the scene of many exquisite dinner parties where he employed his own French maitre d'hôtel and his own chef, Julien, one of the most talented cooks of his day. Beef à la Mode, a superb entrée, was a top round pot roast prepared with bacon, brandy, wine, and seasonings.

The wife of the fourth president, Dolly Madison, a celebrated hostess, often served Beef Collops, which were thin slices of browned beef simmered with cucumber pickles and capers.

Virginia holds so many historic honors that it is difficult to enumerate them. Some of the most decisive battles of the Revolutionary and Civil wars were fought on its soil; and the final surrenders of both wars took place in Virginia. The first permanent English colony was founded at Jamestown in 1607. Although it endured countless hardships, it continued to persevere and planted the seed that eventually grew into a great Tidewater aristocracy of fine culture and tradition.

Fortunately for all of us, a flavor of old Virginia and a taste of its authentic cuisine can be seen and sampled at restored Colonial Williamsburg. A special treat for the connoisseur of fine foods is to visit the village at holiday time, either on Thanksgiving or Christmas. Splendid festivals and bountiful arrays of delicacies are familiar sights on these occasions. One becomes a part of living history and can almost feel the presence of those early colonists, while sampling the old-fashioned turkey soup, baked ham, and carrot loaf at the Williamsburg Inn, or the escalloped oysters and brandied sweet potatoes at the King's Arms Tavern. Many of our finest and most authentic Virginia recipes have been thoroughly researched and are available to us because of the restoration of Colonial Williamsburg.

Geographically, Virginia contains part of the main eastern range of the Appalachian mountain system, but it also boasts of the beautiful gently rolling Piedmont plain in the center section of the state. The Atlantic coastal region, popularly referred to as the Tidewater because of the many bays and rivers and inlets, is a low strip of land approximately one hundred miles wide.

The mild climate and adequate rainfall of this central region helped the agricultural economy of the state to flourish during its early days. Tobacco was usually the main plantation crop. But today, livestock and dairy farming are also important. Along Chesapeake Bay, farmers raise beans, cucumbers, asparagus, lettuce, potatoes, and spinach. Apple, pear, and peach orchards are located in the western valleys.

Virginia is famous for its hickory-smoked Smithfield hams. This curing process is believed to have been taught to the early white settlers by the Indians. Some Virginians say that this dark-red meat should be sliced paper thin and served plain. Others add cider or vinegar, cloves, and brown sugar.

Prepared in any fashion it is delicious, and a special treat when accompanied by Martha Washington's Light Potato Rolls or the famous Sally Lunn bread, baked from a creamy yeast dough.

Another popular Old Dominion specialty is Brunswick stew, usually prepared from chicken, potatoes, okra, tomatoes, and string beans. Other common foods are black-eye peas, corn pudding, and peanuts. Fresh-water fish, such as trout, are prevalent along the inland rivers.

The early plantation wives planted and guarded their kitchen gardens of savory herbs brought from England. Sugar and spices were always a luxury in early colonial days. Desserts were only rare treats among most of the population. One special favorite was Virginia Pound Cake, which used brandy and at least ten eggs and a pound each of butter, flour, and sugar.

Ginger cookies and gingerbread are synonymous with Virginia. The most famous gingerbread recipe was developed by Mary Ball Washington, mother of George, and later perfected by Martha during her reign at Mount Vernon.

Dolly Madison Bouillon

4 pounds juicy beef, cubed
1 veal knuckle
2 small turnips, diced
2 small carrots, diced
1 bunch soup greens
1 small pod red pepper
2 small white onions
1 tablespoon salt
6 quarts water

1. Combine all ingredients in a soup kettle and simmer covered 6 hours.
2. Remove meat and use as desired. Strain liquid through fine sieve; refrigerate until fat congeals. Skim off all the fat.
3. Heat just before serving.

10 to 12 servings

Cream of Turkey Soup

½ cup butter
6 tablespoons flour
½ teaspoon salt

1. Heat butter in a saucepan. Blend in flour, salt, and pepper. Heat until mixture bubbles.
2. Gradually add the cream and 1 cup of the broth,

Few grains black pepper
2 cups cream
3 cups turkey or chicken
    broth
¾ cup coarsely chopped
    cooked turkey

stirring constantly. Bring to boiling; cook and stir 1 to 2 minutes.

3. Blend in remaining broth and turkey. Heat thoroughly (do not boil). Garnish with slivers of **carrot.**

About 6 servings

VIRGINIA

Smithfield Ham

1 ham (10 to 12 pounds)*
  Cold water
2 tablespoons fine cracker
    crumbs
2 tablespoons brown sugar
  Pepper
  Whole cloves

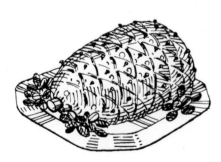

1. Scrub ham thoroughly using warm water. Rinse and put into a kettle. Cover completely with cold water, cover kettle, and bring to boiling. Pour off water and again cover ham with cold water. Cover and bring to boiling. Reduce heat and simmer 4 to 5 hours, or until tender.

2. Cool ham in liquid. Remove skin, place fat side up in a roasting pan, and make crisscross gashes in fat with a sharp knife. Sprinkle cracker crumbs, brown sugar, and desired amount of pepper on top of ham. Stick ham with cloves. (A wineglass of **sherry** sprinkled over top of ham will greatly improve the flavor.)

3. Bake at 450°F 20 minutes until brown.

4. Garnish with **watercress** and **parsley.**

*Allow ¼ to ⅓ pound per serving.

Beef Collops

2½ pounds beef rump
½ cup seasoned flour
2 tablespoons butter
2 cups brown gravy
2 tablespoons butter
1 tablespoon flour
2 teaspoons salt
¼ teaspoon pepper
1 shallot or 3 green
    onions, thinly sliced
4 small pickled
    cucumbers, sliced
1 teaspoon capers, finely
    chopped

1. Cut thin slices of beef from the rump; divide slices into pieces 3 inches long. Pound slices with the blade of a knife, and flour them.

2. Fry collops quickly in 2 tablespoons butter 2 minutes, then put meat into a saucepan and cover with brown gravy.

3. Add remaining 2 tablespoons butter mixed with 1 tablespoon flour along with salt, pepper, shallot, pickle slices, and capers.

4. Cover and simmer about 1 hour, or until meat is tender.

5. Put meat into a hot serving dish.

6. Bring sauce to boiling, stirring constantly; cook 1 to 2 minutes. Pour over meat.

4 to 6 servings

Old Dominion Veal Fricassee

2 **pounds veal loin**
1 **onion, sliced**
2 **stalks celery**
6 **slices of carrot**
  Salt and pepper
  Flour
  Butter or other fat
  Brown Sauce

1. Cut veal into 1-inch cubes, add onion, celery, and carrot. Cover with **boiling water** and simmer until meat is tender, about 30 minutes.
2. Remove meat, season with salt and pepper, dredge with flour, and brown in butter. Serve with Brown Sauce made with the stock.

6 servings

Brown Sauce: Melt **2 tablespoons butter or margarine.** Add **1 small onion, chopped,** and cook until browned. Blend in **2 tablespoons flour** and continue to brown until flour reaches the desired color. Add **1 cup veal stock** gradually with ½ **teaspoon salt** and ¼ **teaspoon pepper.** Boil 3 minutes, stirring constantly. Strain the gravy before using, if desired.

2 cups gravy

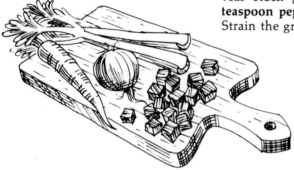

Oysters Royale

6 **tablespoons butter**
½ **clove garlic, minced**
½ **cup diced celery**
½ **cup diced green pepper**
6 **or 7 tablespoons flour**
½ **teaspoon salt**
¼ **teaspoon white pepper**
  Few grains cayenne
    pepper
2 **cups cream**
1½ **pints oysters, drained**
    (reserve ⅓ cup
    liquor)*
1 **teaspoon prepared**
    mustard
2 **ounces Gruyère cheese,**
    cut in pieces
¼ **cup dry sherry**

1. Heat butter in a saucepan. Add garlic, celery, and green pepper; cook about 5 minutes, or until vegetables are crisp-tender. Remove vegetables with a slotted spoon and set aside.
2. Blend flour, salt, and peppers into the butter in saucepan; heat until mixture bubbles. Remove from heat; add cream and reserved oyster liquor gradually, stirring constantly. Continue stirring, bring to boiling, and boil 1 to 2 minutes. Remove from heat.
3. Blend in the mustard and cheese, stirring until cheese is melted. Mix in wine, vegetables, and oysters. Bring just to boiling and remove from heat. (Edges of oysters should just begin to curl.)
4. Serve hot accompanied with a basket of large **toasted buttered bread rounds** sprinkled lightly with **nutmeg.**

10 to 12 servings

*The amount of liquor in a pint of oysters varies. If slightly less liquor is used, the recipe will not be affected.

Carrot Casserole

⅔ cup uncooked rice
2 cups milk
1 cup water
4 eggs
1 to 4 tablespoons sugar
1¼ teaspoons salt
¼ cup chopped toasted
  almonds
3 cups coarsely shredded
  carrots

1. Put rice, milk, and water into top of a double boiler over boiling water. Cook covered 35 minutes, or until rice is tender.
2. Beat eggs with sugar and salt. Mix in cooked rice, almonds, and shredded carrots.
3. Turn into a buttered shallow 1½-quart baking dish. Dot with desired amount of **butter.**
4. Bake at 350°F about 1 hour. Serve hot.

6 to 8 servings

Brandied Sweet Potatoes

6 medium sweet potatoes
  (about 2 pounds)
⅓ cup butter or margarine
⅓ cup firmly packed light
  brown sugar
1 teaspoon cinnamon
¼ teaspoon nutmeg
¼ teaspoon salt
½ cup brandy

1. Cook sweet potatoes in boiling salted water in a covered saucepan 30 to 35 minutes, or until potatoes are just tender. Drain. Cool potatoes, then peel and cut crosswise into 1½-inch-thick slices.
2. Put potato slices into a well-greased shallow baking dish. Dot with butter. Mix brown sugar, cinnamon, nutmeg, and salt. Sprinkle over potatoes. Pour brandy over all.
3. Bake at 375°F 30 minutes.

6 servings

Martha Washington's Light Potato Rolls

2 packages active dry
  yeast
½ cup warm water
  (105°-115°F)
1 cup milk, scalded
½ cup sagar
1½ teaspoons salt
1 cup mashed potato
⅔ cup shortening
2 eggs, well beaten
5 to 6 cups all-purpose
  flour

1. Soften yeast in warm water. Combine milk, sugar, salt, mashed potato, and shortening in a large mixing bowl; beat until thoroughly blended. Cool to luke-warm. Stir in the softened yeast. Beat in the eggs. Add about 3 cups flour, ½ cup at a time, beating vigorously after each addition. Mix in enough remaining flour to make a soft (but not sticky) dough.
2. Turn onto a lightly floured surface, let rest 5 to 10 minutes, and knead until satiny and smooth. Form dough into a ball and put into a greased bowl. Turn to bring greased surface to top. Cover and refrigerate until thoroughly chilled.
3. Remove dough and form into plain rolls or other desired shape. Place on greased baking sheets; cover and let rise in a warm place until double in bulk.
4. Bake at 425°F 12 to 15 minutes. Remove from oven and brush rolls lightly with **melted butter.**

3 to 3½ dozen rolls

VIRGINIA

Old-Fashioned Harrison Cake

⅔ cup shortening
2 cups sugar
3 eggs, well beaten
5 cups sifted cake flour
1 teaspoon baking soda
½ teaspoon cinnamon
½ teaspoon cloves
½ teaspoon allspice
¼ teaspoon salt
1 cup molasses
1½ cups milk
2 cups raisins
½ cup sliced orange peel

1. Cream shortening and sugar; add eggs and mix well.
2. Sift flour, baking soda, spices, and salt together. Combine molasses and milk; add alternately with 4 cups of the flour mixture to the creamed mixture; beat well after each addition. Mix fruits with remaining flour; fold into batter. Turn into 2 waxed-paper-lined 9×5×3-inch loaf pans.
3. Bake at 325°F 1 hour. Turn oven control to 350°F and continue baking 30 minutes.

2 loaf cakes

Sally Lunn

This bread, named after an eighteenth-century pastry cook, has many variations, some made with yeast and others with baking powder. It can be baked in a loaf or cake pan or in muffin pans and is served warm from the oven with plenty of butter.

1 package active dry yeast
¼ cup warm water
½ cup milk, scalded
⅔ cup butter or margarine, softened
2 tablespoons sugar
¾ teaspoon salt
2 cups all-purpose flour
2 eggs, well beaten

1. Soften yeast in the warm water.
2. Pour scalded milk over butter, sugar, and salt in a large bowl; cool to lukewarm. Add about ½ cup flour and beat until smooth.
3. Stir the yeast into the batter; mix well. Add about half of the remaining flour and beat until very smooth. Add eggs; beat thoroughly at least 5 minutes. Scrape down from sides of bowl. Cover; let rise in a warm place until double in bulk (about 45 minutes).
4. When doubled, beat again at least 5 minutes.
5. Turn into a greased 1½-quart ring mold or Turk's-head mold. Cover; let rise again until double in bulk (about 45 minutes).
6. Bake at 350°F 25 to 30 minutes, or until golden brown. Run knife around edge of mold to loosen the loaf and gently remove to wire rack. Serve warm.

1 ring loaf

Hot Buttered Rum

1 small cube sugar
1 tablespoon hot water
⅛ teaspoon allspice
⅛ teaspoon cloves
1½ ounces rum
¼ cup hot water
1 teaspoon unsalted butter

1. Dissolve sugar in 1 tablespoon hot water in a rum glass. Add the remaining ingredients except the butter and stir.
2. Add butter and serve.

One individual portion

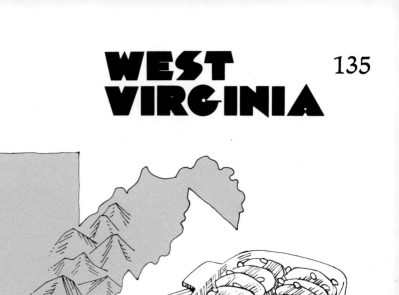

The motto of West Virginia is *Montani Semper Liberi,* or "Mountaineers Are Always Freemen." The words seem very fitting when one travels through the rugged countryside and meets the individualistic people of this valley state. Two thirds of West Virginia, also called the "Mountain State," form part of the great Appalachian plateau and mountain system, and a third is part of the vast valley region stretching from central Alabama to Canada.

Before white settlers arrived in the territory of West Virginia, the Indians were picking wild huckleberries and herbs and hunting the bear and deer and other wild game. Most of the region was forested with trees unknown to the early explorers from Europe. Hickory, persimmon, maple, walnut, chestnut, and cherry trees were providing the Indians with nourishing and tasty foods.

The earliest white settlers concocted stews in large open kettles from bear meat and venison. But conservation regulations were slow in developing, and the wild game remaining today are mainly possum and rabbits.

English and French explorers fought over control of this Appalachian valley region, but the first permanent white settlers were probably of Welsh, Scotch-Irish, and German ancestry who moved into West Virginia from Pennsylvania and Maryland. English pioneers also arrived from Virginia in the early 1700s. Most of the Negroes were brought from North Carolina. The completion of the Cumberland Road in the early 1800s brought even more settlers into the rugged forested territory. Today, 98 percent of the West Virginians were born in their own state, and the majority of these are of English origin.

During the early history of the region, West Virginia and Virginia were united, but the Civil War caused a great cleavage between the eastern and western parts of the territory. By 1863, West Virginia had become the thirty-fifth state and was definitely in the Union camp.

Thus, a few of the traditional southern foods, such as cornmeal mush and hominy grits, are still found on the local tables at mealtime, but much of the state's cookery now favors the North or the "American melting pot" kitchen fare. Numerous West Virginians enjoy home-cured hams, fried chicken, blackberry and raspberry jam on fresh home-baked bread, plenty of potatoes, and common apple desserts.

The Greenbrier, an élite resort hotel, is located in White Sulphur Springs. This world-renowned resort is famous for its elegance in both accommodations and cuisine.

The state boasts of other fine hotels which also feature gourmet fare. Candied sweet potatoes with peanuts is only one example of several distinctive selections from the menus of these attractive inns.

The economy of West Virginia is based on manufacturing and coal mining. The state is well known for its glass and chemical industries. Agriculture plays a diminishing role; the main food crops are apples, turnips, corn, and pumpkins. Blackberries and raspberries are also grown throughout the state. Cream of corn or pumpkin soup, apple chutney, blackberry pie or cake, and salads of crisp turnip greens are a few of the dishes prepared from these indigenous foods.

Deep-fried Cheese Grits Balls

2 cups water
½ teaspoon salt
½ cup quick-cooking
    hominy grits
1 cup shredded sharp
    Cheddar cheese
¼ teaspoon cayenne
    pepper
¼ teaspoon grated nutmeg
    Few grains pepper
2 eggs
1½ teaspoons vegetable oil
1½ cups soft bread crumbs
    Fat for deep frying
    heated to 375°F

1. Bring water and salt to boiling in a saucepan. Stir grits slowly into boiling water. Return to boiling, reduce heat, and cook 2½ to 5 minutes, stirring occasionally. Chill.
2. Mash grits with a fork and stir in cheese, cayenne, nutmeg, and pepper. Shape into about 40 balls.
3. Beat eggs and oil together. Coat balls with egg mixture, then with bread crumbs.
4. Fry in heated fat about 2 minutes, or until golden brown.

40 appetizers

Baked Sliced Ham and Apples

2 large slices ham*
1 teaspoon dry mustard
2 teaspoons vinegar
2 apples
½ cup firmly packed brown
    sugar
1 tablespoon butter

1. Remove bone from ham. Mix mustard and vinegar and spread thinly on ham.
2. Slice apples very thin and spread 2 layers on ham. Sprinkle well with brown sugar.
3. Roll ham the long way. Hold together with metal skewers or tie with string. Place in a baking pan and dot with butter.
4. Bake at 350°F 25 to 30 minutes; baste several times while baking.
*Allow ¼ to ⅓ pound per serving

Cured Pork Gumbo in Rice Ring

1 pound ham or smoked
    pork shoulder roll
1 tablespoon bacon
    drippings
1 onion, chopped
1 green pepper, chopped
1 sprig parsley, chopped
2 or 3 stalks celery,
    chopped
2 cups water
1 quart tomatoes, fresh or
    canned
1 quart sliced okra
    Bay leaf or celery seed
    Salt and pepper
    Baked Rice Ring (page
    138)

1. Cut meat into small pieces and brown in bacon drippings in a saucepot. Add onion, green pepper, parsley, and celery and cook a few minutes. Add water and tomatoes; simmer covered until meat is nearly tender.

2. Add okra and bay leaf; simmer until meat and okra are tender and stew has thickened. Season to taste with salt and pepper. Serve hot in rice ring.

6 servings

Stewed Chicken and Drop Dumplings

1 stewing chicken
1 small onion, diced
    Salt and pepper
1 cup sifted all-purpose
    flour
2 teaspoons baking powder
½ teaspoon salt
    Parsley sprig, minced
½ cup milk

1. Clean and cut up chicken, place in kettle and partly cover with **water;** add onion, salt, and pepper and cook until tender, (2½ to 3 hours).

2. Mix flour, baking powder, salt, minced parsley, and milk to a thick batter and drop from end of spoon into slowly boiling chicken broth; cover tightly and cook 20 minutes without raising lid. Place chicken on platter and surround with dumplings.

6 servings

Fried Chicken à la Southern Belle

1 broiler-fryer chicken
    (2½ to 3 pounds), cut
    in pieces
1½ cups cream
1½ teaspoons savory
1 teaspoon freshly ground
    black pepper
¾ cup all-purpose flour
1½ teaspoons paprika
1½ teaspoons salt
¼ teaspoon freshly ground
    black pepper
    Shortening and butter
    (equal parts)

1. Marinate chicken pieces 1 hour in a mixture of cream, savory, and 1 teaspoon pepper, turning once.

2. Remove chicken from cream. (Cream may be used for gravy.) Coat with a mixture of flour, paprika, salt, and ¼ teaspoon pepper. Set aside 30 minutes.

3. Meanwhile, fill a large heavy skillet one-half full with the fat. Heat to 360°F.

4. Fry only a few chicken pieces at a time 10 to 13 minutes (about 5 minutes for wings), or until tender and browned; turn pieces several times during cooking. Drain over fat a few seconds; remove to absorbent paper. Serve warm.

4 servings

WEST VIRGINIA

Salt Pork, Beans, and Hominy

½ pound navy beans
½ pound hominy
½ pound salt pork
Salt
Pepper
Sweet marjoram

1. Wash beans, cover with water, and soak overnight. Cover hominy with water and also let stand overnight.
2. In the morning, drain off water from both, combine beans and hominy and cover with fresh cold water.
3. Wash salt pork and place in strips on top. Season with salt and pepper and a little sweet marjoram. Simmer about 5 hours, adding more water as necessary.

6 to 8 servings

Candied Sweet Potatoes with Peanuts

6 medium-size sweet potatoes
½ cup firmly packed brown sugar
1 cup boiling water
¼ cup butter
½ teaspoon salt
1½ tablespoons chopped peanuts

1. Pare and slice sweet potatoes crosswise ½ inch thick. Arrange in a 2-quart casserole.
2. Mix brown sugar, water, butter, and salt. Pour over potatoes.
3. Bake at 325°F about 1 hour. Shortly before baking period is over, sprinkle with peanuts and continue baking.

8 servings

Southern Fried Apples

6 large tart cooking apples
5 tablespoons butter or other fat
⅔ cup sugar
1 tablespoon cinnamon
⅛ teaspoon salt

1. Core, but do not pare, apples. Slice ½ inch thick to make perfect rings.
2. Heat butter in a large heavy skillet until light golden brown. Place apple slices in skillet.
3. Mix sugar, cinnamon, and salt. Cover apples with half of this mixture. After 5 minutes turn the slices with a pancake turner to avoid breaking.
4. Cover with remaining sugar mixture. Sauté over low heat until apples are almost transparent. Serve hot.

8 servings

Baked Rice Ring

1 cup uncooked rice
3 medium onions, chopped
¼ cup butter or margarine
1 pound mushrooms, cleaned and sliced
Salt and pepper

1. Cook rice following package directions.
2. Sauté onions in butter. Add mushrooms and cook about 10 minutes.
3. Mix onions and mushrooms with rice and season. Pack mixture into a buttered ring mold.
4. Bake at 350°F 30 minutes.

6 servings

Cornmeal Mush

3 cups water
1½ teaspoons salt
1 cup cornmeal
1 cup cold water

1. Bring water and salt to boiling in a saucepan. Gradually stir in a mixture of cornmeal and cold water. Continue boiling, stirring constantly, until mixture is thickened.
2. Cover, lower heat, and cook slowly 5 minutes or longer for white cornmeal, or 10 minutes or longer for yellow. Serve as a hot breakfast cereal.

6 to 8 servings

Bacon and Cheese Toast

1 egg
3 tablespoons milk
½ teaspoon baking powder
¾ pound Cheddar cheese, shredded
6 slices bread
6 slices bacon

1. Beat egg; add milk, baking powder, and cheese and mix well. Spread on bread and place a strip of bacon on top.
2. Place under broiler with top about 3 inches from heat. Broil until golden brown.

6 servings

Scones

2 cups sifted cake flour
1 tablespoon sugar
½ teaspoon salt
4 teaspoons baking powder
4 tablespoons butter or other shortening
½ cup milk
1 egg, well beaten
Melted butter
Sugar

1. Sift dry ingredients together twice and cut in butter with 2 knives or pastry blender.
2. Add milk to egg, then add to flour mixture gradually, adding more milk if necessary.
3. Knead lightly on a floured board. Pat and roll to ½-inch thickness.
4. Cut in wedges, place on greased baking sheet, brush with melted butter, and dredge with sugar.
5. Bake at 400°F 15 minutes.

About fifteen 4-inch scones

Blackberry Jelly

3 quarts blackberries
1 quart red blackberries
Sugar

1. Sort and wash berries; remove stems and caps. Crush berries and put into a kettle. Add just enough water to come halfway to the top of berries. Cover and bring rapidly to boiling; reduce heat and simmer 5 minutes.
2. Strain the juice through a jelly bag. Measure juice into kettle. For each cup of juice, allow ⅔ cup sugar. Boil juice to jelly stage (mixture sheets from spoon).
3. Remove from heat and skim off foam.
4. Pour jelly immediately into hot sterilized glasses.

About 4 half-pints jelly

Greengage Plum Ice Cream

1½ cups canned greengage
    plums
1 cup sugar
3 tablespoons lemon juice
3 cups milk
2 cups whipping cream

1. Remove pits from plums. Force fruit through a fine sieve into a bowl. Add sugar, lemon juice, milk, and cream; stir until sugar is dissolved.
2. Pour plum mixture into freezer trays and freeze until firm, stirring several times during freezing period.

About 1½ quarts

Raspberry Ice Cream Pie

1 unbaked 9-inch pastry
    shell
16 marshmallows
2 tablespoons crushed
    raspberries
Few drops red food
    coloring
2 egg whites
¼ cup sugar
¼ teaspoon salt
⅔ quart vanilla ice cream
1 cup fresh raspberries
8 or 10 whole raspberries

1. Bake pastry shell; cool.
2. Heat marshmallows with crushed raspberries slowly, folding over and over until marshmallows are half melted. Remove from heat and continue folding until mixture is smooth and fluffy. Add coloring and cool.
3. Beat egg whites until they hold a peak, add sugar slowly, beating constantly. Add salt. Blend lightly with marshmallow mixture.
4. Place ice cream in cool baked pastry shell, cover with raspberries and top with the fluffy marshmallow meringue, swirled attractively.
5. Brown quickly in broiler or in a 450°F oven for ½ minute, or until the tops of the meringue swirls are golden brown. Remove pie from oven, tuck raspberries in the swirls, and serve immediately.

One 9-inch pie

Crunchy Pecan-Topped Pumpkin Pie

1 can (16 ounces) pumpkin
⅔ cup firmly packed brown
    sugar
1 teaspoon cinnamon
½ teaspoon ginger
½ teaspoon nutmeg
⅛ teaspoon cloves
½ teaspoon salt
2 eggs, slightly beaten
2 cups cream, scalded
1 unbaked 9-inch pastry
    shell
3 tablespoons butter
1 cup (about 4 ounces)
    pecan halves
¼ cup firmly packed brown
    sugar

1. Mix pumpkin and brown sugar. Add a blend of spices and salt.
2. Mix in eggs; gradually add scalded cream, stirring until mixture is smooth. Pour into pastry shell.
3. Bake at 400°F about 50 minutes, or until a knife comes out clean when inserted halfway between center and edge. Cool on a rack.
4. Meanwhile, melt butter in small skillet over low heat. Add pecan halves. Occasionally turn pecans until thoroughly coated with butter. Turn nuts into a bowl containing brown sugar; toss to coat thoroughly.
5. When pie is cool, arrange coated pecans, rounded side up, over the top in an attractive design.
6. Place under broiler about 3 inches from heat. Broil 1 to 2 minutes.
7. Serve warm or cold.

One 9-inch pie

Arkansas, (famous for Hot Springs and other vacation playgrounds) is a stronghold of country traditions. Music, crafts, and cookery are elements of yesteryear's culture lovingly preserved, even in the midst of the state's progress and prosperity in agriculture and industry.

Best known for folk art and lore are the Ozark and Ouachita Mountain regions. In many ways the twentieth century has bypassed the more remote highlands, and the relative isolation of the hill people has kept many rustic pioneer customs alive.

The traditional arts, crafts, music, and food are showcased in numerous museums and festivals. The Ozark Folk Center is a living museum of hill-country culture. Visitors enjoy ancient ballads and breakdowns played on musical instruments of the past, and watch as sorghum syrup is cooked from juices squeezed by an old-time mule-drawn mill.

At various festivals and craft shows tourists can see grist milling, spinning, soap making, basket weaving, or log splitting, or join in rousing square dances or lively jigs. The restoration of a quaint mountain village is also a favorite stop for vacationers.

Many hill-country foods of the past remain popular. Sorghum syrup, the basic pioneer sweetener, is still enjoyed, as are smoked country ham, sassafras tea, wild persimmon cakes or pies, apple butter, corn breads, and fried tomatoes.

Northern Arkansas is a vacation mecca. Scenic highways wind over and through the rugged, heavily forested hills. Campers and fishermen from all over the Midwest are drawn to the lakes created by mighty dams built in the 1940s and '50s. Bull Shoals and Lake Norfork are especially noted for bass, while walleye, crappie, and perch are also caught in these and other lakes. In addition,

MIDWEST

ARKANSAS

Arkansas boasts some of the finest trout streams in mid-America.

In the lowlands and river valleys of northwest and west-central Arkansas, wheat fields and apple orchards recall the state's kinship with the Midwest. Other important crops are peaches, Irish and sweet potatoes, beans, tomatoes, and cucumbers.

Spinach is grown commercially in the Fort Smith area. Watermelon patches are found on many farms, but Hempstead County is especially famous for its huge Hope melons.

While the culture of central and western Arkansas has much in common with the midwestern ways of Kansas and Oklahoma, eastern Arkansas is quite different. Here the setting and scenery are reminiscent of the Old South.

The rich, flat, river bottom country is traditionally occupied by huge cotton plantations. The swampy lowlands are ideally suited for the cultivation of rice, which is a staple food in this part of the Mississippi Valley.

A more recent development has been catfish "farming"; fingerlings are raised in fresh-water ponds. Farmers find a ready market, for the South in particular has always had a fondness for the sweet white meat of the channel cat. Frying is the favorite cooking method, and the fish is usually encased in crispy cornmeal.

Eastern Arkansas is also the "land of opportunity" for hunters of migrant waterfowl. Thousands of ducks and geese pass overhead in the Mississippi flyway during their annual migrations. The National Duck Calling Contest is held in Stuttgart on the opening Saturday of each hunting season.

Arkansas shares its borders with deepest-south Mississippi and Louisiana, and with ten-gallon Texas. So it isn't surprising that hickory-smoked barbecue is popular throughout the state.

Channel Catfish Fry

1½ **pounds catfish, fresh or frozen**
1 **egg**
2 **tablespoons water**
½ **cup flour**
½ **cup cornmeal**
1 **teaspoon salt**
   Dash pepper
½ **cup cooking oil**
   Tartar Sauce

1. Thaw frozen fish; pat dry.
2. Beat egg slightly in a shallow dish, stir in water, and set aside.
3. Combine flour, cornmeal, salt, and pepper in another shallow dish.
4. Coat catfish with egg, then coat with flour mixture and place in hot oil in an 8-inch skillet. Brown fish on both sides, cooking until fish flakes easily when tested with a fork.
5. Drain on paper towels and serve with Tartar Sauce.

6 servings

Tartar Sauce: Combine **6 tablespoons mayonnaise, 1 tablespoon sweet pickle relish, 1 tablespoon chopped green olives,** and **1 teaspoon minced onion.** Mix until well blended.

About ½ cup sauce

Barbecued Pork Chops

4 pork chops (1 inch
 thick), trimmed
1 can (5½ ounces) tomato
 juice
¼ cup cooking oil
2 tablespoons vinegar
¼ teaspoon Tabasco
¼ teaspoon Worcestershire
 sauce
⅛ teaspoon crushed basil
1 teaspoon bottled
 vegetable bouquet
 sauce

1. Put pork chops into a shallow dish.
2. Mix tomato juice, oil, vinegar, Tabasco, Worcester-shire sauce, and basil. Pour over chops. Cover; refrigerate overnight.
3. Remove meat from marinade. Blend 2 tablespoons marinade with bouquet sauce and brush generously over both sides of chops.
4. Set chops on grill 3 to 4 inches from moderately hot coals. Grill 15 minutes on each side, or until done.

4 servings

Chicken Baked in Cream

Serve with Piquant Cucumber Slices, biscuits, Peachy Cornbread Shortcake, and iced tea.

1 broiler-fryer chicken
 (about 3 pounds) cut,
 in serving-size pieces
Salt
Pepper
Paprika
1½ cups whipping cream

1. Rinse chicken pieces and pat dry with absorbent paper.
2. Fill a skillet to ¼-inch depth with **butter** or **margarine.** Heat until a drop of water sputters.
3. Add chicken pieces and brown evenly. Cover and cook over low heat until tender, about 15 minutes.
4. Transfer to a shallow baking pan; sprinkle with salt, pepper, and paprika. Pour cream over chicken.
5. Bake at 300°F 30 to 45 minutes, or until cream thickens; baste occasionally.

About 4 servings

Creamed Spinach with Almonds

1 tablespoon flour
¾ teaspoon salt
⅛ teaspoon ground nutmeg
1 tablespoon butter or
 margarine
1 cup half-and-half
2 tablespoons toasted
 almond halves
1 package (10 ounces)
 frozen spinach, cooked
 and drained

1. Blend flour, salt, and nutmeg into hot butter in a saucepan. Heat until bubbly. Gradually add half-and-half, stirring constantly. Bring to boiling; stir and cook 1 to 2 minutes.
2. Add almonds and spinach to sauce; mix lightly to blend. Serve garnished with **tomato wedges.**

About 4 servings

ARKANSAS

Piquant Cucumber Slices

2 tablespoons sugar
1 teaspoon salt
⅛ teaspoon white pepper
1 teaspoon celery seed
¼ cup cider vinegar
1 tablespoon lemon juice
1 cucumber, rinsed (do not pare)
¼ cup coarsely chopped onion
2 tablespoons chopped parsley

1. Combine the sugar, salt, white pepper, celery seed, vinegar, and lemon juice in a bowl; blend thoroughly.
2. Score cucumber by drawing tines of a fork lengthwise over entire surface. Cut into ⅛-inch slices.
3. Add cucumber to vinegar mixture with onion and parsley; toss to coat evenly.
4. Chill thoroughly, turning several times.

About 4 servings

Rice Waffles

A special treat topped with golden sorghum, honey, or maple syrup.

1½ cups sifted all-purpose flour
1 tablespoon sugar
3 teaspoons baking powder
½ teaspoon salt
3 egg yolks
2 cups milk
½ cup butter or margarine, melted
1 cup cooked rice, cooled
3 egg whites

1. Sift flour, sugar, baking powder, and salt together into a large bowl; set aside.
2. Beat egg yolks until thick. Gradually add the milk, mixing well. Blend in melted butter and cooled rice. Add to dry ingredients and mix only until batter is blended.
3. Beat the egg whites until stiff, not dry, peaks are formed. Gently fold into batter.
4. Bake in a waffle baker, following manufacturer's directions.

About 8 servings

Persimmon Pie

2 cups persimmon pulp (see page 158), or 1 can (30 ounces) apricot halves, drained and puréed
1 egg, well beaten
1 cup milk
½ cup sugar
⅛ teaspoon salt
1 tablespoon cornstarch
1 unbaked 8-inch pie shell

1. Mix persimmon pulp, egg, and milk. Mix sugar, salt, and cornstarch and add to first mixture. Pour into unbaked pie shell.
2. Bake at 450°F 10 minutes, then turn oven control to 350°F and bake about 60 minutes longer.

One 8-inch pie

Grilled Steak; Corn-on-the-Cob;
French Fries; Apple Pie

Roast Turkey with Oyster Stuffing, 42

Chocolate Rice Pudding

Cinnamon and cloves subtly spice this luscious dessert.

2 cups milk
2 ounces (2 squares) unsweetened chocolate
⅔ cup sugar
1 tablespoon flour
¼ teaspoon salt
⅛ teaspoon ground cinnamon
⅛ teaspoon ground cloves
3 egg yolks, slightly beaten
1 cup cooked rice
2 tablespoons butter
½ teaspoon vanilla extract

1. Scald 1½ cups of the milk with chocolate in the top of a double boiler over simmering water.
2. Combine in a bowl the sugar, flour, salt, and spices. Add the remaining milk and mix well.
3. Add the scalded milk gradually, stirring constantly. Pour mixture into double-boiler top. Cook and stir until boiling; cook 2 minutes longer.
4. Set over simmering water. Cover and cook 5 to 7 minutes, stirring occasionally.
5. Stir about 3 tablespoons of the hot mixture into the egg yolks; immediately blend into mixture in double boiler. Cook over simmering water 3 to 5 minutes, stirring occasionally.
6. Remove from heat. Fluff rice with a fork and stir into hot mixture. Stir in the butter and vanilla extract. Cover and set pudding aside to cool slightly, stirring occasionally. Serve in sherbet glasses.

6 servings

Peachy Cornbread Shortcake

¾ cup plus 2 tablespoons all-purpose flour
½ teaspoon baking soda
¼ teaspoon salt
1 cup yellow cornmeal
¾ cup firmly packed light brown sugar
1 egg, well beaten
½ cup buttermilk
⅓ cup dairy sour cream
Peach Butter Elégante
Sweetened fresh peach slices

1. Combine the flour, baking soda, salt, cornmeal, and brown sugar in a bowl; set aside.
2. Beat the egg, buttermilk, and sour cream together until well blended. Make a well in center of dry ingredients and add liquid all at one time. Stir until just smooth (do not overmix).
3. Turn into a greased (bottom only) 11×7×1½-inch pan and spread batter evenly to corners and sides of pan.
4. Bake at 425°F about 20 minutes, or until a cake tester or wooden pick inserted in center comes out clean.
5. While still warm, cut cornbread into serving-size pieces, remove from pan, and split into two layers. Spread Peach Butter Elégante generously between layers. Top with peach slices.

9 to 12 servings

Peach Butter Elégante: Using an electric beater, whip **1 cup firm unsalted butter**, gradually beating in **½ cup confectioners' sugar**. Add **1 package (10 ounces) frozen sliced peaches, thawed and cut in pieces**, 1 tablespoon at a time, beating thoroughly.

About 2⅔ cups butter

ARKANSAS

Butterscotch Benchwarmer, 198; Cheerleaders' Choice, 198; Orange Honey Hero, 198; Mexican Chocolate, 212

Oriental Beef Stew, 233

ARKANSAS

Sassafras Tea

2 tablespoons sassafras
1 quart boiling water

Steep sassafras in boiling water in a warm place for about ½ hour. Serve hot.

4 servings

Cherry Watermelon Pickles

Arkansans love watermelon, right down to and including the rind, which is often made into delicious pickles.

3 quarts water
6 tablespoons salt
2 quarts prepared
    watermelon rind* (rind
    of ½ large melon)
2 cups white or cider
    vinegar
6 cups sugar
2 pieces (3 inches each)
    stick cinnamon
1 teaspoon whole cloves
1 jar (8 ounces) red
    maraschino cherries,
    drained

1. Combine water and salt in a 5- or 6-quart Dutch oven. Stir until salt is dissolved. Mix in rind. Set aside for 4 hours; drain, rinse, and drain again. Cover with water and bring to boiling; boil 10 minutes. Remove from heat; drain and reserve rind.
2. Put vinegar and sugar into a saucepan and stir until sugar is dissolved. Add spices tied in a cheesecloth bag. Bring to boiling and boil 10 minutes. Remove from heat and add rind. Cool and refrigerate, covered, overnight.
3. Remove rind from syrup with slotted spoon. Bring syrup to boiling; add rind and cherries and boil 5 minutes. Discard spice bag.
4. Ladle rind and cherries into sterilized jars and pour syrup over rind, leaving headspace; release air bubbles and seal, following manufacturer's directions.
5. Process in boiling water bath 10 minutes.

About 3 pints pickles

*To prepare rind, trim the hard, dark green outer shell and the pink parts from the watermelon rind. Cut into 1-inch cubes.

ILLINOIS 147

Illinois fulfills the promise of its heartland location. Its largest city, towering on the shores of Lake Michigan, is a center of commerce and a leader in shipping agricultural and manufactured products.

Sandburg's "City of the Big Shoulders" still stacks its wheat, though the legendary stockyards are gone. For years the home of the International Livestock Exposition, Chi-cago retains its well-deserved reputation for good beef. Another Chicago specialty is Lake Superior whitefish baked on a sea-soned oak plank and accompanied by duch-ess potatoes.

Chicago offers remarkably cosmopolitan fare. It claims the largest Polish population of any U.S. city, and a thriving Czech com-munity. The Irish are influential, and there are large numbers of Hungarians, Germans, Lithuanians, Greeks, Scandinavians, Ruma-nians, Italians, and Russians.

Thousands of Jewish families also contrib-ute to the culture. Over one million blacks, and more recently Latinos, have added an-other important ethnic dimension. Interest in the old ways is kept alive by festivals, restaurants, bakeries, special markets, and family customs.

Outside Chicago the population is more homogeneous, although Swedes have had a strong impact, particularly in the areas of Rockford and Galesburg (Sandburg's boy-hood home). Illinois is marked by contrasts between the Chicago metropolitan area and largely rural "downstate."

In the Rock River Valley of northwest Illinois is the site of John Deere's blacksmith shop. Here he hammered out the first suc-cessful self-scouring steel plow. This imple-ment broke open the vastly productive mid-western prairies for today's mechanized agriculture. Plowing with the previous iron plows had been a tedious if not impossible task, because the heavy soils stuck to the plows.

In western Illinois historic towns hug the banks of the Mississippi. Among the most interesting is Nauvoo, home of the Mor-

ILLINOIS

mons until their westward trek in the 1840s. A French colony followed and developed vineyards and cheese-making in the area. Now the annual "Wedding of the Wine and Cheese" feast symbolizes the idea that the two are best when enjoyed together.

The prairies of central Illinois include some of the richest farmland in the world, and the state is always near the top in corn and soybean production. Other important crops are wheat, oats, rye, barley, and tomatoes.

Downstate food is characterized by the hearty, simple dishes required by hard-working pioneers and farmers. Here Lincoln grew to greatness, though presumably no credit is due his diet. It is said he took little interest in food beyond mere survival, and sometimes had to be rereminded of that necessity! The frontier diet of the time was based on such staples as ham, salt pork, apples, and biscuits.

Pork—the cornfed variety—remains a favorite meat in the Land of Lincoln, along with beef and chicken. As elsewhere, barbecuing on outdoor grills has become a popular cooking method.

Sweet corn festivals or corn roasts are typical late summer social and/or money-raising events. Sweet, fresh corn-on-the-cob, roasted over coals and dripping with butter, is the main item. It may be accompanied by barbecued pork, chicken, or beef, sliced tomatoes, coleslaw, home-baked bread, pie, and lemonade, iced tea or coffee—any, all, or none of these, depending on the scope of the occasion.

Home gardens are common, and preserving summer's plenty for winter consumption is a time-consuming though rewarding project for many families.

Southern Illinois clings to many of the customs of the Old South, and the cookery reflects this influence. Cairo, Illinois' southernmost city, is farther south than most of Kentucky and Virginia. Magnolias bloom and cotton grows in the fertile river bottoms of "Little Egypt," and apple and peach orchards flourish in the scenic Shawnee Hills.

The traditions of many people have poured into the Illinois melting pot. Combined with the locally grown foods, they have produced a richly varied culinary heritage for the Prairie State.

Standing Rib Roast of Beef

3 rib (6 to 8 pounds) standing rib roast of beef (have meat dealer saw across ribs near backbone so it can be removed to make carving easier)
1½ teaspoons salt
⅛ teaspoon pepper

1. Place roast, fat side up, in a shallow roasting pan. Season with a blend of salt and pepper. Insert meat thermometer so tip is slightly beyond center of thickest part of lean; be sure tip does not rest on bone or in fat.
2. Roast at 300°F to 325°F, allowing 23 to 25 minutes per pound for rare; 27 to 30 minutes per pound for medium; and 32 to 35 minutes per pound for well done meat. Roast is also done when meat thermometer registers 140°F for rare; 160°F for medium; and 170°F for well done.
3. Place roast on a warm serving platter. Remove thermometer.
4. Meat drippings may be used for gravy. For a special treat, serve with Yorkshire Pudding.

8 to 10 servings

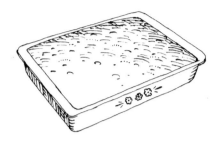

Yorkshire Pudding: Pour ¼ cup hot drippings from roast beef into an 11×7×1½-inch baking dish and keep hot. Add **1 cup milk, 1 cup sifted all-purpose flour,** and ½ teaspoon salt to **2 well-beaten eggs.** Beat with hand rotary or electric beater until smooth. Pour into baking pan over hot drippings. Bake at 400°F 30 to 40 minutes, or until puffed and golden. Cut into squares and serve immediately.

About 8 servings

Corn Roast

Until you have sat before a glowing bonfire on a sandy beach, with the music of water lapping at your feet and above you a golden harvest moon, and in your hands a piping hot cob of corn from which you munch the sweet and succulent kernels, you just haven't lived a full life!

Fresh sweet corn
Cold water
Melted butter
Salt and pepper

1. If using a bonfire, pull back the husks and remove the silks from corn. Then soak the cob, husks and all, in cold water for 20 to 30 minutes. This ensures that the husks are wet through.
2. Drain the cobs, dry them, brush them with melted butter, and tie husks back in place. Roll each cob up in a piece of aluminum foil, sealing it tightly.
3. Place the corn in the glowing coals of the bonfire and let it roast, turning several times, for 20 to 30 minutes, depending on the size of the cob.
4. Shuck the corn, add salt and pepper and more melted butter, if desired, and start getting the next round ready!

Note: If using an outdoor grill, prepare ears of corn as above, omitting butter and aluminum foil. Place ears over glowing coals and roast, turning frequently, until tender (about 15 to 20 minutes).

Freezer Cole Slaw

Provides a bright taste of summer's freshness in the middle of a long, drab winter.

1 teaspoon salt
1 medium head cabbage, shredded
1 carrot, finely chopped
1 green pepper, chopped
1 cup vinegar
¼ cup water
1 teaspoon mustard seed
1 teaspoon celery seed
2 cups sugar

1. Mix salt with cabbage and let stand 1 hour.
2. Squeeze excess moisture out of cabbage; stir in carrot and green pepper.
3. To make dressing, combine vinegar, water, mustard seed, celery seed, and sugar. Boil for 1 minute, stirring constantly.
4. Pour dressing slowly over cabbage mixture, mixing thoroughly.
5. Pack slaw in freezer containers; seal and freeze.
6. Thaw to serve; serve cold.

About 8 servings

ILLINOIS

ILLINOIS

Aunt Hazel's Wedding Salad

This recipe, handed down for several generations, was served at a central Illinois wedding reception in 1919.

¼ cup sugar
1 tablespoon flour
2 tablespoons vinegar
2 egg whites
2 cups whipping cream
1 quart shredded cabbage
4 ounces large marshmallows, cut in pieces
1 can (20 ounces) crushed pineapple, drained
1 cup slivered blanched almonds

1. Combine sugar and flour in a small saucepan; stir in vinegar. Cook until thick. Set aside to cool.
2. Beat egg whites until stiff, not dry, peaks form. Whip cream, 1 cup at a time, until soft peaks form. Fold beaten egg whites and cream into cooled cooked mixture.
3. Combine cabbage, marshmallows, pineapple, and almonds in a large bowl; add dressing and mix well. Chill thoroughly.

About 12 servings

Basic Oats Mix

6 cups sifted all-purpose flour
¼ cup (4 tablespoons) baking powder
4 teaspoons salt
1⅓ cups shortening
2 cups quick or old-fashioned oats, uncooked

1. Sift flour, baking powder, and salt together into large bowl. Cut in shortening until mixture resembles coarse crumbs. Stir in oats.
2. Store mixture in an airtight container in a cool, dry place until ready to use.

9¾ cups mix

Oatmeal Biscuits

2 cups Basic Oats Mix
⅔ cup cold milk

1. Combine Oats Mix and milk in a bowl; stir with a fork to a soft dough.
2. Turn dough onto a lightly floured surface. Knead with fingertips 10 times. Roll out to ½-inch thickness. Cut with a floured 2-inch round cutter. Put onto an ungreased cookie sheet.
3. Bake at 450°F 8 to 10 minutes.

About 16 biscuits

Fluffy Dumplings

2 cups Basic Oats Mix (page
  150)
1 cup milk

Thoroughly combine Oats Mix and milk. Spoon onto boiling stew. Cook, uncovered, over low heat 10 minutes; cover and cook 10 minutes longer.

10 to 12 dumplings

Oatmeal Muffins

2 cups plus 2 tablespoons
  Basic Oats Mix (page
  150)
¼ cup sugar
1 cup milk
1 egg, beaten

1. Combine Oats Mix and sugar in a bowl. Add milk and egg; stir until just blended.
2. Fill 12 greased 2½-inch muffin-pan wells two-thirds full.
3. Bake at 400°F about 20 minutes, or until golden brown.

12 muffins

Quick Applesauce Bread

2¼ cups Basic Oats Mix
  (page 150)
1 cup sugar
1 teaspoon cinnamon
1 cup canned sweetened
  applesauce
1 egg
½ cup milk
½ cup raisins

1. Combine Oats Mix, sugar, and cinnamon in a bowl. Add applesauce, egg, and raisins; stir until mixed.
2. Turn batter into an 8½×4½×2½-inch loaf pan, greased and floured.
3. Bake at 350°F 55 to 60 minutes.
4. Remove from pan and cool completely on a rack before slicing.

1 loaf bread

Irish Scones

1¾ cups sifted all-purpose
  flour
1 tablespoon sugar
1½ teaspoons baking
  powder
½ teaspoon baking soda
½ teaspoon salt
½ cup shortening
½ cup buttermilk

1. Mix flour, sugar, baking powder, baking soda, and salt in a bowl. Cut in shortening with a pastry blender or two knives until particles are the size of rice kernels.
2. Add the buttermilk and stir with a fork until dough follows fork and forms a ball.
3. Turn dough onto a floured surface and knead lightly with fingertips about 8 times. Divide dough in half and shape each into a round about ½ inch thick. Cut each round into 6 wedge-shaped pieces. Place on an ungreased baking sheet.
4. Bake at 450°F 8 to 10 minutes. Serve warm.

1 dozen scones

ILLINOIS

Czechoslovakian Braid (Vanochka)

This raisin-almond yeast braid is a Czechoslovakian Christmas tradition.

¾ cup milk, scalded
½ cup butter or margarine
½ cup sugar
1 teaspoon salt
2 packages active dry yeast
½ cup warm water, 110°F to 115°F
5 cups all-purpose flour
2 eggs
1 tablespoon vanilla extract
1 tablespoon grated lemon peel
½ cup seedless raisins
½ cup blanched almonds, toasted and coarsely chopped

1. Pour scalded milk over butter, sugar, and salt in a mixing bowl; set aside to cool to lukewarm.
2. Sprinkle yeast over warm water; let stand 5 to 10 minutes.
3. Add about ¾ cup flour to milk mixture and beat vigorously until smooth. Stir the yeast and add to the batter, mixing well. Add about one-half the remaining flour and beat until smooth.
4. Beat eggs with vanilla extract and lemon peel and mix into batter. Blend in raisins and almonds. Beat in enough remaining flour to make a soft dough.
5. Turn dough onto a lightly floured surface and let stand 5 to 10 minutes. Knead until smooth. Form dough into a ball and put into a greased bowl. Turn dough to bring greased surface to top. Cover and let rise in warm place (about 80°F) until doubled. Punch dough down, pull edges in to center, and turn dough completely over in bowl. Cover and let rise until nearly doubled.
6. Turn dough onto a floured surface and divide into 9 equal portions. Roll each portion into a 15-inch rope-shaped piece. Braid 4 pieces together; join the ends and place on greased baking sheet. Braid 3 of the remaining pieces together; join ends and place on top of the first braid. Twist remaining pieces together and lay on top of second braid.
7. Brush with **beaten egg** and let rise until doubled (about 45 minutes).
8. Bake at 350°F 45 to 50 minutes, or until golden brown. Cool and, if desired, drizzle with a thin confectioners' sugar icing and sprinkle chopped almonds over top.

1 large braid

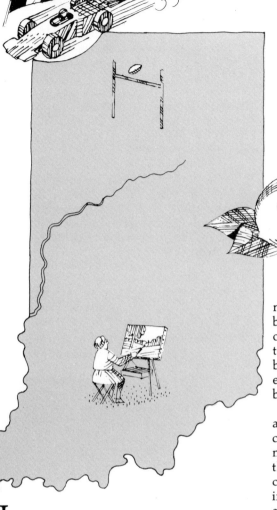

Indiana means many different things to different people. To football fans it's the home of Notre Dame's "Fighting Irish." To racing buffs, the home of the world-famous "Indy 500." To those who have moved away, it's simply *home.* They fondly remember sycamores along the Wabash and the "smell of new-mown hay." But to one and all, it's the "Hoosier State," a word best and uniquely defined in terms of Indiana.

Though in reality a great industrial state, Indiana retains much of its rural character and charm. Its location in the farm belt, plus remnants of the simpler life of yesteryear, combine to produce some of the finest country-style cooking anywhere.

Early English, Irish, and Scotch settlers migrated here from Kentucky and Virginia, bringing preferences for an already developed southern style of cooking still reflected today. This migration pattern was followed by the Lincoln family, who moved to southern Indiana when Abraham was a young boy.

The wooded hills south of Indianapolis are crisscrossed by streams still spanned by covered bridges. This beautiful area attracts many visitors, especially in autumn when the colorful foliage is at its peak and festivals celebrate the harvest. The trees are predominately hardwoods, including oak, maple, and hickory, giving rise to a wealth of recipes using the native nuts.

The American persimmon flourishes near the Ohio River, and although common to much of the southeastern United States, it seems to have a special affinity for Indiana, and Hoosiers for it. Cakes, pies, breads, desserts, preserves (similar to apple butter) as well as the famous Indiana Persimmon Pudding contain the pulp of this sweet, plumlike fruit. Those who live in the colder northern areas of nearby states eagerly await the arrival of summer's first Indiana melons, prized for their luscious flavor.

Central Indiana lies in the corn belt. Here in the "crossroads of America" much of the corn is fed to hogs and cattle, accounting for

INDIANA

the popularity of pork and beef. Other important crops are soybeans, popcorn, and tomatoes. Squash, pumpkins (celebrated in native son James Whitcomb Riley's "When the Frost Is on the Pumpkin"), and other vegetables are abundant. Indeed, where but in a land of such plenty would good cooks deliberately wilt lettuce leaves for a salad?

Another influence traces back to the almost legendary folk hero Johnny Appleseed. Born John Chapman in 1775, he wandered throughout the wilderness of western Pennsylvania, central and northern Ohio, and northeastern Indiana, planting apple seeds and tending the young trees. A park near Ft. Wayne preserves his memory. Apples were very important to frontier families because of their versatility both fresh and dried, and they were relatively easy to grow and care for.

In northern Indiana lakes and marshes share the landscape with the magnificent sand dunes along Lake Michigan's shoreline. A big percentage of the various varieties of mint used in making extracts and flavorings grows here.

While ethnic specialties certainly do exist, basically it's the typical Midwestern farm fare that spells Hoosier hospitality. The regional style is dictated by the generosity of the land, but it boasts a definite Indiana individuality.

Onion Popcorn

⅓ to ½ cup dry onion soup
    mix (1 packet)
½ cup melted butter or
    margarine
3 quarts popped popcorn
    (about)

1. Combine dry onion soup mix with melted butter.
2. Pour over warm popcorn. Toss gently until kernels are coated.

Hoosier Scalloped Tomatoes

3 slices bread
2 medium (about ½
    pound) onions
1 can (28 ounces)
    tomatoes
⅓ cup cheese cracker
    crumbs
1 tablespoon parsley
    flakes
1½ teaspoons sugar
1 teaspoon seasoned salt
1 cup dairy sour cream
2 tablespoons melted
    butter or margarine
    Parsley flakes

1. Grease a 1¼-quart shallow baking dish.
2. Toast bread until very crisp and cut into ½-inch cubes.
3. Peel, rinse, and chop onions.
4. Drain and cut tomatoes into pieces with a spoon.
5. Combine one half the chopped onions, all of the tomatoes, cracker crumbs, parsley flakes, sugar, and salt in casserole. Cover with remaining onion.
6. Spoon sour cream over the mixture in casserole.
7. Toss toast cubes with melted butter and spoon over sour cream. Sprinkle with parsley flakes.
8. Bake at 325°F 20 minutes, or until mixture is thoroughly heated.

6 servings

Pork Shoulder with Apple Stuffing

One of the more economical pork roasts, with an apple-bread stuffing. Pork and apples are natural flavor mates.

1 pork shoulder roast (6 pounds)
¼ pound salt pork, diced
½ cup diced celery
½ cup chopped onion
2 cups diced tart apples
½ cup sugar
1 cup bread crumbs
2 tablespoons minced parsley
½ teaspoon salt
⅛ teaspoon pepper

1. Have bones removed from the pork shoulder, leaving cavity for apple stuffing.
2. For stuffing, cook salt pork until crisp. Remove from pan and cook celery and onion in the fat until onion is tender and a light yellow.
3. Add apples and sugar; cover pan and cook until apples are tender.
4. Combine bread crumbs, parsley, salt, pepper, and salt pork and mix well. Add cooked apple mixture and mix thoroughly.
5. Fill cavity of pork shoulder; fasten opening with poultry pins or skewers.
6. Place in roasting pan; season with salt and pepper.
7. Roast at 350°F until well done. Internal temperature will be 170°F. Allow about 30 to 35 minutes per pound. Add weight of dressing to that of meat in calculating roasting time.
8. When roast is half done, spread with **prepared mustard** and finish roasting.

12 servings

Wilted Lettuce

Especially good with tender leaf lettuce straight from the garden.

4 slices bacon
¼ cup vinegar
2 heads leaf lettuce, chicory, dandelion greens, or fresh spinach
½ cup chopped green onions
Salt and pepper

1. Cut bacon into small pieces, fry, and drain on absorbent paper. Add vinegar to fat in skillet and bring to boiling.
2. Cut lettuce in pieces convenient for eating; add onions and sprinkle with salt and pepper.
3. Pour hot vinegar mixture over lettuce, tossing thoroughly. Sprinkle top with crisp bacon and serve at once.

4 servings

Devil's Food Cake

2 cups sifted cake flour
1 teaspoon baking soda
½ teaspoon salt
½ cup butter
1½ teaspoons vanilla extract
1½ cups sugar or firmly
    packed light brown
    sugar
2 eggs, well beaten
3 ounces (3 squares)
    unsweetened
    chocolate, melted and
    cooled
1 cup milk
½ teaspoon red food
    coloring

1. Sift together flour, baking soda, and salt. Set aside.
2. Cream butter and vanilla extract until softened; add brown sugar gradually, creaming until fluffy after each addition.
3. Add beaten eggs in thirds, beating thoroughly after each addition; stir in cooled chocolate.
4. Add dry ingredients in thirds and milk in halves to creamed mixture, beating only until smooth after each addition. Blend in red food coloring with few final strokes. Turn batter into two 8-inch round layer cake pans.
5. Bake at 350°F 30 to 35 minutes, or until cake tests done. Cool and remove from pans.
6. Fill and frost cooled cake layers with Peppermint Butter Frosting.

Two 8-inch round layers

Peppermint Butter Frosting

½ cup butter
½ teaspoon peppermint
    extract
⅛ teaspoon salt
3½ cups confectioners'
    sugar
1 egg
1 to 2 tablespoons milk or
    cream
Red food coloring

1. Cream together butter, peppermint extract, and salt until softened.
2. Add confectioners' sugar gradually, beating until smooth after each addition.
3. Beat egg in thoroughly; blend in milk if necessary. Beat until frosting is of spreading consistency. Tint to desired color with food coloring.

Enough to frost sides and tops of two 8- or 9-inch cake layers

Apple Upside-Down Cake

¼ cup butter or margarine
⅔ cup firmly packed
    brown sugar
1 teaspoon cinnamon
2 tablespoons chopped
    walnuts
1 medium apple
2 teaspoons lemon juice
1½ cups sifted cake flour
1 teaspoon baking powder
¼ teaspoon baking soda
¼ teaspoon salt
¾ teaspoon cinnamon
¼ teaspoon nutmeg

1. Melt butter in an 8×8×2-inch cake pan.
2. Mix brown sugar and cinnamon; stir in chopped walnuts.
3. Blend sugar mixture into the melted butter and spread evenly in the pan.
4. Wash, quarter, core, pare, and slice apple. Arrange apple slices on the brown sugar mixture. Brush apple slices with lemon juice; set aside.
5. Sift together cake flour, baking powder, baking soda, salt, cinnamon, nutmeg, and allspice; set aside.
6. Cream remaining ⅓ cup butter and vanilla extract until softened; add brown sugar gradually, creaming until fluffy after each addition. Add egg gradually, beating thoroughly after each addition.

¼ teaspoon allspice
⅓ cup butter or margarine
½ teaspoon vanilla extract
¾ cup firmly packed
　　brown sugar
1 egg, well beaten
½ cup buttermilk

7. Beating only until smooth after each addition, alternately add dry ingredients in thirds and buttermilk in halves to creamed mixture. Turn batter over apple slices.
8. Bake at 350°F 40 to 45 minutes, or until cake tests done. Using a spatula, loosen cake from sides of pan and invert immediately on serving plate. Let pan remain over cake a few seconds, so that syrup will drain onto cake. Remove pan. Serve warm.

One 8-inch square cake

Hickory Nut Cookies

1½ cups sugar
1 cup butter or other
　　shortening
3 eggs, well beaten
½ cup molasses
1½ cups raisins
½ cup hickory nuts, finely
　　chopped
　　Sifted flour (about 2
　　cups)
1 teaspoon baking soda
½ teaspoon cinnamon
¼ teaspoon cloves
¼ teaspoon allspice
⅛ teaspoon salt

1. Cream sugar and butter together, add eggs and molasses and beat well. Add raisins and nuts.
2. Sift 1 cup flour, soda, spices, and salt together and add to first mixture. Add enough more flour to make a soft dough.
3. Chill dough, if necessary, until easy to handle.
4. Roll thin on a lightly floured board and cut with cookie cutter.
5. Bake on a greased cookie sheet at 350°F 10 to 12 minutes.

About 4 dozen cookies

Minted Cantaloupe Balls

Indiana cantaloupes are juicy, fragrant, and flavorful. Cantaloupes are a type of muskmelon.

1 large ripe cantaloupe
½ cup sugar
1½ teaspoons cornstarch
　　Few grains salt
¾ cup water
12 fresh mint leaves
1 tablespoon butter or
　　margarine
2 drops green food
　　coloring
　　Mint sprigs

1. Using a melon-ball cutter, cut out balls (about 3 cups) from cantaloupe. Put into a bowl; cover and chill thoroughly.
2. In a saucepan mix sugar, cornstarch, and salt; blend in water and mint leaves (bruise mint by pressing with back of spoon against side of pan). Bring to boiling, stirring constantly, and cook until mixture is slightly thickened.
3. Remove from heat; cool slightly and strain.
4. Mix in butter and food coloring. Chill in refrigerator.
5. To serve, turn chilled melon balls into a chilled serving bowl and pour sauce over them. Garnish with mint sprigs.

About 6 servings

INDIANA

Indiana Persimmon Pudding

1 cup all-purpose flour
1 teaspoon baking soda
½ teaspoon cinnamon
½ teaspoon ginger
¼ teaspoon nutmeg
1 cup sugar
1 cup persimmon pulp*
½ cup milk
2 tablespoons butter, melted and cooled
1 teaspoon vanilla extract
½ cup seedless raisins
1 tablespoon butter, softened
½ cup whipping cream, whipped

1. Stir together flour, baking soda, cinnamon, ginger, and nutmeg; set aside.

2. Add the sugar to the persimmon pulp and mix well with a wooden spoon. Stir in about half the flour mixture. When completely mixed in, stir in ¼ cup milk. Stir in remaining flour mixture and then remaining milk, beating well after each addition. Stir in the melted butter, vanilla extract, and raisins.

3. Spread the softened butter evenly on the bottom and sides of a 1-quart soufflé dish. Pour the batter in the dish, spreading it evenly with a rubber spatula.

4. Bake at 350°F 50 to 60 minutes, or until the pudding begins to shrink away from the sides of the dish, and a wooden pick inserted in the center comes out clean.

5. Serve immediately, directly from the soufflé dish. Top each serving with whipped cream.

4 to 6 servings

*To make 1 cup persimmon pulp, wash **1 pound persimmons** under cold running water and pat dry with paper towels. With a small sharp knife, cut persimmons in quarters and remove the seeds. Purée the fruit through a food mill or in a blender.

Note: If desired, apricots may be substituted for persimmons by draining and puréeing 1 can (17 ounces) apricot halves.

Bread-and-Butter Pickles (Midwestern Style)

Tangy addition to a pot-roast dinner menu.

2 quarts ¼-inch cucumber slices (about 16 cucumbers, 4 to 5 inches each)
½ cup coarse salt
1 quart boiling water
2 cups chopped onion
2 cups chopped green pepper
¾ cup chopped red pepper
2 cups cider vinegar
2 cups sugar
1 teaspoon celery seed
1 teaspoon mustard seed
¾ teaspoon ground turmeric

1. Prepare the cucumber slices and toss with salt in a large bowl. Pour boiling water over cucumbers, cover, and let stand overnight.

2. The next day prepare the chopped vegetables.

3. Combine remaining ingredients in a large saucepot and stir over medium heat until sugar is dissolved. Increase heat and bring to boiling. Add the chopped vegetables and cucumbers and cook gently about 5 minutes.

4. Immediately pack the pickles into clean hot jars. Seal, following manufacturer's directions.

5. Process in boiling water bath 5 minutes.

About 4 pints pickles

A 1940s movie musical celebrated that unique bit of Americana, the State Fair, and presented a portrait of rural Iowa life at the time. Then in the late 1950s composer Meredith Willson put Iowa on the musical map again. "The Music Man" was a loving tribute to early twentieth-century life in an Iowa town.

Iowa, one of the Midwest's most typically rural states, has no really large cities. Its small towns are the very prototype of Americana, with their skylines dominated by those skyscrapers of the plains, the grain elevators. So it is not surprising that much of the state's culture, and in particular the food, is farm oriented.

Iowa is traditionally considered the heart of the Corn Belt, though it usually shares top producing honors with neighboring Illinois. Iowa is also among the leading states in corn-fed pork and beef production.

Iowans prefer pork and beef over other meats; mashed potatoes or noodles with gravy are their usual partners. Chops, roast pork, and ham all take their place at the Iowa table, while beef often shows up in pot roast or meat loaf as well as more sophisticated dishes.

Farm cooking is heavy by city standards, eating habits being dictated by strenuous outdoor work. Tastes are essentially uncomplicated, reflecting Yankee, Pennsylvania Dutch, and European farm backgrounds.

Many Iowa farm homemakers devote more time to "from scratch" cooking than do their urban counterparts, and preserving farm and garden produce is important. In many instances the home freezer has taken over the role formerly reserved for the canning kettle, though canning is enjoying a revival.

The most famous of the various ethnic

IOWA

pockets are the Amana colonies, a series of villages founded in the 1860s as a religious commune. Today most of the communal features have vanished, but the flavor of the Old World German and Swiss life style remains.

Food in the closely knit communities is wholesome and plentiful. German classics such as liver dumplings, sausages, and kuchens are specialties, along with rhubarb wine.

Others who give Iowa food variety and a delicious European accent are the descendants of Norwegian, Swedish, Danish, British, Dutch, and Czech settlers.

Church and club dinners, family reunions and other "covered dish" occasions give Iowa cooks a chance to show off their talents. Here one finds trays of fried chicken, assorted beef and pork dishes, fruit and gelatin salads mixed with or topped by whipped cream, cakes with luscious fillings and frostings, fruit pies and cream pies with meringue or whipped cream toppings.

County fairs and the State Fair in Des Moines also offer a showcase of Iowa cooking. Universally popular fair and carnival snacks are corn dogs, popcorn, and cotton candy. Each Labor Day southeastern Iowa hosts an old-fashioned Steam Threshers' Picnic. Foods of the past and homey skills of yesteryear are featured.

Rolled Pot Roast with Sour Cream Gravy

3 tablespoons fat
4 pounds rolled pot roast of beef
1 teaspoon salt
⅛ teaspoon pepper
1 medium onion, quartered
¼ cup water
1 bay leaf
2 quarts water
1½ teaspoons salt
1½ cups (about 4 ounces) noodles
3 tablespoons melted butter
½ cup water
1 tablespoon flour
1½ cups dairy sour cream
1½ tablespoons lemon juice
1½ teaspoons grated lemon peel
¾ teaspoon sugar

1. Melt fat in a Dutch oven; brown meat slowly on all sides in fat.
2. Season browned meat with a mixture of salt and pepper. Add onion, ¼ cup water, and bay leaf to meat; cover tightly and simmer over low heat about 3 hours. If necessary, add more water during cooking period.
3. For noodles, about 15 minutes before meat is tender, heat 2 quarts water and salt to boiling in a large saucepan. Gradually add noodles, stirring with fork. Boil rapidly, uncovered, 6 to 10 minutes, until tender. Drain and blend butter through noodles. Serve with the pot roast.
4. To make gravy, remove meat from liquid when tender and keep warm. Strain liquid and return to Dutch oven. Set over medium heat.
5. Put ½ cup water and flour into screw-top jar. Shake until mixture is well blended. Gradually stir into liquid in Dutch oven. Bring rapidly to boiling, stirring constantly; cook 3 to 5 minutes longer.
6. Remove Dutch oven from heat. Stirring vigorously, add to mixture in Dutch oven in small amounts a mixture of sour cream, lemon juice, lemon peel, and sugar.
7. Place over low heat and stir constantly until thoroughly heated (about 3 to 5 minutes), but do not boil. Serve with pot roast and noodles.

About 8 servings

Country-Flavored Chicken Halves, 202

Corn Dogs

Cooking oil for deep
   frying
1 cup sifted flour
1½ teaspoons sugar
1 teaspoon salt
½ teaspoon baking powder
⅛ teaspoon garlic salt
   Few grains pepper
⅔ cup cornmeal
2 tablespoons shortening
1 egg, slightly beaten
⅔ cup milk
1 pound frankfurters

1. About 20 minutes before frying, fill a deep sauce-pan one half to two thirds full with cooking oil. Heat slowly to 365°F.
2. Sift together flour, sugar, salt, baking powder, garlic salt, and pepper. Mix in cornmeal.
3. Cut in shortening with pastry blender or two knives until pieces are the size of small peas.
4. Mix egg and milk together thoroughly.
5. Make a well in center of dry ingredients. Add egg mixture and stir until batter is well blended. Using a spatula, spread each frankfurter with batter so that it is evenly coated.
6. Deep-fry only as many coated frankfurters at one time as will float uncrowded one layer deep in fat. Fry 2 or 3 minutes or until golden brown. Turn with a fork as they rise to the surface. Drain over fat before removing to absorbent paper. Insert wooden skewers into one end of each frank.

8 to 10 servings

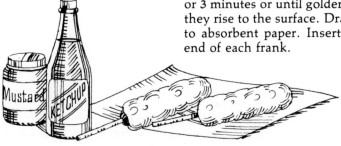

Tomato Salad

Must be prepared ahead of time, so start early. Tomatoes, peppers, onion, and celery marinate in their own juices, and a tangy dressing is added just before serving.

5 or 6 ripe tomatoes, sliced
½ cup chopped green
   pepper
½ cup chopped sweet
   Spanish onion
1 cup chopped celery
   hearts
   Confectioners' sugar
   Salt
1 tablespoon cider vinegar
3 tablespoons salad oil

1. Spread the bottom of a 1-quart earthenware casse-role with a layer of the tomato slices.
2. Mix the chopped pepper, onion, and celery and sprinkle a layer of the mixture over the tomatoes. Sprinkle sugar and salt over all. Start again with a tomato layer, a layer of chopped vegetables, and lightly sprinkle with sugar and salt; repeat in this order until the dish is full, ending with a tomato layer.
3. Cover and place in the refrigerator overnight, or at least 6 hours before serving. This will give the vegetables time to draw their own juice.
4. Just before serving, mix 1 tablespoon cider vinegar with 3 tablespoons of salad oil. Pour over tomato casserole. Serve the salad, over which you drizzle a little extra of the natural juices from the bottom of the bowl.

8 servings

IOWA

Country Fried Potatoes

6 slices pan-fried bacon
6 potatoes, cooked and
    chilled
¼ cup bacon drippings
¾ teaspoon salt
½ teaspoon paprika
⅛ teaspoon pepper

1. Fry bacon; drain on absorbent paper.
2. Peel and slice cooked potatoes.
3. Return ¼ cup bacon drippings to skillet; add potato slices to skillet. Sprinkle with a mixture of salt, paprika, and pepper.
4. Cook potatoes over medium heat, turning only occasionally, until potatoes are well browned.
5. Crumble bacon and mix with potatoes just before serving.

6 servings

Apple Fritters

From the Ox Yoke Inn, Amana, Iowa. Apple rings coated with batter resemble doughnuts when fried. Especially delicious with a generous sprinkling of confectioners' sugar.

1 cup all-purpose flour
2 tablespoons sugar
¼ teaspoon salt
⅔ cup milk
2 eggs, separated
2 tablespoons butter,
    melted
6 large ripe apples, pared
    and cored
3 tablespoons lemon juice
    Fat for deep frying
    heated to 365°F

1. Combine flour, sugar, and salt in a bowl; mix well. Add a mixture of milk, egg yolks, and melted butter; beat with electric or hand rotary beater until smooth.
2. Beat egg whites until stiff, not dry, peaks are formed and fold into batter.
3. Cut apples into ½-inch slices; toss with the lemon juice. Coat each slice with batter.
4. Fry in heated fat until nicely browned. Drain and sprinkle generously with **confectioners' sugar.**

About 8 servings

Rhubarb-Custard Pie

1 unbaked 9-inch pastry
    shell
3 eggs
1 cup sugar
½ cup milk
1 pound fresh rhubarb,
    trimmed, washed, and
    cut in ½-inch pieces*

1. Thoroughly prick pastry shell with a fork. Bake pastry shell at 450°F for 4 minutes.
2. Using a wire whisk, rotary, or electric beater, beat the eggs and sugar together in a deep bowl for 4 to 5 minutes, or until the mixture forms a pale yellow ribbon when it falls from the beaters.
3. Add the milk and beat the mixture until the milk is thoroughly absorbed.
4. Spread the rhubarb evenly in the pastry shell and pour the egg-milk mixture over it.
5. Bake at 350°F 25 to 30 minutes, or until the custard is firm and a knife inserted in the center comes out clean.
6. Cool the pie to room temperature before serving.

One 9-inch pie

*2 cups of frozen rhubarb pieces may be used.

Miniature Kolaches

1 cake (⅝ or ³/₅ ounce)
  compressed yeast
1 cup half-and-half,
  scalded and cooled
½ teaspoon sugar
3 cups sifted all-purpose
  flour
⅛ teaspoon salt
1 cup butter, chilled
4 egg yolks
¼ cup sugar
2 teaspoons grated lemon
  peel
1 can (12 ounces) prune or
  apricot filling

1. Soften yeast in lukewarm half-and-half. Stir in ½ teaspoon sugar and let stand 15 minutes.
2. Blend flour and salt. Cut in butter with a pastry blender or two knives until particles are the size of rice kernels; set aside.
3. Beat egg yolks and ¼ cup sugar together until very thick. Beat in cream mixture and lemon peel.
4. Make a well in the center of the flour-butter mixture; add egg yolk mixture and blend well. Chill dough overnight.
5. Put half of the chilled dough on a lightly floured surface; roll ¼ inch thick. Cut out rounds with a lightly floured 1½-inch cookie cutter; transfer to ungreased cookie sheets.
6. Make a slight depression in the center of each round and fill with about 1 teaspoonful of filling. Repeat, using remaining dough.
7. Cover and allow to stand in a warm place 10 to 15 minutes.
8. Bake at 350°F 15 to 20 minutes, or until lightly browned. Remove cookies to wire racks.

About 7 dozen kolaches

Favorite Vanilla Ice Cream

2 cups milk
1 cup sugar
1 tablespoon flour
¼ teaspoon salt
3 egg yolks, slightly
  beaten
2 cups cream
2 teaspoons vanilla extract

1. Scald milk in double boiler over simmering water.
2. Combine sugar, flour, and salt; mix well. Add gradually to milk, stirring constantly, and cook over direct heat 5 minutes. Remove from heat and vigorously stir about 3 tablespoons of hot mixture into egg yolks. Immediately stir into hot mixture in top of double boiler. Return to heat and cook over simmering water 10 minutes, stirring constantly until mixture coats a metal spoon. Remove from heat and cool.
3. Stir in cream and vanilla extract. Chill in refrigerator.
4. For dasher-type freezer, fill chilled container two-thirds full with ice cream mixture. Cover tightly. Set into freezer tub and, alternating layers, fill with 8 parts crushed ice and 1 part rock salt. Turn handle slowly 5 minutes. Turn rapidly until handle becomes very difficult to turn (about 15 minutes). Remove dasher. Pack down ice cream and cover with waxed paper. Put lid on top again and fill opening for dasher with cork. Repack freezer in ice, using 4 parts ice and 1 part rock salt. Cover with heavy paper or cloth. Let ripen 2 to 3 hours.

About 1½ quarts ice cream

IOWA

Iowa Corn Relish

8 ears fresh corn (about 4 cups corn kernels)
2 cups finely chopped young green cabbage (about ½ small head)
1¼ cups diced sweet red peppers (2 medium peppers)
4 cups finely chopped celery (including edible portion of root and tender leaves)
1 cup finely chopped onion (1 large onion)
1 large clove garlic, minced
1 cup sugar
1 tablespoon salt
1 tablespoon dry mustard
1½ teaspoons celery seed
1 teaspoon turmeric
¼ teaspoon cayenne pepper
2 cups vinegar
2 to 3 tablespoons flour (optional)
½ cup water (optional)

1. Cut kernels from corn.
2. Put corn and cabbage, red peppers, celery, onion, and garlic in a large heavy saucepot or kettle.
3. Combine vegetables and a mixture of sugar, salt, dry mustard, celery seed, turmeric, and cayenne pepper. Stir in vinegar and mix well.
4. Bring mixture to boiling over medium heat; reduce heat and simmer, uncovered, 15 to 20 minutes. (Avoid overcooking. Celery should be crisp-tender.)
5. While relish is cooking, wash and sterilize four 1-pint jars and covers.
6. If consistency of relish is too thin after 20 minutes of cooking, stir in a smooth blend of flour and water. Cook and stir 2 minutes, or until relish is slightly thicker.
7. Quickly ladle into hot clean jars and seal immediately, following manufacturer's directions.
8. Process in boiling water bath 15 minutes.

4 pints relish

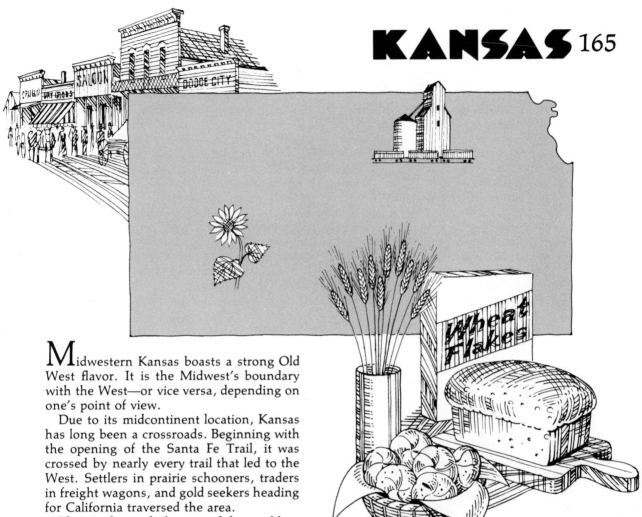

KANSAS

Midwestern Kansas boasts a strong Old West flavor. It is the Midwest's boundary with the West—or vice versa, depending on one's point of view.

Due to its midcontinent location, Kansas has long been a crossroads. Beginning with the opening of the Santa Fe Trail, it was crossed by nearly every trail that led to the West. Settlers in prairie schooners, traders in freight wagons, and gold seekers heading for California traversed the area.

The steady tread of oxen and the rumbling of heavy wagons are now sounds of the past. But in several towns along the old trail routes one can still catch a glimpse of life as it was when the pioneers were forging westward.

Guest ranches and resorts allow visitors to be transported back in time. One company actually conducts overland wagon train treks, retracing old Kansas trails for tourists. Guests "hit the trail" in covered wagons and pioneer costume and enjoy overnight camping as the wagons circle under the stars. One of the highlights of the trip is hearty prairie food, sometimes cooked over a campfire. Typical fare might be stews or chowders, corn-on-the-cob, biscuits, and pie.

Another facet of frontier life was the "wild 'n' wooly" cowtowns like Wichita, Abilene, and Dodge City. When the railroads reached

Kansas in the 1870s these towns became the destination of thundering Texas trail herds. Today, replicas of frontier streets recreate those cattle drivin', gun slingin' days.

In eastern Kansas are the original "tall grass" prairies. Though forests as normally defined don't really exist in Kansas, woodlots do contain oak, black walnut, and hickory trees. And the rustle of cottonwoods along creek banks is a familiar sound.

Here early settlers supplemented meager supplies by gathering wild fruits, berries, nuts, and mushrooms until they could plant gardens and fields. Among the first food crops were corn, pumpkins, root vegetables, green beans, apples, cherries, and rhubarb.

In central and western Kansas are the vast

KANSAS

wheat lands that have earned the title of "the nation's bread basket" for the state. Hard red winter wheat was introduced by Russian Mennonites after the Civil War. It replaced softer eastern varieties and revolutionized the state's agriculture, making possible the sea of golden wheat that now stretches into the horizon at harvest time.

The raising of livestock—cattle, hogs, sheep, and lambs—also plays a key role in Kansas agriculture. The flat, nearly treeless, short-grass high plains of western Kansas are well suited to grazing.

When the state was opened for settlement most of the new residents came from New England, other eastern states, and Missouri. Later they were joined by Civil War veterans and European immigrants. Kansas has never claimed a large foreign-born population, but notable ethnic groups have been the Germans, Russian Mennonites, Irish, English, Swedes, and French.

Many pioneer foods were adapted from eastern recipes. For example, New Englanders brought their love of pie, and prairie homemakers invented substitute fillings when fruits and other familiar ingredients were not obtainable. Dried apples were substituted for fresh apples. And when those ran out, they made "mock apple" pies from soda crackers or potatoes soaked in vinegar!

Kansas's homogeneous population and largely rural life style account for its basically "meat and potatoes" approach to food. And the meat is usually the Kansas favorite, beef.

Dried Beef Tastees

Savory cream cheese balls are rolled in snipped dried beef—the modern, commercial version of the pioneers' jerked meat.

Flavor **cream cheese** with a small amount of **prepared horseradish.** Roll into small balls. Then roll and press balls in **minced dried beef.** Insert wooden or plastic picks.

Dwight D. Eisenhower's Beef Stew

President Eisenhower's deft hand with a frying pan, stew pot, or soup kettle was well known.

3 pounds prime beef round
½ cup cooking oil
2 cans beef bouillon
1 can water
2 teaspoons salt
¼ teaspoon pepper
1 pound small Irish
    potatoes
½ bunch carrots (2 or 3
    medium)
6 small onions
2 large tomatoes, peeled
    and chopped
1 bouquet garni
¼ cup butter
2 tablespoons flour
1 tablespoon cornstarch

1. Cut beef into 1½-inch cubes and brown in cooking oil. Add bouillon, water, salt, and pepper; simmer, covered, until meat is tender.

2. Add the vegetables, except tomatoes, and a bouquet garni (1 bay leaf, 1 whole clove, 2 peppercorns, pinch of thyme, and a bruised clove of garlic tied in a cheesecloth bag). Simmer again until vegetables are tender (about 30 minutes). Stir in tomatoes and heat thoroughly.

3. Strain off 1 cup of liquid and thicken it with a mixture of butter, flour, and cornstarch.

4. Bring stew to boiling and slowly add the stock, stirring constantly; boil 1 to 2 minutes and simmer 10 minutes longer. Remove bouquet garni before serving.

8 servings

Grilled Beef Tenderloin

2 envelopes cheese-garlic
    salad dressing mix
¼ cup salad oil
1 beef tenderloin (3 to 4
    pounds)

1. Blend salad dressing mix with oil.
2. Brush tenderloin generously with dressing mixture.
Place the meat on a greased grill 4 to 6 inches from the
coals.
3. Grill 25 to 35 minutes, or until the tenderloin is done
as desired, turning frequently so that the meat cooks
and browns evenly on all sides.
4. To serve, cut into thin slices.

6 to 8 servings

Flank Steak with Filbert Stuffing

2 tablespoons butter or
    margarine
¼ cup chopped filberts
2 cups ½-inch bread cubes
3 tablespoons chopped
    onion
½ cup diced celery
½ teaspoon salt
⅛ teaspoon pepper
¼ to ½ teaspoon poultry
    seasoning
⅓ to ½ cup hot water
1 flank steak (about 1
    pound)
½ to 1 tablespoon
    shortening or
    drippings
    Beef broth (or hot water)

1. Heat butter in a heavy 8- or 10-inch skillet; add and
sauté filberts until lightly browned. Remove nuts with
slotted spoon and toss with the bread cubes.
2. Add onion and celery to the fat in skillet and cook,
stirring occasionally, 3 to 5 minutes.
3. Toss salt, pepper, poultry seasoning, and hot water
along with bread cubes.
4. Spread stuffing over flank steak; roll and tie securely. Brown roll well on all sides in hot skillet with
shortening. Add a small amount of beef broth. Cover
skillet and simmer until meat is tender, adding additional liquid if needed. Remove meat roll to hot platter
and slice to serve. If desired, meat juice in skillet may
be thickened for gravy.

3 or 4 servings

Picnic Bean Salad

4 cans (15 ounces each)
    kidney beans, drained
8 hard-cooked eggs, diced
2 cups diced celery
1⅓ cups pickle relish
1 cup chopped onion
2 cups (8 ounces)
    shredded sharp
    Cheddar cheese
2 cups dairy sour cream
    Lettuce

1. Mix kidney beans, eggs, celery, pickle relish, onion,
and cheese in a large bowl. Add sour cream and toss
lightly together; chill.
2. Serve on lettuce and garnish with additional hard-
cooked egg, if desired.

About 20 servings

Potluck Potatoes

4 medium-large potatoes,
   pared (about 1½
   pounds)
¼ pound sharp Cheddar
   cheese, shredded
½ medium onion, grated
   (about 2 tablespoons)
¾ teaspoon salt
⅛ teaspoon pepper
1 tablespoon butter
1½ cups milk

1. Cook potatoes in a small amount of boiling salted water 15 minutes; remove and cool. When cool enough to handle, finely shred potatoes (should be about 4 cups).
2. Mix potatoes, cheese, onion, salt, and pepper; turn into a greased 1½-quart casserole or a 10×6½×1¾-inch baking dish. Dot with butter. Pour milk over all.
3. Bake at 300°F 2 hours, or until milk is absorbed and top is browned.

6 servings

Basic White Bread

5½ to 6 cups flour
2 packages active dry
   yeast
2 tablespoons sugar
2 teaspoons salt
1 cup milk
1 cup water
2 tablespoons oil
   Oil or butter

Quick Mix Method
1. Combine 2 cups flour, yeast, sugar, and salt in a large mixing bowl.
2. Heat milk, water, and 2 tablespoons oil in a saucepan over low heat until warm (120° to 130°F).
3. Add liquid to flour mixture; beat on high speed of electric mixer until smooth, about 3 minutes. Gradually stir in more flour to make a soft dough.
4. Turn onto lightly floured surface and knead until smooth and elastic (5 to 10 minutes).
5. Cover dough with bowl or pan; let rest 20 minutes.
6. For two loaves, divide dough in half and roll out two 14×7-inch rectangles; for one loaf roll out to 16×8-inch rectangle.
7. Roll up from narrow side, pressing dough into roll at each turn. Press ends to seal and fold under loaf.
8. Place in 2 greased 8×4×2-inch loaf pans or 1 greased 9×5×3-inch loaf pan; brush with oil.
9. Let rise in warm place until double in bulk (30 to 45 minutes).
10. Bake at 400°F 35 to 40 minutes.
11. Remove from pans immediately and brush with oil; cool on wire rack.

One 2-pound loaf
or two 1-pound loaves

Conventional Method
1. Heat milk, sugar, oil, and salt; cool to lukewarm.
2. In a large bowl, sprinkle yeast over warm water (105° to 115°F); stir until dissolved.
3. Add lukewarm milk mixture and 2 cups flour; beat until smooth.
4. Beat in enough additional flour to make a stiff dough.

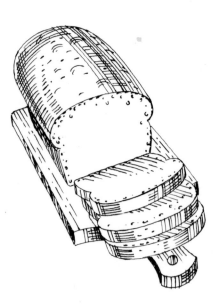

5. Turn out onto lightly floured surface; let rest 10 to 15 minutes. Knead until smooth and elastic (8 to 10 minutes).
6. Place in a greased bowl, turning to grease top. Cover; let rise in warm place until double in bulk (about 1 hour).
7. Punch down. Let rest 15 minutes.
8. Follow same shaping and baking instructions as Quick Mix Method.

Liberal Pancakes

Shrove Tuesday is celebrated as Pancake Day in Liberal, Kansas, when the ladies of the town run a flapjack flippin' race.

1½ cups sifted all-purpose flour
1 tablespoon sugar
1½ teaspoons baking powder
¼ teaspoon salt
2 egg yolks, beaten
1⅓ cups milk
2 tablespoons butter, melted
2 egg whites

1. Combine the flour, sugar, baking powder, and salt in a bowl. Add a mixture of egg yolks and milk; beat until well blended and smooth. Beat in the melted butter.
2. Beat egg whites until stiff, not dry, peaks are formed. Spread over batter and fold together.
3. Lightly grease a preheated griddle (or skillet) only if manufacturer so directs. Pour batter onto griddle from a pitcher or end of a large spoon, in small amounts about 4 inches in diameter, leaving at least 1 inch between cakes. Turn pancakes as they become puffy and full of bubbles. Turn only once.
4. Serve immediately with **butter** and warm **maple syrup.**

About 1 dozen griddlecakes

Spiced Plum Jelly

4 pounds fully ripe tart clingstone plums*
1 cup water
6½ cups sugar
½ teaspoon ground cinnamon
⅛ teaspoon ground allspice
½ bottle liquid fruit pectin
Paraffin

1. Rinse, halve, pit, and crush plums (do not peel). Place in a large saucepan; add the water. Bring to boiling; reduce heat and simmer, covered, 10 minutes.
2. Ladle mixture into a jelly bag, and squeeze out juice. Measure 4 cups of the juice into a very large saucepan. Mix in a blend of sugar and spices.
3. Stir over high heat until mixture comes to a full boil. Immediately stir in fruit pectin and bring to a full rolling boil; boil rapidly 1 minute, stirring constantly.
4. Remove from heat and skim off foam. Pour at once into hot sterilized jelly glasses to within ½ inch of top. Immediately seal with melted paraffin.

About ten 8-ounce glasses jelly

*If using sweet plums or freestone plums, use 3½ cups prepared juice and add ¼ cup lemon juice.

KANSAS

German Molasses Cookies

Spicy and fragrant, these cookies have delighted children for generations.

1 cup butter
1¼ cups light molasses
¾ cup firmly packed light brown sugar
4 cups sifted all-purpose flour
2 teaspoons ground ginger
1 teaspoon baking soda
1 teaspoon salt
1 teaspoon ground cinnamon
½ to ¾ teaspoon ground cloves

1. Melt butter in a saucepan; add molasses and brown sugar and heat until sugar is dissolved, stirring occasionally. Pour into a bowl; cool.
2. Sift remaining ingredients together; add to cooled mixture in fourths, mixing until blended after each addition.
3. Turn dough onto a floured surface and knead until easy to handle, using additional flour if necessary.
4. Wrap in moisture-vaporproof material; refrigerate and allow dough to ripen one or two days.
5. Roll one fourth of dough at a time about ⅛ inch thick on a floured surface; cut with a 3-inch round cutter or fancy cutters. Transfer to ungreased cookie sheets.
6. Bake at 375°F about 10 minutes.

About 8 dozen cookies

Note: For gingerbread men, roll dough ¼ inch thick and cut with a gingerbread-man cutter. Bake about 13 minutes.

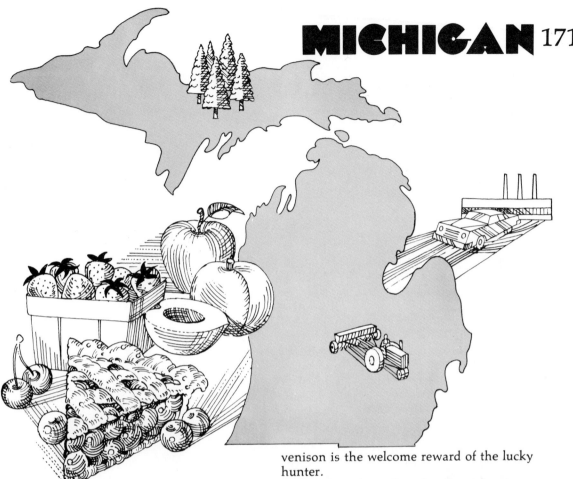

venison is the welcome reward of the lucky hunter.

The "Great Lakes State," Michigan proclaims itself. And justifiably so, for its twin peninsulas are washed by four of the largest bodies of fresh water in the world. Certainly the Great Lakes, thousands of small inland lakes, and miles of streams have influenced Michigan's life style and economy through shipping, recreation, and the attendant tourism.

A food resource taken directly from the cold waters is fish—numerous varieties including bass, smelt, rainbow and lake trout, and more recently salmon, transplanted from the Pacific. Frogs' legs are another gift from the waters. Michigan preference for these delicacies of the marshlands dates from the days of the earliest French explorers.

Dense woodlands and mines of iron and copper share the rugged Upper Peninsula. The forests yield timber, fur-bearing animals, and game. Deer are plentiful, and

Not the mines, but the Cornish miners have contributed another Upper Peninsula specialty, the pasty. The large, sturdy pastry turnovers are filled with cubed beef (or venison), potato, onion, and turnip, rutabaga, or carrot. Pasties migrated with the miners from Cornwall in southwestern England, where it was learned long ago that they would stay hot for hours if wrapped at once in a napkin or bandana and newspaper before being tucked into the lunch pail, or perhaps, the picnic basket.

Across the mighty Mackinac Bridge lower Michigan presents a different picture: one of great industry and productive farming. Indeed, the nation runs on Detroit's wheels, and the surrounding states are supplied with fruits, vegetables, and berries from the fertile southwestern counties.

Lake Michigan tempers the climate of the southern peninsula, enhancing the productivity of the bountiful orchards and fields.

Apples, peaches, blueberries, strawberries, celery, and beans: all are famous beyond the eastern shores of Lake Michigan where they grow in such abundance. Cherries are of primary importance, for Michigan grows more of this tart red fruit than any other state. Local festivals and the multitude of cherry recipes attest to this fact.

A look at Michigan's culinary traditions can't be properly concluded without a salute to the Dutch who settled the area known as "Little Holland." Dutch favorites like Fat Balls (tiny doughnut puffs), apple cake, and green pea soup are almost as well known as the annual Tulip Time celebration, and are especially popular then.

Green Pea Soup (Groene Erwten Soep)

1 cup dried green peas
3 quarts water
1 small pig's foot
⅓ celery root
1 leek
1 onion
1 slice bacon, fried and
    chopped
2 ounces fresh smoked
    sausage, fried
Pepper and salt to taste

1. Soak peas overnight in cold water.
2. In the morning cook peas in 3 quarts of fresh water with remaining ingredients. When the peas are tender remove from heat and add 1 cup of cold water quickly. This helps to soften the skins.
3. Purée everything except the pig's foot and season with pepper and salt.

4 servings

Note: If desired, use veal knuckle instead of pig's foot.

Fried Smelts

2 dozen smelts
1 egg, beaten
1 tablespoon water
Fine bread crumbs
Fat for deep frying heated
    to 360°F

1. Clean the smelts, leaving on the heads and tails; rinse and pat dry.
2. Sprinkle with **salt** and **pepper;** shake in a bag with **flour;** dip in a mixture of the egg and water; roll in crumbs. Let stand about 15 minutes.
3. Fry smelts without crowding in heated fat 3 to 4 minutes. Drain on absorbent paper.
4. Garnish with **parsley;** serve with **tartar sauce.**

4 servings

Peninsula Pasties

Pastry a bit less flaky and fragile than that desirable for pies makes these hardy enough to eat "out of hand." And they're hearty fare for lunch boxes, picnics, or supper at home, accompanied by pickles and/or ketchup.

2 cups sifted all-purpose
    flour
2 teaspoons salt
½ teaspoon baking powder

1. For pastry, sift flour, 1 teaspoon of salt, and baking powder together into a large bowl. Cut in shortening until particles are the size of small peas.
2. Sprinkle water over mixture, a tablespoonful at a

MICHIGAN

⅔ cup shortening
4 to 6 tablespoons cold
  water
1 pound beef round steak,
  cut in ½-inch cubes
2½ cups diced pared potato
  (about 3 medium
  potatoes)
½ cup diced turnip,
  rutabaga, or carrot
½ cup finely chopped
  onion
¼ teaspoon ground black
  pepper

time, mixing lightly with a fork. Add only enough water to hold pastry together.

3. Divide dough into 6 equal parts, shaping into balls. Cover and chill while preparing filling.

4. For filling, stir together steak, potatoes, turnip, onion, remaining 1 teaspoon salt, and pepper.

5. On a lightly floured surface, roll out one ball of dough into a round about 8 inches in diameter. Using an 8-inch pie plate or pot lid as a guide, trim dough to make a neat circle.

6. Place about 1 cup meat filling across center of pastry circle.

7. Fold up one side of pastry over long side of filling. Then turn up opposite side so pastry edges meet as in "drug store wrap." Press edges of dough tightly together at one end; continue pressing edges together to make a seam about ½ inch wide along top of pastry; seal other end. Fold seam over on itself and crimp with fingers. (Pastry should be torpedo-shaped, pointed at both ends.)

8. Transfer pasty to an ungreased baking sheet with a spatula.

9. Repeat steps 5,6,7 and 8 to roll, fill and shape remaining pasties.

10. Bake at 375°F 40 to 50 minutes, or until pastry is golden brown.

Six 8-inch pasties

Honey-Glazed Filbert Roast Chicken

½ package herb-seasoned
  stuffing mix (2 cups)
1 cup toasted filberts,
  chopped
½ cup chopped celery
1 chicken liver, finely
  chopped
½ cup butter or margarine,
  melted
½ cup water
1 roaster-fryer or capon,
  about 5 pounds
½ cup honey
2 tablespoons soy sauce
1 teaspoon grated orange
  peel
2 tablespoons orange juice

1. Combine stuffing mix with the filberts, celery, chicken liver, butter, and water; toss lightly. Stuff cavity of chicken with the mixture, then tie chicken legs and wings with cord to hold close to body.

2. Place chicken, breast up, on rack in a shallow roasting pan. Roast at 325°F 2½ to 3 hours, or until chicken tests done. (The thickest part of drumstick feels soft when pressed with fingers and meat thermometer registers 180° to 185°F.)

3. Meanwhile, combine honey, soy sauce, and orange peel and juice. Brush chicken frequently with the mixture during last hour of roasting.

6 servings

MICHIGAN

Fried Frog Legs

8 pairs large skinned frog legs
½ cup all-purpose flour
1 teaspoon salt
⅛ teaspoon pepper
¼ cup butter or margarine

1. Wash frog legs. Soak legs in salted water (1 tablespoon per 2 quarts water) 15 minutes; drain.
2. Coat legs evenly with a mixture of flour, salt, and pepper, by shaking 2 or 3 at a time in a plastic bag containing flour mixture.
3. Heat butter in a heavy skillet. Add legs and cook over medium heat about 20 minutes, or until legs are golden brown and tender when pierced with a fork. Brown all sides by turning legs as necessary with two spoons or tongs. Drain legs on absorbent paper; set aside and keep warm.
4. Serve with a blend of **½ cup mayonnaise, 2 teaspoons each of chopped chervil, chives, tarragon leaves,** and **parsley.** Garnish with **lemon wedges.**

4 servings

Braised Celery

2 large Spanish onions
Salt and pepper
2 tablespoons chopped parsley
¼ cup butter or margarine
4 cups diagonally sliced celery, cut ½ inch thick
2 cups meat broth or consommé
2 tablespoons water
1 tablespoon cornstarch

1. Peel, thinly slice, and spread onions evenly in bottom of a 1½-quart casserole or baking dish. Sprinkle with salt, pepper, and parsley.
2. Heat butter in a saucepan or skillet; add celery and cook over medium heat until lightly browned, stirring occasionally.
3. Heat meat broth in a saucepan. Combine water and cornstarch to form a smooth paste.
4. Stir paste into the broth, cooking over high heat until mixture comes to boiling. Cook and stir 3 to 5 minutes, or until sauce is thickened and smooth. Combine with the partially cooked celery. Spoon over the onions in casserole.
5. Bake at 325°F about 1 hour.

6 to 8 servings

Sparkling Fresh Peach Mold

2 envelopes unflavored gelatin
¼ cup sugar
¾ cup water
3 cups white grape juice
¼ cup lemon juice
4 medium-size ripe peaches, peeled and sliced
1½ cups red raspberries or blueberries

1. Blend gelatin and sugar in a saucepan. Mix in water; stir over low heat until gelatin and sugar are dissolved.
2. Remove from heat and stir in the grape juice and lemon juice. Chill until mixture is the consistency of thick, unbeaten egg white.
3. Arrange half of the sliced peaches and raspberries in a 1½-quart ring mold. Spoon half of the chilled gelatin over fruit. Arrange the remaining fruit in the mold and spoon remaining gelatin over fruit. Chill until firm.
4. Unmold onto a chilled serving plate.

About 8 servings

Picnic Pear Nut Bread

2 fresh fully ripe Bartlett
    pears
2 large eggs, beaten
1 cup whole bran
1½ cups sifted all-purpose
    flour
½ cup sugar
1 teaspoon baking powder
½ teaspoon salt
½ teaspoon baking soda
¼ cup soft shortening
½ cup chopped walnuts

1. Core and finely chop unpeeled pears to measure 1¼ cups. Combine with eggs and bran; let stand while preparing remaining ingredients.
2. Sift flour with sugar, baking powder, salt, and soda into mixing bowl. Add shortening and pear-bran mixture; mix until all of flour is moistened. Stir in walnuts. Turn into a well-greased 8½×4½×2½-inch loaf pan. Let stand 20 minutes.
3. Bake at 350°F about 1 hour, or until pick inserted in center comes out clean and dry. Let stand 10 minutes, then turn out onto wire rack to cool. If desired, spread with Lemon-Mint Butter.

1 loaf bread

Lemon-Mint Butter: Beat **1 cup softened butter or margarine** with **1 teaspoon grated lemon peel** and **2 tablespoons chopped fresh mint leaves.**

Fat Balls (Oliebollen)

¼ cup shortening
½ cup sugar
1 egg, well beaten
3 cups lukewarm potato
    water
2 cakes compressed yeast
1 cup currants
1 cup raisins
6 to 7 cups sifted flour
1 teaspoon salt

1. Cream shortening with sugar. Add egg, potato water, and yeast. Mix well and add currants, raisins, and flour sifted with salt.
2. Let rise until light. Shape into small balls, using about a teaspoon of dough for each.
3. Fry in hot deep fat (365°F) until brown. Serve with **brown sugar.**

About 72 balls

Cherry Cobbler

4 cups (two 16-ounce cans)
    tart red cherries,
    drained
¾ cup sugar
2 tablespoons flour
1 teaspoon grated lemon
    peel
½ teaspoon cinnamon
1 tablespoon lemon juice
    Butter or margarine
1 can (8 ounces)
    refrigerated biscuits

1. Put one half of drained cherries in a 1½-quart casserole. Sprinkle with one half of a mixture of sugar, flour, lemon peel, and cinnamon. Drizzle one half of lemon juice over cherries and dot with butter.
2. Add remaining cherries to casserole and top with remaining sugar mixture, drizzle with lemon juice, and dot with butter.
3. Bake at 350°F 20 minutes.
4. Remove cherries from oven; set temperature control of oven at 450°F. Arrange biscuits over top of hot cherries. Return casserole to oven.
5. Bake at 450°F 10 to 15 minutes, or until biscuits are lightly browned.
6. Serve warm with **cream.**

6 servings

Dutch Apple Cake

2 cups sifted all-purpose
   flour
3 tablespoons sugar
1 tablespoon baking
   powder
1 teaspoon salt
1 cup chilled whipping
   cream
3 medium-size apples,
   washed, quartered,
   cored, and pared
¼ cup sugar
½ teaspoon ground
   cinnamon
2 tablespoons butter or
   margarine, melted

1. Sift flour, 3 tablespoons sugar, baking powder, and salt together into a bowl.
2. Beat cream until it piles softly. With a fork, lightly blend whipped cream into dry ingredients. Turn into a greased 9×9×2-inch baking pan and spread evenly.
3. Cut each apple quarter into 3 slices. Arrange slices in parallel rows on batter; press into batter. Combine ¼ cup sugar and cinnamon and sprinkle evenly over apples. Pour melted butter over top.
4. Bake at 400°F about 25 minutes, or until cake tests done. Cut into squares.

9 servings

Blueberry Tarts

¾ cup dairy sour cream
1 tablespoon
   confectioners' sugar
1 package instant lemon
   pudding mix
1¼ cups cold milk
6 baked Nutmeg-Sour
   Cream Tart Shells
1 pint fresh blueberries

1. Blend the sour cream and confectioners' sugar.
2. Prepare the pudding mix according to directions on package, using the 1¼ cups milk. Fold in sour cream mixture.
3. Remove tart shells from pans; spoon about ⅓ cup of the pudding into each shell and top with blueberries.

6 tarts

Nutmeg-Sour Cream Tart Shells

Pie crust mix for a
   1-crust pie
1½ teaspoons sugar
1 teaspoon ground
   nutmeg
3 tablespoons dairy sour
   cream

1. Blend the pie crust mix, sugar, and nutmeg in a bowl. Prepare pastry following directions on package, substituting the sour cream for the liquid. Shape pastry into a ball and flatten on a lightly floured surface.
2. Roll pastry to about ¹⁄₁₆-inch thickness and cut 6 rounds about ½ inch larger than overall size of a 3½-inch tart pan. Carefully fit rounds into 6 tart pans without stretching. Fold excess pastry under at edge and flute or press with a fork. Prick bottoms and sides of shells with fork.
3. Bake at 425°F about 8 minutes, or until lightly browned. Cool. Carefully remove from pans.

Six 3½-inch tart shells

Meat-Stuffed Manicotti, 216

Minnesota . . . a land of legends. Its Indian heritage provided the inspiration for Longfellow's "The Song of Hiawatha."

Another Indian legacy is wild rice, one of our native delicacies most prized by gourmets. Though some cultivation and mechanical harvesting have been accomplished, much wild rice is still gathered by Indians poling through the water in canoes, just as it has been for centuries.

The North Woods region is also the setting for many Paul Bunyan stories. The legendary logger and his big blue ox, Babe, were the subjects of some of America's tallest, most colorful folk tales.

It is said that when Paul was hungry he would reach for an enormous frying pan and holler, "Grease it up, boys!" Then six lumberjacks with slabs of bacon strapped to their boots would skate across the skillet!

Like many folk legends, the Bunyan yarns are closely associated with food. The mythical lumber camp's cook was Hot Biscuit Slim, who frequently whipped up giant batches of flapjacks, one of Paul's favorite foods.

The loggers were preceded in the North Woods by the French *voyageurs* who paddled across the waters in canoes searching for beaver and other fur-bearing animals. Their diet was limited to a stew of dried peas or beans with salt pork, plus fish and game and whatever wild berries could be found. Bread, if available at all, was a simple mixture of flour and water, baked in a skillet.

Minnesota's northern wilderness still rewards the skillful angler and hunter. The state claims to be "America's fresh water fishing capital." The streams and thousands of lakes do yield an amazing variety of fish, and waterfowl are plentiful, too.

The farmlands were first settled by other Americans, Germans, and Irish. But it was the Scandinavians migrating to Minnesota after the Civil War who left the most enduring imprint.

Lamb Stew, Continental, 222;
Stuffed Lamb Breasts, 221

MINNESOTA

Though Scandinavians settled throughout the upper Mississippi Valley, they were most influential in the cultural development of Minnesota. Here they found a country much like their homeland; its pine-forested beauty was splashed with lakes and the climate and soil were similar.

Scandinavian homemakers were, and are, famous for their cooking skills. And Minnesota cooks display a real awareness of their culinary heritage.

The traditional smorgasbord, with its assortment of salads, fish, cold meats, cheeses, vegetables, and breads, is usually scaled down for at-home service and is limited to a selection of appetizers. Swedes, Norwegians, Danes, and Finns have individual ways of preparing that universal favorite, meatballs. Dairy products are skillfully employed by all in a tempting array of salads, pastries, puddings, and desserts.

Scandinavians celebrate Christmas with great enthusiasm; it's a time for special recipes using the finest ingredients. Fragrant breads and delectable, buttery cookies are the hallmarks of holiday festivities.

From the rugged arrowhead country of the northeast, through the iron fields and farming regions to the Indian pipestone quarries in the southwest, Minnesota is dominated by its "North Star" spirit of energy and excitement.

Planked Fish Fillet Dinner

1 large fish fillet, weighing about 10 ounces (such as sole, flounder, whitefish, lake trout, or haddock)
1 tablespoon melted butter or margarine
Salt and pepper
Seasoned mashed potatoes
2 broiled tomato halves
4 broiled mushroom caps
Lemon slices
Watercress or parsley

1. If fish is frozen, let thaw on refrigerator shelf or at room temperature. Brush seasoned plank lightly with melted butter.
2. Place fish fillet on plank and brush with remaining butter. Sprinkle lightly with salt and pepper. Bake at 350°F for 20 minutes, or just until fish flakes easily.
3. Remove from oven, and turn oven temperature up to 450°F. Pipe a border of hot mashed potatoes along sides of fish.
4. Return to oven for 10 minutes until potatoes are delicately browned. Place tomato halves and mushroom caps on plank. Garnish with lemon slices and watercress. Serve at once.

2 servings

Baked Steak with Wild Rice Dressing

1 package (6 or 6¾ ounces) seasoned long grain and wild rice mix
1½ pounds round steak, cut ½ to ¾ inch thick
¼ cup flour
1 teaspoon salt
¼ teaspoon pepper

1. Cook rice following package directions.
2. While rice is cooking, coat meat evenly with a mixture of ¼ cup flour, salt, and pepper. Put meat on a flat working surface, pound it repeatedly on one side, turn meat, and repeat on other side. Set aside.
3. For dressing, melt butter in a saucepan. Blend in flour. Heat until bubbly. Add ½ cup of beef broth, stirring constantly. Cook and stir until mixture thickens; cook 1 to 2 minutes longer.

2 tablespoons butter or
    margarine
2 teaspoons flour
1 cup beef broth or
    consommé
¼ cup drained canned
    sliced mushrooms
3 tablespoons fat

4. Remove from heat. Stir in the cooked seasoned rice and mushrooms. Pile rice mixture on one half of steak and fold other half over it. Fasten with skewers.
5. Heat fat in a large skillet. Add steak and brown on all sides. Pour remaining broth into skillet; cover.
6. Bake at 325°F about 1 hour, or until meat is tender when pierced with a fork.

About 4 servings

Swedish Meatballs

1 pound ground round
    steak
½ pound ground pork
½ cup mashed potatoes
½ cup fine dry bread
    crumbs
1 egg, beaten
1 teaspoon salt
½ teaspoon brown sugar
¼ teaspoon pepper
¼ teaspoon ground allspice
¼ teaspoon ground nutmeg
⅛ teaspoon ground cloves
⅛ teaspoon ground ginger
½ cup fine dry bread
    crumbs
3 tablespoons butter or
    margarine

1. Lightly mix in a large bowl the ground meats, potatoes, ½ cup crumbs, egg, and a mixture of the salt, brown sugar, pepper, allspice, nutmeg, cloves, and ginger.
2. Shape mixture lightly into small balls. Roll balls in remaining crumbs.
3. Heat the butter in a large heavy skillet. Add the meatballs and brown on all sides; shake pan frequently to brown evenly and to keep balls round. Cook, covered, about 15 minutes, or until meatballs are thoroughly cooked.

About 10 dozen meatballs

Sylte

You'll want to try this superbly seasoned jellied veal loaf.

½ pound veal
½ pound pork
1 pork shank
½ tablespoon salt
6 peppercorns
3 bay leaves
1 teaspoon paprika
1 teaspoon thyme
1 tablespoon lemon juice
1 tablespoon vinegar

1. Place meat in a kettle with water just to cover. Add dry seasonings and simmer slowly for 1½ to 2 hours, or until tender.
2. Remove meat and chop very fine. Strain liquid.
3. Return meat to liquid, add lemon juice and vinegar. Boil about 5 minutes, then pour into mold and cool.
4. When firm, turn out on platter and serve with boiled **sliced beets** soaked in **vinegar**.

4 to 6 servings

MINNESOTA

Danish Glazed Potatoes

Potatoes with a buttery caramel coating are surprisingly good.

2 to 3 pounds small
    potatoes
6 tablespoons sugar
3 tablespoons butter or
    margarine

1. Cook potatoes until almost tender. Drain and peel. Rinse with cold water; dry with absorbent paper.
2. Heat sugar in a heavy light-colored skillet. With back of a wooden spoon, gently keep sugar moving toward center of skillet until it is melted. Heat until syrup is a light golden brown.
3. Stir in butter and heat until butter and sugar are thoroughly blended.
4. Add potatoes and turn them gently to coat; remove from heat and before serving turn them until coated.

About 8 servings

Rutabaga Soufflé

1 cup mashed cooked
    rutabaga
½ cup hot mashed potatoes
1 cup milk
2 tablespoons cornstarch
½ teaspoon salt
1 tablespoon brown sugar
⅛ to ¼ teaspoon ground
    mace
⅛ teaspoon pepper
3 eggs, separated
2 tablespoons fine dry
    bread crumbs
2 tablespoons shredded
    Parmesan cheese
1 tablespoon butter or
    margarine, melted

1. Beat mashed rutabaga and potatoes together; set aside.
2. Blend milk with cornstarch in a saucepan. Bring to boiling over low heat; stir and cook about 3 minutes. Stir in the salt, brown sugar, mace, and pepper.
3. Add the hot mixture gradually to slightly beaten egg yolks, stirring constantly. Beat into mashed vegetables, blending thoroughly.
4. Beat egg whites until stiff, not dry, peaks are formed. Fold into rutabaga mixture. Turn into a 1½-quart casserole.
5. Toss bread crumbs with cheese and butter. Spoon over top of soufflé.
6. Bake at 325°F about 50 minutes, or until a knife comes out clean when inserted halfway between center and edge of casserole. Serve immediately.

About 6 servings

Swedish Pancakes (Plättar)

These are most often enjoyed as a dessert.

1½ cups sifted all-purpose
    flour
3 tablespoons sugar
½ teaspoon salt
3 eggs
2 cups milk

1. Sift flour, sugar, and salt together.
2. Beat the eggs until thick. Blend in the milk and melted butter. Combine egg mixture with the dry ingredients and beat with hand rotary beater until smooth.
3. For each pancake, spoon 1 tablespoon batter into

2 tablespoons butter or margarine, melted

each round of a greased heated platt pan (Swedish pancake pan available in the housewares section of most department stores). Or, if using a griddle or skillet, form pancakes about 3 inches in diameter.

4. Bake over medium heat until lightly browned on bottom. Loosen edges with a spatula, turn, and lightly brown other side.

5. As pancakes are baked, transfer them to a heated plate. Arrange pancakes in a circle, slightly overlapping each other. In center, serve **preserved lingonberries.**

5 dozen 3-inch pancakes

Buckwheat Pancakes

A stack of these hearty cakes would have appealed to Paul Bunyan, we think.

¾ cup buckwheat flour
¾ cup sifted all-purpose flour
2½ tablespoons sugar
1 teaspoon baking soda
½ teaspoon salt
2 eggs
1 cup buttermilk or sour milk
1 tablespoon melted butter or other shortening

1. Mix dry ingredients together. Beat eggs, add buttermilk and butter, then add to dry ingredients gradually, beating to obtain a smooth batter.

2. Drop from a spoon onto a hot greased griddle and brown on both sides.

18 pancakes

Orange Chiffon Cake

The chiffon cake combines the fluffiness of sponge cakes and the richness of butter-type cakes. It was developed in the kitchens of a large Minneapolis-based milling company, one of several to have national headquarters there.

1 cup plus 2 tablespoons sifted cake flour
½ cup sugar
1½ teaspoons baking powder
½ teaspoon salt
¼ cup cooking oil
2 egg yolks
1 tablespoon grated orange peel
⅓ cup orange juice
½ cup (4 to 5) egg whites
¼ teaspoon cream of tartar
¼ cup sugar

1. Sift flour, ½ cup sugar, baking powder, and salt together into a bowl. Make a well in center and add the oil, egg yolks, and orange peel and juice in order listed. Beat until smooth; set aside.

2. Beat egg whites with cream of tartar until frothy. Gradually add the ¼ cup sugar, continuing to beat until stiff peaks are formed.

3. Slowly pour egg yolk mixture over entire surface of beaten egg white. Gently fold together until just blended. Turn batter into an ungreased 9×9×2-inch baking pan.

4. Bake at 350°F 30 to 35 minutes, or until cake tests done.

5. Immediately invert pan and cool cake completely before removing from pan.

One 9-inch square cake

MINNESOTA

MINNESOTA

Swedish Fruit Soup

This chilled "soup" may be served for breakfast or as a first course or dessert for dinner.

1 cup dried apricots
¾ cup dried apples
½ cup dried peaches
½ cup prunes
½ cup dark seedless raisins
2 quarts water
¼ cup sugar
3 tablespoons
   quick-cooking tapioca
1 piece (3 inch) stick
   cinnamon
1 teaspoon grated orange
   peel
1 cup red raspberry fruit
   syrup

1. Rinse dried fruits with cold water; remove pits from prunes. Place fruits in a large kettle with the water; cover and allow to soak 2 to 3 hours.
2. Add the sugar, tapioca, cinnamon, and orange peel to the fruits. Bring mixture to boiling; cover and simmer 1 hour, or until fruit is tender.
3. Stir in syrup; cool, then chill thoroughly.
4. Serve with **whipped cream** and **slivered blanched almonds.**

About 3 quarts soup

Swedish Punch (Glögg)

A potent beverage guaranteed to warm the holidays. Wherever Swedes are during the Christmas season they traditionally raise glasses of steaming glögg.

1 bottle (25 ounces)
   Aquavit
1 bottle (25 ounces) claret
1 cup (about 5 ounces)
   blanched almonds
6 cinnamon sticks (2½
   inches each)
1 cup (about 4 ounces)
   dark seedless raisins
6 pieces candied orange or
   lemon peel
12 whole cloves
12 cardamom seeds, peeled
1 cup lump sugar

1. Bring all ingredients except sugar slowly to boiling in a large saucepan. Reduce heat and simmer 10 minutes.
2. Remove from heat. Put sugar into a large sieve. Place over saucepan. Ladle some of mixture from saucepan over sugar. Ignite the sugar and continue to ladle the liquid over the sugar until sugar is completely melted. The liquid should be flaming. (If necessary, extinguish the flame by placing cover over pan.)
3. Serve hot in mugs or punch glasses. Be sure there are some raisins and almonds in each serving.

10 to 15 servings

Note: Glögg may be prepared days in advance and stored in bottles. When ready to serve, heat thoroughly (do not boil).

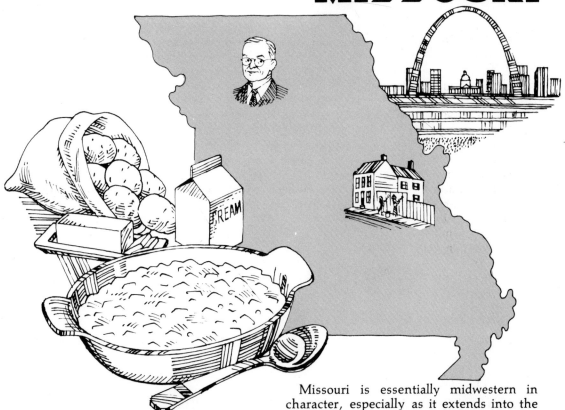

Tom Sawyer and Huckleberry Finn, Mark Twain's youthful adventurers, are timeless reminders of the delights of growing up in Missouri. Twain's nineteenth-century portrait of life on the Mississippi captured a spirit that endures today. His hometown of Hannibal overlooks the mighty river; the nearby islands where Tom and Huck played pirates and the caves they explored beckon still. And visitors enjoy touring Twain's memorabilia-filled boyhood home, bordered by the famous whitewashed fence.

Samuel Clemens (Mark Twain's real name, of course) was an ardent advocate of home-cooked American food. When traveling in Europe he often championed American cooking, and described special dishes—even entire meals—in letters and manuscripts. Among Twain's favorites were beef (preferably a juicy broiled steak), creamed potatoes, cornbreads, biscuits, fruit pies, baked apples with cream, and coffee.

Missouri is essentially midwestern in character, especially as it extends into the Corn Belt in the north and blends into the Kansas wheat fields in the west. The southern counties, particularly in the southeast corner, like their cooking southern style, while the Ozarks have a flavor all their own.

Certain little tricks are identified with country cooks everywhere. Things like flavoring vegetables or breads with bacon, baking pork chops or chicken in milk or cream, and a generally generous use of butter and cream (dating from the time when most families had at least one cow) are universally employed.

Missouri was the nineteenth-century "gateway to the west," now symbolized by the magnificent Gateway Arch on the St. Louis riverfront. Westport Landing (now Kansas City) marked the beginning of several westbound wagon trails, and St. Joseph was the eastern terminus of the famed Pony Express.

The first settlers in the Louisiana Territory were predominately French. In the early

1800s immigrants from the British Isles and Germany swelled the population; the Germans in particular exerted a strong influence on St. Louis food and culture. At about the same time farmers migrated to Missouri from the South.

Missouri has been an important farming state since pioneer times. Today about three fourths of the state's agricultural income derives from livestock: cattle, hogs, dairy products, poultry, and eggs. (Excellent Missouri country-smoked hams are nationally known.) Important field crops are corn, wheat, oats, soybeans, potatoes, apples, melons, and peaches.

Two of the Midwest's most dynamic cities are in Missouri—one on its eastern edge, the other on its western boundary. Old St. Louis was a fur-trading center and steamboat landing. The palatial riverboats that plied the Mississippi between St. Louis and New Orleans were floating examples of antebellum gourmet cuisine.

Kansas City is situated on the great Missouri River, also known as "Old Muddy." Early Kansas City was instrumental in trade with the plains and mountain regions of the West, supplying army posts and the Colorado mines. Modern Kansas City claims important wholesale grain and cattle markets, accompanied by stockyards and meat-packing plants.

To the south of St. Louis and Kansas City are the Ozarks, home of some of America's most colorful folk beliefs and practices. The hills were settled by southern Appalachian mountain people who retain much of their ancestral culture.

The Ozarks, occupying about a third of the state, contain areas of great natural beauty, including huge Lake of the Ozarks and other fine fishing lakes.

Sauerbraten

The famous German spiced pot roast is often served with potato dumplings.

3- to 4-pound beef blade pot roast
1 clove garlic, halved
2 teaspoons salt
¼ teaspoon pepper
2 cups cider vinegar
2 cups water
2 onions, sliced
2 bay leaves
1 teaspoon peppercorns
¼ cup sugar
2 tablespoons lard

1. Rub meat with cut surface of garlic, then with salt and pepper. Put meat and garlic into a deep casserole having a cover.
2. Heat the vinegar, water, onions, bay leaves, peppercorns, and sugar just until boiling; pour over meat and allow to cool. Cover and refrigerate 4 days, turning meat each day.
3. Remove meat; strain and reserve liquid for cooking the meat.
4. Brown meat in heated lard in a Dutch oven, turning to brown evenly. Add half of the reserved liquid; cover and simmer 2 to 3 hours, or until meat is tender, adding additional liquid as needed. Slice meat; serve with Gingershap Gravy, if desired.

6 to 8 servings

Gingersnap Gravy: Stir ¾ **cup crushed gingersnaps** and **1 tablespoon sugar** into cooking liquid in Dutch oven. Simmer 10 minutes; stir occasionally.

Skillet Franks 'n' Noodles

1 pound frankfurters, cut
in half diagonally
½ cup chopped onion
½ teaspoon basil or
oregano leaves,
crushed
2 tablespoons butter or
margarine
1 can (10¾ ounces)
condensed cream of
celery or mushroom
soup
½ cup milk
½ cup chopped canned
tomatoes
2 cups cooked wide
noodles
2 tablespoons chopped
parsley

1. In a skillet, brown frankfurters and cook onion with basil in butter until tender.
2. Stir in remaining ingredients. Heat, stirring occasionally.

4 to 6 servings

Spicy Ham Loaf with Apricot Topping

1½ pounds ground cooked
ham
½ pound ground veal
½ pound ground pork
2 eggs, fork beaten
½ teaspoon salt
⅛ teaspoon black pepper
½ teaspoon ground
nutmeg
½ teaspoon dry mustard
¼ teaspoon ground thyme
¼ cup finely chopped
onion
½ cup finely chopped
green pepper
2 tablespoons finely
chopped parsley
¾ cup soft bread crumbs
¾ cup apple juice
Apricot Topping

1. Combine ground meat with eggs, salt, pepper, nutmeg, dry mustard, and thyme in a large bowl. Add onion, green pepper, and parsley and toss.
2. Add the crumbs and apple juice; mix thoroughly but lightly. Turn into a 9×5×3-inch loaf pan and flatten top.
3. Bake at 350°F 1 hour. Remove from oven; drain and reserve juices. Unmold loaf in a shallow baking pan and spoon some of the juices over loaf. Spoon the topping over loaf; return to oven 30 minutes.
4. Remove loaf to a warm platter.

1 meat loaf

Apricot Topping: Blend ⅔ cup packed light brown sugar, 2 teaspoons cornstarch, 1 teaspoon dry mustard, and 1 teaspoon ground allspice in a small saucepan. Add ⅔ cup apricot nectar, 3 tablespoons lemon juice, and 2 teaspoons cider vinegar. Bring rapidly to boiling and cook about 2 minutes, stirring constantly. Reduce heat and simmer 10 minutes.

About 1¼ cups topping

MISSOURI

Creamed Potatoes

Creamed potatoes were a favorite of Mark Twain's family. We're sure they would have approved of this richly flavored version.

2 pounds (6 or 7 medium) potatoes
2½ cups Medium White Sauce (page 43)

1. Wash, pare, and cook potatoes, covered, in boiling salted water about 20 minutes, or until potatoes are tender when pierced with a fork.
2. Meanwhile, prepare white sauce.
3. Drain potatoes. Peel and cut into ½-inch cubes. Stir potatoes into sauce, being careful not to break cubes.

6 servings

Note: Leftover cooked potatoes may be diced and creamed. If this is done, use 4 cups potatoes to 2 cups Medium White Sauce. Heat together in top of double boiler over simmering water, stirring gently.

Herbed Onions

10 medium-size onions, peeled
1 cup vegetable broth
½ teaspoon salt
1 teaspoon sugar
¼ teaspoon oregano, crushed
¼ teaspoon basil, crushed
¼ teaspoon garlic powder
2 whole cloves
1 large sprig parsley
½ small bay leaf
1 tablespoon olive oil

1. Put onions into a skillet. Add a mixture of the broth and remaining ingredients. Cover tightly and bring to boiling. Reduce heat and simmer until onions are crisp-tender (about 25 minutes).
2. Season with **salt** and **pepper.** Serve hot.

6 to 8 servings

Hot Cinnamon Apples

Another Twain favorite, now dressed up in a cinnamon-spiced sauce.

3 cups sugar
1½ cups water
⅔ cup red cinnamon candies
½ teaspoon red food coloring
6 small tart apples, cored and pared

1. Combine sugar, water, cinnamon candies, and food coloring in a large deep saucepan; bring to boiling, stirring until candies are dissolved.
2. Add apples to syrup and simmer, uncovered, until apples are tender, about 10 minutes; turn frequently. Remove from heat and allow to stand about 20 minutes or until apples are evenly colored, turning frequently.
3. Serve hot as a meat accompaniment.

6 servings

Turnip-Carrot-Cabbage Slaw

1 cup shredded white
    turnip
1 cup shredded carrot
2 cups finely shredded
    cabbage
¼ cup finely chopped onion
¼ cup chopped parsley
¼ teaspoon salt
⅛ teaspoon pepper
3 tablespoons mayonnaise

1. Toss vegetables together gently with a mixture of salt, pepper, and mayonnaise until vegetables are evenly coated.
2. Chill, covered, in refrigerator until ready to serve.

About 6 servings

Corn Dodger

This simple, old-fashioned cornbread was a favorite of westward-bound pioneers.

2 cups cornmeal
1 teaspoon salt
2 teaspoons fat
2 cups boiling water

1. Combine cornmeal, salt, and fat; add boiling water and beat thoroughly. Spread ½ to ¾ inch thick in pie plates.
2. Bake at 400°F 30 minutes, or until crisp and brown.
3. Serve hot with butter, gravy, or stew.

Two 8-inch dodgers

Cornmeal Muffins

¼ cup butter or margarine
1½ cups white cornmeal
½ cup all-purpose flour
1 tablespoon sugar
1 tablespoon baking
    powder
¾ teaspoon salt
1 egg, well beaten
1 cup milk

1. Melt butter and set aside to cool.
2. Mix cornmeal, flour, sugar, baking powder, and salt in a bowl. Make a well in center of dry ingredients.
3. Blend melted butter, egg, and milk. Add all at one time to dry ingredients. Beat with rotary beater until just smooth, being careful not to overmix.
4. Cut against side of bowl with spoon to get enough batter at one time to fill each muffin-pan well two-thirds full. Place spoon in well and push batter off with another spoon or spatula.
5. Bake at 425°F 20 to 25 minutes, or until muffins are an even golden brown. Remove muffins from wells.

1 dozen muffins

MISSOURI

Ozark Pudding

Both Missouri and Arkansas claim this homey baked apple dessert. This is Mrs. Harry Truman's recipe, an easy, tasty version.

1 egg
¾ cup sugar
¼ cup all-purpose flour
1¼ teaspoons baking powder
⅛ teaspoon salt
½ cup chopped nuts
½ cup chopped apple
1 teaspoon vanilla extract

1. Beat together egg and sugar until thoroughly blended and smooth. Blend flour, baking powder, and salt; mix into the egg-sugar mixture.
2. Stir in chopped nuts, chopped apple, and vanilla extract. Turn into a greased 8-inch pie pan.
3. Bake at 350°F about 35 minutes.
4. Serve warm or cold with **whipped cream or ice cream.**

6 servings

Angel Food Cake

It's said that Angel Food Cake was first made in St. Louis, but its popularity has certainly spread throughout the country.

1 cup sifted cake flour
¾ cup sugar
1½ cups (about 12) egg whites
1 teaspoon cream of tartar
½ teaspoon salt
1 teaspoon vanilla extract
½ teaspoon almond extract
¾ cup sugar

1. Sift flour and ¾ cup sugar together four times; set aside.
2. Beat egg whites with cream of tartar, salt, and extracts until stiff, not dry, peaks are formed. Lightly fold in remaining sugar, 2 tablespoons at a time.
3. Gently folding until blended after each addition, sift about 4 tablespoons of the flour mixture at a time over meringue. Carefully slide batter into an ungreased 10-inch tube pan, turning pan as batter is poured. Cut through batter with knife or spatula to break large air bubbles.
4. Bake at 350°F about 45 minutes, or until cake tests done.
5. Immediately invert pan and cool cake completely before removing from pan.

One 10-inch tube cake

Diversity and balance have been key ingredients in Ohio's success, beginning with the land itself. A gracefully rolling terrain reveals surprises around every curve in the road.

Ohio maintains a desirable balance between industry and agriculture, as well as considerable diversity. The economically important centers are well scattered throughout the state.

Agriculture is well diversified, and many of the family-size farms are models of mechanization. Chief field crops are corn, soybeans, oats, soft red winter wheat, popcorn, sugar beets, potatoes, and tomatoes. Grapes, greenhouse vegetables, and maple syrup are also principal products.

Cattle, hog, and sheep farms are located primarily in the west, where feed grains are grown. Most of the dairy farms are concentrated in the northeast (excluding the fruit and truck farming area along the Lake Erie shoreline).

One of Ohio's greatest resources is its people—drawn there because of the variety of opportunity. The first permanent settlers were English, French, Scotch, and Irish colonists who pushed west when Ohio, Kentucky, and Tennessee comprised the frontier. Germans helped build Cincinnati, and its German flavor persists even today. New Englanders settled Connecticut's Western Reserve in the northeast. A second wave of immigration brought eastern and southern Europeans to the industrial areas.

Ohio, particularly Tuscarawas County, was a haven for freedom-seeking religious sects in the eighteenth and nineteenth centuries. The restored Moravian mission of Schoenbrunn is open to visitors, as is nearby Zoar, a commune founded by German Separatists. Neighboring Holmes County has a large concentration of Amish and Mennon-

OHIO

ites who preserve the Pennsylvania Dutch style of cooking.

Sugarcreek, in western Tuscarawas County, hosts the Ohio Swiss Festival each autumn. Features are yodeling, gay Swiss costumes, parades, dancing, and Swiss foods—with the accent on the local cheese. Apple fritters, Swiss cookies, and a local sausage called "trail bologna" are other specialties.

The Shakers founded communities at North Union (now Shaker Heights, a Cleveland suburb) and Union Village, north of Cincinnati. Another "plain people," the Shakers were of English origin. Pious and celibate, they lived on communal farms and pioneered many scientific agriculture practices. Their foods were of excellent quality, and their diet, making ingenious use of fruits, vegetables, and herbs, was highly nutritious. Though the Shakers have vanished, many of their recipes are worth noting today, for they make the best possible use of natural ingredients. Many Ohioans share a renewed interest in more natural foods, with whole-grain breads and cereals gaining particular favor.

As in other states where food is so abundant, Ohioans celebrate that bounty with many festivals. The Circleville Pumpkin Show annually presents pumpkins and squash in countless shapes, sizes, and colors; recipes for pumpkin dishes are almost as numerous. Maple syrup, sweet corn, apple butter, and other products all have special days.

German Meatballs (Koenigsberger Klops)

These German meatballs have a distinctive gravy with a mildly tart flavor and the surprise of capers.

1 cup soft bread crumbs
¼ cup milk
½ cup chopped onion
2 tablespoons butter or margarine
1 pound ground beef
¼ pound ground veal
4 anchovy fillets, mashed
1 egg, fork beaten
1 teaspoon salt
¼ teaspoon pepper
3 cups water
2 tablespoons chopped onion
1 bay leaf
1 whole clove
2 peppercorns
¼ teaspoon salt
2 tablespoons butter or margarine
2 tablespoons flour
2 tablespoons lemon juice
1 tablespoon chopped capers

1. Put bread crumbs and milk into a large bowl.
2. Cook ½ cup onion in 2 tablespoons hot butter in a skillet until golden, stirring occasionally.
3. Add the contents of the skillet, the ground meat, anchovies, egg, 1 teaspoon salt, and pepper to the bread crumb mixture; mix lightly. Shape meat mixture into 2-inch balls.
4. Bring water, 2 tablespoons chopped onion, bay leaf, clove, peppercorns, and ¼ teaspoon salt to boiling in a saucepan. Put meatballs into boiling liquid. Return to boiling and simmer 20 minutes. Remove meatballs with a slotted spoon; keep hot. Strain cooking liquid and reserve 2 cups.
5. Heat remaining butter in the saucepan. Mix in flour and heat until bubbly. Stir in reserved liquid, lemon juice, and capers. Bring rapidly to boiling, stirring constantly. Cook and stir 1 to 2 minutes.
6. Return meatballs to gravy and heat thoroughly.

6 to 8 servings

Balkan Lamb and Eggplant Casserole

Moussaka is the Greek name for this tasty dish. Lamb and eggplant are popular ingredients in Balkan and Near Eastern cookery.

3 cloves garlic, minced
2 large onions, chopped
1 large green pepper, chopped
1 tablespoon olive oil
1½ pounds lean ground lamb
1½ teaspoons salt
Freshly ground black pepper
2 teaspoons paprika
2 large eggplant, pared and cut in ½-inch slices
4 egg yolks, beaten
1 cup yogurt
½ cup flour

1. Cook garlic, onion, and green pepper 3 minutes in hot oil in a large skillet. Add ground lamb and season with salt, pepper, and paprika. Separate meat and cook until pink color is gone. Using a slotted spoon, remove mixture from skillet; set aside.
2. Coat eggplant with **flour.** Lightly brown slices in hot **butter** or **margarine** in the skillet.
3. In a 3½-quart casserole, alternate layers of eggplant and meat; cover.
4. Bake at 350°F 45 minutes.
5. Mix remaining ingredients and spoon over mixture in casserole. Cover and continue baking 15 minutes; uncover and brown top under broiler.

8 to 10 servings

Shaker Corn

The Shakers were well known for their development of various food preservation methods. Dried corn is still frequently made and enjoyed by many families. The old method, still sometimes used, is to dry the corn in the sun. The modern method is to cook the corn, then oven-dry it.

Water
Corn on the cob*

1. *To prepare dried corn,* fill a large kettle with water, bring to boiling, and add corn. Bring to boiling again and cook 5 minutes. Remove corn from water; cool.
2. Cut kernels from cobs. Spread kernels one layer deep in a large shallow pan.
3. Dry in a 200°F oven 5 to 6 hours, or until thoroughly dry, stirring every hour.
4. Pack in sterilized jars and seal. Store at room temperature.
5. *To serve dried corn,* soak overnight in water. Add salt to taste and simmer 1 hour. Add **butter** or **cream.**

*10 large ears of corn will yield about 6 cups of fresh kernels and about 1½ cups dried kernels. Allow about ¼ cup dried corn per serving.

OHIO

Baked Swiss Cheese Fondue

2 tablespoons flour
½ teaspoon salt
Pinch black pepper
2 tablespoons butter or
margarine
1 cup milk
4 egg yolks, fork beaten
8 ounces Swiss cheese,
finely shredded
1 cup ¼-inch soft bread
cubes
2 teaspoons grated onion
½ clove garlic, minced
¼ cup snipped parsley
4 egg whites
Ground nutmeg

1. Blend a mixture of flour, salt, and pepper into hot butter in a saucepan. Heat until bubbly. Add milk gradually, stirring constantly. Bring to boiling; boil 1 to 2 minutes. Remove from heat.
2. Blend a small amount of sauce into egg yolks; stir into remaining sauce. Mix in the cheese. Add bread cubes, onion, garlic, and parsley; mix thoroughly.
3. Beat egg whites until stiff, not dry, peaks are formed. Gently fold with cheese mixture.
4. Turn into a buttered 1½-quart shallow baking dish. Sprinkle top with nutmeg.
5. Bake at 325°F 40 to 45 minutes, or until top is golden brown.

About 6 servings

Farmer's Chop Suey

1 large firm cucumber
1 cup sliced red radishes
6 green onions (use some
green tops)
3 medium tomatoes
¼ teaspoon salt
⅛ teaspoon pepper
1½ cups chilled dairy sour
cream

1. Rinse, pare and cut cucumber into small cubes. Wash, cut off root and stem ends, and thinly slice radishes. Peel, cut off roots, rinse and cut green onions crosswise. Put cucumber, radishes, and green onions into a bowl; cover tightly and set in refrigerator to chill for at least 1 hour.
2. Rinse tomatoes and chill in refrigerator.
3. Just before serving, remove tomatoes from refrigerator, cut out stem ends, cut tomatoes into chunks and toss gently with chilled vegetables.
4. Season with a mixture of salt and pepper.
5. Pour sour cream over the salad and mix lightly. Serve immediately.

6 servings

Ohio Lemon Pie

2 lemons, very thinly sliced
2 cups sugar
Pastry for a 2-crust pie
4 eggs

1. Put sliced lemon into a bowl and add sugar; mix well. Let stand at least 2 hours.
2. Prepare pastry. Roll out enough pastry to line a 9-inch pie pan; line pie pan. Roll out remaining pastry for top crust; slit pastry. Set aside.
3. Beat eggs until blended; add to lemon mixture and mix well. Pour into pastry shell. Cover with top crust; seal and flute edge.
4. Bake at 450°F 15 minutes. Turn oven control to 350°F and bake 45 minutes.
5. Serve warm.

One 9-inch pie

Planked Halibut Dinner, 228

Schnecken

Popular Pennsylvania Dutch cinnamon rolls may be baked with or without pecans.

1 package active dry yeast
¼ cup warm water
1 cup milk or
    half-and-half, scalded
½ cup sugar
1 teaspoon salt
5 cups all-purpose flour
2 eggs, well beaten
½ cup butter or margarine,
    softened
⅔ cup butter or margarine,
    melted
1 cup pecan pieces,
    coarsely chopped
1 cup packed brown sugar
¼ cup currants
1 tablespoon ground
    cinnamon
1 cup small pecan halves

1. Soften yeast in the warm water.
2. Pour the scalded milk over sugar and salt in a large bowl; stir until sugar is dissolved. Cool to lukewarm.
3. Blend in 1 cup of the flour and beat until smooth. Stir in yeast. Add about half the remaining flour and beat until very smooth. Beat in the eggs. Vigorously beat in the ½ cup softened butter, 2 to 3 tablespoons at a time. Beat in enough remaining flour to make a soft dough.
4. Turn dough onto a lightly floured surface. Cover and let rest 10 minutes.
5. Knead until smooth and elastic. Form into a ball and put into a greased deep bowl; turn dough to bring greased surface to top. Cover; let rise in a warm place until doubled (about 1 hour).
6. Punch dough down; pull edges of dough in to center and turn over completely in bowl. Cover; let rise again until nearly doubled (about 45 minutes).
7. Lightly grease twenty-four 2½-inch muffin-pan wells. Put about 1 teaspoon of the melted butter into each well; reserve remaining butter. Mix the chopped nuts, brown sugar, currants, and cinnamon. Spoon 2 teaspoons into each well and gently press 3 or 4 pecan halves onto mixture.
8. Again punch dough down; form into 2 balls. Roll ball into a rectangle ¼ to ⅓ inch thick, 6 to 8 inches wide, and 12 inches long. Brush top surface of dough with half the remaining melted butter and sprinkle evenly with half the remaining brown sugar mixture. Beginning with longer side, roll dough tightly into a long roll. Cut roll into 12 slices. Place a slice, cut side down, in each well. Repeat with second ball. Cover; let rise again until doubled (about 45 minutes).
9. Bake at 375°F 15 to 20 minutes. Invert muffin pans on wire racks, set on waxed paper or aluminum foil, leaving pans over Schnecken 5 minutes. Remove from pans and cool on racks, glazed side up. To store, wrap tightly in foil. Reheat just before serving.

2 dozen Schnecken

OHIO

Grape Arbor Pie

Wines and sparkling grape juice are also produced from Ohio's Concord grapes.

3 cups Concord grapes
1 cup sugar
3 tablespoons cornstarch
¼ teaspoon salt
2 teaspoons grated orange
     peel
1 tablespoon orange juice
1 tablespoon lemon juice
1 tablespoon butter or
     margarine
     Pastry for a 2-crust pie

1. Rinse and drain the grapes; slip off skins and chop; set aside in bowl.
2. Bring skinned grapes to boiling in a saucepan; lower heat and simmer 5 minutes, or until seeds are loosened.
3. Drain pulp, reserving juice. Force pulp through fine sieve or food mill into bowl with chopped grape skins; set aside. Discard the seeds.
4. Thoroughly mix sugar, cornstarch, and salt in a saucepan. Stir in the reserved grape juice until well blended. Bring mixture to boiling; stir and cook 3 minutes.
5. Remove from heat; stir in the pulp mixture, orange peel, and the juices.
6. Prepare an 8-inch pie shell and lattice strips for top crust.
7. Turn filling into pie shell. Dot with butter. Top with lattice strips and flute edge.
8. Bake at 450°F 10 minutes; turn oven control to 350°F and bake 20 to 25 minutes, or until pastry is lightly browned.
9. Cool on wire rack.

One 8-inch pie

Shaker Sugar Pie

From the menu of The Golden Lamb in Lebanon, Ohio, not far from one of the original Shaker communities.

1 unbaked 9-inch pie shell
¾ cup firmly packed light
     brown sugar
¼ cup flour
2 cups half-and-half
1 teaspoon vanilla extract
     Few grains ground
     nutmeg
½ cup butter or margarine,
     softened

1. Prick pie shell and bake at 450°F 5 minutes. Set aside. Reduce oven temperature to 350°F.
2. Mix brown sugar with flour until blended. Spoon over bottom of partially baked pie shell.
3. Combine half-and-half, extract, and nutmeg; pour over sugar in pie shell. Dot with the butter.
4. Bake at 350°F about 55 minutes, or until crust is lightly browned and filling is set.

One 9-inch pie

"America's Dairyland" is a prime example of the nation's melting pot in action. As in most other midwestern states, Wisconsin's food traditions are newer and younger than those of New England and the South, for it was settled more than a century later. The cookery retains more of its Old World character.

In the forests of the north, where the lakes teem with fish and the woods yield wild berries and game animals, one finds truly "native" fare. There is a Scandinavian flavor, especially around Superior, where many Finns settled.

One of Wisconsin's most picturesque communities is the Door Peninsula, an area reminiscent of New England, as bluffs fall away to snug little harbors where fishing villages nestle. The scenic countryside and quaintly named towns attract thousands of tourists and a thriving artists' colony.

The peninsula, bounded by Green Bay on the west and Lake Michigan on the east, is the setting for a unique midwestern event. The Door County Fish Boil is Wisconsin's counterpart of the New England clambake.

The fish boil was the invention of early loggers and fishermen. Public fish boils conducted by church groups, civic organizations, and resorts draw big crowds, for they are dramatic and provide wonderful eating.

The fish is cooked in huge iron pots over open fires. First baskets of potatoes and onions are lowered into the boiling water. Shortly before the vegetables are done, steaks of lake trout or whitefish are added.

The drama comes just as the fish is done. A small amount of kerosene is thrown on the fire, causing a momentary burst of flame and a boil-over of the water, carrying away the fish oils and foam.

The delicately flavored fish plus the potatoes and onions are served with a generous splash of melted butter. Traditional accompaniments are coleslaw, homemade bread, cherry pie, and beverage. Truly a delectable feast!

WISCONSIN

Scattered through the state are the peaceful, prosperous dairy farms that give Wisconsin its greatest fame. The Germans, Swiss, and Danes who settled the farmlands had come from dairy country and recognized the possibilities of their new land. They set about developing a dairy industry, and the pastoral beauty of the area speaks well of their success.

Green County is known as Wisconsin's "Little Switzerland," and the state's Swiss cheese industry is centered here. New Glarus (named for the Swiss canton which was the homeland of many early settlers) focuses on the area's Swiss heritage and history; it hosts a William Tell Pageant, Heidi Festival, and Volkfest each summer.

Farther west, Welsh and Cornishmen came to the lead-mining area shared by Wisconsin, Iowa, and Illinois. Saffron-scented breads, currant cakes, and pasties are reminders of the region's past.

Skipping back across the state to its eastern edge we find Milwaukee, known far and wide for its *gemütlichkeit* spirit. Though basically a German-flavored city, it is also much more. Traditions, restaurants, and life styles reflect the varied ethnic backgrounds of its people, including Polish, Czech, Hungarian, and Ukrainian.

The famous breweries owe their beginnings to the German settlers. The German fondness for sausages of all types is very visible, too. In southeastern Wisconsin savory grilled bratwurst nestled in crusty rolls rival the ubiquitous hot dog in popularity.

Beef Lindstrom

The Finnish name for this Scandinavian counterpart of the hamburger is Lindstromin Pihvi.

1½ pounds lean beef,
    ground twice
2 egg yolks, beaten
¼ cup half-and-half
2 tablespoons chopped
    onion
1 tablespoon capers
1 teaspoon salt
¼ teaspoon pepper
3 medium-size cooked
    potatoes, diced
½ cup finely diced pickled
    beets
3 tablespoons butter or
    margarine

1. Lightly toss the ground beef, egg yolks, half-and-half, onion, capers, salt, and pepper in a bowl. Add potatoes and beets and mix well. Refrigerate 1 to 2 hours.
2. Shape the mixture into patties about ¾ inch thick. Brown on both sides in heated butter in a heavy skillet. Serve immediately.

6 to 8 servings

Home-Style Fish Boil

10 to 12 medium potatoes
    (red are best)
10 to 12 pounds whole fresh
    lake trout or other fish
2 cups salt
    Onions, bay leaves,
      peppercorns (optional)
    Melted butter or
      margarine

1. Use at least a 12-quart pot with insert for food. Bring 8 quarts water to full boil.
2. Meanwhile, cut potatoes in half, if large, or take nick off small for flavor penetration. Add half the salt to water.
3. Put potatoes in insert; lower into water. Onions and cheesecloth bag of bay leaves and peppercorns can be added for more flavor, if desired. Return to boil, cover and boil about 20 minutes, until almost done.

4. Cut head and tail from fish; gut; wash; cut across backbone into 2-inch-wide sections. Do not remove skin or bone. Add remaining salt to pot; put fish on potatoes.

5. Quickly return to boiling, cover, and gently boil 8 to 10 minutes. If fish is not under water, add more boiling water to cover, and corresponding amount of salt. (At least 2 tablespoons per quart.) Skim off foam during cooking, if necessary.

6. Test fish a few minutes early. When it flakes easily with fork, it is done. Remove basket; drain. Serve immediately with lots of melted butter. It traditionally is served with **cole slaw, bread,** and **cherry pie.**

10 to 12 servings

Potato Pancakes

6 medium potatoes
Fat for frying
2 tablespoons flour
1½ teaspoons salt
¼ teaspoon baking powder
⅛ teaspoon pepper
2 eggs, well beaten
1 tablespoon grated onion
1 tablespoon minced parsley

1. Pare and grate potatoes; set aside.
2. Put fat (enough to make a layer ¼ inch deep) into a heavy skillet; set over low heat.
3. Blend the flour, salt, baking powder, and pepper. Mix into beaten eggs along with onion and parsley.
4. Drain liquid from grated potatoes; add potatoes to egg mixture and beat thoroughly with a spoon.
5. When fat is hot, increase heat to medium. For each pancake, spoon about 2 tablespoons potato mixture into hot fat; leave about 1 inch between pancakes. Cook until golden brown and crisp on one side. Turn carefully and brown other side. Drain on absorbent paper. Repeat until all potato mixture is used.
6. Serve with **applesauce** and **sour cream.**

About 20 medium-size pancakes

Welsh Rabbit

Many tales have been told about the origin of this dish, but one fact is clear. It makes delicious use of two of Wisconsin's finest products: sharp Cheddar cheese and beer.

2 eggs
1 teaspoon Worcestershire sauce
½ teaspoon dry mustard
¼ teaspoon salt
¼ teaspoon paprika
2 tablespoons butter
1 pound sharp Cheddar cheese, shredded
1 cup beer or ale

1. Beat eggs lightly, just enough to mix yolk and white. Add Worcestershire sauce, dry mustard, salt, and paprika to eggs and set aside.
2. Melt butter at a low temperature in an electric fry pan and add the cheese. Stir until the cheese is melted. Stirring must be constant from this step until completion of the dish.
3. Slowly stir in beer or ale. When blended, slowly stir in the egg mixture. (Whether you are using a double boiler or electric fry pan, do not let egg mixture overheat or eggs will curdle.)
4. When mixture is thick and warmed through, spoon over slices of **toast.**

6 servings

WISCONSIN

Cranberry-Orange Nut Bread

2 cups sifted all-purpose
flour
1 cup sugar
1½ teaspoons baking
powder
½ teaspoon baking soda
1 teaspoon salt
1¼ cups cranberries, cut in
pieces
½ cup coarsely chopped
walnuts
1 egg, well beaten
1 teaspoon grated orange
peel
¾ cup orange juice
2 tablespoons butter or
margarine, melted

1. Sift flour, sugar, baking powder, baking soda, and salt together into a bowl. Mix in cranberries and walnuts.
2. Combine egg, orange peel, orange juice, and melted butter. Add liquid mixture to flour mixture; stir only enough to moisten flour. Turn into a greased 9×5×3-inch loaf pan and spread evenly.
3. Bake at 350°F 40 to 45 minutes.
4. Cool bread 10 minutes in pan on wire rack; remove from pan and cool completely before slicing or storing.

1 loaf bread

Lattice-Top Cherry Pie

Cherry pie is the traditional dessert for the Wisconsin Fish Boil; cherries were once widely grown on the Door Peninsula.

¾ to 1 cup sugar
2½ tablespoons cornstarch
⅛ teaspoon salt
2 cans (16 ounces each)
pitted tart red
cherries, drained
(reserve ¾ cup liquid)
1 teaspoon lemon juice
¼ teaspoon almond extract
4 or 5 drops red food
coloring
Pastry for 2-crust pie
1 tablespoon butter or
margarine

1. Combine sugar, cornstarch, and salt in a heavy saucepan; stir in the reserved cherry liquid. Bring to boiling and boil 2 to 3 minutes, stirring constantly.
2. Remove from heat; stir in lemon juice, extract, and food coloring, then the cherries. Set aside.
3. Meanwhile, prepare an 8-inch pie shell and lattice strips for top crust; set aside.
4. When filling is cool, spoon into unbaked pie shell. Dot with butter. Arrange pastry strips in a lattice design over filling. Crimp edge of pie crust.
5. Bake at 450°F 10 minutes; turn oven control to 350°F and bake about 35 minutes, or until pastry is lightly browned.
6. Remove pie to wire rack to cool.

One 8-inch pie

Swiss Apple Pie

One of the most delectable apple desserts ever. Apple orchards are a common sight throughout the state.

- 6 tablespoons butter
- 1½ cups all-purpose flour
- 3 to 4 tablespoons cold water
- 1 tablespoon ground toasted almonds
- 1 tablespoon fine dry bread crumbs
- 1½ pounds tart apples, pared and thinly sliced
- 2 eggs
- 2 egg yolks
- 2 cups whipping cream
- ½ cup sugar
- 2 tablespoons butter, melted
- ¼ cup sugar

1. Cut butter into flour with a pastry blender or two knives until the pieces are size of small peas. Add water gradually, mixing with a fork until pastry holds together. Shape into a ball.
2. Roll pastry about ⅛ inch thick on a lightly floured surface. Line a 10-inch pie pan with pastry; flute edge. Sprinkle a mixture of almonds and crumbs over bottom; cover with apples.
3. Bake at 350°F 5 minutes.
4. Meanwhile, beat eggs and egg yolks slightly; add cream and ½ cup sugar; blend well. Pour half of the mixture over the apples.
5. Bake until firm, about 30 minutes. Pour remaining mixture over apples and continue baking about 45 minutes, or until a metal knife inserted halfway between center and edge of pie comes out clean.
6. Remove pie from oven and pour melted butter evenly over the top. Sprinkle with remaining sugar and return to oven for 5 minutes. Cool before serving.

One 10-inch pie

Honey Cakes (Lebkuchen)

These German honey cookies boast rich, spicy flavor.

- 3 cups sifted all-purpose flour
- ¼ teaspoon baking soda
- 1 teaspoon ground cinnamon
- ½ teaspoon ground allspice
- ½ teaspoon ground cloves
- ½ teaspoon ground nutmeg
- 2 eggs
- 1 cup sugar
- ½ cup honey
- ¾ cup unblanched almonds, finely chopped
- 2 ounces candied orange peel, finely chopped
- 2 ounces candied lemon peel, finely chopped
- Glaze

1. Sift flour, baking soda, and spices together; set aside.
2. Beat eggs with sugar until very thick. Add honey gradually, beating well.
3. Add flour mixture in fourths, folding until blended after each addition. Mix in almonds and candied peels. Turn into a greased 15×10×1-inch jelly-roll pan and spread evenly.
4. Bake at 350°F 25 to 30 minutes.
5. Remove pan to wire rack and cool slightly. Spread Glaze evenly over warm surface. Cut into bars.

About 3 dozen cookies

Glaze: Blend thoroughly **⅓ cup confectioners' sugar, 1 tablespoon water,** and **1 teaspoon lemon juice.**

Note: More traditionally, Lebkuchen is a rolled cookie which is cut into bars before baking.

WISCONSIN

Orange Honey Hero

4 cups milk
½ cup instant vanilla
    pudding mix
6 tablespoons thawed
    frozen orange juice
    concentrate
1 tablespoon honey

1. Combine milk, pudding mix, orange juice concentrate, and honey in a 2-quart saucepan and heat to serving temperature, stirring occasionally.
2. Pour into glasses with handles or mugs and garnish with **orange slices.**

About 5 cups beverage

Butterscotch Benchwarmer

4 cups milk
½ cup butterscotch pieces
    Miniature marshmallows

1. Combine milk and butterscotch pieces in a 2-quart saucepan.
2. Heat until butterscotch pieces are melted, stirring occasionally.
3. Serve topped with marshmallows.

About 1 quart beverage

Cheerleaders' Choice

½ cup water
¼ cup red cinnamon
    candies
¼ cup sugar
2 tablespoons whole cloves
⅛ teaspoon salt
4 cups milk
    Cinnamon sticks

1. Combine water, cinnamon candies, sugar, whole cloves, and salt in a 2-quart saucepan.
2. Simmer over low heat about 5 minutes, stirring occasionally.
3. Add milk and heat to serving temperature.
4. Pour into four glasses with handles, or mugs. Serve with cinnamon sticks.

About 1 quart beverage

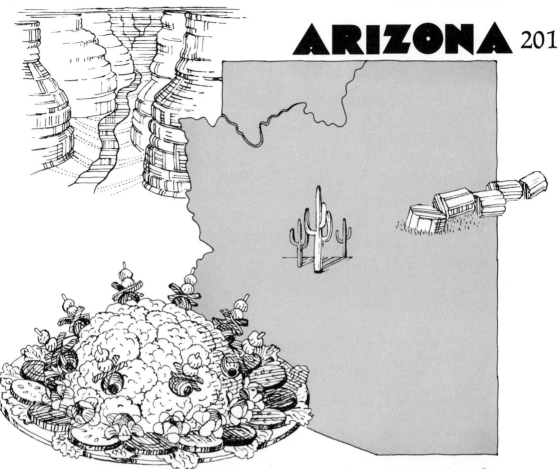

Basking in the sun belt, Arizona is a colorful patch in the southwestern border of our country. As the forty-eighth state to be admitted to the Union, it was long known as the "newest state," but passed that title along when Hawaii and Alaska gained statehood.

Arizona's economy is said to be based on the five "C's"—copper, cotton, cattle, climate, and citrus. That order says something about the relative importance of agriculture in the state. Until modern irrigation made farming possible, it was even farther down the line. Cotton is by far the biggest cash crop, with citrus fruits and vegetables falling in behind.

To those five "C's", add a "see" for its scenery. Arizona boasts such wonders as the Grand Canyon on the Colorado River, the Painted Desert, and the Petrified Forest. These attractions bring multitudes of visitors to the state each year, and make tourism a thriving business.

While the stars and stripes have flown over Arizona for a relatively short time, it has a long and colorful history. It has been home to Indian cultures for at least 2,500 years.

Since ancient times, the Indians have cultivated corn, or more specifically, maize. "Corn," to the European settlers, meant the primary grain crop in any area. In England, the word referred to the grain we call wheat. The exact place of the origin of maize is unknown, but it is thought that Indians of Central America may have carried it northward through Mexico and into what is now the United States, since it is not wind-borne and does not seed itself.

Corn was one of the gifts of the New World that Columbus carried back to the Spanish people. It was also one of the bequests of the American Indian to the new settlers. The Indians showed the white man how to grow, harvest, and cook with corn. One recipe with both Indian and Mexican roots is the tamale.

SOUTHWEST

Prior to statehood in 1912, the Arizona territory was frontier land, and a reminder of that time is the lingering popularity of cowboy boots and hats. The backyard grill and swimming pool are commonplace, with so much of the year favoring outdoor activity. But in contrast to this informality is a growing sophistication. The symphony, art museums, and theater have a loyal following in the state.

Arizona is characterized by a diversity in life-style. In addition to the Indian population which have retained many of their age-old recipes and customs, there are other ethnic influences. Mexican Americans have contributed to the cuisine of Arizona through dishes often redolent of chili and highly seasoned tomato sauces. Dishes such as flan and almendrado are reminders of the Spanish heritage.

Pozole (Pork and Hominy Soup)

This hearty soup comes from Mexico. Pozole is always served with a variety of crisp vegetable garnishes which are sprinkled on top of the hot soup.

2 pork hocks, split in two or three pieces each
1 large onion, sliced
2 cloves garlic, minced
Water
1 stewing chicken, cut in serving pieces
1 pound pork loin, boneless, cut in 1-inch chunks
2 cups canned hominy or canned garbanzos
1 tablespoon salt
½ teaspoon pepper
1 cup sliced crisp radishes
1 cup shredded cabbage
1 cup shredded lettuce
½ cup chopped green onions
Lime or lemon wedges

1. Put split pork hocks, onion, and garlic into a kettle, cover with water and cook until almost tender (about 3 hours).
2. Add chicken and pork loin and cook 45 minutes, or until chicken is almost tender.
3. Add hominy, salt, and pepper. Cook about 15 minutes, or until all meat is tender.
4. Remove pork hocks and chicken from soup. Remove meat from bones and return meat to soup.
5. Serve in large soup bowls. Accompany with a relish tray offering the radishes, cabbage, lettuce, green onions, and lime or lemon wedges as garnishes.

8 to 10 servings

Country-Flavored Chicken Halves

1 package 15-minute chicken marinade
1 cup cold water
1 broiler-fryer (2½ to 3 pounds), cut in half

1. In a shallow pan, thoroughly blend chicken marinade and water. Place well-drained chicken in marinade; turn, pierce all surfaces of chicken deeply with fork. Marinate only 15 minutes, turning several times. Remove chicken from marinade and arrange skin side up in a shallow ungreased pan just large enough to accommodate the chicken.
2. Bake, uncovered, at 425°F for 45 to 55 minutes, until thoroughly cooked.

4 servings

Tamale Perfection

¼ pound bulk pork
    sausage
1½ teaspoons cold water
1 pound ground beef
1 cup (about 2
    medium-size) finely
    chopped onion
½ cup finely chopped
    celery
⅓ cup finely chopped
    green pepper
2½ cups canned tomatoes,
    sieved
1¼ cups (12 ounce can,
    drained) whole kernel
    corn
1 tablespoon salt
2 teaspoons chili powder
¼ teaspoon pepper
1 cup cold water
½ cup yellow cornmeal
1 cup sliced ripe olives
¾ cup (3 ounces) shredded
    sharp Cheddar cheese
Whole ripe olives

1. Put pork sausage into a large, heavy, unheated skillet. Break into small pieces with fork and add water. Cover and cook slowly 8 minutes. Remove cover and pour off fat. Mix ground beef in with fork, breaking meat into pieces.

2. Brown meat over medium heat, stirring occasionally. Pour off fat as it collects. When meat begins to brown, add onion, celery, and green pepper. Cook until meat is well browned and onion is tender, stirring occasionally.

3. Add slowly and mix in tomatoes and corn. Blend in a mixture of salt, chili powder, and pepper. Cover and bring mixture to boiling over high heat. Reduce heat and simmer about 15 minutes.

4. Mix together thoroughly cold water and cornmeal. Bring mixture in skillet to boiling; add cornmeal mixture gradually, stirring constantly. Cook over medium heat until thickened, stirring slowly. Stir in the sliced olives. Turn mixture into a greased 2-quart casserole.

5. Bake at 350°F 1 hour. Remove from oven and sprinkle with cheese.

6. Return to oven and bake 5 minutes longer, or until cheese is melted. Garnish with whole ripe olives.

8 servings

Burritos

Burritos are a type of taco made with wheat flour tortillas. The filling may be refried beans alone, or combined with meat as in the following recipe.

12 wheat flour tortillas
1½ cups hot refried beans
    (use canned beans or
    see recipe on page
    210)
1½ cups hot Ground Beef
    Filling (page 204)
    Oil for frying (optional)

1. Spread each tortilla with about 1 tablespoon refried beans, spreading only to about ½ inch of edge. Spoon a heaping tablespoon of filling along one side. Fold in ends about 1 inch to cover filling, then roll up tortilla starting with side on which meat has been placed. Serve at once.

2. Or, fry in hot oil until crisp, placing each burrito in skillet with open flap on bottom to start, then turning to fry top and sides. Drain on absorbent paper. Serve hot.

12 burritos

Enchiladas con Chili Verde

1 can (8 ounces) tomato
   sauce
1 package (1⅝ ounces)
   enchilada sauce mix
1½ cups water
1 pound ground beef
¼ cup finely chopped
   onion
½ teaspoon salt
   Dash pepper
12 corn tortillas
   Oil for frying
1½ cups shredded longhorn
   cheese
1 tablespoon chopped
   parsley

1. Combine tomato sauce, enchilada mix, and water in saucepan. Stir to blend.
2. Bring to boiling. Reduce heat and simmer, uncovered, 15 minutes, stirring occasionally.
3. Brown beef in hot skillet. Stir in onion, salt, pepper, and a little water, if necessary, to keep beef from sticking to pan.
4. Stir meat mixture into enchilada sauce.
5. In same skillet, fry tortillas quickly in hot oil, turning once; adding more oil if necessary.
6. Place half the tortillas in a shallow 3-quart baking dish. Cover with half the meat sauce. Sprinkle with half the cheese. Repeat with remaining tortillas, sauce, and cheese.
7. Bake at 375°F 30 minutes, or until casserole is hot and cheese is melted. Sprinkle with parsley, cut into squares, and serve.

6 to 8 servings

Ground Beef Filling

This filling may be used alone, but is particularly good sprinkled with shredded mild Cheddar cheese.

1½ pounds ground beef
½ cup chopped onion
1 clove garlic, minced
1 teaspoon salt
¼ teaspoon pepper
1 teaspoon chili powder
½ teaspoon cumin
   (optional)
1 cup canned tomato
   sauce

1. Crumble beef into skillet and brown well; if beef is very fat, pour off excess fat.
2. Add onion and garlic and cook about 5 minutes until onion is soft, stirring frequently.
3. Stir in dry seasonings, then tomato sauce. Continue cooking about 15 minutes longer.

About 3 cups filling

Sweet Potatoes with Orange

4 medium-size (about 1½
   pounds) sweet
   potatoes, scrubbed
¼ cup sugar
4 teaspoons grated orange
   peel
½ teaspoon salt
¼ teaspoon cinnamon

1. Grease a 1½-quart casserole having a tight-fitting cover. Scrub potatoes.
2. Cook potatoes, covered, in boiling salted water for 10 minutes. Drain. Shake pan over low heat to dry potatoes. Peel. With a sharp knife, cut into crosswise slices ⅛ inch thick. Set aside.
3. Mix together sugar, orange peel, salt, and cinnamon.

ARIZONA

2 large oranges
¼ cup butter or margarine
½ cup orange juice

4. Wash oranges, cut away peel, and cut into crosswise slices ¼ inch thick.
5. Arrange one half of the potato slices in an even layer in the casserole. Cover with one half of the orange slices and sprinkle with one half of the sugar mixture. Dot with 2 tablespoons of butter. Repeat layering. Pour orange juice over all. Cover.
6. Bake at 375°F about 40 minutes, or until potatoes are tender when pierced with a fork.

About 4 servings

Coliflor Acapulco

Mexico has contributed this flamboyant salad.

1 large head cauliflower
  Marinade
1 can (15 ounces)
    garbanzos, drained
1 cup pimento-stuffed olives
  Pimentos, drained and cut
    lengthwise in strips
  Lettuce
1 jar (16 ounces) sliced
    pickled beets, drained
    and chilled
1 large cucumber, thinly
    sliced and chilled
  Radish roses
  Guacamole I

1. Cook the cauliflower in boiling **salted walter** about 10 minutes, or just until tender; drain. Place cauliflower, head down, in a deep bowl and pour the marinade over it. Chill several hours or overnight; occasionally spoon marinade over all.
2. Shortly before serving, thread garbanzos, pimento-stuffed olives, and pimento strips onto wooden picks for decorative kabobs. Set aside while arranging salad.
3. Drain the cauliflower. Line a chilled serving plate with crisp lettuce and place cauliflower, head up, in the center. Arrange the pickled beet and cucumber slices around the base, tucking in **parsley sprigs** and the radish roses.
4. Spoon and spread Guacamole over cauliflower. Decorate with **cashew nuts** and the kabobs. Serve cold.

6 to 8 servings

Marinade: Combine **1½ cups salad oil, ½ cup lemon juice, 1½ teaspoons salt, and 1 teaspoon chili powder.** Shake the marinade well before pouring it over the cauliflower.

Guacamole I: Mix **1½ cups mashed ripe avocado, 2 to 3 teaspoons lemon juice, ½ teaspoon salt, 3 tablespoons minced onion, and ⅓ cup finely chopped, peeled, and seeded ripe tomato.** Cover tightly and chill until ready to serve.

Date Milk Shake

½ cup chopped pitted dates
1 cup milk
  Vanilla ice cream (about
    1 pint)

1. Whirl dates and milk in an electric blender until puréed.
2. Add ice cream, a spoonful at a time, blending until shake is desired consistency.

About 2 cups

ARIZONA

Southwestern Salad Bowl

Creamy avocado slices, juicy grapefruit sections, and onion rings—mmmm! A perfect pickup for days when the Arizona mercury soars.

Bibb lettuce or leaf lettuce (enough to line the salad bowl)
1 large grapefruit
1 large avocado

1. Rinse lettuce, discarding bruised leaves, pat dry and chill.
2. With a sharp knife, cut away peel from grapefruit.
3. Remove sections by cutting on either side of dividing membrane, working over a bowl to save the juice. Set aside.
4. Rinse avocado, peel, cut into halves, and remove and discard pit. Slice into bowl containing the grapefruit juice. Toss slices gently to coat with juice (this helps to prevent discoloring).
5. Arrange the slices of avocado alternately with grapefruit sections on lettuce in salad bowl. Cover and chill in refrigerator.
6. Just before serving, garnish with thin **onion rings.** Serve with **French dressing.**

4 to 6 servings

Almendrado

The colors of the Mexican flag and the Mexican eagle are represented in this red, white, and green layered gelatin dessert served with creamy custard sauce.

1 tablespoon unflavored gelatin
½ cup sugar
1 cup cold water
4 egg whites
½ teaspoon almond extract
Red and green food coloring
1 cup finely ground almonds
Custard Sauce with Almonds

1. Mix gelatin and sugar in a saucepan. Stir in water. Set over low heat and stir until gelatin and sugar are dissolved. Chill until slightly thickened.
2. Beat egg whites until stiff, not dry, peaks are formed. Fold into gelatin mixture along with almond extract. Beat until mixture resembles whipped cream. Divide equally into 3 portions. Color one portion red, another green, and leave the last one white.
3. Pour red mixture into an 8-inch square dish or pan. Sprinkle with half of the almonds. Pour in white mixture and sprinkle with remaining almonds. Top with green layer. Chill thoroughly.
4. Cut into portions and serve with custard sauce.

12 servings

Custard Sauce with Almonds: Scald **2 cups milk.** Mix **4 egg yolks** and **¼ cup sugar** in the top of a double boiler. Add scalded milk gradually, stirring constantly. Cook over boiling water, stirring constantly until mixture coats a spoon. Remove from water and stir in **¼ teaspoon almond extract** and **½ cup toasted sliced almonds.** Cool; chill thoroughly.

About 2½ cups

C ompared to the explorers and conquistadores who have paraded across New Mexico's history, the pinto bean may seem lowly indeed. Yet, some call it the cornerstone of New Mexican history. The pinto played a major role in feeding the Indian tribes of the Southwest for centuries, and later, the Spanish-American settler.

The pink pinto bean, called *frijoles* in Spanish, is nicknamed "the Spanish strawberry." Particularly among the Spanish-American population of New Mexico, it has been a diet staple. It is still important in New Mexican menus, from plain to fancy. There are dozens of ways to prepare them, perhaps as many as there are cooks to devise them.

Physically, New Mexico is a plateau, with rivers cutting deep gorges. Of these rivers, the Rio Grande is the biggest and best known. Running through the state from north to south are the Rocky Mountains. In the eastern sector of the state are the Great Plains. While formerly arid country, irrigation has made these fertile.

Fray Jacinto de San Francisco is said to

have been the first to apply the name of New Mexico to this region, which had been inhabited by Pueblo Indians for centuries. Spanish influence extended into the nineteenth century, and the state is now largely comprised of the Indians and "Anglo-Americans" as well as Spanish-Americans. Each of these has made its impact on the way of life, including the cooking, of the state.

A list of prominent New Mexican recipes is lyrical with Spanish names such as Chiles Rellenos. Our Chili-Beef Bake is an adaptation. Tacos are a Mexican contribution, and come with a variety of fillings, often based on beef or chicken. Another favorite from south of the border is Mexican Chocolate, a fancy dress-up for familiar cocoa.

From the Anglo-American segment of the

population comes such homespun stand-bys as Spiced Grape Jelly and Stay-Popped Popovers. These hot breads make good use of one of New Mexico's leading products, wheat flour.

Since vast stretches of New Mexico are suitable only for grazing, the raising of livestock is the state's main agricultural activity. Thus the barbecue, capitalizing on the state's top-grade meat and accommodating weather, has become an institution. A menu of barbecued beef, accompanied by the ubiquitous bean, and closing with pecan pie, delights natives and visitors alike.

Bacon-Wrapped Shrimp

½ cup butter or margarine
1½ teaspoons chili powder
1 clove garlic, minced or crushed in a garlic press
8 slices bacon
1 pound cooked shrimp
Lemon wedges
Parsley
Bottled seafood sauce

1. Combine in a small saucepan butter, chili powder, and garlic. Set over low heat, stirring occasionally, until butter is melted and heated thoroughly. Remove from heat and set aside.
2. Cut bacon slices in halves. Wrap one-half slice around each shrimp and secure with a wooden pick.
3. Set temperature control of range at Broil (500°F or higher). Arrange shrimp on broiler rack. Brush with the butter sauce. Place rack in broiler so tops of shrimp are about 3 inches from source of heat.
4. Broil 5 minutes, brushing once with sauce. Carefully turn shrimp, brush with sauce, and broil second side 5 minutes, or until bacon is cooked, brushing once again during cooking.
5. Place on a warm platter; garnish with lemon wedges and parsley. Serve immediately with seafood sauce.

About 16 appetizers

Chili-Beef Bake

½ pound ground beef
½ large clove garlic, minced
½ onion, finely chopped
½ teaspoon Worcestershire sauce
½ teaspoon salt
2 cans (4 ounces each) green chilies, drained, seeded, and chopped
6 ounces longhorn cheese, shredded
6 eggs, beaten
¾ teaspoon salt
Green Chili Sauce with Meat (page 210)

1. Cook ground beef with garlic and onion until beef is browned and onion is soft. Stir in Worcestershire sauce and ½ teaspoon salt.
2. Spread half of chilies in a 15×10×1-inch jelly-roll pan. Top with half the beef mixture, then sprinkle on half the cheese. Repeat layering with remaining chilies, meat, and cheese.
3. Beat eggs well with ¾ teaspoon salt and pour over meat mixture.
4. Bake at 350°F for 15 to 20 minutes, or until eggs begin to brown and are firm.
5. Divide into 6 to 8 portions; place on individual serving plates and top with Green Chili Sauce.

6 to 8 servings

Ham Loaf en Brioche, 232;
Sherry-Coconut Chiffon Cake, 236

Pork Chops with Chili Caribe Sauce

3 large dried hot red
   chilies
½ cup chopped onion
¼ teaspoon ground cumin
1 teaspoon oregano
2 cloves garlic
¼ teaspoon Worcestershire
   sauce
½ teaspoon salt
¼ teaspoon pepper
2 cups water
½ cup flour
¼ teaspoon salt
6 boneless pork loin chops,
   cut 1 inch thick
3 tablespoons butter or
   margarine

1. For sauce, toast chilies in a 400°F oven 3 to 4 minutes.
2. Remove chilies from oven and cool. Split chilies, remove stems, seeds, and any thick veins inside (see Note). Rinse chilies in cool water; drain and cover with hot water. Let stand 1 hour.
3. Drain chilies and place in an electric blender jar with onion, cumin, oregano, garlic, Worcestershire sauce, ½ teaspoon salt, ¼ teaspoon pepper, and water. Blend until smooth. Pour sauce into a saucepan and cook over medium heat 20 minutes.
4. Season the flour with ¼ teaspoon salt, and lightly coat pork chops. Brown chops in butter in a skillet; cover and cook until done (about 45 minutes).
5. Spoon some sauce over bottom of a shallow 2½-quart baking dish. Place pork chops on top of sauce. Cover with remaining sauce.
6. Bake at 250°F 30 minutes.

6 servings

Note: Wash hands thoroughly after peeling chilies; oil in chili veins and seeds will irritate skin and eyes.

Mexican Chili Chicken Casserole

¼ cup instant minced
   onion
½ teaspoon instant minced
   garlic
⅓ cup water
1 can (17 ounces) whole
   kernel corn
2 tablespoons oil
1 can (16 ounces)
   tomatoes, drained and
   broken up
1 can (8 ounces) tomato
   sauce
4 teaspoons chili powder
1 teaspoon oregano
   leaves, crumbled
⅛ teaspoon salt
1 tablespoon cornstarch
½ cup pitted ripe olives,
   sliced
1½ pounds boned cooked
   chicken, chunked
8 bacon slices, cooked
   crisp

1. Combine minced onion and garlic with water; let stand for 10 minutes to rehydrate. Drain and reserve liquid from corn; set corn and liquid aside separately.
2. In a large saucepan, heat oil. Add onion and garlic; sauté for 5 minutes. Stir in tomatoes, tomato sauce, chili powder, oregano leaves, and salt.
3. Mix cornstarch with reserved corn liquid; stir into saucepan. Simmer, uncovered, for 15 minutes, stirring occasionally. Remove from heat; add olives.
4. In a large casserole, place in layers chicken, reserved corn, and sauce. Repeat procedure, ending with corn. Garnish with crisp bacon slices over top.
5. Bake at 400°F until casserole is bubbly (about 20 minutes).

8 servings

Beef Kabobs with Vegetables, 245

NEW MEXICO

Green Chili Sauce with Meat

¼ pound coarsely ground
  beef
1 teaspoon chopped onion
½ clove garlic, minced
¼ teaspoon salt
  Few grains pepper
¼ teaspoon Worcestershire
  sauce
1 can (4 ounces) hot green
  chilies, drained and
  chopped
2 cups water
1 tablespoon cornstarch

1. Cook beef with onion and garlic in a skillet until meat is no longer pink. Pour off excess fat. Season meat with salt and pepper. Add Worcestershire sauce, chilies, and water; mix. Cook 10 minutes.

2. Blend some of cooking liquid with cornstarch to make a smooth paste. Return to beef mixture and cook, stirring, until mixture is thickened.

About 2 cups sauce

Refried Beans (Frijoles Refritos)

2 to 3 cups cooked kidney
  beans or pinto beans
½ cup lard or bacon
  drippings
1 cup chopped onion
1 clove garlic, minced
½ cup cooked tomatoes or
  tomato sauce
1 teaspoon chili powder
  Salt and pepper

1. Mash beans with a potato masher with half of the lard or bacon drippings (drippings make the best-flavored beans).

2. Heat remaining lard or drippings in skillet. Add onion and garlic and cook until onion is soft (about 5 minutes). Add mashed beans and continue cooking until all fat is absorbed by beans, stirring constantly to prevent sticking. Stir in tomatoes, chili powder, and salt and pepper to taste.

3 to 4 cups beans

Chicken Tacos

  Soft tortillas
2 cups diced cooked chicken
1 cup Guacamole II or 1
  fresh avocado, peeled
  and sliced in thin strips
1 large fresh tomato,
  peeled, cored, and
  chopped

1. Heat tortillas on medium-hot ungreased griddle, turning several times.

2. Combine chicken and Guacamole.

3. To assemble tacos, spoon chicken onto tortillas (top with avocado slices, if using). Spoon on a little chopped tomato and close tacos.

Guacamole II: Peel **2 very ripe avocados** and mash pulp, leaving a few small lumps throughout. Peel and chop **1 medium fresh tomato** and add to mashed avocado. Add **1 small onion, chopped, 2 tablespoons lemon juice, 1 teaspoon salt,** and **1 to 2 teaspoons chili powder** to taste; mix well. If not serving immediately, refrigerate in covered bowl, with avocado pits immersed in guacamole; this is said to help keep avocado from darkening on standing.

About 2 cups

Ground Beef Tacos

Soft tortillas
Ground Beef Filling (page 204)
Shredded mild Cheddar cheese

1. Heat tortillas on medium-hot ungreased griddle, turning several times. Immediately place in towel-lined bowl and wrap to keep hot.
2. To prepare tacos, spoon 2 tablespoons of filling onto center of hot tortilla, sprinkle with desired amount of cheese, and fold or roll up to enclose the filling.

Note: If desired, place filling on one side of soft tortilla. Roll up to completely enclose filling. Fry in hot oil until crisp, starting with open flap on underside, then turning to fry top and sides.

Stay-Popped Popovers

1 cup sifted all-purpose flour
3 eggs
1 cup milk
2 tablespoons cooking oil
½ teaspoon salt

1. Grease thoroughly with cooking oil eight 5-ounce heat-resistant custard cups or wells of an iron popover pan; preheat pan 15 minutes in oven.
2. Measure flour and set aside.
3. Beat eggs slightly in a small mixing bowl. Beat in milk, cooking oil, and salt until blended.
4. Add flour to liquid ingredients and beat with rotary beater until batter is smooth. Divide the batter evenly among the custard cups or wells of popover pan.
5. Bake at 400°F 35 to 40 minutes, or until popovers are a deep golden brown. Serve hot with **butter.**

8 popovers

Note: If a drier interior is desired, make a slit in the side of each baked popover to allow the steam to escape. Return popovers to oven with the heat turned off and allow them to dry for about 10 minutes.

Pecan Pie

3 tablespoons butter
1 teaspoon vanilla extract
¾ cup sugar
3 eggs, well beaten
1 cup dark corn syrup
⅛ teaspoon salt
½ cup (about 2 ounces) pecan halves
1 unbaked 9-inch pastry shell
½ cup (about 2 ounces) pecan halves

1. Cream butter and extract. Gradually add sugar, creaming well.
2. Add eggs in thirds, blending well after each addition. Thoroughly blend in the corn syrup, salt, and chopped pecans; turn into the pastry shell.
3. Bake at 450°F 10 minutes. Arrange pecan halves on top of pie filling. Turn oven control to 350°F and bake 30 to 35 minutes longer, or until a knife comes out clean when inserted halfway between center and edge of filling. Cool on wire rack.

One 9-inch pie

NEW MEXICO

Mexican Chocolate

2 ounces (2 squares)
    unsweetened
    chocolate
½ cup strong coffee
½ cup sugar
1 teaspoon ground
    cinnamon
1/16 teaspoon ground
    allspice
    Few grains salt
3 cups milk
1½ teaspoons vanilla extract
    Whipped cream

1. Heat chocolate and coffee together in a heavy saucepan, stirring until chocolate is melted and mixture is smooth. Cook 2 minutes, stirring constantly.
2. Mix in sugar, cinnamon, allspice, and salt. Gradually add milk, stirring until blended; heat thoroughly.
3. Remove from heat; blend in vanilla extract. Top each serving with whipped cream.

About 4 servings

Spiced Grape Jelly

3 pounds Concord grapes
½ cup cider vinegar
2 teaspoons ground
    cinnamon
1 teaspoon ground cloves
7 cups sugar
½ bottle liquid fruit pectin
    Paraffin

1. Rinse grapes, discard stems and blemished grapes. Drain and put into a large kettle. Crush grapes thoroughly.
2. Mix vinegar and spices and blend with grapes. Bring rapidly to boiling; reduce heat, cover kettle, and simmer mixture 10 minutes. Strain through a jelly bag.
3. Measure 4 cups of the strained juice into a large saucepan; cook over high heat until very hot. Add sugar and stir until dissolved. Bring rapidly to boiling and stir in pectin. Boil vigorously 1 minute, stirring constantly.
4. Remove from heat; skim off foam. Pour into hot sterilized jelly glasses and cover with melted paraffin.

Eight 8-ounce glasses jelly

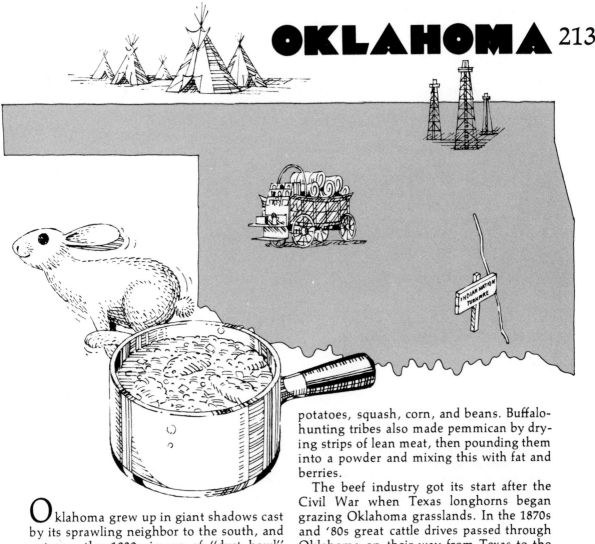

Oklahoma grew up in giant shadows cast by its sprawling neighbor to the south, and outgrew the 1930s image of "dust bowl" refugees streaming westward. Today it is a proud, bountiful land where Indian and cowboy cultures intermingle.

Loosely translated, Oklahoma means "land of the red man." And Indian it is, in beginnings and spirit as well as in name.

The government Indian Territory had its origin in the early 1800s when the Cherokees, Chickasaws, Choctaws, Creeks, and Seminoles were moved along the Trail of Tears to the wilderness west of the Mississippi. People of great courage, wisdom, and ability, they created new homes, established schools, and founded the first newspaper in the Territory.

In Oklahoma as elsewhere, the Indian diet contained such native foods as sweet potatoes, squash, corn, and beans. Buffalo-hunting tribes also made pemmican by drying strips of lean meat, then pounding them into a powder and mixing this with fat and berries.

The beef industry got its start after the Civil War when Texas longhorns began grazing Oklahoma grasslands. In the 1870s and '80s great cattle drives passed through Oklahoma on their way from Texas to the railroads in Kansas.

Cooks in outpost cow camps, explorers, and settlers adapted the Indian method of preparing meat. Strips of buffalo, venison, or beef were sun-dried to make jerky. Jerky, beans, bacon, dried fruits, and biscuits—accompanied by scalding coffee—were the staples of cowboy cookery.

The plains of western Oklahoma were the domain of Apache, Comanche, Cheyenne and Kiowa buffalo hunters, then of cowboys astride tough ponies. Though today's cow hands may ride trucks as often as horses, the long, straight roads still lead past grazing cattle and ranches where children practice tossing ropes as readily as others skip them.

OKLAHOMA

By 1889 pressure to open the Indian lands led the federal government to organize the first "run" into Indian territory. Thousands of homesteaders poured across the boundaries. Some impatient settlers crossed the line and staked claims "sooner" than allowed, hence the state nickname.

Land cultivation followed, and today northern Oklahoma is a vast green carpet in the spring as waving wheat spreads away to the limitless horizon. In the summer it ripens, ready for the men, combines, and trucks that harvest it. Though wheat is dominant, soybeans, oats, rye, barley, peanuts, pecans, and sweet potatoes are also important food crops.

In eastern Oklahoma timber-clad hills form the western ridges of the Ozark and Ouachita mountains. Here settlers built log cabins, fished the streams, and hunted deer and rabbit. The land still retains its rustic charm, though much has been cleared for farming.

Throughout the state museums and galleries house fine collections of western art and artifacts. Events and activities also recall Oklahoma's "cowboy and Indian" past. Rodeo riders test their skills in events that were once matter-of-fact daily tasks for range hands.

Indian Pow-Wows are ceremonial gatherings where traditional dances are performed in full regalia. At the American Indian Exposition in Anadarko visitors may view the ceremonies and share the customs and heritage of many tribes.

Rodgers and Hammerstein caught the excitement of the Sooner State in *Oklahoma!*, giving immortality to its atmosphere of frontier friendliness and vigor.

Chili and Bean Dip

1 cup pork and beans with
    tomato sauce
¼ cup mayonnaise
2 tablespoons dry onion
    soup mix
1 tablespoon chili powder
1 wedge onion
    Dairy sour cream (about
    ½ cup)

1. Put all ingredients except sour cream into an electric blender container. Cover and blend.
2. Transfer mixture to a serving dish and stir in sour cream to taste.
3. Serve **potato chips** and **corn chips** as dippers.

About 2 cups dip

Tenderfoot Hamburgers

These tender, juicy burgers are mildly seasoned.

1 pound ground beef
1 cup fine cracker or fine
    dry bread crumbs
½ cup finely chopped onion
½ cup tomato juice
1 egg, well beaten
½ teaspoon salt
¼ teaspoon pepper

1. Combine ground beef, cracker crumbs, onion, tomato juice, egg, salt, and pepper; mix lightly. Shape meat mixture into patties ¾ to 1 inch thick.
2. Arrange patties on broiler rack. Place under broiler with tops of patties about 3 inches from heat. Broil 10 to 12 minutes. Turn and brown other side of patties. Serve on split and toasted **hamburger buns**.

6 servings

OKLAHOMA

Beef Jerky

1 pound very lean top
    round steak
4 teaspoons salt
1 teaspoon pepper
1 teaspoon chili powder
1 teaspoon garlic powder
1 teaspoon onion powder
¼ teaspoon cayenne pepper
3 dashes liquid smoke
½ cup water

1. Trim the meat, removing any fat or connective tissue, and place in the freezer to freeze partially (about 1 hour).
2. Meanwhile, mix salt, pepper, chili powder, garlic powder, onion powder, cayenne, and liquid smoke in a bowl. Add water and stir to blend.
3. When the meat has firmed enough to slice easily, cut across the grain in slanting slices about ⅛ inch thick. Put the strips into the marinade, stir, cover, and chill several hours or overnight, stirring occasionally.
4. Remove strips from marinade, drain, and spread on wire racks placed on baking sheets. Place in a 200°F oven with door slightly ajar. Dry until a piece cracks when bent but does not break in two (5½ to 6 hours).
5. Cool on racks, then store in a covered container at room temperature or in the refrigerator.

About 8 ounces jerky

Rabbit Stew

Rabbits, both cottontails and jack rabbits, are plentiful in Oklahoma.

2½ cups water
1 cup (about ½ pound)
    dried large lima beans
2 tablespoons butter or
    margarine
2 medium (about ½
    pound) onions, thinly
    sliced
1 rabbit, 2½ to 3 pounds
    ready-to-cook weight,
    cleaned and cut in
    serving-size pieces
¼ cup chopped cooked
    ham
    Hot water (enough to
    half cover the rabbit)
1 tablespoon salt
¼ teaspoon pepper
⅛ teaspoon thyme
1 clove garlic, finely
    minced
1 bay leaf, crushed
1 pound carrots, sliced
2 green peppers, sliced in
    rings

1. Heat water to boiling in a large saucepan.
2. Meanwhile, sort and rinse lima beans thoroughly. Add beans gradually to water so boiling will continue. Simmer 2 minutes and remove saucepan from heat. Cover saucepan; set beans aside to soak 1 hour.
3. Heat butter in a large kettle or saucepot with a tight-fitting cover; add onion slices and cook over medium heat until just tender. Add rabbit pieces, chopped ham, and enough hot water to half cover the rabbit. Add salt, pepper, thyme, garlic, and bay leaf; cover and simmer 45 minutes.
4. Drain lima beans and add with sliced carrots to kettle. Continue cooking about 45 minutes, or until rabbit and vegetables are tender. Add more boiling water as needed.
5. During last 15 minutes of cooking time, add green pepper rings. Thicken cooking liquid with ¼ cup flour blended with ½ cup water, if desired.

6 to 8 servings

Meat-Stuffed Manicotti

2 tablespoons olive oil
½ pound fresh spinach, washed, dried, and finely chopped
2 tablespoons chopped onion
½ teaspoon salt
½ teaspoon oregano
½ pound ground beef
2 tablespoons fine dry bread crumbs
1 egg, slightly beaten
2 tablespoons tomato paste
8 manicotti shells (two-thirds of 5½-ounce package), cooked
1½ tablespoons butter or margarine, softened
Grated Parmesan or Romano cheese (about 2 tablespoons)

1. Heat olive oil in a skillet. Add spinach, onion, salt, oregano, and meat. Mix well, separating meat into small pieces. Cook, stirring frequently, until meat is no longer pink.
2. Set aside to cool slightly. Add bread crumbs, egg, and tomato paste; mix well. Stuff manicotti with mixture. Put side by side in a greased 2-quart glass baking dish.
3. Spread butter over stuffed manicotti and sprinkle with cheese. Cover dish.
4. Bake at 425°F 12 to 15 minutes, or until lightly browned.
5. If desired, serve topped with tomato sauce and additional cheese.

4 servings

Fried Corn

4 cups corn kernels
¼ cup chopped green pepper
2 tablespoons chopped onion
½ teaspoon salt
⅛ teaspoon pepper
¼ cup butter or margarine

1. Cut kernels from ears of cooked sweet corn, enough to yield 4 cups.
2. Combine corn in a bowl with green pepper, onion, salt, and pepper.
3. Heat butter in a skillet; add corn mixture and cook over medium heat about 20 minutes; stirring occasionally.

6 servings

Buckaroo Beans

Beans are cooked leisurely in a kettle, as they would have cooked over the campfire of a remote cow camp of yesteryear. They absorb a wonderful flavor from the rich brown sauce formed during cooking.

1 pound dried pinto or red beans
6 cups water
2 medium-size onions, thinly sliced

1. Wash beans, drain, and place in heavy kettle or saucepot with the water; bring rapidly to boiling. Boil 2 minutes and remove from heat. Set aside covered 1 hour. (If desired, pour the water over the washed beans in kettle, cover, and let stand overnight. Do not drain.)

2 large cloves garlic, thinly
    sliced
1 small bay leaf
1 teaspoon salt
½ pound salt pork, slab
    bacon, or smoked ham
1 can (16 ounces) whole
    tomatoes (undrained)
½ cup coarsely chopped
    green pepper
2 tablespoons brown sugar
2 teaspoons chili powder
½ teaspoon dry mustard
¼ teaspoon crushed
    oregano or cumin

2. Stir in the onion, garlic, bay leaf, and salt. (If salt pork is used, add salt later.)
3. Wash salt pork thoroughly. Slice through pork or bacon twice each way, not quite to the rind. Cut ham into ½-inch cubes, if used. Add meat to beans and bring rapidly to boiling. (To prevent foam from forming, add **1 tablespoon butter** or **margarine**.) Cover tightly and cook slowly about 1½ hours.
4. Stir in tomatoes, green pepper, and a mixture of the remaining ingredients. Bring rapidly to boiling and reduce heat. Season to taste with salt and simmer, covered, 6 hours or longer; remove cover the last hour of cooking, if desired. If necessary, gently stir beans occasionally to avoid sticking on bottom of kettle. There should be just enough liquid remaining on beans to resemble a medium-thick sauce.
5. Serve piping hot in soup plates.

About 6 servings

OKLAHOMA

Apache Bread

Cornbread baked in green cornhusks stays moist and flavorful, thanks to a steaming effect.

1 cup white cornmeal
1 cup yellow cornmeal
1 teaspoon salt
½ teaspoon red pepper
1 cup boiling water
½ cup bacon drippings
    Green cornhusks

1. Mix dry ingredients; add boiling water and bacon drippings.
2. Form into small rolls and wrap in green cornhusks.
3. Bake at 350°F 1 hour.

12 rolls

Peanut Blonde Brownies

½ cup chunk-style peanut
    butter
¼ cup butter or margarine
1 teaspoon vanilla extract
1 cup firmly packed light
    brown sugar
2 eggs
½ cup sifted all-purpose
    flour
1 cup chopped salted
    peanuts
    Confectioners' sugar

1. Cream peanut butter with butter and vanilla extract. Gradually add brown sugar, beating well. Add eggs, one at a time, beating until fluffy after each addition.
2. Add flour in halves, mixing until blended after each addition. Stir in peanuts. Turn into a greased 8×8×2-inch baking pan and spread evenly.
3. Bake at 350°F 30 to 35 minutes.
4. Remove pan to wire rack to cool 5 minutes before cutting into 2-inch squares. Remove from pan and cool on rack. Sift confectioners' sugar over tops.

16 squares

OKLAHOMA

Freezer Bran Muffins

3 cups whole bran cereal
1 cup boiling water
½ cup shortening
1½ cups sugar
2 eggs
2 cups buttermilk
3 cups sifted all-purpose
   flour
2½ teaspoons baking soda
½ teaspoon salt

1. Put bran cereal into a bowl. Pour in boiling water. Set aside until cool.

2. Put shortening and sugar into a large mixer bowl. Beat until thoroughly blended. Beat in eggs one at a time. Alternately mix in the soaked bran and buttermilk.

3. Sift flour, baking soda, and salt together; add to the bran mixture and mix gently until ingredients are thoroughly moistened (do not overmix).

4. *To freeze batter:* Pour batter into jars or other containers (leave headspace), cover tightly, and place in freezer for up to 6 weeks.

5. *To thaw batter:* Remove jars from freezer and thaw in the refrigerator or at room temperature only until batter is of pouring consistency.

6. Pour batter into well-greased 2- to 2½-inch muffin-pan wells, filling each about two thirds full.

7. Bake at 400°F 15 to 18 minutes, or until muffins test done.

About 3 dozen muffins

Note: The batter may be stored, tightly covered, in the refrigerator up to 3 weeks, instead of being frozen. When ready to use, remove the batter from refrigerator and immediately pour into greased muffin-pan wells and bake.

Variations: **Chopped raisins, dates,** or **nuts** (about ½ cup for each quart of batter) may be folded into batter before pouring into muffin wells.

Watermelon Punch

Especially refreshing on those Oklahoma days when the temperature may soar to well over 100°F!

2½ cups water
¼ cup lemon juice
1 cup sugar
3 cups watermelon juice*
2 cups orange juice
6 tablespoons lemon juice
   Lemon, lime, and
      orange slices

1. Combine one half of the water, lemon juice, and sugar in a saucepan; mix well. Bring to boiling and boil 3 minutes; cool.

2. Mix in remaining water and fruit juices. Chill thoroughly.

3. Pour over decorative ice block in a punch bowl. Garnish with fruit slices.

About 2 quarts punch

*To prepare watermelon juice, extract juice from diced watermelon (about 5½ cups) by pressing it against the sides of a fine sieve. If desired, strain juice through cheesecloth.

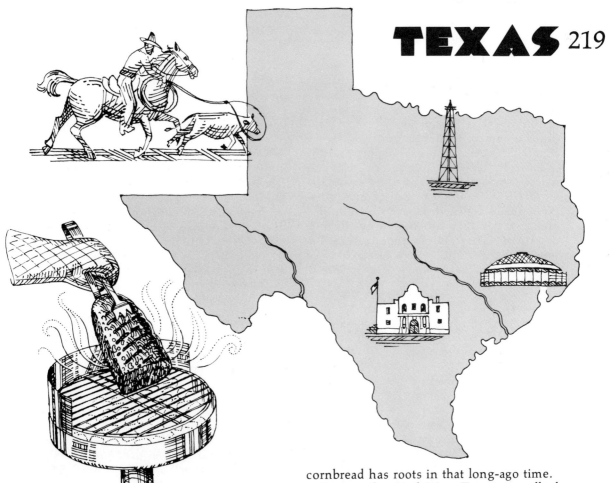

Texas is famous for its hospitality. "Y'all come" is sincerely meant, and the latchstring is always out. Hostesses make it a practice to prepare for more guests than they've invited, so there is never an "unexpected" guest.

For years the biggest state in the nation, Texas has been edged out of first place by Alaska, but still offers plenty of wide open spaces. Mountainous in the northwest, it slopes off to sea level at the Gulf of Mexico.

Texas became a part of Mexico in 1821, and later that year Stephen Austin led the first Anglo-American colonists into the area. Austin is now called the "Father of Texas," and the capital is named for him.

Texas later rebelled against Mexico and became a republic before joining the Union, but it retains its Mexican heritage in its cooking. The popularity of such dishes as chili con carne, sopapillas, and jalapeña cornbread has roots in that long-ago time.

During the Civil War, Texas was allied with the South. Even today there is much that is southern in its cuisine and life-style. Along with such Deep-South favorites as spoon bread are dishes with Creole overtones, such as gumbo and pralines.

Because the width of Texas spreads into the southwestern sun belt, there are western influences in its cookery, too. The barbecue is an outgrowth of the frontier days chuckwagon-style "grub."

Beef and lamb are Texas barbecue favorites, and ranching is as much a part of the state's economy as of its image. Today's methods are a far cry from the fabled cattle drives over the Chisholm Trail. Now Interstate 35 parallels that historic route. Open ranges are a thing of the past, and the Texas Longhorn has been replaced by other breeds, but Texas remains the nation's leader in both cattle and sheep production.

Grains are important in Texas agriculture,

too. The wheat and rice fields are both big producers. Jefferson County, bordering Louisiana and the Gulf of Mexico, leads the country in rice production. Texans have found a number of innovative ways to serve it; rice pilaf makes a fancy side dish.

The seacoast plays a big role in Texas life; a fact sometimes overlooked by outsiders. Galveston, where Jean Laffite and other pirates once made headquarters, is now a major seaport. Shrimp boats bring in a delicious haul. They are often manned by Cajuns (Acadians with French heritage). Red snapper and other seafoods give variety to the Texas table.

The turn of the century was a turning point in Texas history, when oil was discovered at Spindletop. "Black gold" gave an upturn to the state's economy and brought prospectors in vast numbers.

Northeast Texas boasts two of the state's largest cities: Dallas and Fort Worth. Between the two is one of the state's favorite tourist spots, Six Flags Over Texas. Those six flags symbolize the colorful past under Spain, France, Mexico, the Republic, the Confederacy, and the present as part of the United States. Each nationality has contributed to the cookery, as well as the folkways of Texas.

Smoked Barbecued Beef

1 tablespoon coarsely
    ground sage
1 teaspoon paprika
1 tablespoon ground
    summer savory
½ teaspoon chili powder
1 beef rib eye roast (5
    pounds)

Sauce:
½ cup butter
2 tablespoons lemon juice
5 tablespoons
    Worcestershire sauce
6 tablespoons ketchup
2 tablespoons soy sauce
2 tablespoons French
    dressing
1 teaspoon salt
1 teaspoon bottled steak
    sauce

1. Combine sage, paprika, savory, and chili powder. Rub meat with the mixture, wrap in plastic wrap, and place in refrigerator 12 to 24 hours.
2. For sauce, combine butter, lemon juice, Worcestershire sauce, ketchup, soy sauce, French dressing, salt, and steak sauce in a saucepan. Heat and stir until blended.
3. Place meat over low coals; never over direct flames. When meat has browned well and is dry on surface, brush with sauce. Continue to apply sauce and turn meat every 30 minutes. When turning meat, use a spatula or tongs, for a fork will cause the juices to run out.
4. After roast has been cooking 3 hours, begin to check the temperature of the meat, and continue cooking until desired temperature is reached (140°F for rare, 160°F for medium, and 170°F for well done).

10 to 15 servings

Pedernales River Chili *(Lyndon B. Johnson's favorite)*

4 pounds ground beef
    (chuck)
1 large onion, chopped
2 cloves garlic, minced
1 teaspoon ground oregano

1. Put meat, onion, and garlic in a large, heavy boiler or skillet. Cook until vegetables are tender and all pink color is gone from meat. Add oregano, cumin, chili powder, tomatoes, salt to taste, and hot water. Bring to boiling. Lower heat.

1 teaspoon cumin seed
6 teaspoons chili powder, more if needed
2 cans (16 ounces each) tomatoes (undrained)
   Salt
2 cups hot water

2. Simmer about 1 hour. Skim fat as necessary.
3. Serve with a side dish of **jalapeño peppers**.

About 8 servings

Stuffed Lamb Breasts

5 strips bacon
½ cup finely chopped onion
6 cups bread cubes with crusts removed
⅓ cup chopped pepperoni
3 tablespoons fresh parsley, or 1½ tablespoons dried parsley
1 teaspoon dried sweet basil
½ teaspoon salt
¼ teaspoon pepper
3 eggs, well beaten
½ cup milk
2 lamb breasts with pockets (about 5 pounds)
   Brown Sauce
2 tablespoons cornstarch
½ cup water

1. Cook bacon in skillet until crisp; drain, then crumble and set aside. Sauté onion in bacon fat until tender, but do not brown.
2. In large bowl, combine bread, onion, pepperoni, parsley, sweet basil, salt, pepper, and bacon. Toss lightly until well mixed.
3. In small bowl, mix beaten eggs and milk; then add to bread mixture and toss lightly until well mixed. Spoon half of stuffing into each lamb breast; then close opening with skewers. Place lamb breasts on rack in shallow roasting pan. Sprinkle lightly with additional salt and pepper.
4. Roast in a 350°F oven 15 minutes. Meanwhile make Brown Sauce. Generously baste lamb with Brown Sauce and continue to roast for 2 hours longer, or until lamb breasts are tender, basting lamb with Brown Sauce about every 15 minutes.
5. Remove lamb to heated platter. Skim fat from pan juice; stir in cornstarch dissolved in water. Cook over medium heat, stirring continuously, until thickened, adding more water if needed.
6. Carve lamb into slices and serve with pan gravy.

6 servings

Brown Sauce: In a 2-cup saucepan, mix **1½ cups water or bouillon** with **1 teaspoon prepared mustard, 1 teaspoon Worcestershire sauce, 1 teaspoon bottled beef sauce, ½ teaspoon celery salt, 1 bay leaf, and 2 whole cloves.** Add **1 medium onion, halved,** and simmer over low heat for 15 minutes. Remove onion halves and place on top of lamb breasts. Baste meat with sauce.

TEXAS

Lamb Stew, Continental

2 pounds lamb shoulder,
   boneless, cut in
   1½-inch cubes
2 tablespoons oil
½ cup chopped onion
½ teaspoon salt
½ teaspoon basil
½ teaspoon oregano
1 bay leaf, crushed
1 can (16 ounces) tomatoes
   (undrained)
1 can (8 ounces) tomato
   sauce
2 cloves garlic
1 teaspoon sugar
½ green pepper, cut in
   strips

1. Brown lamb cubes in oil in a large skillet. Add onion and cook, stirring frequently, until onion is soft. Drain off excess fat. Add salt, basil, oregano, bay leaf, tomatoes, tomato sauce, garlic, and sugar. Simmer covered 1½ hours.
2. Add green pepper, cover, and simmer 15 minutes, or until meat is tender.
3. Remove cover and cook, stirring as necessary, until sauce is reduced to desired consistency. Remove garlic.

About 6 servings

Shrimp and Rice au Gratin

1½ tablespoons butter
1 tablespoon flour
1½ cups milk
½ pound American cheese,
   cut in small pieces
½ teaspoon salt
1 teaspoon curry powder
   Dash of paprika
1 cup cooked shrimp, cut
   in halves
1 cup cooked rice
1 cup fine, soft bread
   crumbs

1. Melt butter and add flour, blending well. Add milk gradually and cook until thickened.
2. Add half of cheese and all seasonings; cook until cheese is melted, stirring constantly. Mix shrimp with rice and sauce.
3. Place in buttered baking dish, sprinkle with crumbs, and cover with remaining cheese.
4. Bake at 350°F 15 minutes, or until crumbs are browned and cheese is melted.

6 servings

Cowboy Crumb Cake

2½ cups sifted cake flour
½ teaspoon salt
2 cups brown sugar
⅔ cup shortening
½ teaspoon cinnamon
½ teaspoon nutmeg
½ teaspoon baking soda

1. Combine flour, salt, and brown sugar; add shortening and cut in with a pastry blender or 2 knives until mixture is very crumbly. Reserve ½ cup of these crumbs for top of cake.
2. To the remaining crumbs add mixed spices, baking soda, and baking powder.
3. Beat eggs, combine with buttermilk, and add to the

2 teaspoons baking
    powder
2 eggs, well beaten
1 cup buttermilk

crumb mixture. Beat until smooth. Spread batter in 2 well-greased cake pans and sprinkle top with the reserved crumbs.

4. Bake at 350°F 20 minutes. Serve hot.

Two 9-inch layers

Jean Lafitte Salad

1 cup diced, chilled cooked
    meat or poultry
½ cup diced cooked potato
½ cup diced cooked carrots
½ cup cut cooked green
    beans
2 tablespoons chopped
    sweet pickle
½ teaspoon salt
⅛ teaspoon pepper
½ cup French dressing
1 hard-cooked egg

1. Toss meat and vegetables with a mixture of pickle, salt, and pepper. Add French dressing and toss until meat and vegetables are well coated.

2. Chill in refrigerator at least 1 hour.

3. Chop hard-cooked egg. Add egg to mixture and mix thoroughly.

·*About 6 servings*

Sopaipillas

Sopaipillas are little pillow-shaped deep-fried pastries. They may be served plain as a bread, or as suggested here, sprinkled with cinnamon-sugar as a dessert. Sometimes they are topped with syrup.

2 cups sifted all-purpose
    flour
2 teaspoons baking powder
1 teaspoon salt
2 tablespoons shortening
⅔ to ¾ cup cold water
    Oil or shortening for
    deep frying heated to
    365°F
    Cinnamon-sugar

1. Sift flour, baking powder, and salt together into a bowl. Cut in shortening until mixture resembles coarse crumbs. Sprinkle water over top and work in gradually until dough will just hold together (as for pie pastry).

2. Turn out on a lightly floured surface and knead gently about 30 seconds. Roll out as thin as possible. Cut into 2-inch squares.

3. Fry one or two at a time in heated fat, turning until puffed and golden brown on both sides.

4. Drain on absorbent paper. Sprinkle with cinnamon-sugar while still hot.

2½ to 3 dozen

TEXAS

Cornbread Pie

1 cup soft butter or
    margarine
1 cup sugar
4 eggs
2 cups (16-ounce can)
    cream-style corn
1 cup shredded Monterey
    Jack
½ cup (4-ounce can) green
    chilies, drained,
    seeded, and chopped
1 cup yellow or white
    cornmeal
1 cup sifted all-purpose
    flour
4 teaspoons baking powder
½ teaspoon salt

1. Cream butter and sugar until light and fluffy. Beat in eggs, one at a time. Stir in corn, cheese, chilies, and cornmeal.
2. Sift flour, baking powder, and salt together and stir into batter.
3. Pour into greased 13×9-inch baking pan or two 9-inch pie pans.
4. Bake at 300°F 60 to 70 minutes, or until a wooden pick inserted in center comes out clean.
5. To serve, cut while still hot into squares or wedges. Serve with butter, if desired.

6 to 8 servings

Watermelon Pickles

2 pounds prepared
    watermelon rind
½ cup salt
2 quarts water
1 teaspoon whole allspice
1 teaspoon whole cloves
¼ teaspoon mustard seed
5 pieces (2 inches each)
    stick cinnamon
3 cups vinegar
2 cups water
2 pounds sugar
    Green or red food
    coloring (optional)

1. Pare the watermelon rind, removing all green and pink portions. Cut the rind into 2x1x½-inch pieces.
2. Prepare a brine of the salt and 2 quarts water; pour over rind. Cover and let stand overnight.
3. Drain rind; cover with fresh water and cook until tender when pierced with a fork. Remove from heat and let stand several hours; drain.
4. Tie the spices loosely in a spice bag or cheesecloth. Put into a large saucepot with the remaining ingredients. Bring to boiling and cook 5 minutes. Add the drained watermelon rind and cook gently until rind is clear and transparent. If desired, several minutes before end of cooking time, add enough green or red food coloring to the syrup to delicately tint the pickles. Remove and discard the spice bag.
5. Pack pickles in clean, hot jars. Fill with hot syrup to within ½ inch of top of jar. Remove air bubbles and add more syrup, if needed, to fill jars to within ½ inch of top.
6. Seal, following manufacturer's directions.
7. Process in boiling water bath 10 minutes.

About 3 pints pickles

Potato-Frosted Meat Loaf, 251

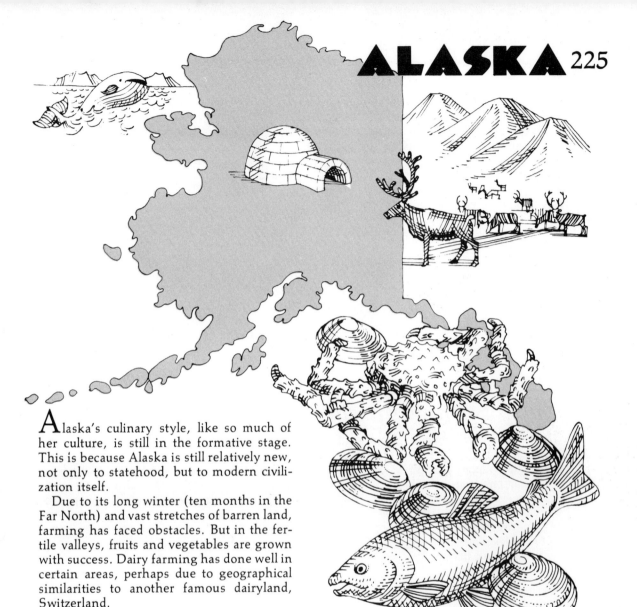

Alaska's culinary style, like so much of her culture, is still in the formative stage. This is because Alaska is still relatively new, not only to statehood, but to modern civilization itself.

Due to its long winter (ten months in the Far North) and vast stretches of barren land, farming has faced obstacles. But in the fertile valleys, fruits and vegetables are grown with success. Dairy farming has done well in certain areas, perhaps due to geographical similarities to another famous dairyland, Switzerland.

Alaska makes its greatest culinary contribution in seafood. Salmon is by far the biggest catch, but halibut, herring, clams, crabs, shrimp, and cod all help to make fishing the state's main source of income.

The climate seems almost unendurable, with winter temperatures dropping to 70°F below zero and summer heat reaching 100°F above in the interior. Yet Alaska has been populated for centuries. Early Russian explorers to the Aleutians found a society that had lived there for at least four thousand years.

Just as with the weather, it is difficult to discuss Alaska except in superlatives. It is the biggest state, with more than twice the land area of Texas. It claims the highest mountain in America, Mt. McKinley, which rises to an elevation of 20,320 feet. It has the smallest population, giving each Alaskan the most space per person of all the fifty states.

The gold strike in Juneau in 1880 started the rush to Alaska. It was some time before the next large-scale immigration. During the depression of the 1930s, the federal government helped a number of farm families from the Midwest to resettle in the Matanuska Valley.

ALASKA

The present Alaskan population is drawn mainly from the western United States, with Eskimos and Aleutians together accounting for about 10 percent. Some of the earliest settlers came from western Canada; others from the Scandinavian and Balkan countries. Other ethnic groups include Japanese, Filipinos, and Indians from the interior and from the coastal areas. Each has made an impact on the culinary as well as the cultural melting pot.

The early gold prospectors often carried a starter of sourdough in their knapsacks. In time, the term "sourdough" came to mean the miners themselves, as well as their bread.

Sourdough, sometimes called the wilderness yeast, has a history that goes back centuries before the Alaskan gold rush. It is said that an Egyptian left some flour out in the open that got wet and then fermented. The bubbles caused by the fermentation forced the dough to rise. He baked the loaf, and discovered that it was a great improvement over the flat cakes to which he was accustomed. For centuries this was the only method known to leaven bread, and the one that served, and still serves, many frontiersmen.

Another source of food for both the early settlers and present-day Alaskas is game. Moose, caribou, and reindeer all provide meat for the Alaskan table. Alaskans also take pride in their delicious and plentiful wild berries, such as cranberries and blueberries.

Nutty Shrimp Spread

¾ cup chopped cooked shrimp
¼ cup chopped ripe olives
¼ cup chopped walnuts
3 to 4 tablespoons mayonnaise-type salad dressing
1 tablespoon lemon juice
¼ teaspoon thyme
¼ teaspoon salt
Few grains cayenne pepper

1. Combine all ingredients and blend well. Refrigerate until thoroughly chilled.
2. To serve, spread on crisp **crackers,** and if desired, sprinkle with additional chopped walnuts. Garnish each with a piece of **shrimp,** a whole **small shrimp,** or a sprig of **parsley.**

About 1⅓ cups spread

Salmon Nuggets

¼ cup mashed potato
2 ounces sharp Cheddar cheese
1 can (7¾ ounces) salmon (about 1 cup, flaked)
1 tablespoon butter or margarine
1 tablespoon finely chopped onion
1 tablespoon finely chopped celery

1. Set out a deep saucepan or automatic deep-fryer and heat fat to 375°F.
2. Set out mashed potato. Cut cheese into ½-inch cubes and set aside.
3. Drain, flake, and set aside salmon.
4. Heat butter in a small skillet over low heat. Add and cook slowly over medium heat until onion and celery are transparent, stirring frequently.
5. Mix with the flaked salmon the mashed potato, onion, celery, Worcestershire sauce, and a mixture of salt and pepper.

1 teaspoon Worcestershire
  sauce
¼ teaspoon salt
⅛ teaspoon pepper
1 egg, beaten
⅓ cup fine, dry bread·
  crumbs

6. Use about 2 teaspoons of the salmon mixture and one cheese cube for each nugget. Shape the salmon around the cheese to form a ball about 1 inch in diameter.
7. Dip the nuggets in beaten egg. Coat nuggets by rolling in bread crumbs.
8. Deep-fry only as many nuggets at one time as will float uncrowded one-layer deep in fat. Deep-fry 1 minute, or until golden brown. Turn once or twice to brown evenly. Drain over fat for a few seconds; remove to absorbent paper.
9. Insert a wooden pick into each nugget and serve immediately.

About 1½ dozen appetizers

Broiled Elk Steak

2 pounds elk steak, 1 inch
  thick
1 clove garlic
2 tablespoons butter or
  other fat, melted
4 large mushroom caps
  Salt and pepper ·
  Parsley and watercress

1. Wipe steak with a damp cloth. Rub both sides with cut surfaces of garlic and brush with butter.
2. Place on a greased broiler rack in a hot broiler and cook for 5 minutes; turn and brush with butter and broil 5 to 8 minutes longer.
3. Broil mushroom caps. Season steak with salt and pepper and garnish with mushroom caps, parsley, and watercress.

4 servings

Filet of Venison

6 venison filets, cut 2
  inches thick
  Instant meat tenderizer
  (seasoned)
  Olive oil
1 clove garlic, split
1 tablespoon butter or
  margarine
1 tablespoon olive oil
3 tablespoons Madeira
1 tablespoon lemon juice
1 firm banana with
  all-yellow peel, cut
  diagonally in slices
  Butter or margarine

1. Prepare the meat as follows: Moisten each side of meat with water and sprinkle evenly with the instant meat tenderizer on all sides, using about ½ teaspoon per pound. Pierce meat deeply with a fork at approximately ½-inch intervals.
2. Heat a small amount of olive oil with garlic in a heavy skillet. Remove garlic before adding meat to the hot oil. Fry filets until they are brown outside but rare inside, about 20 minutes. Transfer to a hot platter and keep hot while preparing the sauce.
3. Add 1 tablespoon each butter and olive oil to the skillet with Madeira. Simmer about 2 minutes, stirring constantly. Pour over the filets just before serving.
4. Drizzle lemon juice evenly over the banana slices and fry slices in hot butter until thoroughly heated.
5. Garnish each filet with a banana slice and serve with Candied Cranberries (page 230).

6 servings

ALASKA

Planked Halibut Dinner

4 halibut steaks, fresh or
    thawed frozen (about 2
    pounds)
¼ cup butter, melted
2 tablespoons olive oil
1 tablespoon wine vinegar
2 teaspoons lemon juice
1 clove garlic, minced
¼ teaspoon dry mustard
¼ teaspoon marjoram
½ teaspoon salt
⅛ teaspoon ground black
    pepper
2 large zucchini
1 package (10 ounces)
    frozen green peas
1 can (8¼ ounces) tiny
    whole carrots
    Au Gratin Potato Puffs

1. Place halibut steaks in an oiled baking pan.
2. Combine butter, olive oil, vinegar, lemon juice, garlic, dry mustard, marjoram, salt, and pepper. Drizzle over halibut.
3. Bake at 450°F 10 to 12 minutes, or until halibut is almost done.
4. Meanwhile, halve zucchini lengthwise and scoop out center portion. Cook in boiling salted water until just tender.
5. Cook peas following directions on package. Heat carrots.
6. Prepare Au Gratin Potato Puffs.
7. Arrange halibut on wooden plank or heated ovenware platter and border with zucchini halves filled with peas, carrots, and potato puffs. Dot peas and carrots with **butter.**
8. Place platter under broiler to brown potato puffs. Sprinkle carrots with **chopped parsley.**
9. Garnish with sprigs of **parsley** and **lemon wedges** arranged on a skewer.

4 servings

Au Gratin Potato Puffs: Pare 1½ **pounds potatoes;** cook and mash potatoes in a saucepan. Add **2 tablespoons butter** and ⅓ **cup milk;** whip until fluffy. Add **2 slightly beaten egg yolks,** ½ **cup shredded sharp Cheddar cheese, 1 teaspoon salt,** and **few grains pepper;** continue whipping. Using a pastry bag with a large star tip, form mounds about 2 inches in diameter on plank. Proceed as directed in recipe.

Seafood Pie

⅓ cup butter or margarine
⅓ cup flour
½ teaspoon salt
2 cups liquid made of fish
    liquor and milk, fish
    stock, or diluted cream
    of mushroom soup
2 tablespoons chopped
    onion
1 cup frozen carrots, peas,
    or celery; or a
    combination of these
1 can (16 ounces) salmon,
    drained and flaked
    Pastry for a 2-crust pie or
    3 cups mashed potatoes

1. Melt butter in a large saucepan or skillet. Stir in flour and salt, blend until smooth. Add liquid gradually and cook until thickened, stirring constantly. Add onion, vegetables, and salmon. Blend thoroughly.
2. Line the bottom and sides of a well-greased 2-quart casserole with half of the pastry or 2 cups of the mashed potatoes. Pour in the filling, and top with remaining dough or potatoes.
3. Bake at 425°F about 30 minutes, or until crust is lightly browned and casserole is heated through.

6 servings

Note: If desired, 2 to 3 cups halibut, cooked and flaked, may be substitued for salmon. The mixture may also be turned into a greased 1½-quart casserole and topped with pastry for a 1-crust pie or 1 cup mashed potatoes, and baked.

Pimento Crab Meat Strata Supreme

1 can (7½ ounces) Alaska
    king crab meat,
    drained and flaked
½ cup finely chopped celery
¼ cup finely chopped onion
¾ cup mayonnaise
    Few grains cayenne
    pepper
12 slices white bread, crusts
    removed
    Butter or margarine,
    softened
3 jars or cans (4 ounces
    each) whole pimentos,
    each pimento cut in 2
    or 3 large pieces
1 pound Swiss cheese,
    shredded
5 eggs
3 cups milk
1 teaspoon salt
⅛ teaspoon pepper
¼ teaspoon dry mustard

1. Mix crab meat, celery, and onion. Blend in a mixture of mayonnaise and cayenne pepper. Set aside.
2. Spread both sides of the bread slices with butter. Place half of the bread in one layer in a greased 3-quart shallow baking dish; reserve remainder.
3. Arrange half of the pimento pieces over the bread, half of the crab mixture, and a third of the shredded cheese. Repeat layering, using remainder of crab mixture, pimento, and second third of the cheese. Cover with reserved bread and sprinkle with the remaining cheese.
4. Beat remaining ingredients together until frothy and blended. Pour over all. Let stand 1 hour.
5. Bake at 325°F 1 hour, or until puffed and browned.
6. Garnish top with three well-drained whole **pimentos** arranged in a bell cluster with **green pepper strips** between the bells. Nestle a small **parsley bouquet** at center.

6 to 8 servings

Sourdough Starter

2 cups all-purpose flour
1 package active dry yeast
1 tablespoon sugar
2 cups warm potato water
    (105°F to 115°F)

1. Combine flour, yeast, and sugar in a nonmetal mixing bowl. Stir in potato water.
2. Cover; let stand in a warm place (80°F to 85°F) for 48 hours.
3. Store in covered jar in refrigerator.
To use in recipe: Stir well before use. Pour out required amount called for in recipe and use as directed.
To replenish remaining starter: Mix in 1 cup each flour and warm water until smooth. Let stand in warm place a few hours until it bubbles again before covering and replacing in refrigerator.

Note: Use in recipe or remove 1 cup starter and replenish every week.

ALASKA

Golden Sourdough Bread

1 package active dry yeast
1¼ cups warm water
¼ cup firmly packed
    brown sugar
2 teaspoons salt
⅓ cup butter or margarine
3½ to 4 cups all-purpose
    flour
1½ cups Sourdough Starter
    (page 229)
3½ cups uncooked oats

1. Soften yeast in ½ cup warm water. Pour remaining 1 cup water over sugar, salt, and butter in a large bowl. Stir in 2 cups of flour, Sourdough Starter, oats, and softened yeast. Stir in enough additional flour to make a stiff dough.
2. Knead dough on a floured surface until smooth and elastic (about 10 minutes). Round dough into a ball; place in a greased bowl. Lightly grease surface of dough. Cover; let rise in a warm place until nearly double in bulk (about 1 hour).
3. Punch dough down; shape into 2 round loaves. Place on greased cookie sheets. Let rise in a warm place until nearly double in bulk (about 40 minutes). Slash tops with sharp knife or kitchen shears.
4. Bake at 400°F 35 to 40 minutes. Cool on wire racks.

2 loaves

Blueberry Buckle

½ cup sugar
2 cups all-purpose flour
2½ teaspoons baking
    powder
¼ teaspoon salt
1 egg
¼ cup butter or margarine,
    melted
½ cup milk
1 pint fresh blueberries,
    rinsed and drained
½ cup sugar
⅓ cup all-purpose flour
¼ cup butter
½ teaspoon cinnamon

1. Sift together ½ cup sugar, 2 cups flour, baking powder, and salt; set aside.
2. Beat together egg, melted butter, and milk. Make a well in the middle of the dry mixture, pour the liquid in the well, and stir just enough to mix with the dry ingredients.
3. Spread mixture in a well-greased 13×9-inch shallow baking dish and cover with blueberries.
4. Combine ½ cup sugar, ⅓ cup flour, ¼ cup butter, and cinnamon. Crumble this mixture over the blueberries.
5. Bake at 350°F 40 to 50 minutes.

12 servings

Candied Cranberries

2 cups fresh cranberries
1 cup sugar

1. Wash cranberries and spread over bottom of a shallow baking dish. Sprinkle with sugar and cover tightly.
2. Bake at 350°F 1 hour, stirring occasionally.
3. Chill before serving.

The gold rush that lured the Forty-niners westward also inspired California's nickname, "The Golden State." But the label fits for other reasons, too. There is the vibrant color of the citrus orchards, the gilt edge of a sunset on the Pacific sands, and of course, Hollywood's Midas touch on the state's economy.

California's cooking is so diverse that it is more appropriate to speak of its cuisines in the plural than in the singular. It is not uncommon to find, in a single locale, menus typical of the Spanish, Mexican, French, Oriental, and American Indian cooks who have settled there. Californians have no difficulty shifting culinary gears, ordering a French gourmet feast at one meal, a Creole dinner the next, and so on.

Much of California is now wine country. The wine industry goes back farther than statehood, which didn't formalize until 1850. A year later, Count Haraszthy, a Hungarian nobleman, introduced the great *Vitis vinifera* varietal vines to Calfornia. These included the now famous Zinfandel vines, which produce one of the state's most popular red wines. As it is produced nowhere else in the world, Californians take special pride in it. The finest of California's dry table wines are produced in the Napa Valley of northern California.

Located on the eastern edge of the wine country is San Francisco, a cosmopolitan diamond springing out of the rough crag of seacoasts. The whole span of the American melting pot is found in the population of San Francisco, and therefore, in its cooking.

Among the delights awaiting a visitor to San Francisco is a trip to Chinatown. A stroll down Grant Avenue is popular with tourists, but more authentic Chinese restaurants are found on nearby side streets. Hangtown Fry, a recipe that merges Oriental style with California ingredients, is a piquant oyster omelet. In San Francisco it might be served at brunch with toast and fresh strawberries from the Napa Valley.

CALIFORNIA

The Nisei, or Japanese Americans, are well represented among San Franciscans, too. A sample of Japanese fare is rumaki, the appetizer tidbits of chicken livers and water chestnuts broiled in bacon.

San Francisco is well known for its continental dining establishments; Crab Louis is the sort of dish that belongs in that ambience. There is some debate about the identity of Louis, for whom the dish is named, but absolutely none about its elegance. It combines two of California's most popular foods, avocado and crab.

More crab, and a vast array of other gifts from the sea, are to be savored at Fisherman's Wharf, another of San Francisco's culinary attractions. More than a mere tourist attraction, Fisherman's Wharf is a genuine commercial pier.

Even at-home entertaining in San Francisco calls for long skirts and candlelight. Shift the scene to Los Angeles and the attire, as well as the cooking, is more apt to be casual. The grill, often alongside the backyard swimming pool, is a favorite setting for both family and company meals.

That California was once part of Spanish Mexico is clearly evident in Los Angeles. Old Mexico itself spills over into such intriguing byways as Olvera Street, where enchiladas and tacos are available along with other Mexican attractions.

Los Angeles, like San Francisco, is made up of many cultural groups, and newcomers are still moving in. Perhaps at some future date the culinary style of California can be more precisely defined; in these changing times, its diversity is part of its charm.

The valleys of lower California are both fruit and vegetable baskets for the nation. They have inspired such writers as Nobel prize winner John Steinbeck and pop poet Rod McKuen, just as they have inspired artistry in the kitchen.

Ham Loaf en Brioche

Wine and ripe olives are two ingredients that identify this as a California recipe. The French sophistication is typical of San Francisco cuisine.

Brioche Dough:
- 1 package (13¾ ounces) hot roll mix
- ¼ cup warm water
- ⅓ cup milk
- ⅓ cup butter or margarine
- 2 tablespoons sugar
- 3 eggs, beaten

Ham Loaf:
- 2 cups ground cooked ham
- 1 pound ground veal or lean beef
- 2 eggs, beaten
- 2 cups fine soft bread crumbs
- ¾ cup California Sauterne
- ½ teaspoon dry mustard
- ½ teaspoon salt
- ¼ teaspoon pepper
- ½ cup coarsely chopped ripe olives

1. For brioche dough, combine yeast from packet in hot roll mix with warm water.
2. Scald milk and cool to lukewarm.
3. Cream butter and sugar. Add eggs and yeast; mix well. Stir in flour mixture from mix alternately with milk, beating until smooth after each addition. Cover tightly; let rise in a warm place until light (about 1 hour). Stir down and set in refrigerator until thoroughly chilled.
4. Meanwhile, prepare ham loaf.
5. For ham loaf, combine all ingredients and mix well. Turn into a greased fluted brioche pan, about 8½ inches across top and about 1-quart capacity; pack into pan and round up center.
6. Bake at 350°F 1 hour. Cool in pan about 10 minutes, then turn out of pan and cool thoroughly.
7. Divide chilled brioche dough in half. Roll each portion into a round about 10 inches in diameter. Turn cooled ham loaf upside down and fit a round of dough over bottom and sides. Trim off excess dough. Holding dough in place, quickly invert loaf and fit other round

CALIFORNIA

¼ cup diced pimento
1 tablespoon instant
    minced onion

of dough over top and sides. Trim edges evenly.

8. Place dough-wrapped loaf in a well-greased brioche pan a size larger than one used for ham loaf, about 9½ inches in diameter across top and about 2-quarts capacity.

9. Shape dough trimmings into a ball and place on top of loaf. Let rise in a warm place about 30 to 45 minutes, or until dough is light.

10. Set on lowest shelf of 375°F oven. Bake 10 to 15 minutes, or until top is browned. Place a piece of brown paper or aluminum foil over top of loaf. Continue baking about 25 minutes, or until nicely browned and baked through (test brioche with wooden pick).

11. Turn loaf out of pan and serve warm or cold, cut in wedges.

About 8 servings

Oriental Beef Stew

1¼ pounds boneless beef
    (round sirloin, sirloin
    tip, or rump), cut ½
    inch thick
    Seasoned instant meat
    tenderizer
3 tablespoons cooking oil
1 green pepper, cut in
    thin strips
1 sweet red pepper, cut in
    thin strips
2 celery stalks, cut
    lengthwise in thin
    strips, then into
    2-inch pieces
2 small onions, thinly
    sliced
6 fresh mushrooms (about
    2 ounces), sliced
    lengthwise through
    caps and stems
1 can (5 ounces) water
    chestnuts, drained and
    sliced
2 tablespoons cornstarch
2 teaspoons sugar
¾ teaspoon ground ginger
1½ cups water
3 tablespoons Japanese
    soy sauce (shoyu)
1 beef bouillon cube

1. Tenderize meat according to the directions; cut into 2×¼-inch strips.

2. Heat 1 tablespoon of the oil in a large skillet. Add beef strips and stir-fry over high heat about 2 minutes, or until well browned. Remove and set aside.

3. Add remaining oil and heat. Add vegetables and cook, turning frequently, about 3 minutes, or until vegetables are crisp-tender. Remove from heat and return meat to skillet.

4. In a saucepan, thoroughly blend cornstarch, sugar, and ginger; stir in water and soy sauce; add bouillon cube. Bring the mixture to boiling and boil 3 minutes, stirring frequently.

5. Pour sauce over meat and vegetables; toss lightly to coat well. Heat thoroughly. Serve immediately.

About 4 servings

CALIFORNIA

Rumaki

½ pound chicken livers
1½ tablespoons honey
1 tablespoon soy sauce
2 tablespoons cooking oil
½ clove garlic, minced
1 can (5 ounces) water chestnuts, drained and cut in quarters or slices
Bacon slices, halved

1. Rinse chicken livers with running cold water and drain on absorbent paper; cut into halves and put into a bowl.
2. Pour a mixture of honey, soy sauce, oil, and garlic over the liver pieces. Cover and let stand about 30 minutes, turning pieces occasionally. Remove from marinade and drain.
3. Wrap a piece of bacon around a twosome of liver and water chestnut pieces, threading each onto a wooden pick or small skewer.
4. Put appetizers on rack in broiler pan and broil with top about 3 inches from source of heat about 5 minutes. Turn with tongs and broil until bacon is browned. Serve hot.

About 1½ dozen appetizers

Avocado Voisin

4 tablespoons butter
1½ tablespoons minced onion
1½ tablespoons minced celery
¾ teaspoon curry powder
¾ cup uncooked white rice
1½ cups chicken or beef broth
Salt
White pepper
1 small bay leaf
2 tablespoons flour
1 cup milk
1 egg yolk
2 cans (about 6½ ounces each) crab meat, drained
2 tablespoons chutney, finely chopped
3 large avocados
Lemon juice

1. Melt 1½ tablespoons butter in skillet. Add onion and celery; cook until tender, about 4 minutes, stirring occasionally.
2. Add curry powder to vegetables and blend thoroughly. Stir in rice, mixing to coat each grain. Add broth, few grains each salt and white pepper, and bay leaf. Bring to boiling, cover, lower heat, and simmer until moisture is absorbed and rice is tender (about 20 minutes).
3. In a saucepan, melt 1½ tablespoons butter. Blend in flour and a few grains each salt and white pepper. Cook slowly for 5 minutes, not allowing mixture to brown. Remove pan from heat and stir milk gradually into flour mixture. Return pan to heat, cook until sauce is thickened (about 10 minutes), stirring constantly.
4. Beat a small amount of hot mixture into egg yolk, then return to mixture in saucepan. Heat just to boiling. Remove from heat, cover, and keep warm.
5. Sauté crab meat in 1 tablespoon butter 1 minute. Add chutney and mix well. Combine cooked rice and crab meat, tossing lightly to mix. Keep warm.
6. Halve avocados, remove seeds, and peel. Cut small slice from bottoms so that avocados will be flat. Put

CALIFORNIA

3 tablespoons grated
    Parmesan cheese
Parsley and lemon
    wedges for garnish

cut-off slices in avocado cavities, and brush cut surfaces of avocado with lemon juice.

7. Arrange avocado halves in a shallow baking dish. Pile crab-rice mixture into avocado halves. Spoon sauce over each stuffed avocado. Sprinkle with Parmesan cheese.

8. Bake at 300°F 10 to 15 minutes.

9. Garnish with parsley and lemon wedges.

6 servings

Hangtown Fry

6 tablespoons butter
8 large oysters, fresh,
    frozen, or canned
2 cups sliced fresh
    mushrooms
½ cup chopped green onion
8 eggs
½ cup water
1 teaspoon salt
½ teaspoon paprika
¼ teaspoon pepper
3 slices bacon, crisply
    cooked and crumbled

1. Melt butter in a large skillet. Add oysters and sauté until cooked and browned. Stir in mushrooms, cooking until slightly browned. Add onion, mix with oysters and mushrooms, and cook until just tender.

2. Beat eggs with water, salt, paprika, and pepper, until mixed. Sprinkle bacon over oyster mixture in skillet, then pour egg mixture over bacon.

3. Cook over medium heat, lifting from bottom and sides of skillet to allow uncooked egg to go under cooked mixture.

4. When eggs are cooked but not dry, cut in fourths and serve.

4 servings

Monterey Artichokes

Ninety-eight percent of all artichokes consumed in the United States are grown north of Monterey.

4 large artichokes
3 quarts boiling salted
    water
¼ cup tarragon vinegar
10 whole allspice
1 bay leaf
    Dilled Mayonnaise

1. Rinse and cut stems of artichokes. Place on side on cutting board and cut 1 inch off top. Using kitchen shears, snip off prickly top of each leaf.

2. Immerse in boiling salted water. Add vinegar, allspice, and bay leaf. Cover.

3. Cook 20 minutes, or until one of outer leaves of artichoke pulls off easily. Remove from water and drain upside down.

4. Serve warm or chilled with Dilled Mayonnaise.

4 servings

Dilled Mayonnaise: Blend together **½ cup mayonnaise, 1 tablespoon lemon juice,** and **1 teaspoon dill weed.**

CALIFORNIA

Sherry-Coconut Chiffon Cake

2 cups sifted all-purpose
   flour
1-½ cups sugar
1 tablespoon baking
   powder
1 teaspoon salt
⅔ cup cooking oil
2 egg yolks
½ cup water
¼ cup California Sherry or
   Muscatel
2 teaspoons vanilla extract
½ cup flaked coconut
1 cup egg whites (7 or 8)
½ teaspoon cream of tartar
   Confectioners' sugar
   (optional)

1. Sift flour, 1 cup sugar, baking powder, and salt into a bowl. Make a well and add, in order, oil, egg yolks, water, sherry, and vanilla extract. Beat to a smooth batter. Mix in coconut.
2. Pour egg whites into a very large mixing bowl. Sprinkle cream of tartar over egg whites. Whip until soft peaks are formed. Add remaining ½ cup sugar gradually, beating until very stiff peaks are formed. Do not underbeat (whites should be stiffer than for angel food cake or meringue).
3. Pour batter slowly over whites, gently folding with rubber spatula or large spoon just until blended.
4. Turn immediately into an ungreased 10x4-inch tube pan.
5. Bake at 325°F 1 hour and 10 minutes, or until top surface springs back when lightly touched with finger and cracks look dry.
6. Remove from oven and turn upside down. Cool completely in pan.
7. Loosen cake from sides and center tube. Turn pan over and hit edge sharply on table to loosen.
8. Put cake on a serving plate. If desired, sift confectioners' sugar over top.

One 10-inch tube cake

Champagne Punch

Ice Ring
3 jiggers brandy
3 jiggers curaçao
1 quart chilled champagne
1 quart sparkling water

1. At serving time, turn Ice Ring into a punch bowl.
2. Add brandy, curacao, champagne, and sparkling water. Serve in punch cups.

About 2 quarts punch

Ice Ring: Fill a ring mold with water and freeze the night before the party. If desired, arrange mint leaves and maraschino cherries in mold to form a wreath effect.

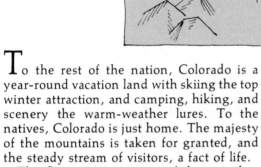

To the rest of the nation, Colorado is a year-round vacation land with skiing the top winter attraction, and camping, hiking, and scenery the warm-weather lures. To the natives, Colorado is just home. The majesty of the mountains is taken for granted, and the steady stream of visitors, a fact of life.

The flat, eastern section of the state has much in common with its midwestern neighbors. Cattle farms prosper, and grains such as corn and wheat dominate the crops. Fruits and vegetables grow well, too, in the fertile, irrigated sections.

Off to the west, Colorado-style is apt to mean Western. Sage gives a purple hue to the rocky landscape, which is unsuited for conventional farming.

The Rocky Mountains crest in the west-central part of the state at the Continental Divide. They slope off to the east through foothills and on to wide expanses of plains. To the west, river beds have cut gorges through flat-topped hills called mesas. The Mesa Verde is the best known of these; it was home to prehistoric Indians.

The south central part of Colorado has much in common with the Spanish southwest. In 1848, when the western half of the state was ceded to the United States by Mexico, Spanish-speaking colonists from New Mexico moved into the San Luis Valley. The area became for a time an extension of the old Spanish agricultural communities of the south. A taste for highly seasoned south-of-the border dishes has spread from here throughout the state.

Another group of settlers rushed into the state when gold was discovered near Denver. The prospectors were a mixed band, contributing further to the cultural and cooking style. Colorado became a territory in 1861; statehood followed in 1876. Thus it won the inevitable nickname, "The Centennial State."

Coloradoans are, for the most part, outdoor people who make good use of the endowments of nature. Skiing is a favorite

COLORADO

sport, and Aspen, Vail, Snowmass, and Winterpark are just a few of the famous runs that have helped to make Colorado the ski capital of North America. Hot drinks and hot appetizers are popular with the après-ski set.

A few old mining towns, such as Central City, have been restored to give visitors a look at early-day life. Other "ghost" towns are sprinkled through the old mining areas, a reminder of the days when the gold strikes were frequent and the prospectors prospered. Little remains but broken-down buildings, but tourists delight in poking through them.

Colorado cooking, as all mountain cooking, varies from that of the lowlands in one respect; the altitude requires a conversion in length of cooking time due to the difference in atmospheric pressure.

Colorado is a leading producer of sugar beets and an important refiner of sugar. Another treat for which the state is famous is mountain trout. Quick pan-frying is the favored cooking method. Side dishes of Colorado-grown sweet corn, sliced tomatoes, and perhaps melon for dessert make a summer meal to remember.

Come wintertime, the cooking style may highlight après-ski with such favorites as quiche or fondue to accompany a warming beverage.

Chili con Queso Dip

1 cup chopped onion
2 cans (4 ounces each) green chilies, chopped and drained
2 large garlic cloves, mashed
2 tablespoons cooking oil
1 pound process sharp Cheddar cheese, cut in chunks
1 teaspoon Worcestershire sauce
¼ teaspoon paprika
¼ teaspoon salt
½ cup tomato juice

1. Sauté onion, green chilies, and garlic in oil in a heavy skillet until onions are tender.
2. Reduce heat to low, and add remaining ingredients except tomato juice. Cook, stirring constantly, until cheese is melted.
3. Add tomato juice gradually until dip is the desired consistency.

3¼ cups dip

Beef Brisket with Horseradish Sauce

1 fresh beef brisket (6 to 7 pounds)
4½ teaspoons seasoned salt
4 to 5 tablespoons flour
½ cup chili sauce
½ cup ketchup
1 jar (5 ounces) prepared horseradish
1 cup boiling water

1. Sprinkle the beef with seasoned salt; coat evenly with flour. Set on a rack in a roasting pan. Roast at 450°F 30 minutes.
2. Combine the chili sauce, ketchup, and horseradish; mix well and spoon over meat.
3. Pour boiling water into bottom of pan; cover. Reduce oven temperature to 350°F and return meat to oven. Continue roasting about 3 hours, or until meat is tender.
4. If desired, thicken cooking liquid for gravy.

10 to 12 servings

Cucumber Soup

A featured treat served at the Copper Kettle in Aspen, Colorado.

½ cup chopped onion
¼ cup sliced carrot
4 cups chopped celery
   (with leaves)
1 tablespoon butter
3 cucumbers, pared and
   diced
¼ teaspoon thyme
½ teaspoon tarragon leaves,
   crushed
6 cups chicken broth
2 eggs, slightly beaten
1 cup whipping cream
2 tablespoons dry sherry
1 teaspoon lemon juice

1. In a kettle, cook onion, carrot, and celery with butter until vegetables are soft (about 5 minutes). cover and cook 10 minutes. Cool slightly.
3. Pour half of mixture into an electric blender container; blend until smooth. Repeat with remaining half. Pour purée back into kettle; heat thoroughly.
4. Blend beaten eggs with cream. Slowly stir in about ½ cup of hot purée, then stir into remaining hot purée. Blend in sherry and lemon juice.
5. Serve soup immediately in mugs or bowl. Sprinkle with **paprika** and **toasted seasame seed**.

About 2 quarts soup

Frankly Outdoor Stew

1 pound frankfurters, cut
   in ½-inch chunks
2 tablespoons minced
   onion
½ clove garlic, minced
   (optional)
¾ cup coarsely chopped
   pitted ripe olives
1 can (6 ounces) tomato
   juice
1 teaspoon Worcestershire
   sauce
½ teaspoon celery salt
1 can (16 ounces) kidney
   beans, drained and
   rinsed
1 can (16 ounces) whole
   kernel corn
1 cup shredded Cheddar
   cheese

1. Combine franks, onion, garlic, olives, tomato juice, seasonings, and vegetables in a large saucepan. Cook over medium heat until thoroughly heated.
2. Remove from heat; add cheese and stir until melted.
3. Serve on buttered slices of **French bread** or **rusks**.

6 servings

COLORADO

COLORADO

Peach 'n' Pork Chop Barbecue

6 pork chops, cut 1 inch
    thick
1 tablespoon fat
¼ cup lightly packed brown
    sugar
1 teaspoon ground
    cinnamon
½ teaspoon ground cloves
1 can (8 ounces) tomato
    sauce
6 canned cling peach
    halves, drained
    (reserve ¼ cup syrup)
¼ cup cider vinegar
¾ teaspoon salt
¼ teaspoon pepper

1. Brown chops on both sides in hot fat in a large, heavy skillet.
2. Meanwhile, blend a mixture of brown sugar, cinnamon, and cloves with the tomato sauce, reserved peach syrup, and vinegar.
3. Pour off excess fat from skillet. Sprinkle chops with a mixture of salt and pepper. Place a peach half on each chop. Pour sauce over all. Cover skillet and simmer about 30 minutes, or until pork is tender; baste occasionally with the sauce.

6 servings

Rocky Mountain Trout

6 cleaned fresh trout, 8 to
    10 ounces each
1 cup all-purpose flour
1 teaspoon salt
¼ teaspoon pepper
    Cooking oil

1. Remove heads and tails from trout, if desired; rinse quickly under cold running water and pat dry with absorbent paper. Do not scale.
2. Combine dry ingredients in a shallow bowl or pie plate. Coat trout with mixture.
3. Pour oil to a depth of ½ inch into a skillet and heat to 350°F. Place fish in oil (do not crowd) and cook until golden on both sides, turning only once.

6 servings

Swiss Cheese-Onion Quiche

6 slices bacon
1 cup chopped onion
1 unbaked 9-inch pie shell
½ pound Swiss cheese, cut
    in ½-inch cubes
3 eggs, slightly beaten
½ cup milk
¼ cup dairy sour cream
½ teaspoon salt
    Dash pepper

1. Fry bacon until crisp and drain on paper towels.
2. Pour off all but 1 tablespoon bacon drippings from skillet. Stir-fry chopped onion in drippings until tender; drain.
3. Crumble bacon into bottom of pie shell. Add onion and cheese cubes evenly over the bacon.
4. Combine beaten eggs, milk, sour cream, salt, and pepper in a mixing bowl. Pour over bacon-onion-cheese mixture in pie shell.
5. Bake at 375°F for 25 to 30 minutes, or until center is set. Do not overbake.

One 9-inch pie

Salsa de Chili Colorado

6 **dried red chilies**
  Water (about 2 cups)
1 **pound ripe tomatoes or 1**
  can (16 ounces)
  tomatoes
2 **large cloves garlic**
3 **tablespoons olive oil**
½ **teaspoon oregano**
¼ **teaspoon ground cumin**

1. Place chilies under broiler, about 5 inches from heat, and broil about 3 minutes. Watch carefully, as they burn easily.
2. Remove stems, shake out seeds, place in saucepan, cover with water, and bring to boiling. Remove from heat and let stand 20 minutes.
3. Put chilies into a blender jar with the cooking liquid and whirl until smooth; or chilies may be pressed through a strainer. Return chilies and liquid to saucepan.
4. Whirl tomatoes in blender or press through a strainer and add to chilies. Press garlic and add to sauce with olive oil, oregano, and cumin.
5. Simmer sauce 15 to 20 minutes. If desired, sauce may be thickened with a mixture of ½ tablespoon butter and ½ tablespoon flour. Stir in, bring to boiling, and cook 1 to 2 minutes.
6. Use as a sauce for Burritos (page 203).

3 cups sauce

COLORADO

Zucchini Pickle Slices

2½ **pounds zucchini,**
  scrubbed, rinsed, and
  cut in ¼-inch slices
  (2½ cups)
¾ **pound onions, thinly**
  sliced (2½ cups)
2 **cups cider vinegar**
1 **cup sugar**
4 **to 5 tablespoons salt**
1½ **teaspoons celery seed**
¼ **to ½ teaspoon ground**
  turmeric

1. Prepare vegetables and set aside.
2. Mix remaining ingredients in a heavy saucepan. Cook and stir over medium heat until sugar is dissolved and mixture comes to boiling. Remove from heat. Immediately add the vegetables; cover and let stand about 1 hour.
3. Bring the vegetable mixture to boiling rapidly; reduce heat and cook gently, uncovered, about 3 minutes. Remove from heat.
4. Pack vegetables in clean, hot jars; add hot pickling liquid to within ½ inch of top, being sure that vegetables are completely covered. Remove air bubbles and add more syrup, if needed, to fill jars to within ½ inch of top.
5. Seal, following manufacturer's directions.
6. Process in boiling water bath 15 minutes.

About 4 pints pickles

COLORADO

Cantaloupe Preserves

1 large, unripe cantaloupe
1 quart water
2 cups sugar
½ lemon, thinly sliced
2 tablespoons thinly sliced
   crystallized ginger

1. Cut cantaloupe into wedges, discarding seedy portion. Pare wedges and cut orange portion into 1-inch pieces. (There should be 3½ to 4 cups cantaloupe pieces.)
2. Cover cantaloupe in a bowl with a salt solution (1 tablespoon salt dissolved in 2 quarts cold water). Cover and let stand 8 hours, or overnight.
3. Drain cantaloupe in a colander and rinse with cold water; cook 8 to 10 minutes, or until cantaloupe is tender, but not soft. Drain thoroughly.
4. Meanwhile, mix the water and sugar in a saucepan. Bring to boiling, stirring until sugar is dissolved; boil, uncovered, about 5 minutes. Add the cantaloupe, lemon, and ginger. Cook rapidly until cantaloupe is translucent, 30 to 40 minutes. Remove from heat; cover tightly and set aside.
5. The next day, reheat the preserves to boiling and ladle into clean, hot jars. Seal immediately, following manufacturer's directions.
6. Process in boiling water bath for 10 minutes.

4 half-pints preserves

Apple Jelly

4 pounds tart apples
4 cups water
  Sugar
  Paraffin

1. Rinse, remove stem ends, and quarter apples. (Do not core or pare fruit.) Add the water to apples in a large kettle. Cover and cook gently until fruit is soft, stirring occasionally.
2. Strain fruit through a jelly bag. The pulp remaining in the bag may be used to make apple butter, if desired.
3. To prepare jelly, measure not more than 4 cups of apple juice into saucepan. Measure ¾ cup sugar for each cup of juice. Heat the juice to boiling and stir in the sugar. Return to boiling and cook rapidly until mixture tests done.*
4. Remove from heat; skim off foam.
5. Pour into hot, sterilized glasses. Seal with paraffin or lids, following manufacturer's directions.

5 half-pints jelly

*To test for jelly, dip a small amount of boiling syrup from saucepan with a cool metal spoon and slowly pour it back into saucepan from edge of spoon. Jelly is sufficiently cooked when drops of syrup run together and fall from spoon in a sheet. Remove from heat while testing.

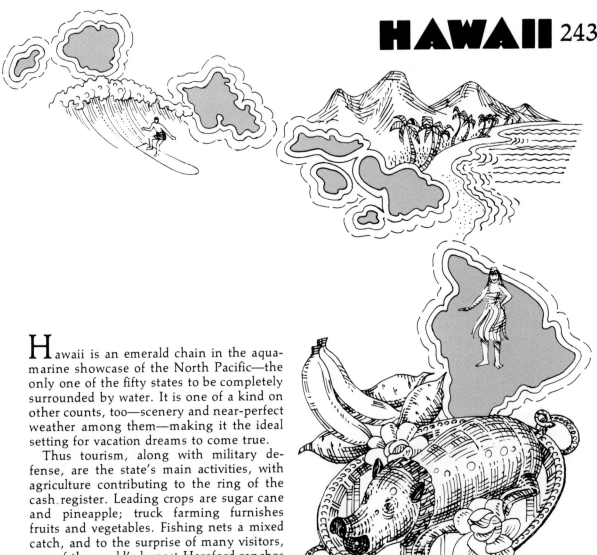

Hawaii is an emerald chain in the aquamarine showcase of the North Pacific—the only one of the fifty states to be completely surrounded by water. It is one of a kind on other counts, too—scenery and near-perfect weather among them—making it the ideal setting for vacation dreams to come true.

Thus tourism, along with military defense, are the state's main activities, with agriculture contributing to the ring of the cash register. Leading crops are sugar cane and pineapple; truck farming furnishes fruits and vegetables. Fishing nets a mixed catch, and to the surprise of many visitors, one of the world's largest Hereford ranches is located on the island of Hawaii. Poultry and hogs also help to put meat on the table.

The largest of the island chain is called Hawaii, and is located at the southern tip. Oahu is only the third largest of the islands, but leads the others in importance as it houses the capital city, Honolulu, and four fifths of the population.

From today's historical viewpoint, it is surprising that Hawaii was not discovered long before it was. Not until 1778 (after American mainland colonists had declared their independence) did Captain James Cook, an Englishman, come across the islands. He named the chain for his patron, the Earl of Sandwich, and they were known

for a time as the Sandwich Islands. They were quickly brought into a complex Pacific trade pattern, with sandalwood their main export.

The people whom Captain Cook found on the islands were Polynesians, and it is believed that their forefathers arrived in the islands around A.D. 750. Early in the nineteenth century, American missionaries set sail for Hawaii, carrying the work ethic along with their religion. Hawaii was annexed to the United States in 1898, and in

HAWAII

1959 the fiftieth star was added to our flag.

Cuisine in the islands is varied, but the feast that spells "Hawaii" to visitors is the luau. The early luaus were held in a spirit of thanksgiving to the gods. They were given as wedding feasts, birthday parties, house-warmings, or to welcome guests. Today they are a ritual for tourists, starting with pupus, tidbits served with cocktails. Won ton, tempting fillings deep-fried in pastry wrappers, are popular pupus.

The focal point of the luau is the kalua pig, which is prepared in an underground oven. (A simplified luau could substitute barbecued ribs with pineapple.) Poi, the taro-root paste, and limu, or seaweed, are also traditional on the islands, but can be skipped where they are unavailable. Other dishes, just as authentic, can be made from more accessible ingredients. These include pansit (noodles with pork) and teriyaki. The luau might end with fresh pineapple in rum sauce or bananas in pineapple sauce.

Since the Hawaii of today is a mixture of Polynesians, Orientals, mainland Americans, Filipinos, and a sprinkling of Europeans, its cuisine is best described as melting-pot cookery.

Chinese Crisp Won Ton

½ pound cooked pork, ground
1 can (4½ ounces) medium size shrimp, rinsed and drained
1 stalk green onion, finely chopped, or 1 tablespoon instant minced onion
½ teaspoon salt
¼ teaspoon sugar
2 packages (12 ounces each) won ton skins
Oil for frying

1. Combine all of the ingredients except the won ton skins and oil. Chop the mixture coarsely.
2. Place 1 teaspoon of the mixture in each won ton skin, dampen the edges with water, and fold diagonally, forming a triangle. Dampen the two corners of the triangle which are opposite each other, and fold to the center, where they should just meet. Press tightly.
3. Fold the remaining corner of the triangle towards the side opposite the side where the other corners meet. Press to secure shut.
4. Fry in hot (365°F) oil, turning once, until golden. Drain on paper towel. Serve with a **sweet-and-sour sauce** or **mustard sauce**.

About 100 filled won ton

Indonesian Shrimp Balls

2 cups cooked shrimp, minced
2 eggs, beaten
1 clove garlic, minced
¼ cup bread crumbs
⅛ teaspoon pepper
½ teaspoon salt
1 tablespoon minced parsley
Few grains nutmeg
Oil for frying

1. Mix all ingredients together except oil. Form in balls the size of a large marble.
2. Heat oil to 365°F, and fry balls until golden. Drain on paper towel. Serve on cocktail picks.

About 3 dozen balls

Note: If using canned shrimp, rinse before using.

Teriyaki

An oriental appetizer of Japanese origin.

1 teaspoon ground ginger
⅓ cup soy sauce
¼ cup honey
1 clove garlic, minced
1 teaspoon grated onion
1 pound beef sirloin tip,
    cut in 2×½×¼-inch
    strips
3 tablespoons cooking or
    salad oil
1 tablespoon cornstarch
½ cup water
⅛ teaspoon red food
    coloring

1. Blend ginger, soy sauce, honey, garlic, and onion in a bowl. Add meat; marinate about 1 hour.
2. Remove meat, reserving marinade, and brown quickly on all sides in the hot oil in a skillet.
3. Stir a blend of cornstarch, water, and food coloring into the reserved marinade in a saucepan. Bring rapidly to boiling and cook 2 to 3 minutes, stirring constantly.
4. Add meat to thickened marinade to glaze; remove and drain on wire rack.
5. Insert a frilled wooden pick into each meat strip and serve with the sauce.

About 24 appetizers

Beef Kabobs with Vegetables

3 tablespoons light brown
    sugar
¼ teaspoon dry mustard
1 cup soy sauce
½ cup water
3 tablespoons dry sherry
¼ teaspoon Tabasco
1 tablespoon grated onion
1 clove garlic, minced
1½ to 2 pounds beef sirloin,
    cut in 1½-inch cubes
Tomato wedges
Green pepper squares
    (about 1 to 1-½
    inches)
Small onions, peeled

1. Mix brown sugar, mustard, soy sauce, water, sherry, Tabasco, onion, and garlic in a bowl.
2. Place meat in glass baking dish, pour marinade over beef, and allow to marinate in refrigerator overnight. Remove meat and reserve marinade.
3. Alternate meat and vegetables on skewers.
4. Place kabobs on grill about 5 inches from hot coals. Brush generously with marinade. Grill 7 to 10 minutes, then turn and baste with more marinade. Continue cooking until meat is done as desired.

About 6 servings

Note: The beef often requires a longer cooking period than the vegetables. If desired, place all beef on 2 or 3 skewers, and place all vegetables on other skewers. Place vegetables on grill towards end of cooking time of beef. Meat and vegetables may be rearranged on skewers for serving.

HAWAII

HAWAII

Barbecued Ribs with Pineapple

4 pounds spareribs, cracked through center and cut in serving-size pieces
2 tablespoons cornstarch
6 tablespoons brown sugar
⅔ cup light or dark corn syrup
⅔ cup Hawaiian barbecue sauce (a sweet-tart bottled sauce)
⅓ cup thawed frozen orange juice concentrate
2 tablespoons cider vinegar
2 large cloves garlic, minced
6 tablespoons finely chopped crystallized ginger
1 lemon, thinly sliced and slices quartered
1 can (8½ ounces) crushed pineapple

1. Put spareribs into a heavy saucepot. Add water to cover and bring to boiling; cover and reduce heat. Simmer 1 hour, or until almost tender; drain.
2. Meanwhile, prepare sauce. In a large bowl, mix the cornstarch and brown sugar. Blend in the corn syrup, Hawaiian barbecue sauce, orange juice concentrate, and vinegar. Stir in the garlic, ginger, lemon, and pineapple with syrup.
3. Add the drained cooked ribs to sauce, turn to coat, and marinate at least ½ hour.
4. Put spareribs in a single layer in a large shallow pan or jelly-roll pan and place under broiler with tops of ribs about 5 inches from source of heat. Broil 5 to 10 minutes, or until richly browned, turning and brushing several times with the sauce.
5. Arrange ribs on a heated serving platter and accompany with **hot cooked rice** and remaining sauce.

6 to 8 servings

Kalua Pig *(Pit-Roasted Whole Pig)*

One pig, cleaned and drawn
Soy sauce
Lemon
Garlic
White wine
Banana leaves
Bananas
Yams

1. Dig the pit (imu) according to the size of pig purchased, and prepare as for a closed-pit barbecue.
2. Line the bottom of pit with round smooth stones, build and start a wood fire, and add some extra stones (for cavity of pig). Add more wood as the fire burns to ashes (allow 4 to 5 hours).
3. To prepare the pig, rub well inside and out with soy sauce, lemon, garlic, and white wine.
4. Place the extra heated stones in the cavity of the pig and tie legs together.
5. Rake the ashes from the fire and reserve in a large can or tub. Cover surface thoroughly with banana leaves. Lower the pig into the pit (in a wire basket, if desired) and surround it with heavy-duty aluminum foil-wrapped bananas, yams, and if desired, serving portions of fish, allowing one of each per person. Cover with additional leaves or layers of aluminum foil, then with a layer of hot ashes, and with some burlap bags or a sheet of metal. Cover completely with earth.

HAWAII

6. Roast pig about 5 hours.
7. When ready to serve, uncover the pig and remove packets of cooked food. Remove the pig to a board or table for carving.
8. Serve with **poi** (a paste of cooked and fermented taro root).

Curry of Chicken

⅓ cup butter or margarine
3 tablespoons chopped onion
3 tablespoons chopped celery
3 tablespoons chopped green apple
12 peppercorns
1 bay leaf
⅓ cup flour
2½ teaspoons curry powder
¼ teaspoon sugar
⅛ teaspoon ground nutmeg
2½ cups milk
2 teaspoons lemon juice
½ teaspoon Worcestershire sauce
3 cups cubed cooked chicken
¼ cup cream
¼ teaspoon Worcestershire sauce

1. Heat butter in a heavy 3-quart saucepan. Add onion, celery, apple, peppercorns, and bay leaf; cook until onion is golden.
2. Blend in a mixture of flour, curry powder, sugar, and nutmeg; heat until bubbly.
3. Gradually add milk, stirring constantly. Bring to boiling, stirring until mixture thickens; cook 1 to 2 minutes.
4. Remove from heat; stir in lemon juice and the ½ teaspoon Worcestershire sauce. Strain through a fine sieve, pressing vegetables against sieve to extract all sauce.*
5. Return sauce to pan; blend in cream and the ¼ teaspoon Worcestershire sauce. Add chicken and cook over medium heat 2 to 3 minutes, or until thoroughly heated.
6. Serve with **fluffy cooked rice** and accompaniments such as **chutney, golden raisins, preserved kumquats,** and **cashew nuts.**

About 4 servings

*If desired, this sauce may be prepared ahead of time and stored, covered, in the refrigerator for several hours. If this is done, reheat sauce and proceed with step 5 just before serving.

Pansit

1 package (4 ounces) fine noodles
1 tablespoon vegetable oil
1 clove garlic, sliced
1 small onion, sliced
1 pound pork, cubed
½ pound shrimp, fresh or frozen
1 teaspoon salt
⅛ teaspoon pepper

1. Cook noodles in boiling salted water until tender. Drain thoroughly. Set aside.
2. Heat vegetable oil in a large skillet; add garlic. Cook garlic a few minutes, then remove. Stir in onion; fry until partially cooked. Stir in pork. When half cooked, stir in shrimp, salt, and pepper. Continue cooking until pork is tender.
3. Add noodles to the pork and shrimp mixture, and place on a large chop plate. Garnish with finely **ground roasted peanuts,** or **bacon rinds, slices of lemon, finely chopped onion, Chinese parsley,** and **strips of slightly beaten egg fried in tissue thin sheets.**

6 servings

HAWAII

Egg Foo Yong

These omelet-type pancakes are served in just about every restaurant where Chinese food is featured.

1 cup finely diced cooked
  ham, roast pork, or
  chicken
1 cup drained canned bean
  sprouts
¾ cup chopped onion
1 tablespoon soy sauce
¼ to ½ teaspoon salt
  (smaller amount with
  ham)
6 eggs, slightly beaten
  Fat or cooking oil (about
  ¼ cup or enough to
  form an ⅛-inch layer)
  Sauce

1. Mix the ham, bean sprouts, onion, soy sauce, and salt. Stir in the eggs.
2. Heat the fat in a large, heavy skillet. Drop ¼-cup portions of the mixture into the hot fat to form patties. Cook about 5 minutes, or until browned on one side; turn and brown other side.
3. Lift from skillet with a pancake turner or slotted spoon; drain over fat a few seconds. Transfer to a warm heat-resistant platter; keep warm in a 200°F oven while cooking remaining patties.
4. Pour hot Sauce over the patties on the platter. Serve with **fluffy cooked rice** and additional soy sauce.

5 or 6 servings

Sauce: Blend **2 teaspoons cornstarch, 1 tablespoon cold water, 2 teaspoons soy sauce,** and **1 teaspoon bead molasses** in a small saucepan. Stir in **1 cup chicken broth.** Bring to boiling, stirring constantly. Boil 3 minutes, or until sauce is thickened. Keep hot.

¾ cup sauce

Pineapple Chutney

1 pineapple
8 ounces raisins
7 ounces golden raisins
2 tablespoons finely
  chopped ginger root
2 tablespoons finely
  chopped garlic
3 cups chopped sweet red
  pepper
1½ cups vinegar
1½ cups golden brown
  sugar
1 tablespoon salt
1 cup chopped macadamia
  nuts or almonds
  Paraffin

1. Pare pineapple, remove core, and cut in small pieces to make 4 cups chopped pineapple.
2. In a large saucepan, combine pineapple pieces, raisins, golden raisins, ginger root, garlic, red pepper, vinegar, brown sugar, and salt. Cook slowly until pineapple is tender.
3. Stir in nuts and cook until chutney is desired consistency.
4. Fill sterilized glass jars with chutney, and seal while hot with melted paraffin.

4 pints

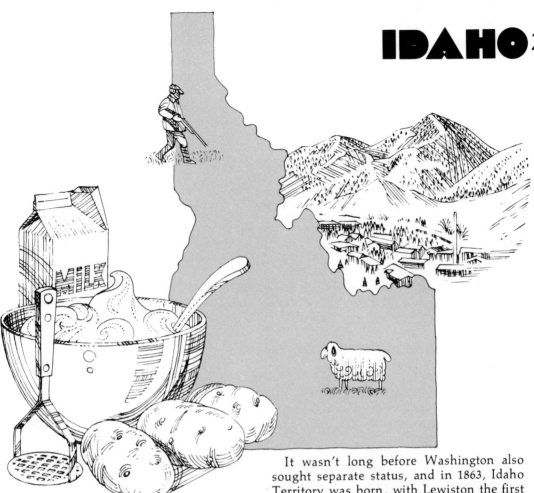

Mountains, forests, and lakes in northern Idaho validate its membership in the general area known as the Northwest. This part of the state has more in common with Washington and Oregon than it does with its own arid southeast corner.

As it happened, natural geographical factors had little to do with setting state borders for Idaho. The southern and northern boundaries were drawn at the forty-second and forty-ninth parallels by a man who had never visited the area, John Quincy Adams.

The uneven eastern and western borders outlined the leftovers when other states were carved away. Originally a part of the Oregon country, Idaho was divided between Oregon and Washington when they became territories. In 1859, Oregon became a state and gave up its share of Idaho to Washington.

It wasn't long before Washington also sought separate status, and in 1863, Idaho Territory was born, with Lewiston the first capital. The capital shifted to Boise the next year, but Lewiston retains importance for its position on the Snake River. Thanks to dams on the Columbia and Snake which opened up river traffic to the Pacific, Lewiston is "Idaho's first seaport."

Barges now pass through the locks, carrying local produce downstream and foreign imports back. Such traffic was impossible before the Columbia was harnessed, and gives a cosmopolitan flavor to the Idaho marketplace.

One attraction that brought settlers into Idaho was the construction of the Northern Pacific Railroad in the 1860s. The railroad, wishing to bring workers to the land it was opening up, set up tourist bureaus in eastern cities. It also did massive recruitment in Britain, Sweden, Denmark, Holland, and Germany, which helps to explain the immigration from those countries.

IDAHO

Other Idahoans had first spent a generation or so in other midwestern states before continuing the journey west. People often moved laterally westward across the country; perhaps out of familiarity with the climate and the crops it produced.

The mere mention of "Idaho" brings "potato" to mind, so it's not surprising to learn that the state leads the nation in this crop. Other crops of importance are wheat, peas, beans, lentils, sugar beets, apples, and prunes.

Sheep and beef are raised in Idaho; the sheep in the hillier parts and the cattle on the plains. A contingent of sheep herders long ago migrated from the Spanish and French Pyrenees to Idaho, and their descen-

dants are still among the livestock producers of today. The Spanish and French influence in the cooking of Idaho can be attributed to them.

Today tourism follows agriculture in importance to the state's economy. With its scenic setting and good fishing and hunting, Idaho is an ideal vacation spot for the outdoorsman. Bringing home a bag of game, the sportsman with gourmet flair can set his sights on new adventures at the table.

Cooks of game birds and animals suggest that treating them in the same manner as "less tender" cuts from the market gives the best results, since the age and musculature of the meat is uncertain. Thus, slow cooking in a sauce is advised.

Potato Soup

4 potatoes, pared and cut in pieces
1 large onion, peeled and cut in pieces
3 stalks celery, cut in pieces
1½ cups water
1 quart milk
1 teaspoon butter
Salt and pepper

1. Cook potatoes with onion and celery in a covered saucepan until vegetables are tender.
2. Mash vegetables without draining and add milk and butter. Season with salt and pepper. Heat thoroughly.

4 servings

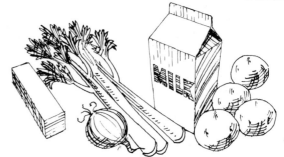

Creamy Carrot Soup

¼ to ½ cup chopped onion
6 tablespoons butter or margarine
2 cups thinly sliced pared carrots
1 teaspoon salt
3 chicken bouillon cubes
3 cups boiling water
¼ cup uncooked rice
2 cups milk

1. Lightly brown onion in heated butter in a saucepan. Add carrots and salt; toss to coat with butter. Cook, tightly covered, over low heat 20 minutes, stirring occasionally.
2. Add bouillon cubes, water, and rice. Cover and simmer 1 hour, stirring occasionally.
3. Pour the mixture into an electric blender container and blend until smooth.
4. Return to saucepan; stir in the milk and heat thoroughly. Serve hot.

About 1¼ quarts soup

Potato-Frosted Meat Loaf

1½ pounds ground beef
½ cup chopped onion
2 teaspoons salt
¼ teaspoon pepper
⅛ teaspoon oregano
⅔ cup quick or
    old-fashioned oats,
    uncooked
1 egg, beaten
½ cup milk
2 cups hot mashed
    potatoes*

1. Thoroughly combine all ingredients except mashed potatoes. Pack firmly into a 8½ × 4½ × 2½-inch loaf pan.
2. Bake at 350°F about 1 hour. Drain off excess fat. Let stand a few minutes; remove from pan.
3. Place on broiler rack. Frost loaf with mashed potatoes.
4. Place under broiler 5 to 7 inches from heat 2 to 3 minutes. Serve immediately.

8 servings

*Four medium-size potatoes will yield about 2 cups mashed potatoes.

Party Lamb Chops

6 lamb loin chops, about 2
    pounds
½ teaspoon salt
⅛ teaspoon pepper
2 tablespoons butter
2 tablespoons prepared
    mustard
1 can (16 ounces) quartered
    hearts of celery
1 cup tomato juice
½ cup dry white wine, such
    as sauterne
¼ cup finely chopped
    parsley

1. Sprinkle chops with salt and pepper.
2. Brown chops on both sides in butter in skillet. Spread mustard on chops.
3. Add celery and liquid from can, tomato juice, and wine. Cover and simmer 1 hour over low heat until chops are tender. Place chops on platter and keep warm.
4. Pour pan juice into blender and whirl until smooth, or beat with a rotary beater in small bowl. Pour back into skillet and reheat until bubbly and thick. Spoon over chops. Sprinkle chops with parsley.

6 servings

Pheasant and Apple Casserole

½ cup flour
½ teaspoon salt
⅛ teaspoon pepper
1 pheasant, dressed and cut
    in serving pieces
¼ cup butter or margarine
½ teaspoon salt
½ teaspoon thyme
⅛ teaspoon pepper
2 large apples, pared,
    cored, and sliced
1 cup apple cider
2 tablespoons wine vinegar

1. Combine flour, ½ teaspoon salt, and ⅛ teaspoon pepper in a plastic bag. Place pheasant in the bag, a few pieces at a time, and coat with the flour mixture.
2. Melt butter in a skillet and brown the pheasant in the butter over medium heat.
3. Transfer pheasant to a 3-quart casserole. Sprinkle ½ teaspoon salt, thyme, and ⅛ teaspoon pepper over pheasant.
4. Add apples and mix gently. Pour cider and vinegar over pheasant and apples. Cover casserole.
5. Bake at 350°F 1¼ hours.

About 4 servings

IDAHO

Paella

1 cup olive oil
1 broiler-fryer chicken (2 pounds), cut in serving-size pieces
½ cup diced boiled ham or smoky sausage
1 tablespoon finely chopped onion
2 cloves garlic, minced
2 ripe tomatoes, peeled and coarsely chopped
1½ pounds fresh shrimp, shelled and deveined
12 small clams in shells, shells scrubbed
1½ teaspoons salt
2 cups uncooked rice
4 cups hot water
1 cup fresh or frozen green peas
¼ cup coarsely chopped parsley
Few shreds saffron
1 rock lobster tail cooked and meat cut in pieces, or 1 package frozen crab meat, thawed, drained, and bony tissue removed
1 can or jar (7 ounces) whole pimentos

1. Heat oil in paellera or large skillet. Add chicken and ham and cook about 10 minutes, turning chicken to brown on all sides.
2. Add onion and garlic and cook 2 minutes; add tomatoes, shrimp, clams, and salt; cover and cook 5 to 10 minutes, or until clam shells open. Remove clams and keep warm.
3. Stir rice into mixture. Add water, peas, parsley, and saffron. Cover and cook 25 minutes, or until rice is just tender, stirring occasionally.
4. Mix in lobster or crab meat, half of the pimento, and the clams in shells; heat until very hot. Serve garnished with the remaining pimento.

8 to 10 servings

Split-Pea Stuffed Peppers

1 cup yellow or green split peas, sorted and washed
2⅓ cups water
½ teaspoon salt
1 small bay leaf
1 small clove garlic
¾ cup minced onion
2 tablespoons butter
2 cans (8 ounces each) tomato sauce
⅛ teaspoon poultry seasoning

1. Place split peas, water, salt, bay leaf, and garlic in a large saucepan. Cook 45 minutes, or until split peas are tender and water is evaporated. Remove bay leaf and garlic.
2. Sauté onion in butter until onion is clear, but not brown. Add onion, 1 can tomato sauce, and poultry seasoning to split peas; mix well.
3. Brown the pork sausage in a heavy skillet, breaking it apart, then add to split peas.
4. Remove tops, seeds, and membranes of peppers. Cook peppers in boiling salted water about 3 minutes, drain, and cool.
5. Place peppers in a shallow baking pan, stuff with

1 pound bulk pork
   sausage
8 medium-size green
   peppers
   Shredded cheese

split pea mixture, and sprinkle cheese on top of each pepper.

6. Combine other can of tomato sauce and ½ cup water. Pour around stuffed peppers. Baste peppers with sauce, if desired.

7. Bake at 350°F 45 minutes. Serve immediately.

8 servings

Note: To freeze stuffed peppers, follow recipe through step 4. Put peppers in freezer until they are frozen. Remove and wrap individually, or together in a foil pan, in foil or plastic wrap. May be stored 2 to 3 months. To serve, remove wrapping, place partially thawed peppers in shallow pan, add sauce, and bake as directed.

IDAHO

Baked Lentils

2⅓ cups lentils, sorted and
   washed
1 onion stuck with 3
   whole cloves
1 bay leaf
5 cups water
2 teaspoons salt
½ cup ketchup
¼ cup dark molasses
2 tablespoons light brown
   sugar
1 teaspoon dry mustard
¼ teaspoon Worcestershire
   sauce
2 tablespoons minced
   onion
4 slices bacon, cut in
   thirds

1. In a Dutch oven combine lentils, onion, bay leaf, water, and salt. Bring to boiling, cover, and simmer 30 minutes.

2. Without draining lentils, add ketchup, molasses, brown sugar, dry mustard, Worcestershire sauce, and onion to Dutch oven. Mix thoroughly. Top with bacon and cover.

3. Bake at 350°F 1 hour. Uncover last few minutes to brown bacon.

12 servings

Note: If desired, omit bacon, and 10 minutes before casserole should be done, sprinkle liberally with **shredded Cheddar cheese.** Return to oven to melt and brown cheese. **Parboiled link sausage** may be substituted for bacon; allow sausage to brown on top of lentils, as with bacon.

Baked Idaho Potatoes

Potatoes
Butter
Salt
Pepper

1. Wash and dry potatoes thoroughly, and rub well with shortening if a soft skin is desired.

2. Bake at 400°F 45 to 60 minutes, or until potatoes are soft when pressed together with the fingers. Remove from oven and make 2 gashes in the center of the potatoes, in the form of a cross; press potatoes with the fingers.

3. Insert a large piece of butter, season with salt and pepper, and serve piping hot. Allow 1 potato per person.

IDAHO

Stuffed Potatoes

6 medium-size baking
    potatoes, baked
½ cup coarsely chopped
    onion
½ cup coarsely chopped
    green pepper
3 tablespoons butter or
    margarine
1 medium-size tomato,
    chopped
2 tablespoons milk
2 tablespoons butter or
    margarine
2 teaspoons salt
¼ teaspoon white pepper
1 teaspoon paprika
¼ teaspoon crushed
    rosemary leaves

1. While potatoes are baking, cook onion and green pepper in 3 tablespoons hot butter in a skillet. Add tomato and cook 1 minute.

2. Cut a thin lengthwise slice from each baked potato. With a spoon, scoop out each potato without breaking skin. Thoroughly mash or rice scooped-out potato. Whip in milk with remaining ingredients until potatoes are fluffy. Blend in vegetable mixture.

3. Pile mixture lightly into potato shells. Arrange on baking sheet. Sprinkle with **paprika.**

4. Bake at 400°F 20 minutes, or until thoroughly heated and lightly browned.

6 servings

Apricot Bread

½ cup hot water
1 cup dried apricots, cut
    fine
2 cups sugar
2 eggs
¼ cup butter or margarine,
    melted
1 cup orange juice
4 cups sifted all-purpose
    flour
1 teaspoon baking soda

1. Add hot water to apricots in a bowl; beat in sugar thoroughly. Add eggs, one at a time, beating well after each addition. Beat in melted butter, then orange juice.

2. Sift flour and baking soda together and add about ½ cup at a time to apricot mixture, mixing only until blended after each addition. Turn into 4 greased 7×4×2-inch loaf pans and spread evenly.

3. Bake at 350°F about 30 minutes.

4. Cool bread 10 minutes in pans on wire rack; remove from pans and cool completely. To store, wrap and refrigerate.

4 small loaves bread

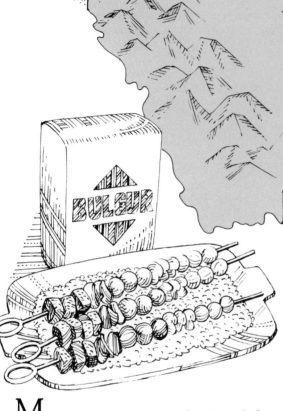

Montana's name is a reflection of the many people who have called it home. The Indians first called it the "Land of the Shining Mountains." Later, the Spanish explorers shortened this to Montana, their word for mountain. The later arrivals kept the Spanish word, as it is the mountains that still shape the life of the natives, both at work and at play.

But early in our country's history, the mountains discouraged settlers. The Rockies, cutting through the state diagonally in the west, made movement difficult, and the arid plains in the east were almost as uninviting.

Then, in the 1850s, valuable ore was found; the cry went up, "There's gold in them thar hills!" It was the mountains that brought the flow of newcomers to the area. They included many Scandinavian, British, and Canadian immigrants.

In size, Montana is the largest of the Rocky Mountain states, but is one of the least populated, having under a million residents. A list of the state's cities and towns shows several communities with fewer than ten residents.

Much of the state retains a primitive look, with eleven national forests and thirteen areas classified simply "wilderness." In addition, there are state parks and recreation areas, providing the vacationer with the unspoiled pleasures of the great outdoors—hunting, fishing, hiking, camping, and the enjoyment of incomparable views.

Farming is carried on, for the most part, in the eastern and middle sections of the state. The leading crop is wheat. Its yield makes Montana the nation's third largest producer, following North Dakota and Kansas. As for its other crops, they could be sung to the childhood jingle, "Oats, peas, beans, and barley grow . . ."

One use made of wheat is the production of bulgur, a food that for centuries was the "daily bread" of Near and Middle Eastern countries. In the past, bulgur was made by boiling whole wheat grains in open vessels with a little water until the kernels were soft and tender. They were then spread in thin layers to dry in the sun. The coarse bran was removed and the hard inner grain was cracked between stones or in a crude mill. Today's production, while using modern facilities, is basically the same. Bulgur is cooked with a small amount of water, or with broth and seasonings, to make pilaf. The wheat of the New World can be used to good advantage in such traditional dishes from the Old.

Lamb from Montana is ideally suited to such Middle Eastern dishes as shish kebab, which go well with pilaf. It is also popular in more American forms, such as barbecued and broiled dishes.

MONTANA (vertical)

Beef Soup

1½ pounds beef for stew
1 soup bone
1½ to 2 teaspoons salt
½ teaspoon pepper
2 bay leaves
4 medium-size carrots, pared and sliced
1 cup chopped cabbage
1 cup chopped celery
½ cup chopped onion
1 can (15 ounces) Italian-style tomatoes
1 tablespoon Worcestershire sauce
1 beef bouillon cube
Pinch oregano (or other herb desired)

1. Put meat and soup bone in a heavy 3-quart kettle; cover with cold water (about 4 cups). Add salt, pepper, and bay leaves. Bring rapidly to boiling. Reduce heat. Add carrots, cabbage, celery, and onion; cover and simmer until meat is tender, about 2½ hours.
2. Remove and discard bone and bay leaves. Cut meat into bite-size pieces and return to soup. Mix in tomatoes, Worcestershire sauce, bouillon cube, and oregano. Cover and simmer 30 minutes.

6 servings

Scotch Broth with Bulgur

2 lamb shanks, about 1 pound each
3 quarts water
1 cup bulgur, uncooked
1 cup diced or shredded carrots
½ cup chopped onion or leeks
1 cup sliced celery
¼ cup snipped parsley
1 teaspoon salt
¼ teaspoon pepper
½ teaspoon curry powder
2 tablespoons butter
¼ cup flour

1. Place lamb shanks and water in a large pot. Bring to boiling, lower heat, and simmer 2 to 3 hours. Remove meat and bones from broth and skim off all fat.
2. Add bulgur, vegetables, and seasonings to broth. Cover and cook until vegetables are tender (15 to 20 minutes). Remove meat from bones, dice, and return to soup.
3. Blend butter and flour over low heat. Stir 1 cup of soup into flour and butter mixture, then return mixture to large pot of soup. Cook until thickened (about 3 minutes).

6 to 8 servings

Spanish Beef Stew with Olives, 262

MONTANA

Shish Kabobs with Pilaf

2 pounds lamb (loin, leg,
   or shoulder), boneless,
   cut in 1½-inch cubes
   and fat removed
½ cup lemon juice
½ cup olive oil
1 teaspoon oregano
1 teaspoon rosemary
   leaves, coarsely
   crushed
1 teaspoon salt
½ teaspoon pepper
2 cloves garlic, sliced
   Green pepper chunks
   Onions, quartered, or
   left whole if small
   Mushroom caps
   Butter for sautéeing
   Cherry tomatoes
   Bulgur Pilaf

1. Place lamb in a large shallow pan.
2. Combine lemon juice, olive oil, dry seasonings, and garlic and pour over lamb. Cover and marinate overnight in refrigerator.
3. Sauté green pepper, onion, and mushroom caps in butter briefly.
4. Remove lamb from marinade and put on skewers. Place about 4 to 5 inches from hot coals, and cook 15 to 20 minutes, turning occasionally.
5. Put green pepper, onion, and mushroom caps on skewers (do not crowd), and cook an additional 10 to 15 minutes. Place tomatoes on skewers for last 5 minutes of cooking.
6. Remove lamb and serve while still pink and juicy, on a bed of Bulgur Pilaf.

6 servings

Bulgur Pilaf: Mix **2 cups dry bulgur, 4 cups chicken stock, broth, or bouillon, 1 teaspoon salt,** and **½ teaspoon pepper** together in a large saucepan. Simmer until all liquid is absorbed. Slice **¼ pound butter** over top and let melt. Stir to fluff, cover, and let stand a few minutes. Just before serving, crush **1 cup chow mein noodles** in hands, add to pilaf, and stir in carefully.

Deviled Lamb Spareribs

2½ cups lemon juice
1 tablespoon grated onion
8 cloves garlic, sliced
4 teaspoons salt
4 teaspoons dry mustard
4 teaspoons chili powder
2 teaspoons ground cumin
1 teaspoon thyme,
   crushed
½ teaspoon seasoned
   pepper
9 to 10 pounds lamb
   spareribs
   Paprika

1. Mix lemon juice, grated onion, garlic, and a mixture of salt, dry mustard, chili powder, cumin, thyme, and seasoned pepper. Pour over lamb in a large shallow dish or pan. Cover and marinate in refrigerator 6 to 8 hours, or overnight; turn occasionally.
2. Remove spareribs from marinade and place on rack in a shallow roasting pan. Roast at 325°F 1½ hours, basting occasionally with marinade.
3. Sprinkle spareribs with paprika; roast ½ hour longer, or until tender.
4. Place ribs in a serving dish and garnish with **parsley sprigs.**

About 12 servings

Grilled Lamb Spareribs: Marinate spareribs as directed in recipe for Deviled Lamb Spareribs. Remove from marinade and arrange on skewers; sprinkle with paprika. Grill 6 or 7 inches from source of heat 20 minutes on each side, or until done as desired, basting occasionally with marinade.

Arroz con Pollo, 270

MONTANA

Marinated Onion-Topped Burger Loaf

1 medium sweet Spanish
   onion
½ cup clear French dressing
1 tablespoon chopped
   parsley
¾ pound ground beef
1 teaspoon pepper
¼ teaspoon garlic salt
1 teaspoon Worcestershire
   sauce
   French bread
   Prepared mustard
4 slices American cheese,
   cut crosswise in
   triangles

1. Peel and thinly slice onion. Separate into rings. Combine French dressing with chopped parsley and marinate onion rings.
2. Combine ground beef and seasonings.
3. Cut French bread in half lengthwise. Spread bottom half with desired amount of prepared mustard. Spread ground beef filling evenly over surface. Place under broiler and broil until meat is done as desired. Toast cut side of top half.
4. Arrange cheese triangles on top of hamburger. Place under broiler again until cheese melts.
5. Drain onion rings and arrange over cheeseburger filling. Put top on loaf. To serve, cut into crosswise slices.

About 4 servings

Savory Onion Topper

3 cups chopped sweet
   Spanish onion
3 tablespoons butter
1¼ cups chili sauce
¼ cup bottled meat sauce

1. Sauté onion in butter in a skillet until tender. Mix in chili sauce and meat sauce; heat thoroughly.
2. Serve over grilled or broiled hamburgers.

About 2½ cups sauce

Crispy French Fried Onion Rings

2 sweet Spanish onions
1 cup pancake mix
¾ cup beer
   Oil for deep frying
     heated to 375°F
   Salt

1. Peel onions and cut into ½-inch-thick slices; separate into rings.
2. Combine pancake mix and beer to make a smooth, thick batter.
3. Dip onion rings in batter and fry, a few at a time, in hot fat until golden brown. Drain on absorbent-paper-lined baking sheets.
4. Keep fried onion rings hot in oven until all rings are fried.

Note: To freeze fried onion rings, leave onion rings on lined baking sheets, place in freezer, and freeze quickly. Then carefully remove rings to moisture-vaporproof containers with layers of absorbent paper between layers of onions. Cover container tightly and freeze. To heat frozen onion rings, place rings on a baking sheet and heat in a 375°F oven for several minutes.

Onion Confetti Relish

2 cups chopped sweet
   Spanish onion (1
   large)
½ green pepper, diced
3 tablespoons diced
   pimento
½ cup vinegar
¼ cup water
¼ cup sugar
2 teaspoons caraway seed
½ teaspoon salt

1. Combine onion with green pepper and pimento.
2. Combine vinegar, water, sugar, caraway seed, and salt. Bring to boiling and simmer 5 minutes. Pour over onion mixture. Refrigerate several hours.
3. Serve with grilled or broiled hamburgers.

2½ cups relish

Coffee Bread (Vetebröd)

1 cup milk or cream
1 package active dry yeast
¼ cup warm water, 105° to
   115°F
   (Or, if using
   compressed yeast,
   soften 1 cake in ¼ cup
   lukewarm water, 80° to
   85°F)
½ cup butter
½ cup sugar
1 teaspoon salt
3 to 3½ cups sifted
   all-purpose flour
1 egg, well beaten
   Egg white, slightly
   beaten
½ cup chopped almonds
⅓ cup sugar

1. Scald milk.
2. Meanwhile, soften yeast in warm water; set aside.
3. Combine in a large bowl butter, sugar, and salt. Immediately pour scalded milk over ingredients in bowl. When lukewarm, blend in 1 cup flour, beating until smooth. Stir softened yeast and add, mixing well.
4. Add about 1 cup of the flour to the yeast mixture and beat until very smooth.
5. Beat in egg. Then beat in enough remaining flour to make a soft dough. Turn dough onto a lightly floured surface and allow dough to rest 5 to 10 minutes.
6. Knead dough 5 to 8 minutes, until smooth and elastic. Form dough into a large ball and put it into a greased deep bowl. Turn dough to bring greased surface to top. Cover with waxed paper and towel and let stand in warm place (about 80°F) until dough is doubled.
7. Punch down with fist; pull edges of dough in to center and turn dough completely over in bowl. Cover and let rise again until nearly doubled. Punch down and turn dough out onto lightly floured surface. Divide dough into two portions and shape into oblong loaves.
8. Lightly grease two baking sheets. Place loaves on baking sheets and brush with egg white. Sprinkle each loaf with one half of a mixture of chopped almonds and sugar. Cover and let rise about 45 minutes, or until dough is doubled.
9. Bake at 375°F 20 to 25 minutes. Cool completely on wire racks.

2 loaves bread

MONTANA

Unbaked Fruitcake

MONTANA

8 ounces (1½ cups) raisins
1 cup chopped figs
1 cup chopped dried pears
1 cup chopped walnuts
6 ounces (1 cup) chopped
  candied pineapple
6 ounces (1 cup) chopped
  candied cherries
4 ounces (½ cup) chopped
  candied citron
8 ounces (1 cup) chopped
  candied orange peel
¾ cup butter or margarine
1 tablespoon grated orange
  peel
¾ cup confectioners' sugar
3 dozen vanilla wafers,
  finely crushed (about 7
  cups crumbs)
¼ teaspoon salt
1 cup honey

1. Pour 2 cups boiling water over dried fruits; bring to boiling and drain. Mix with walnuts and candied fruits.
2. Cream butter with orange peel; gradually add confectioners' sugar, creaming well. Blend in crumbs, salt, and honey. Mix with fruit-nut mixture. Press into a well-greased 2-quart fluted mold.
3. Refrigerate 2 to 3 days before unmolding to serve.

About 5 pounds fruitcake

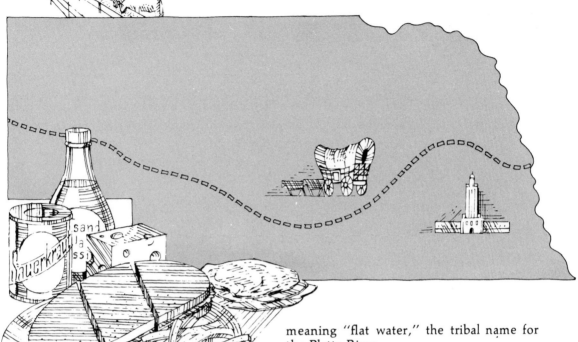

meaning "flat water," the tribal name for the Platte River.

The Homestead Act of 1862 brought many newcomers to the state. Their numbers included Scandinavians, Germans, French, Italians, and Poles. After the Civil War came an influx of southerners who chose to leave the devastated conditions "down home." All brought with them their cooking traditions and treasured heirloom recipes.

The first railroad to join the eastern and western halves of the nation was the Union Pacific, now headquartered at Omaha. On May 10, 1869, the Union Pacific construction team met that of the Central Pacific at Promontory, Utah, and a golden spike was driven to mark the occasion.

Population in the state grew, thanks to the new railroad accommodations, the free land offer, and the end of serious Indian wars around 1880. The state has always been primarily agricultural; its only sizeable cities are Omaha and Lincoln, the capital.

Nebraska's grains help to fill the nation's breadbasket. While today most Nebraska homemakers buy their bread, as elsewhere in the country, there are still those who

Many localities claim to be "the place where the West begins," but the spot could well be in Nebraska, where rolling cornfields subtly change to level prairies of wheat and feeder ranches. Buffalo Bill's homestead and other western memorabilia that show up midstate add to the illusion.

Nebraska is better known as "the Cornhusker State." While lagging behind its neighbor to the east, Iowa, in total production, corn is still the major agricultural product of the state. Wheat takes second place. Other Nebraska crops are oats, sugar beets, potatoes, and beans. The raising of hogs and beef cattle figures large in the state's agricultural life, too.

The Missouri River forms a natural border for Nebraska on the east, and the Platte cuts through its center, east to west. The word Nebraska comes from an Indian word

NEBRASKA

make time to turn out their own. Nebraska cooks have applied their ingenuity to beef dishes also, making the most of such economical cuts as short ribs and ground beef.

The Nebraska farm wife of the past kept her canning cellar well stocked. Canning is now coming back into its own, not out of necessity, but because today's homemaker finds it creative.

Rarely is a really new recipe created, but one was born in Nebraska back in the nineteen-twenties. Reuben Kay, a Nebraska wholesale grocer, is credited with the concoction that bears his first name. It combines rye bread, sauerkraut, corned beef, and Swiss cheese. For years, only a few of Kay's card-playing friends shared his discovery. Then in 1956 an Omaha waitress entered it in the National Sandwich Idea Contest—and won. Now, the Reuben has a permanent place in the sandwich hall of fame.

Reuben Sandwich

18 slices Russian rye bread
1¼ cups thousand island dressing
12 slices Swiss cheese (about 12 ounces)
½ cup sauerkraut
24 slices cooked corned beef (about 12 ounces)
Butter or margarine

1. Spread bread with dressing. On each of 12 bread slices, arrange 1 cheese slice, 2 teaspoons sauerkraut, and 2 slices corned beef.
2. Stack these bread slices to make 6 sandwiches. Cover with remaining bread slices. Secure with picks.
3. Spread outside surfaces with butter and grill until cheese is melted and sandwich is heated through. Cut diagonally into three pieces. Serve with **French fried potatoes.**

6 sandwiches

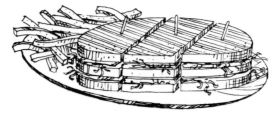

Spanish Beef Stew with Olives

2 tablespoons olive or salad oil
3½ pounds beef stew meat, cubed
1 teaspoon salt
⅛ teaspoon pepper
2 medium onions, sliced
2 large cloves garlic, crushed
2 cups beef broth
2 cups dry red wine
4 tomatoes, peeled and quartered
1 bay leaf
4 parsley sprigs
½ teaspoon thyme leaves

1. Heat oil in a large kettle or Dutch oven. Add meat, a few pieces at a time, and brown well on all sides. Remove meat and season with salt and pepper. If drippings in kettle are too brown, drain off and add additional 2 tablespoons oil.
2. Add onions and cook until tender and lightly brown. Add garlic, broth, wine, one of the tomatoes, and herbs (tied in cheesecloth). Add browned meat and bring to boiling.
3. Cover and simmer, or bake in a 350°F oven, 2 hours, or until meat is tender. Add olives and potatoes and continue cooking 30 minutes.
4. Remove meat and vegetables to serving dish; keep warm. Drain cooking liquid into saucepan and skim off fat; bring to boiling.
5. Blend flour with water; stir into boiling liquid. Add

1½ cups pimento-stuffed
    olives
2½ pounds potatoes, pared
    and halved
  2 tablespoons flour
  3 tablespoons water
    Parsley (optional)

remaining tomatoes and simmer 10 minutes. Pour
liquid over meat and vegetables; top with tomatoes.
Garnish with parsley, if desired.

8 to 10 servings

Nebraska Hospitality Dish

  2 cups dried lima beans,
    sorted and washed
  5 cups boiling water
  4 strips bacon, chopped
1¼ cups chopped onion
⅔ cup chopped green
    pepper
1¾ cups chopped celery
  1 pound ground beef
    round
  1 teaspoon salt
½ teaspoon oregano
  1 can (4 ounces) sliced
    mushrooms, drained
  1 can (8 ounces) tomato
    sauce
  1 can (6 ounces) tomato
    paste
¼ cup light brown sugar
½ teaspoon allspice
½ teaspoon ground cloves

1. Add lima beans to boiling water gradually so boiling
will not stop. Simmer 2 minutes. Remove from heat;
set aside 1 hour.
2. Bring beans to boiling. Simmer 1 hour, stirring
occasionally. Remove from heat.
3. In a large skillet, fry bacon briefly. Stir in onion,
green pepper, and celery. Cook until tender, but not
brown. Add ground round, breaking up into pieces,
and cook until meat loses pink color. Add remaining
ingredients, mixing well.
4. Drain beans, reserving ½ cup liquid. Add beans and
liquid to skillet mixture, stirring gently. Transfer mixture to 3-quart casserole.
5. Bake at 300°F 30 to 45 minutes, or until bubbly.

4 to 6 servings

Beef and Eggplant Bake

  1 large eggplant
  2 teaspoons salt
½ cup cooking oil
  1 pound ground beef
  2 cups chopped onion
  1 clove garlic, minced
  1 can (16 ounces)
    tomatoes, cut up
⅓ cup uncooked rice
¼ teaspoon pepper

1. Pare eggplant; cut in 1-inch-thick slices. Sprinkle
with 1 teaspoon salt and let stand 20 minutes.
2. In a large skillet, heat oil until very hot. Add
eggplant slices and brown lightly on both sides. Remove from skillet and set on paper towels to drain.
3. Using same skillet, brown ground beef, onion, and
garlic, stirring frequently. Stir in tomatoes, rice, 1
teaspoon salt, and pepper. Bring to boiling; remove
from heat.
4. In a buttered 2½-quart baking dish, place half the
eggplant slices. Top with half the beef mixture. Repeat
layering and cover dish.
5. Bake at 350°F 1 hour.

6 servings

Barbecued Turkey Drumsticks

1 can (8 ounces) tomato
   sauce with tomato bits
¼ cup molasses
¼ cup lemon juice
1 tablespoon
   Worcestershire sauce
¼ teaspoon Tabasco
1 tablespoon chopped
   chives
1 teaspoon marjoram
   leaves
¼ teaspoon salt
6 turkey drumsticks (about
   1 pound each)
Salt and pepper
Butter

1. For sauce, combine tomato sauce, molasses, lemon juice, Worcestershire sauce, Tabasco, chives, marjoram, and salt. Refrigerate overnight to blend flavors.
2. Put each turkey leg on a piece of heavy-duty aluminum foil. Sprinkle with salt and pepper and dot with butter. Wrap securely, using a drugstore fold and sealing ends.
3. Set packages on grill 3 to 6 inches from heat. Grill about 2 hours, or until fork-tender, turning them occasionally.
4. Remove foil and brush drumsticks with sauce. Grill about 20 minutes, turning frequently and brushing with sauce.

6 servings

Note: Sauce may be used as a brushing sauce for hamburgers or frankfurters during grilling.

Zucchini Slippers

6 medium zucchini
Boiling, salted water
2 eggs, well beaten
1½ cups shredded sharp
   cheese
½ cup cottage cheese
2 tablespoons chopped
   fresh parsley
½ teaspoon salt
¼ teaspoon pepper

1. Cook zucchini in boiling water about 10 minutes, or until tender.
2. Drain and carefully remove zucchini to cutting board. Slice in half lengthwise; scoop out pulp into mixing bowl. Mash slightly with wooden spoon.
3. Add to the pulp the eggs, cheeses, parsley, salt, and pepper.
4. Arrange shells in a buttered 13×9-inch baking pan and fill with mixture.
5. Bake at 350°F 15 minutes; turn oven control to 450°F and bake until top is brown.

6 servings

German Noodle Ring

1 cup medium noodles,
   cooked and drained
3 tablespoons flour
½ teaspoon salt
½ teaspoon paprika
3 tablespoons butter or
   margarine
1½ cups milk

1. Spoon noodles into a buttered 1½-quart ring mold.
2. Blend flour, salt, and paprika into hot butter in a saucepan. Heat until bubbly. Remove from heat. Add milk gradually, stirring constantly. Bring to boiling; cook 1 to 2 minutes.
3. Remove from heat and add cheese all at one time; stir rapidly until cheese is melted. Reserve half of sauce to use later.

6 ounces Swiss cheese,
   cut in pieces
2 eggs, well beaten

4. Add beaten eggs gradually to remaining sauce, blending well. Pour over noodles in mold.
5. Set mold in a pan in a 350°F oven. Pour hot water into pan to a depth of 1 inch. Bake about 40 minutes, or until mixture is set.
6. Unmold onto a large platter and pour remaining cheese sauce over mold.

About 8 servings

Swedish Rye Bread (Limpa)

Anise seed, orange peel, molasses, brown sugar, and rye flour all contribute to the exceptional flavor of this bread.

2 packages active dry
   yeast
½ cup warm water
½ cup packed dark brown
   sugar
⅓ cup molasses
2 tablespoons butter or
   margarine
1 tablespoon salt
4 teaspoons grated orange
   peel
¾ teaspoon anise seed
1½ cups hot water
2½ cups medium rye flour
3½ to 4 cups all-purpose
   flour
Cornmeal

1. Soften yeast in the warm water.
2. Combine brown sugar, molasses, butter, salt, orange peel, and anise in a large bowl. Add the hot water and blend. Cool to lukewarm.
3. Beat in 1 cup of the rye flour until smooth. Stir in yeast. Gradually add all of the rye flour, beating vigorously. Mix in enough of the all-purpose flour (2½ to 3 cups) to make a soft dough, beating until the dough comes away from the sides of bowl.
4. Turn onto a lightly floured surface and let rest about 10 minutes.
5. Knead in enough remaining flour to make a smooth elastic dough which does not stick to kneading surface. Form into a ball and put into a greased deep bowl. Turn dough to bring greased surface to top. Cover; let rise in a warm place until doubled.
6. Punch down dough; pull edges into center and turn dough completely over in bowl. Cover; let rise again until almost doubled.
7. Punch down again and turn onto a lightly floured surface. Divide dough into halves and shape into smooth balls. Place on a greased baking sheet sprinkled with cornmeal. Cover; let rise again until doubled (about 30 minutes).
8. Bake at 375°F 25 to 30 minutes. Remove to a wire rack and immediately brush lightly with milk. Cool.

2 loaves bread

Note: 2 teaspoons **caraway seed** may be substituted for orange peel. Decrease anise to ½ teaspoon.

NEBRASKA

NEBRASKA

Bacon-Nut Corn Sticks

1 cup sifted all-purpose
    flour
1 cup yellow cornmeal
¼ cup sugar
1 teaspoon baking powder
½ teaspoon baking soda
½ teaspoon salt
⅓ cup coarsely chopped
    pecans
6 to 8 slices crisply fried
    bacon, drained on
    absorbent paper and
    crumbled
1 egg, well beaten
1 cup buttermilk
5 tablespoons melted
    shortening

1. Combine the flour, cornmeal, sugar, baking powder, baking soda, and salt in a bowl, mix well and stir in pecans and bacon.
2. Add a mixture of egg, buttermilk, and melted shortening; stir only until flour is moistened. Spoon mixture into 12 preheated greased corn-stick pan sections (15×1½ inches).
3. Bake at 425°F 10 to 15 minutes.

1 dozen corn sticks

Brown Sugar Doughnuts

The warm sweet smell of fresh doughnuts and the dark fragrance of freshly brewed coffee—a time-tried invitation to comfort and cheer.

5 to 5½ cups sifted
    all-purpose flour
2 teaspoons baking powder
2 teaspoons baking soda
2 teaspoons cinnamon
4 eggs
2 cups firmly packed brown
    sugar
½ cup dairy sour cream
    Fat for deep frying
    heated to 365°F
½ cup confectioners' sugar

1. Sift together 5 cups flour, baking powder, baking soda, and cinnamon; set aside.
2. Beat eggs until thick and piled softly. Add brown sugar gradually, beating thoroughly after each addition. Blend in dry ingredients alternately with sour cream. Stir lightly until well blended. Dough will be soft. If dough seems very sticky, measure ½ cup flour; add enough of the flour to make an easily handled but soft dough. Save remainder for rolling. Chill dough in refrigerator for 1 hour.
3. Turn dough onto lightly floured surface. Handling very lightly, roll dough ½ inch thick and cut with a lightly floured doughnut cutter.
4. Deep-fry doughnuts and "holes" in heated fat. Fry only as many doughnuts at one time as will float uncrowded one layer deep in the fat. Turn doughnuts with a fork as they rise to surface and several times during cooking (do not pierce). Fry 2 to 4 minutes, or until lightly browned. Drain doughnuts and "holes" over fat for a few seconds before removing to absorbent paper.
5. Serve plain or shake 2 or 3 warm doughnuts at a time in plastic bag containing confectioners' sugar.

About 3 dozen doughnuts plus "holes"

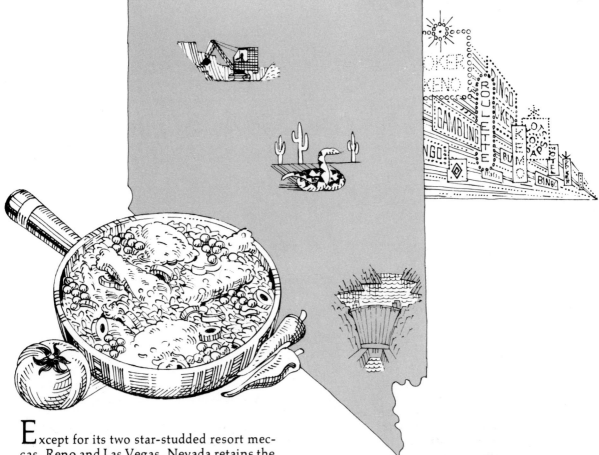

Except for its two star-studded resort meccas, Reno and Las Vegas, Nevada retains the look and feel of the frontier. Nevadans outside the cities live the rural life of their grandfathers, free from urban pressures.

Nevada reflects strong influences from outside. From the California side come the glitter and night life, superimposed on the Nevada scene where gambling is legal and divorce laws are lax. At any given time, a large percentage of the people in the state are nonresidents, enjoying the luxury of the hostelries and the roller-coaster excitement of the casinos.

The Mormon church, pulling from the Utah side, is the other strong influence on Nevada. In the mid-nineteenth century, Nevada's Carson Valley was a center of the Mormon faith, and Mormons still make up a large share of the Nevada population. The cooking in Mormon homes is substantial,

filling food for the large numbers that often make up the family.

Other settlers were attracted to Nevada after the discovery of the Comstock Lode. Gold seekers rushed in, and in 1861 Nevada became a territory. Statehood followed in 1864.

Mining has always been a leading factor in the state's economy. More recently, irrigation has made farming possible. The state's agriculture is dominated by large cattle and sheep ranches.

A number of Basques from the French and Spanish Pyrenees carry on the sheep-raising heritage of their ancestors. Italy has also contributed to the cultural heritage of the state, as have Germany, France, the British Isles, and Greece. Both of our neighbors,

NEVADA

Mexico and Canada, are well represented in the state's makeup.

While Nevada is largely desert and mountains, irrigated fields do produce some crops. Forage crops produce feed for the state's livestock. Grains, including barley, wheat, and oats, are grown, as well as potatoes and some vegetables. Nevada has proportionately less land devoted to farming than any other state.

While the glittering restaurants of Nevada's cities produce food to suit eclectic tastes, the cooking of that other, "real" Nevada has much in common with rural cooking everywhere. It combines the heritage of the individual cook with the food at hand. Lemony Meat Sauce with Spaghetti, for example, serves the state's plentiful meat in a savory sauce over pasta, an Italian innovation. From south of the border come dishes such as Arroz con Pollo. Simply translated, that's "rice with chicken," but through the addition of vegetables and seasonings, it becomes an attention-getter.

Split Pea Vegetable Soup

1 **pound green split peas,**
   rinsed
4 **leeks, washed thoroughly**
   and cut in large pieces
2 **large dry onions, peeled**
   and cut in large pieces
1 **bunch green onions,**
   diced
4 **large carrots, pared and**
   diced
2 **teaspoons salt**
⅛ **teaspoon black pepper**
4 **quarts water**
1 **package (10 ounces)**
   frozen cut okra
1 **package (10 ounces)**
   frozen whole kernel
   corn
2 **cans (10½ ounces each)**
   condensed beef broth
2 **cans (about 13 ounces**
   each) chicken broth
½ **cup butter or margarine**
½ **pound fresh mushrooms,**
   cleaned and diced
   Dairy sour cream
   Fresh parsley, snipped

1. Put split peas into a large saucepot or Dutch oven. Add leeks, dry onions, green onions, carrots, salt, pepper, and water; stir. Cover; bring to boiling, reduce heat, and simmer about 2 hours, stirring occasionally.
2. Add okra, corn, beef broth, and chicken broth; stir. Bring to boiling and simmer, covered, about 1 hour, stirring occasionally.
3. Meanwhile, heat butter in a skillet. Add mushrooms and cook until lightly browned, stirring occasionally.
4. Mix mushrooms into soup. Simmer, covered, about 30 minutes.
5. Ladle hot soup into bowls. Top with sour cream and parsley.

About 4 quarts soup

Herbed Lamb Kidneys in Rice Ring

¾ cup butter or margarine
1 clove garlic, crushed
½ pound fresh mushrooms,
   sliced lengthwise
1 large onion, sliced
¼ teaspoon salt
⅛ teaspoon pepper
3 to 4 tablespoons lemon
   juice
1 tablespoon crushed
   rosemary
12 lamb kidneys, cut in half
   lengthwise and
   trimmed
   Parsley Rice Ring

1. Heat butter in a large skillet. Add garlic, mushrooms, onion, salt, and pepper; cook until mushrooms and onion are lightly browned, stirring occasionally. Remove vegetables; keep warm.
2. Mix lemon juice and rosemary into butter remaining in skillet. Add kidneys and cook about 10 minutes, or until kidneys are tender but still slightly pink in center; turn frequently.
3. Return vegetables to the skillet and mix lightly with the kidneys. Spoon into center of rice ring. Serve remaining sauce in a gravy boat.

6 to 8 servings

Parsley Rice Ring: Bring **4 cups chicken broth** to boiling; add **2 cups uncooked rice** and **2 teaspoons salt.** Cover and cook over low heat for about 25 minutes, or until rice is tender and liquid is absorbed. Stir **¼ cup butter** and **½ cup snipped parsley** into the cooked rice until well blended. Pack into a lightly buttered 5½-cup ring mold. Let stand 10 minutes; unmold onto a warm serving plate.

Ham-Veal Loaf with Saucy Topping

1½ pounds ground cooked
   ham
½ pound ground veal
½ pound ground pork
2 eggs, fork beaten
½ teaspoon salt
⅛ teaspoon black pepper
½ teaspoon ground
   nutmeg
½ teaspoon dry mustard
¼ teaspoon ground thyme
¼ cup finely chopped
   onion
½ cup finely chopped
   green pepper
2 tablespoons finely
   chopped parsley
¾ cup soft bread crumbs
¾ cup apple juice
   Topping

1. Combine ground meats with eggs, salt, pepper, nutmeg, dry mustard, and thyme in a large bowl. Add onion, green pepper, and parsley and toss.
2. Add crumbs and apple juice; mix thoroughly but lightly. Turn into a 9×5×3-inch loaf pan and flatten top.
3. Bake at 350°F 1 hour. Remove from oven; drain and reserve juices. Unmold loaf in a shallow baking pan and spoon some of the juices over loaf. Spoon the Topping over loaf; return to oven 30 minutes.
4. Remove loaf to a warm platter.

1 meat loaf

Topping: Blend ⅔ cup packed light brown sugar, 2 teaspoons cornstarch, 1 teaspoon dry mustard, and 1 teaspoon ground allspice in a small saucepan. Add ⅔ cup apricot nectar, 3 tablespoons lemon juice, and 2 teaspoons cider vinegar. Bring rapidly to boiling and cook about 2 minutes, stirring constantly. Reduce heat and simmer 10 minutes.

About 1¼ cups topping

NEVADA

NEVADA

Arroz con Pollo

2 pounds chicken parts
2 tablespoons salad oil
1 can (13½ ounces) chicken broth
1 can (16 ounces) tomatoes, cut up
½ cup chopped onion
2 medium cloves garlic, minced
1 teaspoon salt
¼ teaspoon saffron or turmeric
⅛ teaspoon pepper
1 bay leaf
1 package (10 ounces) frozen peas
1 cup uncooked regular rice
¼ cup sliced pimento-stuffed or ripe olives

1. In a skillet, brown chicken in oil; pour off fat. Add broth, tomatoes, onion, garlic, salt, saffron, pepper, and bay leaf.
2. Cover; cook over low heat 15 minutes. Add remaining ingredients.
3. Cover; cook 30 minutes more or until chicken and rice are tender; stir occasionally. Remove bay leaf.

4 servings

Ranch Baked Bean Casserole

1 pound ground beef
1 package dry onion soup mix
½ cup water
1 cup ketchup
2 tablespoons prepared mustard
2 teaspoons vinegar
2 cans (about 16 ounces each) pork and beans
1 can (about 16 ounces) kidney beans, drained

1. Brown the beef in a large skillet. Stir in the remaining ingredients and pour into a 2-quart casserole.
2. Bake at 400°F 30 minutes.

10 to 12 servings

Lemony Meat Sauce with Spaghetti

2 pounds ground beef
1½ cups finely chopped onion
1¼ cups chopped green pepper
2 cloves garlic, minced
¼ cup firmly packed brown sugar

1. Put meat, onion, green pepper, and garlic into a heated large heavy saucepot or Dutch oven. Cook 10 to 15 minutes, cutting meat apart with fork or spoon.
2. Stir in brown sugar, salt, pepper, thyme, basil, water, tomato sauce, and tomato paste. Cover and simmer 2 to 3 hours, stirring occasionally. About 30 minutes before serving, mix in mushrooms with liquid and lemon peel and juice.

1 teaspoon salt
¼ teaspoon ground black
    pepper
1 teaspoon thyme,
    crushed
½ teaspoon basil, crushed
2 cups water
2 cans (8 ounces each)
    tomato sauce
2 cans (6 ounces each)
    tomato paste
1 can (6 ounces) sliced
    broiled mushrooms
    (undrained)
1 tablespoon grated
    lemon peel
¼ cup lemon juice
1 pound spaghetti
    Shredded Parmesan
    cheese

3. Meanwhile, cook spaghetti following package directions; drain.
4. Spoon sauce over hot spaghetti and sprinkle generously with cheese.

10 to 12 servings

NEVADA

Turkey Spoon Bread

¾ cup yellow cornmeal
2 tablespoons flour
1 teaspoon salt
4 cups turkey or chicken
    broth, cooled*
¼ cup butter or margarine
4 egg yolks
3 cups chopped cooked
    turkey
4 egg whites

1. Mix cornmeal, flour, and salt in a heavy saucepan. Stirring constantly, gradually add broth and bring to boiling. Continue cooking and stirring until mixture is thickened and smooth. Blend in butter. Turn into a large bowl and set aside to cool.
2. Beat egg yolks until thick and lemon colored; stir into cornmeal mixture. Blend in turkey.
3. Beat egg whites until rounded peaks are formed; gently fold into turkey mixture. Turn into a greased 2-quart shallow baking dish.
4. Bake at 375°F about 40 minutes, or until top is golden brown.

About 8 servings

Onion Casserole

½ cup milk
¼ cup butter
¼ teaspoon salt
⅛ teaspoon pepper
1½ pounds onions, peeled
    and thickly sliced
2 egg yolks, fork beaten
½ cup dairy sour cream
1 cup finely shredded
    sharp Cheddar cheese
⅓ cup dry bread crumbs

1. Heat milk, butter, salt, and pepper in a saucepan. Add onion and cook covered until tender (about 15 minutes).
2. Turn onion mixture into a 1-quart casserole and pour a mixture of egg yolks, sour cream, and cheese over onions. Top with bread crumbs.
3. Heat in a 350°F oven 10 to 12 minutes.

About 6 servings

NEVADA

Cauliflower-Spinach Sensation

⅓ cup chopped watercress
2 tablespoons chopped
  parsley
½ teaspoon tarragon,
  crushed
1 package (10 ounces)
  frozen chopped
  spinach, cooked (do
  not drain)
½ cup mayonnaise
½ cup whipping cream,
  whipped
1 package (10 ounces)
  frozen cauliflower,
  cooked, drained, and
  cooled

1. Stir watercress, parsley, and tarragon into un-drained cooked spinach. Cook 1 minute.
2. Drain spinach mixture thoroughly and force through a food mill or sieve.
3. Blend mayonnaise and whipped cream. Mix with sieved spinach and cooled cauliflower. Chill.

About 4 servings

Avocado Mousse

1½ cups mashed ripe
  avocado
1 teaspoon grated lemon
  peel
2 tablespoons lemon juice
2 tablespoons orange juice
¼ teaspoon salt
8 drops green food
  coloring
1 envelope unflavored
  gelatin
½ cup milk
¼ cup confectioners' sugar
1½ cups whipping cream,
  whipped

1. Blend the avocado, lemon peel and juice, orange juice, salt, and food coloring; set aside.
2. Soften gelatin in milk in a small saucepan. Stir over low heat until dissolved. Blend into the avocado mixture. Chill about 45 minutes, or until mixture becomes slightly thicker.
3. Blend confectioners' sugar into whipped cream. Fold into the avocado mixture. Turn into a 5-cup fancy mold. Freeze until firm.
4. To serve, unmold on a chilled serving plate and allow to stand about 1 hour to soften slightly.

10 to 12 servings

Pear Salad Gazpacho, 283

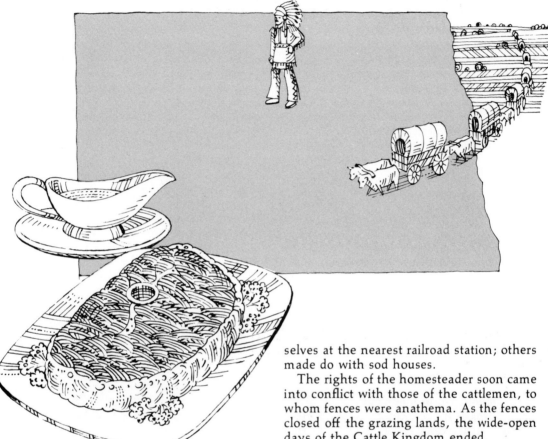

The New World may have held out the dream of a home for the homeless, but it was the Homestead Act that gave it substance. President Lincoln signed the act in 1862, granting 160 acres of unclaimed land to anyone agreeing to cultivate it for five years.

With an early sense of public relations, North Dakota issued a pamphlet billing itself "The Land of Golden Grain. . . . The Lake-Gemmed, Breeze-Swept Empire of the New Northwest." The immigrants took heed. There followed a mixed band of Scandinavians, Germans, Scots, English, Russians, Icelanders, Poles, and French Canadians.

What they found was a wide expanse of treeless plains. Those with enough money to buy lumber for homes supplied themselves at the nearest railroad station; others made do with sod houses.

The rights of the homesteader soon came into conflict with those of the cattlemen, to whom fences were anathema. As the fences closed off the grazing lands, the wide-open days of the Cattle Kingdom ended.

But both the farmer and the cattleman are still well represented in North Dakota. The state produces about half the nation's spring wheat and 80 percent of its durum. Other grains—oats, barley, and rye—also burgeon from its fields. So do potatoes, which along with the beef from the ranches make North Dakota "meat and potatoes" country.

But there is nothing prosaic about the cooking of the state. Largely due to the ethnic mix, the food is a collage of foreign specialities.

When the Scandinavians have a lutefisk supper, it's a good bet everyone will go. Lutefisk is cod cured in lye in a process that takes days and has little appeal for modern homemakers on an individual basis; for special occasions the preparation becomes a community affair. The Norwegians like their lutefisk with drawn butter sauce; the

Swedes, with cream sauce and meatballs. Both like it with lefse (mashed potatoes fried in thin cakes). Lingonberries are traditional at these feasts, but cranberries are often substituted as they are more available.

Scottish settlers came to the Red River Valley in the early nineteenth century. They brought with them their taste for oatmeal porridge, salt fish, and shortbread. Scottish food specialties can still be savored on such occasions as the Highlanders Frolic at International Peace Gardens on the Canadian border.

The Icelandic contribution to the North Dakota table is rich and varied. Skyr, their version of yogurt, is heavenly served with fresh berries. It is made with a special culture said to have been kept alive since the colonization of Iceland in A.D. 930. Icelandic desserts are both tongue-twisting and mouth-watering; pönnukökur and kleinur are two special treats.

In the late nineteenth century a group of French Canadians joined the other settlers in the Red River Valley. They have retained such Gallic specialties as cassoulet, a bean casserole fortified with pork and goose.

In towns where there is a large representation of Scandinavian groups, holiday baking is important. Long before Christmas, Norwegian women start turning out Christmas cookies. In Fargo, the Norwegian children parade through the streets in traditional masks and costumes, visiting homes where they are served special holiday treats.

Many customs are clustered about the Swedish Christmas observance, too. Homemade potato and blood sausages are two Swedish specialties, and their cookie tray spills over with tempting morsels. On Christmas eve, glögg is served, and the family joins hands to dance through the house to carols while Father Christmas leaves his surprises under the tree.

Barbecued Pot Roast

3-pound arm or blade pot roast of beef, cut 2 inches thick
2 teaspoons salt
¼ teaspoon pepper
3 tablespoons fat
1 can (8 ounces) tomato sauce
½ cup water
3 medium-size onions, thinly sliced
2 cloves garlic, minced; or crushed in a garlic press
¼ cup ketchup
¼ cup vinegar
¼ cup lemon juice
2 tablespoons dark brown sugar
1 tablespoon Worcestershire sauce
½ teaspoon dry mustard
¼ teaspoon paprika

1. Season meat with a mixture of salt and pepper.
2. Heat fat in a Dutch oven over medium heat; add the pot roast and brown on both sides.
3. Add to browned meat, tomato sauce, water, onions, and garlic; bring liquid rapidly to boiling; reduce heat (do not boil), cover, and simmer 1½ hours.
4. Meanwhile, blend together ketchup, vinegar, lemon juice, brown sugar, Worcestershire sauce, dry mustard, and paprika. Pour mixture over meat and simmer 1 hour longer, or until meat is tender when pierced with a fork.
5. Remove meat to warm platter. Skim fat from liquid; pour liquid into serving dish and serve with the meat.

About 6 servings

Smoked Beef Tongue (Rökt Tunga)

3- to 4-pound smoked beef
   tongue
   Whole apple
   Celery leaves

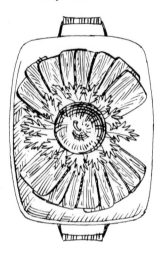

1. Put tongue into a large kettle or a saucepot having a tight-fitting cover.
2. Add enough **boiling water** to cover the tongue. Cover and simmer 3 to 4 hours, or until tender. (If necessary, add more boiling water to keep the tongue covered during cooking period.) Or follow cooking directions on the wrapper.
3. When tongue is tender, slit skin on underside of tongue and peel it off. Cut away roots and gristle. (Plunging tongue into cold water after cooking helps to loosen the skin.) Return tongue to cooking liquid to complete cooling. Drain and chill in refrigerator.
4. Cut chilled tongue into thin slices and arrange on a serving platter. Garnish with whole apple and celery leaves.

9 to 12 servings

Cassoulet

1 pound dried white beans
   (navy or Great
   Northern)
1 to 2 teaspoons salt
2 garlic cloves, minced
¼ pound smoked bacon (or
   salt pork)
1 garlic-flavored sausage
½ pound pork shoulder,
   diced
½ pound mutton, cut in
   cubes
   Lard or other shortening
2 medium onions, chopped
1 bay leaf
1 can (10 ounces) tomato
   purée
   Salt
   Pepper
   Thyme
   Coarse dry bread crumbs
   Butter or margarine

1. Soak beans overnight in about 6 cups water in a saucepot.
2. The next day, add salt and just enough water to cover beans; add garlic, bacon, and sausage. Bring to boiling.
3. In a skillet, brown cubed meat in several tablespoons lard along with onion and bay leaf. Add to the saucepot.
4. Stir in tomato purée and season mixture with salt, pepper, and thyme.
5. Cover and cook gently until meat and beans are tender (about 2 hours). Remove bacon and sausage; slice and return to beans.
6. Turn mixture into an ovenproof casserole; cover with bread crumbs; dot with butter.
7. Bake at 400°F 10 minutes, or until well browned. (Or, if desired, brown crumbs under broiler heat.) Fold under the crusty surface; sprinkle again with crumbs; dot with butter and return to oven to brown; repeat this procedure.

About 6 servings

NORTH DAKOTA

NORTH DAKOTA

Lefse

This is an indispensable side dish at the traditional Scandinavian lutefisk supper.

6 medium-size (about 2 pounds) potatoes, cut in halves
¼ cup butter
¼ cup milk
1½ teaspoons salt
1 teaspoon sugar
⅛ teaspoon pepper
2½ to 3 cups sifted all-purpose flour
Butter, softened

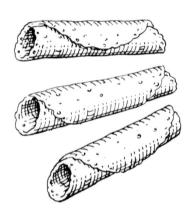

1. Wash, pare and cook potatoes. Cook about 20 minutes, or until tender when pierced with a fork. Drain. To dry potatoes, shake pan over low heat.
2. Mash or rice potatoes thoroughly. Whip in butter, milk, and a mixture of salt, sugar, and pepper until potatoes are fluffy. Cool potatoes; chill in refrigerator.
3. Set a griddle or heavy skillet over low heat. Remove chilled potatoes from refrigerator. Add about one-half the flour and beat until smooth. Beat in enough remaining flour to make a soft dough. Shape dough into a ball and turn onto a lightly floured surface. Roll into a round about ⅛ inch thick. Cut into 6-inch rounds.
4. Test griddle; it is hot enough for baking when drops of water sprinkled on surface dance in small beads. Do not grease the griddle.
5. Place lefse on griddle and cook until lightly browned. Turn and lightly brown other side. Then, turning frequently, continue cooking until lefse are browned and dry. Remove to a clean, dry towel. Cool lefse completely.
6. Spread cold lefse with softened butter. Roll loosely and serve.

About 2½ dozen lefse

Homesteaders' Pancakes

The usual way to eat these is to butter them lavishly, then add maple syrup, corn syrup, or brown sugar. But westerners often eat them with a jelly made from wild berries.

2 eggs
½ cup sugar
½ cup evaporated milk
½ cup water
1 teaspoon vanilla extract
1 cup all-purpose flour
2½ teaspoons baking powder
1 teaspoon ground nutmeg
½ teaspoon salt

1. Beat eggs and add sugar, evaporated milk, water, and vanilla extract; beat well.
2. Mix flour, baking powder, nutmeg, and salt; add to liquid mixture and beat until blended.
3. Drop batter by spoonfuls onto a lightly greased hot griddle; turn when batter begins to bubble.

1 to 2 dozen pancakes

Pickled Beets (Inlagd Rödbetor)

1 pound (about 5)
    medium-size beets
1 medium-size onion
¾ cup cider vinegar
¾ cup reserved beet liquid
1 whole clove

1. Leaving on 1- to 2-inch stem and the root end, cut off leaves from beets. Scrub beets thoroughly. Cook in water to cover 30 to 45 minutes, or until just tender. When beets are tender, drain, reserving liquid in a measuring cup for liquids.
2. Plunge beets into running cold water; peel off and discard skin, stem, and root end. Cut beets into slices ¼ inch thick.
3. Thinly slice onion and separate the slices into rings. Put a layer of beets into a shallow bowl. Cover with some of the onion rings. Repeat layers of beets and onions, ending with the beets.
4. Pour over a mixture of vinegar, beet liquid, and clove.
5. Cover and chill thoroughly in refrigerator several hours or overnight, to blend flavors.

8 to 10 servings

Ponnukökur

2 cups all-purpose flour
1 teaspoon salt
1 teasooon baking soda
1 teaspoon baking powder
¼ teaspoon nutmeg
¼ teaspoon cinnamon
1 cup sugar
4 eggs
1½ cups sour milk (in a
    glass measure,
    combine 4 teaspoons
    vinegar and milk to
    fill to 1½-cup line)
1 cup half-and-half
    Confectioners' sugar

1. Blend flour, salt, baking soda, baking powder, nutmeg, and cinnamon in a large mixing bowl. Stir in sugar.
2. In a small mixing bowl, beat eggs until light. Add sour milk and half-and-half, and combine well.
3. Add liquid mixture to dry ingredients, mixing no more than necessary to make a thin batter. (If too thick, add more milk.)
4. Bake on a lightly greased round 8-inch griddle or frying pan with handle. Spoon about ¼ cup of batter onto griddle, and rotate pan to spread batter over the surface. When a delicate brown at the edges, flip over with a spatula and bake the other side. Repeat until all batter is used, greasing griddle as needed.
5. Transfer to plate and stack, sprinkling generous amounts of confectioners' sugar on each cake.
6. When all batter is used, roll each sheet, and cut into two pieces. Sprinkle on more confectioners' sugar as rolls are arranged in bowl or on a plate. Keep warm until serving.

About 30 pönnukökur

Note: If desired, serve as follows: Place one pönnukökur on a dessert plate. Spread one half of circle with a **tart jelly** or **jam.** Top jelly with **whipped cream.** Fold unspread half over, then spread half (of the half) with jelly and cream and fold over, making a quarter-circle shape.

NORTH DAKOTA

NORTH DAKOTA

Icelandic Kleinur

4 eggs
2 cups sugar
1¼ cups milk
¼ cup melted butter
2 teaspoons baking
      powder
1 teaspoon salt
½ teaspoon ground
      cardamon
8 cups all-purpose flour
   Oil for deep frying
   Confectioners' sugar

1. Beat eggs and sugar until very thick. Combine milk with melted butter and add to egg mixture very slowly, stirring well.
2. Stir baking powder, salt, and cardamon into ½ cup flour. Stir into egg-milk mixture. Continue adding flour, ½ cup at a time, until dough is stiff.
3. Heat oil to 365°F in a deep saucepan.
4. Roll dough, a portion at a time, very thin, about ⅛ inch thick. Using a kleinur cutter, pastry wheel, or floured knife, cut dough in 3×1-inch strips. Cut one end of strip at a diagonal, cut a lengthwise slit in center of strip, put slanted end through slit, and pull through.
5. Place kleinur in hot oil (do not crowd). Fry 1 or 2 minutes, turning once, until golden brown. Drain on paper towels and dust with confectioners' sugar.

About 10 dozen kleinur

Note: If doughnut-type kleinur is desired, roll dough ¼ to ½ inch thick.

Scottish Grasmere Shortbread

2 cups sifted all-purpose
      flour
6 tablespoons sugar
2 tablespoons cornstarch
½ teaspoon ground ginger
¾ cup butter
½ cup finely chopped
      crystallized ginger
   Ginger Filling

1. Sift flour, sugar, cornstarch, and ground ginger into a bowl. Cut in butter until mixture becomes a soft dough (requires working beyond the stage when particles are the size of rice kernels). Mix in crystallized ginger.
2. Shape dough into a ball; knead lightly with fingertips until mixture holds together.
3. Roll a fourth of dough at a time ⅛ inch thick on a floured surface; cut with a 2-inch fluted round cutter. Put on ungreased cookie sheets.
4. Bake at 350°F 12 minutes. Cool.
5. Spread Ginger Filling over bottoms of half the cookies; cover with remaining cookies.

About 3 dozen cookies

Ginger Filling: Cream **¼ cup butter** and **1 teaspoon vanilla extract**; add **2 cups confectioners' sugar** gradually, beating until fluffy. Stir in **1 tablespoon milk** until of spreading consistency. Stir in **2 tablespoons grated crystallized ginger**.

About ⅔ cup

Before the expedition of Lewis and Clark, "Oregon Country" existed largely in the imagination. There was hopeful speculation that, among other prizes, it would provide a Northwest Passage through which ships could sail from the Atlantic to the Pacific.

But on November 7, 1805, those rumors were laid to rest. Lewis and Clark worked their way down the Columbia River for the first official look at the Pacific. The next year they reported back that although there was no cross-continent waterway, a lush and fertile land awaited settlers on the continent's western shore.

It hardly started a land rush. Almost a half century passed before the covered wagons of settlers followed the path of the explorers in appreciable numbers. East and West eventually defied the old axiom by meeting in the ethnic mix that make up Oregon's population. Chinese and Japanese represent the East; Europe and the British Isles provide the western complement.

After the Civil War, many discouraged southerners headed west; today many Dixie specialties are still served in Oregon—southern fried chicken, baked ham and hominy grits, and hot biscuits.

The settlers depended heavily on sourdough bread in Oregon, as others did in Washington and Alaska. Game was plentiful, and hunting provided meat for the table.

Many pioneers carried seeds from eastern orchards as part of their dowry to the new land. Their foresight has resulted in the wide variety of fruits now available in the state. The pear family alone provides an array of choices, with such colorful subdivisions as Bosc, Comice, Eldorado, Forella, Anjou and Bartlett. Other Oregon fruits include apples, plums, and berries in abun-

OREGON

dance. The huckleberry was one of the wild fruits the pioneers found waiting for them in the wilderness.

The moist, sandy coastal area and the fertile land in the valleys are made to order for vegetable farming, but much is done east of the Cascades, too. Beans, lentils, rhubarb, squash, potatoes, and tomatoes are part of Oregon's production.

Vast acreages in western Oregon are grain lands. The state ranks first in hops production and harvests a considerable amount of wheat, too.

Oregon's dairies produce excellent cheese to complement her fruits. And those with sophisticated palates are giving high marks to her new wine industry.

The coastal location gives Oregon a generous supply of such seafood as salmon, tuna, sardines, halibut, and herring. Shellfish include clams, crabs, oysters, and shrimp.

The Oregon clambake was well established before the covered wagons arrived; the Indians had their own version. Stones were heated in fires on the beach. Once the flames died down, the stones were covered with leaves, clams were laid in and covered with a mat. Sweet corn in the husk and new potatoes in their skin cooked alongside. Today's clambake is similar, but the modern cook often uses a steamer. Butter for dipping and beer for washing down the clams are basics.

Each spring at Seaside there is a public "crab feed." Cracked Dungeness crabs are served in great quantities—plain or with a choice of sauces.

Zesty Shrimp Tempters

2 cups cider vinegar
½ cup water
¼ cup salt
¼ teaspoon black pepper
2 tablespoons sugar
3 bay leaves
½ teaspoon whole allspice
½ teaspoon whole cloves
½ teaspoon whole mustard seed
⅛ teaspoon paprika
3 medium-size onions, sliced
4 pounds large fresh shrimp, cooked, peeled, and deveined

1. Combine the vinegar and water in a saucepan. Bring to boiling. Remove from heat and stir in salt, pepper, and sugar until dissolved. Stir in bay leaves, allspice, cloves, mustard seed, paprika, and onion.
2. Put cooked shrimp into a large bowl (not metal). Add vinegar mixture and mix gently. Cover; refrigerate 24 hours.
3. Before serving, drain shrimp thoroughly. Arrange on a bed of frilly **green lettuce leaves.** Accompany with fancy cocktail picks.

About 4 dozen shrimp

Lentil Soup

1 package (16 ounces) dried lentils, rinsed
¼ pound smoked sausage
Thin slice garlic
1 small onion, minced
¼ cup diced celery
3 quarts water

1. Place lentils in a kettle with sausage, garlic, onion, celery, and water. Cover.
2. Simmer 3 to 4 hours, adding more water as necessary.

6 servings

Fresh Pear and Pork Chop Skillet

6 pork chops, cut ¾ to 1
   inch thick
½ teaspoon salt
⅛ teaspoon pepper
6 thin lemon slices
12 thin onion slices
3 Anjou pears, halved and
   cored
¾ cup lightly packed brown
   sugar
½ cup lemon juice
½ cup water
⅓ cup soy sauce
½ teaspoon ground ginger

1. Brown chops on both sides. Drain off any fat.
2. Season chops with salt and pepper. Put a lemon slice and two onion slices on each chop. Place pear halves cut-side down in skillet around chops.
3. Combine brown sugar with the lemon juice, water, soy sauce, and ginger and pour over all. Cover; basting frequently with sauce, cook over low heat about 20 minutes; then turn pears cut-side up and cook 20 minutes longer, or until pork is tender.

6 servings

OREGON

Steak Diablo

2 beef round steaks, 1½
   pounds each
1 teaspoon salt
1 teaspoon pepper
½ teaspoon paprika
1 jar (4½ ounces) sliced
   mushrooms, drained
1 large onion, thinly sliced
1 jar (2 ounces) pimento,
   drained
1 cup fine bread crumbs
½ cup butter or margarine,
   melted
1 tablespoon boiling water
1 egg
10 large pimento-stuffed
   olives
¼ cup butter
½ cup flour
2 cups red wine

1. Pound steaks until thin. Rub with salt, pepper, and paprika. Overlap steaks on cutting board, making 1 large steak. Spread with layers of mushrooms, sliced onions, and pimento. Sprinkle with bread crumbs.
2. With an electric mixer, combine melted butter with boiling water and egg. Drizzle egg mixture over bread crumbs. Arrange stuffed olives in a row along one edge of steak. Begin rolling meat at the end with olives. Tie firmly with string.
3. Melt ¼ cup butter in a deep casserole. Flour steak and brown in the butter. Add wine and cover.
4. Bake at 350°F 2 hours, or until tender.
5. To serve, place steak on hot platter and surround with **quartered tomatoes** and **parsley sprigs**.

8 servings

OREGON

Oriental Chicken Wings

10 chicken wings
⅓ cup soy sauce
2 tablespoons sugar
1 tablespoon dry sherry
½ teaspoon anise seed
⅓ cup water

1. Cut tips off wings and discard. Cut wings in two at joints. Wash in warm water and dry.
2. In a heavy saucepan, combine chicken wings and rest of ingredients. Bring to boiling, lower heat, cover, and simmer 20 minutes. Stir occasionally.
3. Remove cover and simmer another 15 minutes, basting frequently until about ½ cup liquid remains. Spoon liquid on wings and serve chicken either hot or cold.

20 pieces

Note: The wings have more flavor if made a day ahead and allowed to stand in sauce overnight.

Crab Meat Mousse

1½ tablespoons unflavored gelatin
¼ cup cold water
¼ cup lemon juice
1 teaspoon salt
¼ teaspoon paprika
Few grains pepper
2 cups crab meat, flaked
1 cup whipping cream, whipped

Cucumber Mayonnaise:
1 cup mayonnaise
2 tablespoons lemon juice
1 tablespoon minced parsley
1 medium cucumber, pared and finely chopped

1. Sprinkle gelatin over cold water and lemon juice in a bowl; dissolve over hot water. Mix in salt, paprika, and pepper. Remove from heat and place over ice water about 5 minutes, stirring frequently.
2. Stir in crab meat, then fold in whipped cream. Turn into a 1-quart mold and chill until firm.
3. Unmold onto a chilled plate and serve with Cucumber Mayonnaise.
4. For dressing, blend mayonnaise, lemon juice, and parsley, then mix in cucumber.

About 8 servings

Back-Yard Clambake

This is a modernized version of the old-fashioned clambake, adapted for the grill.

18-inch heavy-duty aluminum foil, 28-inch length
Cheesecloth
Seaweed or rockweed (available at fish market), thoroughly washed

1. For each packet, line the length of foil with a piece of cheesecloth several inches longer than foil.
2. Form three layers on the piece of cheesecloth, using seaweed, clams, and chicken, in that order. Tuck in the corn ear (halves, if long) and potato quarters. Sprinkle lightly with salt and grind pepper over all. Bring the cheesecloth up to cover the food. Bring two opposite edges of foil together over mixture and wrap securely,

1 dozen unopened steamer
    clams, well scrubbed
    and rinsed
Half of a 2½-pound
    broiler-fryer chicken
    (split lengthwise),
    rinsed
1 ready-to-cook ear of corn
    (fresh or frozen)
1 baking potato, scrubbed,
    rinsed, and cut
    lengthwise in quarters
Salt and pepper

using a drugstore fold; turn up ends and fold to seal.
3. Set packet on a hot grill and cook 1 hour, or until chicken is tender. (Cover grill with hood if necessary during cooking.)
4. Carefully pour the broth from packet into a cup for dunking the clams or for drinking. Accompany with **melted butter** or **margarine.** Serve with **crusty bread,** which has been wrapped in foil and heated on grill; slice before serving.

1 serving

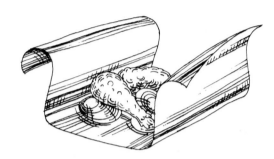

Pear Salad Gazpacho

4 fresh California Bartlett
    pears
1 clove garlic, peeled
1 teaspoon salt
1½ tablespoons sugar
½ teaspoon tarragon,
    crumbled
½ teaspoon basil,
    crumbled
¼ teaspoon paprika
¼ cup red wine vinegar
¼ cup olive oil
¼ cup water
1 tablespoon sherry
1 cup chopped celery
1 cup chopped green
    pepper
½ cup chopped or sliced
    green onion
2 large firm, ripe
    tomatoes chopped (2
    cups)
1 quart shredded western
    iceberg lettuce

1. Rinse and chill pears.
2. Mash garlic with salt and sugar. Combine with herbs, paprika, vinegar, oil, water, and sherry in a pint jar. Cover tightly and shake well to blend (shake again before using). Let stand an hour or longer to blend flavors. (If a creamy-type dressing is desired, measure dressing ingredients into top of blender jar. Cover and whirl at high speed until well blended.)
3. Prepare and chill vegetables.
4. When ready to serve, toss celery, green pepper, onion, and tomato with half of dressing. Cut pears in half lengthwise and remove cores. Arrange 2 pear halves for each serving on shredded lettuce on chilled salad plates. Fill with mixed vegetables and spoon on remaining dressing.

4 servings

OREGON

Pizza

1 package active dry yeast
2 tablespoons lukewarm
water
1 cup boiling water
2 tablespoons shortening
1½ teaspoons salt
3 cups sifted all-purpose
flour
3 tablespoons olive oil
½ cup grated Parmesan
cheese
¾ pound mozzarella
cheese, sliced
2 cups diced, peeled ripe
tomatoes
1 clove garlic, minced
½ teaspoon salt
⅛ teaspoon pepper
½ teaspoon dried oregano
or thyme

1. Sprinkle yeast in the lukewarm water. Let stand 5 to 10 minutes to completely dissolve.
2. Pour boiling water over shortening and salt in a large bowl. Stir to melt shortening Cool to lukewarm. Stir up yeast and add to shortening mixture.
3. Add half of the flour to yeast mixture; beat with a spoon until smooth. Add remaining flour; beat smooth.
4. Place dough on floured board; pat gently into two 11-inch rounds or one 13-inch round, leaving edges slightly thicker. Place on greased cookie sheet and let rise in a warm place (85°F) until double in height.
5. Brush dough with 1 tablespoon olive oil. Sprinkle with Parmesan cheese, then layer on one third of the mozzarella cheese.
6. Mix together tomatoes, garlic, salt, and pepper. Pour on pizza; arrange rest of mozzarella on top. Sprinkle on oregano, then drizzle 2 tablespoons olive oil on top.
7. Bake at 450°F 25 to 30 minutes, or until crust is golden brown.

*One 13-inch or
two 11-inch pizzas*

Note: Anchovies may be added if all oil and cheeses are omitted. Dot tomatoes with **1 can (2 ounces) anchovy fillets,** finely minced, and drizzle oil from anchovies on top. Garnish with slices of **green pepper.** Bake as above.

Upside-Down Pear Coffee Cake

1 tablespoon butter
¼ cup light brown sugar
½ teaspoon cinnamon
⅛ teaspoon ground cloves
2 tablespoons chopped nuts
4 ripe pears
2 cups biscuit mix
¼ cup granulated sugar
1 egg, beaten
½ cup milk

1. Melt butter in bottom of an 8-inch round baking pan.
2. Combine brown sugar, spices, and nuts; set aside. Pare and core pears. Slice 2 pears in 8 slices each, and arrange petal fashion in butter in pan. Sprinkle with brown sugar mixture.
3. Finely chop remaining 2 pears, and combine with biscuit mix and granulated sugar. Combine egg and milk and stir into dry ingredients just until moistened. Spread batter over pears in pan.
4. Bake at 400°F 35 minutes. Cool 2 minutes, run a knife around edge, and invert on plate.

One 8-inch coffee cake

Almost every variety of landscape on earth—and even the moon—can be found in South Dakota. There are the heights of the Black Hills, rolling prairie in the midlands, and lush valley land along the Red River. And an eerie, lunar expanse of rock awaits the visitor to the Bad Lands.

The cultural make-up of the state is almost as varied. The Danes, Swedes, Norwegians, and Finns who answered the call of the Homestead Act in 1862 still give the state a distinctively Scandinavian flavor. Many other Europeans, including German Mennonites who migrated by way of Russia, brought influences from their homelands. Those first settlers, the American Indians, are still an important component of the population.

The story of the Indian is inseparable from the history of the state; "Dakota" or "Sioux" was the name of one of those tribes that made this land their home. Those early-day Indians based their meals on corn, squash, and other plants they found growing wild, as well as on game.

South Dakota's past is as rich and colorful as a TV western; indeed, its history has provided story lines for many. In 1817 the first trading post was set up at Pierre, now the capital.

Today the state is largely agricultural, and while corn is still an important crop, wheat has taken over first place. The raising of livestock and poultry is a significant part of the life of the state.

From Nebraska's Scandinavian community comes some of the state's most interesting food customs. In their homes the smorgasbord, a meal served buffet-style at a long table, is an institution. Some traditional smorgasbord recipes are given here; others are in the chapters on North Dakota and Minnesota, states which also boast a large Scandinavian population.

The Swedish smorgasbord is traditionally a feast in four courses beginning with cheese, and offering hot dishes to balance the cold. Homemade sausages, pickled herring, lutefisk (cod that has been soaked in lye), salads, and rye breads belong in the Swedish smorgasbord. So do trays of deviled eggs, and the rice porridge that signals the meal's conclusion.

The Danish kolde bord—cold table—is similar to the smorgasbord but features makings for do-it-yourself smorrebrod, or open-faced sandwiches. Pumpernickel is popular with the Danes, but all shades of bread, from white to dark brown, are set out, along with bits of meat, fish, poultry, vegetables, and egg.

Visitors to the state can set up headquarters in the Black Hills, and in just a few side trips see some of the country's most interesting sights: the Bad Lands, Wind Cave, and the Mount Rushmore Memorial among them.

From miles away, travelers are urged to visit the Wall Drug Store, made famous by a small businessman during the depression. In order to stimulate trade in those lean days, he posted signs far and near inviting tourists to stop in for a free glass of water (not uncommon in those days). From a simple one-room store, Wall's has grown into a busy complex.

Another attraction awaits the tourist in Mitchell—the famous Corn Palace. This is an imposing building, covered with a mosaic of grain, and housing exhibits celebrating the state's achievements. Each September it hosts the Corn Palace Festival.

Savory Pot Roast

3-to 4-pound beef pot roast
2 tablespoons flour
2 tablespoons paprika
2 teaspoons salt
⅛ teaspoon black pepper
3 tablespoons fat
4 onions, thinly sliced

1. Coat meat with a mixture of the flour, paprika, salt, and pepper. Brown meat on all sides in hot fat in a large skillet or Dutch oven.
2. Lift out meat and put about one third of the onions in a layer in bottom of a skillet or Dutch oven. Return meat and cover with remaining onions.
3. Cover tightly and cook over low heat about 3 hours, or until meat is tender.

6 to 8 servings

Lamb Olé

1 package chili seasoning mix
2 tablespoons flour
2 teaspoons salt
4 lamb shanks
3 tablespoons cooking oil
1 can (28 ounces) tomatoes (undrained)
1 can (15 ounces) chili style beans
1 can (15 ounces) golden hominy (optional)
2 tablespoons cornmeal

1. Combine 2 tablespoons chili seasoning mix, flour, and salt. Place in a large plastic bag; add shanks to bag and shake to coat with flour mixture.
2. Heat oil in a large skillet; add shanks and brown on all sides.
3. Place lamb in casserole dish; mix tomatoes with remaining chili seasoning; pour over shanks.
4. Bake at 325°F 1 hour. Remove casserole from oven; skim off fat. Add beans, hominy (if desired) and cornmeal to casserole, stirring gently to combine.
5. Return to oven and continue to bake 1½ hours, or until sauce is slightly thickened and lamb is tender.

4 servings

SOUTH DAKOTA

Roast Pheasant

2 young pheasants, about
    2 pounds each
Wild Rice with
    Mushrooms (page
    289)
1½ teaspoons salt
¼ cup unsalted butter,
    melted

1. Cut off necks of birds close to bodies, leaving neck skin on to help hold the stuffing. Remove any pin feathers; singe if necessary. Rinse inside and out in warm water; drain; pat dry with absorbent paper.
2. Cover giblets (except liver) and neck with water; bring to boiling, then simmer until tender (about 1 hour). During last 15 minutes, add desired amount of salt and the livers.
3. Prepare Wild Rice with Mushrooms for stuffing. Rub pheasant cavities with the salt. Lightly fill neck and body cavities with stuffing. Close cavities with skewers and lace with cord.
4. Place birds, breast up, on rack in roasting pan. Brush with melted butter.
5. Roast at 325°F 1½ to 2 hours, or until pheasants test done; baste frequently.
6. Reserve liquid from giblets for gravy; finely chop the hearts, gizzards, and livers.
7. Transfer birds to platter and keep warm while making gravy, if desired.

4 servings

Liver Loaf

1 pound beef liver
6 tablespoons butter or
    margarine
2 tablespoons chopped
    onion
½ cup flour
1 cup milk
1½ cups cooked oats or
    bulgur
2 eggs, slightly beaten
2½ teaspoons salt
¼ teaspoon pepper
½ teaspoon dry mustard
¼ teaspoon sage
1 teaspoon Worcestershire
    sauce
Sour Cream Sauce

1. Cover liver with boiling water and let stand 10 minutes. Drain liver and put through medium blade of food grinder.
2. Melt butter in a saucepan. Sauté onion until golden.
3. Blend in flour. Reduce heat and add milk, stirring constantly until mixture thickens.
4. Add liver, oats, eggs, and seasonings, blending well. Turn mixture into a lightly greased 8×4-inch loaf pan.
5. Bake at 325°F 1 hour. Let cool in pan 15 to 20 minutes before unmolding on serving platter. Serve with Sour Cream Sauce.

8 to 10 servings

Sour Cream Sauce: Melt **2 tablespoons butter** in a saucepan. Blend in **2 tablespoons flour.** Remove from heat and add **1 cup beef stock** and **1 cup dairy sour cream.** Bring to boiling, stirring constantly. Stir in ½ **teaspoon salt,** ¼ **teaspoon pepper,** and **1 teaspoon Worcestershire sauce.** Serve hot.

About 2 cups

SOUTH DAKOTA

Ham Loaf with Savory Horseradish Sauce

3 pounds ground smoked
    ham
3 pounds ground pork
3 eggs
1 can (13 ounces)
    evaporated milk
1 can (10¾ ounces)
    condensed tomato soup
1 cup cracker crumbs
    Savory Horseradish Sauce

1. Combine ham and pork.
2. Beat eggs. Blend in evaporated milk, condensed tomato soup, and cracker crumbs. Add meat and mix well.
3. Pack into two 9×5×3-inch loaf pans. Place loaf pans in a ½-inch depth of water in a large pan.
4. Bake at 350°F 1½ hours. Serve with chilled sauce.

24 servings

Savory Horseradish Sauce: Combine **1 jar (5 ounces) horseradish** with **½ cup mayonnaise, 2 teaspoons prepared mustard,** and **¼ cup chopped parsley.** Fold in **2 cups dairy sour cream** until well blended. Chill.

Fish Balls (Fiskekroketer)

  Oil for deep frying
2 tablespoons butter
¼ cup all-purpose flour
1 teaspoon salt
⅛ teaspoon pepper
1 cup cream
3 cups flaked cooked fish
    (cod, trout, fillet of
    sole, whitefish)
1 egg yolk, beaten
2 eggs, slightly beaten
1 cup fine dry bread
    crumbs

1. Fill a deep saucepan or automatic deep-fat fryer one half to two thirds full with oil. Heat fat to 350°F.
2. Meanwhile, heat butter over low heat in a saucepan. Blend in flour, salt, and pepper.
3. Heat until mixture bubbles. Add cream gradually, stirring constantly.
4. Cook rapidly, stirring constantly, until mixture thickens. Remove from heat; cool.
5. When sauce is cool, blend in fish and beaten egg yolk. Shape mixture into balls 1 inch in diameter.
6. Dip balls into slightly beaten egg. To coat evenly, roll balls in bread crumbs.
7. Deep-fry fish balls in heated fat. Deep-fry only as many balls at one time as will float uncrowded one layer deep in the fat. Turn balls often. Deep-fry 2 minutes, or until lightly browned. Drain; remove to absorbent paper. Keep fish balls warm for the smorgasbord.

About 5 dozen fish balls

Bulgur and Eggplant Casserole

⅓ cup chopped onion
¼ teaspoon minced garlic
2 tablespoons cooking oil
1 can (16 ounces)
    tomatoes (undrained)
¼ teaspoon basil
1¼ teaspoons salt

1. Sauté onion and garlic in 2 tablespoons hot oil until golden in color. Add tomatoes and liquid, basil, salt, pepper, and sugar. Cover and simmer 30 minutes. Set aside.
2. Dip eggplant slices in flour and fry in ½ cup oil until golden brown on each side. Set on paper towel to drain.

⅛ teaspoon pepper
½ teaspoon sugar
1 medium eggplant, pared and sliced ½ inch thick
2 to 3 tablespoons flour
½ cup cooking oil
2 cups cooked bulgur
4 to 6 ounces mozzarella cheese, thinly sliced
½ cup grated Parmesan cheese

3. In a 2-quart baking dish, layer the eggplant, bulgur, sauce, and mozzarella cheese. Sprinkle Parmesan cheese on top.
4. Bake at 350°F about 30 minutes.

6 servings

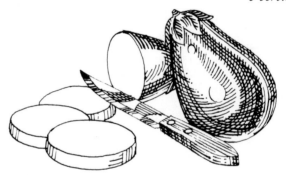

SOUTH DAKOTA

Wild Rice with Mushrooms

½ pound fresh mushrooms, sliced
2 tablespoons finely chopped onion
¼ cup butter or margarine
1 cup wild rice, cooked and drained
⅓ cup melted butter or margarine

1. Cook mushrooms and onion in ¼ cup butter in a skillet until mushrooms are lightly browned.
2. Combine mushrooms, wild rice, and melted butter; toss gently until mushrooms and butter are evenly distributed throughout rice.

8 servings

Corn-Gold Fritters

1⅓ cups sifted all-purpose flour
1 teaspoon baking powder
¾ teaspoon salt
⅛ teaspoon pepper
⅔ cup milk
1 teaspoon Worcestershire sauce
1 teaspoon cooking or salad oil
2 eggs, well beaten
1 can (12 ounces) whole kernel corn, drained
Fat for deep frying heated to 365°F

1. Blend flour, baking powder, salt, and pepper in a bowl.
2. Mix milk, Worcestershire sauce, and oil with eggs. Add all at one time to the dry ingredients and beat with a rotary beater just until smooth. Mix in corn.
3. For each frying, drop batter by tablespoonfuls into the hot fat until surface is covered. Fry 2 to 3 minutes, or until golden brown, turning frequently. Drain fritters over fat for a few seconds before removing to absorbent paper. Allow 2 fritters per serving.

About 6 servings

SOUTH DAKOTA

Whole Wheat Bread

3 cups whole wheat flour
3⅓ cups (about) all-purpose flour
3 tablespoons sugar
4 teaspoons salt
2 packages active dry yeast
1½ cups water
¾ cup milk
⅓ cup molasses
⅓ cup margarine or other shortening

1. Combine the flours, blending thoroughly. Into a large bowl measure 2½ cups of the flour mixture. Add sugar, salt, and undissolved yeast; mix well.
2. Combine the remaining ingredients in a saucepan and place over low heat until liquids are warm (fat need not be melted).
3. Add liquids gradually to dry ingredients, beating constantly at medium speed of electric mixer; scrape sides of bowl occasionally. Add ½ cup flour mixture or enough to make a thick batter. Beat at high speed 2 minutes, scraping sides of bowl when necessary.
4. Stir in enough additional flour to make a soft dough. (If more flour is needed, add all-purpose flour to obtain desired dough.)
5. Turn onto a lightly floured surface and knead until smooth and elastic (about 8 minutes).
6. Put into a greased deep bowl; turn dough to bring bottom surface to top. Cover; let rise in warm place until doubled (about 1 hour).
7. Punch down dough; turn onto a lightly floured surface. Divide into halves and shape into loaves. Put into 2 greased 8×4×2-inch loaf pans. Cover; let rise again until doubled (about 1 hour).
8. Bake at 400°F about 30 minutes, or until done. Remove from pans to wire racks; brush loaves lightly with melted shortening, if desired. Cool thoroughly before storing.

2 loaves bread

Swedish Christmas Porridge *(Risgrynsgröt)*

This rice porridge is served at Christmastime. According to Swedish custom the person who finds the almond will marry within the next year. When the porridge is served, each person makes up a rhyme as he takes a spoonful. This continues around the table until all the porridge is eaten. At other times of the year the porridge is served only with a fruit sauce and the almond is omitted.

6 cups milk
1 cup rice
3 tablespoons sugar
½ teaspoon salt
1 whole blanched almond
Cool milk
Sugar
Cinnamon

1. Put milk, rice, sugar, and salt into the top of a double boiler. Cover and cook over simmering water 2½ to 3 hours, or until rice is entirely soft when a kernel is pressed between fingers and mixture is quite thick. Remove cover for last 10 minutes if mixture is not thick enough.
2. Mix in almond just before serving.
3. Serve with milk, sugar, and cinnamon, or with a **fruit sauce.**

6 servings

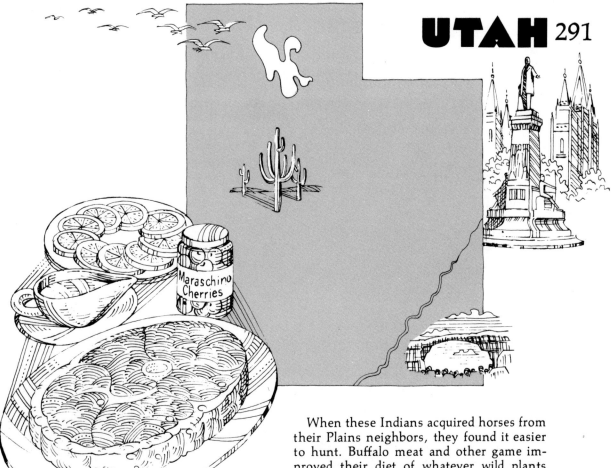

Lying miles inland, the Great Basin of Utah hardly looks like an ocean bed. Yet that is exactly what it was, and there are the lacy prints of sea fossils to prove it. Melting glaciers long ago filled low areas with water, eventually forming salt lakes in the Basin, including the one that gives the state capital its name.

Religion has been a guiding force in the development of Utah. The land was first explored by Catholic priests seeking to expand the frontiers of their faith. And it was eventually settled by another religious band, the Mormons, seeking asylum after having been driven from one place to another.

Before the arrival of the white man, the land was inhabited by Indians of the Shoshonean group. One tribe was the Ute, for whom the state was later named.

When these Indians acquired horses from their Plains neighbors, they found it easier to hunt. Buffalo meat and other game improved their diet of whatever wild plants they could find, such as the sego lily.

In 1847, the Mormons entered the area under the leadership of Brigham Young. The following year, the territory that included Utah was ceded to the United States by Mexico in the Treaty of Guadalupe Hidalgo.

In the beginning, life was difficult for the Mormon settlers. Their first lodgings were often little more than dirt dugouts or wooden lean-tos. Their food was not much better. They sometimes made do with roots, thistle greens, wild birds, and molasses. In time, they learned how to cook such local fare as milkweed, wild lettuce, and spinach. From forays into California, they introduced wheat and some vegetables.

Despite the fact that Utah is considered 90 percent nonarable, the Mormons literally made the desert bloom through irrigation and good management. By 1860 they had 150 self-sustaining colonies with a population of 40,000 people.

UTAH

The hub of their settlement was, and is, Salt Lake City. On July 24, a visitor will be caught up in the state's annual holiday, a reenactment of the Mormons' entry into the state. Other towns in the state also mark the occasion with rodeos, parades, and celebrations, complete with local food specialties.

Family life is important to the Mormons, and large families have been part of their tradition. Thus the cooking has come to be hearty, substantial fare. The potato, almost as important in Utah as in neighboring Idaho, has proved appetite-satisfying in combination with the meat for which the state is also known. Pigs, cattle, and sheep are raised on the plains which are less suited to crop farming.

Ham is prized in Mormon cookery; it is often served with a mustard sauce. Biscuits and other breads, made from local wheat, disappear rapidly from the Mormon table. Fruit orchards in the fertile Utah valleys provide numerous treats such as prune cake and apple pancakes.

Scenery is one of Utah's most valuable resources, and it brings caravans of tourists to the state each year. They bring with them the paraphernalia for outdoor cooking that has become the hallmark of the camper and backpacker.

Cheddar Puffs

¼ cup butter or margarine, softened
8 ounces shredded sharp Cheddar cheese (about 2 cups)
1¼ cups sifted all-purpose flour
¾ teaspoon paprika
¼ teaspoon dry mustard
⅛ teaspoon cayenne pepper

1. Blend butter and cheese until smooth. Mix in a blend of flour, paprika, dry mustard, and cayenne pepper.
2. Shape dough into rolls about 1¼ inches in diameter. Wrap in waxed paper and chill.
3. Cut into ¼-inch slices. Place about 1 inch apart on lightly greased baking sheets.
4. Bake at 400°F about 8 minutes. Serve hot.

About 4 dozen puffs

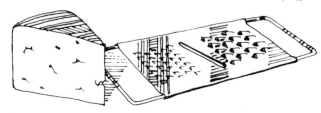

Baked Ham Slice

1 smoked ham slice (about 1 pound), cut about ½ inch thick
Whole cloves
2 tablespoons brown sugar
2 tablespoons fine dry bread crumbs
1 teaspoon grated orange peel
½ teaspoon dry mustard
1 orange
Maraschino cherries, cut in rings
¾ cup orange juice

1. Place ham slice in an 11×7×2-inch baking dish.
2. Insert cloves in ham slice at 1-inch intervals.
3. Sprinkle a mixture of brown sugar, bread crumbs, orange peel, and dry mustard over ham.
4. Rinse orange and cut into ¼-inch slices. Arrange slices on ham over sugar mixture. Garnish with maraschino cherries, cut in rings. Carefully pour orange juice over top of ham slice.
5. Bake at 300°F about 40 minutes. Remove cloves from ham slice before serving.

2 or 3 servings

Mountain Lamb Chops

6 tablespoons olive oil
2 tablespoons lemon juice
1½ teaspoons salt
1 teaspoon dried oregano
    leaves, crushed
½ teaspoon freshly ground
    pepper
4 lamb shoulder chops
    (about 2 pounds), cut
    1 inch thick

1. Combine oil, lemon juice, salt, oregano, and pepper in a large, shallow pan. Add lamb chops. Marinate 3 to 4 hours in refrigerator.
2. Transfer lamb chops to a large skillet, reserving the marinade.
3. Cook the meat on both sides over medium-low heat, adding marinade if liquid is needed. For medium rare, cook the meat 10 minutes on each side. For well-done, cook the meat 15 minutes on each side. If desired, serve with buttered rice, sliced beets, corn, and green salad.

4 servings

Camper's Egg-in-a-Bag

2 slices bacon
1 egg

1. Cover the bottom of a small brown paper bag with bacon.
2. Crack egg and drop in bag over bacon.
3. Roll sack down in 1-inch folds and shove sharp-pointed stick through paper bag.
4. Place over coals for 5 to 10 minutes, depending upon firmness of egg desired.

1 serving

German Apple Pancakes

¼ cup butter or margarine
3 small, firm cooking
    apples, cored, pared,
    and thinly sliced
    (about 2½ cups)
2 tablespoons sugar
1 teaspoon ground
    cinnamon
4 eggs
⅓ cup milk
½ cup flour
1 tablespoon sugar
¼ teaspoon salt
6 tablespoons butter or
    margarine
    Confectioners' sugar

1. Heat the ¼ cup butter in a 10-inch skillet; add apple slices, cover, and cook over medium heat until apples are almost tender, turning slices several times during cooking. When almost tender, sprinkle a mixture of the 2 tablespoons sugar and the cinnamon evenly over apples. Continue cooking, uncovered, until apples are just tender. Turn into a bowl and keep warm.
2. Beat eggs thoroughly and blend in milk. Add a mixture of flour, 1 tablespoon sugar, and salt and beat with a rotary beater until smooth.
3. Heat 3 tablespoons of butter in the skillet until moderately hot. Pour in enough batter to cover bottom of skillet. Spoon about one half of the apple mixture evenly over batter. Pour in just enough batter to cover apples.
4. Bake pancake over medium heat until golden brown on bottom. Loosen edges with spatula; carefully turn and brown other side.
5. When pancake is baked, remove skillet from heat and brush pancake generously with **melted butter.** Roll up and transfer to a warm serving platter. Sift confectioners' sugar over the top. Keep pancake hot. Repeat procedure with remaining batter and apples.

2 apple pancakes

UTAH

Garbanzo Bean Salad

2 cans (15 ounces each)
   garbanzos, drained
   (about 4 cups)
1 cup cut celery
2 green peppers, diced or
   slivered
2 or 3 tomatoes, peeled
   and cut in small pieces
½ cup finely chopped sweet
   onion
1 cup radish slices
¼ cup snipped parsley
1 cup quartered pitted ripe
   olives
1 envelope Italian salad
   dressing mix
2 teaspoons Worcestershire
   sauce
1 teaspoon ground
   coriander
¾ teaspoon lemon pepper
   marinade

1. Combine the vegetables, parsley, and olives in a bowl; toss lightly and refrigerate to chill.
2. Meanwhile, prepare salad dressing following package directions, using **wine vinegar** and adding Worcestershire sauce and remaining ingredients with the mix. Shake thoroughly before using.
3. About 1 hour before serving, toss salad ingredients lightly with dressing until well mixed, then chill.

10 to 12 servings

Gourmet Potato Salad

5 cups cubed cooked
   potatoes
½ teaspoon salt
⅛ teaspoon ground black
   pepper
4 hard-cooked eggs,
   chopped
1 cup chopped celery
⅔ cup sliced green onions
   with tops
¼ cup chopped green
   pepper
1 cup large curd cottage
   cheese
¼ teaspoon dry mustard
½ teaspoon salt
   Few grains black pepper
⅔ cup (6-ounce can)
   undiluted evaporated
   milk
½ cup crumbled blue cheese
2 tablespoons cider vinegar
   Lettuce

1. Put potatoes into a large bowl and sprinkle with salt and pepper. Add eggs, celery, onions, and green pepper; toss lightly.
2. Put cottage cheese, dry mustard, salt, pepper, evaporated milk, blue cheese, and vinegar into an electric blender container. Blend thoroughly.
3. Pour dressing over mixture in bowl and toss lightly and thoroughly. Chill before serving to blend flavors.
4. Spoon chilled salad into a bowl lined with lettuce. Garnish as desired.

About 8 servings

Utah Coleslaw

1 cup mayonnaise
¼ cup French dressing
1 teaspoon salt
Dash freshly ground
pepper
4 cups shredded cabbage
1 cup diced, unpeeled
tomatoes
½ cup chopped celery
¼ cup chopped green onion
¼ cup sliced radishes
¼ pound Cheddar cheese,
cubed

1. Combine mayonnaise, French dressing, salt, and pepper; mix until blended well.
2. Add remaining ingredients and toss lightly.

6 to 8 servings

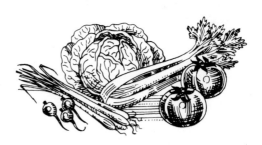

Indian Fry Bread

4 cups all-purpose flour
1 tablespoon salt
1 tablespoon baking
powder
1½ cups water (more, if
needed)
Oil for frying

1. In a large bowl, combine flour, salt, and baking powder. Mix well. Stir in water, about ¼ cup at a time, until mixture forms a stiff dough.
2. Knead about 5 minutes, until the dough is thick and elastic. Pinch off about 2 tablespoons dough and form very thin round patties, using a rolling pin or hands.
3. Fry in hot (365°F) oil, turning once, until brown on each side.

24 individual breads

All-American Cookies

1 cup shortening, soft
1 cup firmly packed
brown sugar
½ cup sugar
2 eggs
¼ cup milk
1 teaspoon vanilla extract
1½ cups sifted all-purpose
flour
1 teaspoon baking powder
½ teaspoon baking soda
½ teaspoon salt
3 cups uncooked oats

1. Beat together shortening and sugars until creamy. Add eggs, milk, and vanilla extract. Beat until well blended.
2. Sift flour, baking powder, baking soda, and salt together. Add to creamed mixture; mix well. Stir in oats.
3. For variations, divide batter into three equal parts. To first part, add chocolate pieces. To the second, add pecans. To the third, add coconut.
4. Drop by rounded teaspoonfuls onto cookie sheets.
5. Bake at 350°F 12 to 15 minutes, or until lightly browned.

About 7 dozen cookies

Variations:
⅓ cup semisweet chocolate
pieces
¼ cup chopped pecans
¼ cup flaked or shredded
coconut

UTAH

Fruit-a-Plenty Pie

1 can (30 ounces) apricot halves
1 package (12 ounces) frozen pineapple chunks, thawed
1 package (8 ounces) cream cheese
2 tablespoons butter or margarine
1 cup all-purpose biscuit mix
½ cup sugar
2 tablespoons cornstarch
¼ teaspoon salt
¼ cup lemon juice
¼ teaspoon grated lemon peel
1 pint strawberries, rinsed and halved
1 bunch seedless grapes (about 1½ cups)

1. Drain apricots, reserving syrup. Drain pineapple chunks, reserving syrup. Set all aside.

2. To make crust, cut 3 ounces cream cheese (reserve remaining 5 ounces for use in cream cheese spread) and butter into biscuit mix until mixture resembles coarse crumbs; with hands form into a ball. Pat out dough on a lightly greased 12-inch pizza pan; flute edge. (Crust will be very thin.) Bake in a 425°F oven for about 8 minutes, or until crust is lightly browned; cool.

3. To make glaze, combine in a small saucepan ¼ cup sugar, cornstarch, and salt. Add 1 cup reserved apricot syrup, ½ cup reserved pineapple syrup, and lemon juice. Cook over medium-high heat, stirring constantly, until mixture thickens and begins to boil. Boil and stir 1 minute; cool.

4. To make cream cheese spread, stir remaining cream cheese, 2 tablespoons reserved apricot syrup, remaining ¼ cup of the sugar, and lemon peel until smooth; spread on cooled crust.

5. To assemble pie, arrange fruits in circles on cream cheese spread as follows: Place apricots around outer edge of pie, overlapping slightly. Next, make circle of halved strawberries, then circle of grapes, finally a circle of pineapple chunks. Arrange 3 apricot halves in center of pie. Brush some of the glaze over fruits. Cut pie into wedges; serve with remaining glaze mixture.

10 to 12 servings

WASHINGTON

To the bands in covered wagons who made the trip cross-country, the coastal area of Washington must have looked like the Promised Land. After roughing it over frigid mountains, they were rewarded with a lush coastline, set in a moderate year-round climate.

Yet not all of Washington is so verdant. East of the Cascade Mountain Range the land is parched, with some sections getting as little as seven inches of rainfall in a year. The Cascades form a natural barrier, keeping the moisture on the coast and leaving the inland dry.

The Yakima area, east of the Cascades, is desertlike, except for areas that have been irrigated. Almost half of the nation's pears are grown here, and a quarter of the apples. Peaches, apricots, plums, cherries, and nuts all spill from the state's cornucopia.

But even larger than the fruit production is Washington's wheat crop; it can be grown without irrigation. The central part of the state is wheat country.

Grapes for wine production have long been grown in the Puget Sound area. These are from the *Vitis labrusca* stock that produces wine of the sweet, red kosher type. A newer undertaking is the planting of *Vitis*

vinifera vines of European origin. The resulting wines are like those of the famous continental varieties.

In the early days, beef jerky and sourdough bread were common among the rations of the Washington pioneer. Today, the outdoorsman has replaced the pioneer, but his need for lightweight, high-energy food is much the same.

Washington's natural attractions of seacoast and mountains make the state popular with vacationers. Skiiers, skippers of small craft, and campers can enjoy their sports many months of the year.

The fishing is great in Washington, both for sportsmen and as an occupation. Salmon, oysters, crabs, shrimp, halibut, and many other fish and shellfish abound.

The town of Dungeness, for which the

WASHINGTON

famous crabs are named, spreads over a point in the Juan de Fuca Strait. Powerboats ply the coastal waters for the crabs, but sportsmen go after them with long-handled nets, raking the ocean bottom at low ebb.

But Washington has its urban side, too. Seattle, Spokane, and Tacoma are all major cities. Orientals, Scandinavians, Mexicans, and Europeans contribute to their population and influence the cooking style.

In Seattle, a famous Japanese restaurant is the Bush Garden. Guests leave shoes at the door, Japanese fashion, and enjoy a quiet silk-and-bamboo setting. Sukiyaki, pre-

pared at the table by a gracious Japanese cook, is an experience not to be missed.

Seattle also has its own version of Fisherman's Wharf, where the many-splendored catch is served in a variety of ways. Its oldest eatery is Ivar's Acres of Clams. Ivar Haglund offers a spectacular array of fish in addition to the clams for which he is famed. A favorite is Baked Fillet of King Salmon, Ivar Style.

The cities offer a selection of continental fare, too. Restaurant menus list dishes that combine sophistication with the natural bounty of the Northwest.

Mr. Seko's Sukiyaki

1 cup soy sauce
1 cup water
½ cup sake (rice wine)
3 tablespoons sugar
1 can (5 ounces) bamboo
shoots
4 cups green onion,
including tops, cut in
1½-inch lengths
3 large dry onions, sliced
2½ pounds sukiyaki beef
strips (beef slices ⅛
inch thick from the
"eye" of prime rib)

1. Combine soy sauce, water, sake, and sugar. Mix well and set aside.
2. In a large frying pan, place bamboo shoots, green onion, and dry onion. Spread meat over vegetables evenly. Pour on enough sauce so the meat and vegetables are half submerged.
3. Bring to boiling, lower heat, and simmer uncovered until meat is almost done (about 3 minutes). Mix contents of frying pan and remove from heat.
4. Allow to stand 3 to 5 minutes before serving. Serve over hot fluffy **rice**.

8 servings

Note: If desired, drain 1 can shirataki (yam threads) and add to frying pan along with bamboo shoots.

Barbecued Lamb

6- pound lamb leg
1 teaspoon ginger (ground)
1 teaspoon dry mustard
Salt and pepper
Flour
2 onions, sliced
1 clove garlic
2 tablespoons chili sauce
1 tablespoon Worcestershire
sauce
1 tablespoon vinegar
2 tablespoons olive oil
1 cup boiling water

1. Rub lamb with mixture of spices; dredge with flour.
2. Place lamb in a baking pan, surround with sliced onion, and add garlic.
3. Bake at 325°F 25 to 30 minutes per pound, or until the internal temperature is 170°F.
4. Meanwhile, mix remaining ingredients. Baste every 15 minutes with sauce.

12 servings

Pork Chops en Casserole

6 lean pork chops
2 onions, sliced
2 tomatoes, sliced
2 green peppers, sliced
½ cup uncooked rice
2 teaspoons salt
¼ teaspoon pepper
½ cup boiling water

1. Sear the chops on both sides in hot skillet.
2. Place chops in a casserole or baking dish with cover. On each chop arrange in this order the following: 1 slice of onion, 1 slice of tomato, a ring of green pepper. Fill the pepper ring with rice. Season and add water. Cover tightly.
3. Bake at 350°F 1½ hours.

6 servings

Boiled Dungeness Crabs

3 live Dungeness crabs
8 quarts boiling water
½ cup salt
   Butter or margarine,
      melted, or mayonnaise

1. Dress crabs by inserting a table knife under the back of the top shell and prying it off. Remove spongy parts under shell (gills, stomach, and intestines) and wash body cavity.
2. Place in boiling salted water. Cover and return to boiling point. Simmer for 15 minutes. Drain.
3. Crack the claws and legs. Serve hot with butter, or chill and serve with mayonnaise.

6 servings

Baked Fillet of King Salmon, Ivar Style

4 slices bacon, diced
1½ cups diced celery
1½ cups diced onion
½ teaspoon sage
1 loaf (16 ounces) bread,
   2 or 3 days old
3 eggs, beaten
⅛ teaspoon salt
⅛ teaspoon pepper
1 cup chicken stock
½ cup dry white wine
⅓ cup fresh lemon juice
⅓ cup dry white wine
⅓ cup butter or margarine,
   melted
8 salmon fillets or steaks
2 lemons, quartered

1. Fry bacon until brown and crisp; remove from pan. Add celery, onion, and sage to bacon drippings. Sauté vegetables until golden brown (about 10 minutes).
2. Tear bread into bite-size crumbs. Combine with bacon, vegetables, and bacon drippings, mixing well.
3. Combine eggs, salt, pepper, chicken stock, and ½ cup wine. Stir into the crumb mixture. Spoon dressing into a 13×9-inch baking pan.
4. Combine lemon juice, ⅓ cup wine, and butter. Dip fillets in sauce and arrange on top of dressing.
5. Bake uncovered at 350°F 25 to 30 minutes, or until fish is tender, basting frequently with lemon sauce. Spoon any remaining sauce over fillets just before serving. Serve with quartered lemons.

8 servings

WASHINGTON

WASHINGTON

Oriental Barbecued Chicken

As in other West Coast states, Orientals have made important contributions to local cooking.

1 broiler-fryer chicken
   (2½ to 3 pounds), cut
   in serving-size pieces
½ cup soy sauce
¼ cup sugar
1½ teaspoons ginger
   Few grains paprika
1 clove garlic, minced; or
   crushed in garlic press
8 slices bacon

1. Rinse chicken pieces and drain on absorbent paper.
2. Mix together in a large, shallow dish soy sauce, sugar, ginger, paprika, and garlic.
3. Turn chicken pieces in the soy-sauce marinade. Cover and refrigerate several hours or overnight, turning pieces occasionally. Remove chicken from marinade. (Reserve marinade for basting.)
4. Wrap each chicken piece with a bacon slice. Secure slices with wooden picks. Place chicken pieces in a large, shallow baking dish.
5. Bake at 350°F 1½ hours, frequently turning pieces and basting with reserved marinade, or until thickest pieces of chicken are tender when pierced with a fork.

4 servings

Apple-Covered Ham in Claret

2 smoked ham center
   slices, fully cooked,
   about ¾ inch thick
   (about ½ pound each)
   or 1 large center cut,
   1½ inches thick
½ teaspoon dry mustard
3 to 4 medium Golden
   Delicious apples, cored
   and cut in rings
4 orange slices
¾ cup dry red wine, such as
   claret
½ cup packed brown sugar
   Parsley sprigs

1. Place ham slices in a large, shallow baking dish. Sprinkle each slice with ¼ teaspoon mustard.
2. Cut unpared apple rings in half and place around outer edge of ham, slightly overlapping slices.
3. Place two orange slices in center of each ham slice.
4. Pour wine over top of ham and fruit. Then sprinkle brown sugar over all.
5. Cover; cook in a 350°F oven 45 minutes. Serve on platter or from baking dish, and garnish with parsley.

6 to 8 servings

Herbed Carrots with Grapes

1½ pounds carrots
½ teaspoon salt
1 teaspoon basil
½ cup butter or margarine
1 small clove garlic,
   minced
½ teaspoon thyme
¼ teaspoon celery salt
1 cup seedless grapes

1. Wash and pare carrots; cut in 3×¼-inch strips. Put into a saucepan; add the ½ teaspoon salt, basil, and enough **boiling water** to almost cover. Cook covered 12 to 15 minutes, or until carrots are crisp-tender.
2. Meanwhile, melt butter and add garlic, thyme, and celery salt. Set aside.
3. When carrots are cooked, remove from heat immediately. Add grapes and let stand covered 1 to 2 minutes; drain off liquid.

1 tablespoon lemon juice
⅛ teaspoon salt
Few grains pepper

4. Stir lemon juice into garlic butter and pour over hot carrots. Season with salt and pepper; toss mixture gently.

6 to 8 servings

Make-Ahead Mashed Potatoes

5 pounds potatoes (about 10 medium), pared
½ cup margarine
2 packages (3 ounces each) cream cheese, softened
1 cup dairy sour cream
4 ounces extra sharp Cheddar cheese, shredded (optional)
½ cup grated Parmesan cheese
4 green onions, chopped
1 tablespoon salt
1 teaspoon pepper

1. Cook potatoes until tender. Mash or rice while hot. Add remaining ingredients and beat well. Turn into a 3-quart greased casserole. Cover and store in refrigerator up to 2 weeks.
2. Remove casserole from refrigerator 1 hour before baking. If desired, fluff up potatoes with a little **milk.**
3. Bake uncovered at 350°F 45 minutes, or until heated through.

10 to 12 servings

Spinach-Mushroom Salad

1 bag (10 ounces) fresh spinach
6 slices bacon
1 box (5 ounces) fresh mushrooms
1 bunch green onions (6 to 8)
½ cup salad oil
2 tablespoons lemon juice or wine vinegar
1 clove garlic, minced
1 teaspoon salt
½ teaspoon dry mustard
¼ teaspoon sugar
¼ teaspoon pepper
1 egg yolk

1. Wash spinach and pat dry on absorbent paper; discard stems. Chill until serving time.
2. Fry bacon until crisp and remove to absorbent paper to drain; crumble.
3. Clean mushrooms; slice lengthwise through caps and stems.
4. Clean green onions; chop onions, using some of the green tops for color.
5. For dressing, put remaining ingredients into an electric blender and run on medium speed until well blended.
6. At serving time, combine spinach, mushrooms, onion, and bacon in a salad bowl. Add dressing and toss.

6 servings

WASHINGTON

Wine Fruit Compote

1 can (16 ounces) pear
    halves
1 can (16 ounces) cling
    peach halves
1 can (13½ ounces)
    pineapple chunks
½ lemon, thinly sliced and
    quartered
2 cups fruit juices and
    water
5 whole cloves
1 stick cinnamon
1 package (3 ounces)
    strawberry-flavored
    gelatin
2 teaspoons lemon juice
1 cup cherry kijafa wine

1. Drain fruit and reserve juice. Arrange fruit in a shallow 1½-quart dish. Scatter lemon slices over top.
2. Combine juices from fruit and water, cloves, and cinnamon in a saucepan. Heat to boiling. Simmer for 5 minutes. Strain.
3. Dissolve gelatin in the hot liquid. Add lemon juice and cherry wine. Pour over fruit. Chill 1 to 1½ hours, or until gelatin is only partly set. Baste fruit occasionally with gelatin mixture while chilling.

6 to 8 servings

Apple Candy

8 medium apples, cored
    and pared
¼ cup cold water
2 cups firmly packed light
    brown sugar
2 tablespoons unflavored
    gelatin
½ cup cold water
1 cup chopped walnuts
1 tablespoon lemon juice
½ cup confectioners' sugar
1 tablespoon cornstarch

1. Cut apples into small pieces. Add ¼ cup water.
2. Cook until tender; put through food mill or sieve and add sugar. Cook over medium heat until thick (about ½ hour), stirring frequently.
3. Soften gelatin in ½ cup water and add to hot mixture; stir until dissolved.
4. Chill until slightly thickened; stir in nuts and lemon juice.
5. Pour into a pan to a depth of about ½ inch. Chill until firm. Cut into squares.
6. Combine confectioners' sugar and cornstarch. Coat squares with mixture.

The "purple mountains' majesty and amber waves of grain" that help make America the Beautiful are spectacular in Wyoming. Even with the occasional golden arch and hamburger palace that mark the modern highway, beauty is still a natural resource in this state.

In its early days, Wyoming was home to a number of Indian tribes, including the Cheyenne for whom the state capital is named. The Lewis and Clark expedition passed through Wyoming, but there were no pioneer settlements until the 1830s.

The entry of the Union Pacific Railroad into the Wyoming Territory brought increasing numbers of settlers. Cities sprang up along the path of the rails; Cheyenne, Laramie, Rawlins, and others grew, especially after gold was discovered in 1870.

Cattlemen followed the prospectors, grazing their herds on the open land. As farmers moved in, tension grew between those who fenced in the land and those seeking open pasture. Their battles, as well as those with the Indians, have been recorded in numerous sagas of the West. Eventually, smaller farmers who raised both cattle and feed supplanted the big cattlemen, and the day of the open range was gone.

Today, the natural beauty of the state is among its leading attractions, drawing many visitors from other parts of the nation. Yellowstone Park in the northwest is famed for wonders such as Old Faithful, the geyser that performs on schedule. South of Yellowstone is the Grand Teton National Park.

Many pageants and rodeos are held in Wyoming each year, including the famous Frontier Days at Frontier Park in Cheyenne, and Jubilee Days at Laramie. Visitors are invited to sample the local fare, mainly of the "meat and potatoes" variety.

While the dry climate of the state is well suited to tourism, it makes farming difficult. Ninety percent of the state's agricultural

WYOMING

area is devoted to cattle and sheep raising. The local preference is for beef; much of the sheep is shipped to eastern markets.

On the remaining cropland, wheat, sugar beets, beans, barley, oats, corn, and potatoes are grown. As one use for its plentiful wheat, natives are getting acquainted with bulgur, a wheat product popular in the Mideastern countries. Bulgur and Corn Soup uses two of Wyoming's leading products in a form that has wide appeal.

Many of Wyoming's visitors like to combine hunting with their sightseeing. Pheas-

ant and wild ducks both offer sophisticated eating after a day of outdoorsmanship.

Those who visit Wyoming in a camper during the summer—and their numbers are mounting—like to cook *alfresco,* not losing a moment of the gorgeous scenery. They are enthusiastic users of such recipes as beef kabobs cooked on the grill.

Petite Marmite is a recipe that makes good use of both beef and chicken in a soup with French overtones. There is a growing interest in foreign cookery in Wyoming, common to creative cooks everywhere.

Petite Marmite

3 pounds beef brisket
1 frying chicken, cut up
3 quarts beef stock
1 tablespoon salt
2 carrots, sliced
2 celery stalks, cubed
2 white turnips, pared and cubed
2 onions, sliced
1 marrow bone, cut in 1-inch lengths
1 cup grated Gruyère cheese

1. Place beef brisket and chicken in a large soup kettle; add beef stock and stir in salt. Bring to boiling, skim surface, reduce heat, and simmer 2 hours.
2. Add carrots, celery, turnips, and onions to soup pot. Simmer 1 hour, skimming occasionally.
3. Place marrow bone in a separate saucepan, and cover with cold water. Bring to boiling, remove from heat, and let stand in water. Remove bones from water, and remove marrow from bones.
4. When ready to serve, remove the meat and vegetables from the soup, and place on serving platter.
5. Serve broth topped with bone marrow and grated Gruyère cheese.

6 to 8 servings

Corn and Bulgur Soup

2 tablespoons oil
2 cloves garlic, minced
1 cup uncooked bulgur
½ cup nonfat dry milk solids
2 cups water
2 cans (17 ounces each) cream-style corn
5 cups chicken broth
1 teaspoon salt
⅛ teaspoon black pepper
¼ cup chopped green pepper

1. Heat oil in a large saucepan or Dutch oven. Sauté garlic until golden. Add bulgur and blend well. Add rest of ingredients and mix thoroughly.
2. Bring to boiling, lower heat, and simmer, covered, 25 minutes.

6 servings

Fruit-a-Plenty Pie, 296

WYOMING

Barbecued Beef Chuck Steak

1 beef chuck steak (1½
    pounds), 1½ inches
    thick
½ cup chutney
3 tablespoons lemon juice
⅓ cup ketchup
    Salt and pepper

1. Trim fat from edges of beef. Put steak into a shallow pan.
2. Combine chutney, lemon juice, and ketchup in an electric blender; blend until smooth.
3. Pour chutney mixture over steak. Turn to coat both sides. Allow to stand an hour or longer.
4. Drain steak well and reserve marinade.
5. Grill steak over charcoal, sprinkling with salt and pepper. Grill 10 minutes on each side, or until a small cut near the center of steak shows the color you desire.
6. Heat remaining marinade and serve as sauce. Slice steak in diagonal strips to serve.

4 servings

Corned Beef

6-pound beef brisket
    corned, boneless
2 teaspoons whole cloves
½ cup firmly packed light
    brown sugar
¼ cup sherry

1. Put the meat into a saucepot and add enough water to cover meat. Cover saucepot lightly and bring water just to boiling over high heat. Reduce heat and simmer about 4 hours, or until meat is almost tender when pierced with a fork.
2. Remove from heat and cool in liquid; refrigerate overnight.
3. Remove meat from liquid and set on rack in roasting pan. Stud with cloves. Put brown sugar over top and press firmly.
4. Roast at 325°F 1½ hours. After roasting 30 minutes, drizzle with sherry.
5. To serve, carve meat into slices.

About 12 servings

Lamb Chops Mint Julep

2 teaspoons dried mint
4 lamb double loin chops
½ teaspoon salt
¼ teaspoon pepper
2 teaspoons butter
4 canned pineapple slices
    Bourbon whiskey

1. Press mint into surface of lamb chop. Season with salt and pepper.
2. Broil 3 to 4 inches from source of heat, about 8 minutes on each side (broiling time depends upon how well done you want the chops).
3. About 5 minutes before chops are done, heat butter in an electric skillet or large chafing dish. Add pineapple slices and brown lightly on each side. (Or brown pineapple on foil under broiler.) Put pineapple slices on lamb chops. Sprinkle with desired amount of whiskey; ignite and serve.

4 servings

Apple-Covered Ham in Claret, 300

WYOMING

Roast Leg of Lamb, Jardinière

6-pound lamb leg
Salt and pepper
1 clove garlic (optional)
2 small heads cooked
    cauliflower
16 stalks cooked asparagus
8 artichoke bottoms, filled
    with small green peas,
    heated
8 sugar-glazed cooked new
    potatoes
8 mint-glazed cooked
    carrots (page 307)
Parsley sprig garnish
Hollandaise Sauce

1. Season lamb with salt and pepper; rub with a clove of garlic if you wish. Place the leg, fat side up, on rack in a shallow roasting pan. Insert meat thermometer in fleshy part, away from bone or fat.
2. Roast uncovered in a 300°–325°F oven until meat thermometer reaches 140°F for rare, 160°F for medium-done, 180°F for well-done. Or allow 25 to 30 minutes per pound for roasting medium-done. Remove lamb to a heated, extra-large platter and allow to stand 10 minutes.
3. Meanwhile, arrange on platter 2 small cooked cauliflower heads, cooked asparagus, artichoke bottoms with peas, sugar-glazed new potatoes, mint-glazed carrots, all heated, and a few sprigs of parsley as garnish. Vegetables should be piping hot, accompanied by a sauceboat of Hollandaise Sauce for the cauliflower, asparagus, artichoke-peas.

8 servings

Chicken Breasts with Noodles

8 whole chicken breasts,
    flattened
Salt and pepper to taste
Dash of crushed
    marjoram
Butter to cover skillet
3 pounds fresh mushrooms
½ pound butter
12 ounces noodles
2 tablespoons butter
2 cups Medium White
    Sauce (page 43)
1 cup cold milk
1 cup chicken stock
Hollandaise Sauce (page
    307)
½ cup dry white wine
Parmesan cheese, grated

1. Season chicken breasts with salt, pepper, and marjoram. Sauté in butter until breasts are fully cooked.
2. While chicken is cooking, wash mushrooms and cut into small pieces, then sauté in ½ pound of butter.
3. Cook noodles until done; drain and work 2 tablespoons of butter gently into the noodles.
4. Make 2 cups of basic white sauce; add to it the cold milk and chicken stock. Cook mixture until thickened. Reserve while making Hollandaise Sauce.
5. Carefully blend hollandaise with the white sauce mixture; stir in dry white wine.
6. Butter a small, covered roasting pan. Place noodles in bottom; add the mushrooms and place chicken breasts on top of the mushrooms. Pour the sauce over all.
7. Set in a 325°F oven about 45 minutes, or until thoroughly heated. Remove from oven, sprinkle with grated Parmesan cheese, and place under broiler to brown.

8 servings

Note: This recipe may be increased to include 12 chicken breasts without changing the other ingredients.

Hollandaise Sauce

2 egg yolks
2 tablespoons cream
¼ teaspoon salt
  Few grains cayenne
    pepper
2 tablespoons lemon juice
    or tarragon vinegar
½ cup butter

1. In the top of a double boiler, beat egg yolks, cream, salt, and cayenne pepper until thick with a whisk beater. Set over hot (not boiling) water. (Bottom of double-boiler top should not touch water.)
2. Add the lemon juice gradually, while beating constantly. Cook, beating constantly with the whisk beater, until sauce is the consistency of thick cream. Remove double boiler from heat, leaving top in place.
3. Beating constantly, add the butter, ½ teaspoon at a time. Beat with whisk beater until butter is melted and thoroughly blended in.

About 1 cup

Note: If necessary, the sauce may be kept hot 15 to 30 minutes over hot water. Keep covered and stir occasionally.

Roast Wild Ducks

3 wild ducks, about 2
    pounds each
  Salt
  Raisin-Orange Stuffing
6 slices bacon, cut in halves
1 cup orange juice
  Orange Sauce

1. Singe and clean ducks. Cut out oil sac at base of tail; cut off neck at body, leaving on neck skin. Wash ducks under cold running water; dry.
2. Rub cavities with salt. Lightly stuff the cavities with Raisin-Orange Stuffing.
3. Place ducks, breast side up, on rack in a shallow roasting pan. Lay four bacon pieces over breast of each bird.
4. Roast, uncovered, in a 450°F oven 15 minutes for very rare, 20 minutes for medium rare, and 25 minutes for medium well. Baste ducks occasionally with orange juice during roasting.
5. Place ducks on heated platter; reserve drippings for Orange Sauce to serve over ducks.

6 servings

Orange Sauce

2 tablespoons fat in
    roasting pan
3 tablespoons flour
½ cup water
⅔ cup orange juice
½ teaspoon grated orange
    peel
½ teaspoon grated lemon
    peel

1. Heat the fat in roasting pan. Add flour and stir until smooth. Add the water gradually, stirring constantly. Continue to stir, bring to boiling, and cook 1 to 2 minutes. Blend in the orange juice and heat to boiling.
2. Serve sauce topped with the grated peel.

About 1¼ cups sauce

WYOMING

Raisin-Orange Stuffing

6 cups ¼-inch bread cubes
   (slightly dry)
1 cup seedless raisins
½ cup chopped onion
1 cup thinly sliced celery
½ cup butter
1 tablespoon grated orange
   peel
1 teaspoon salt
½ teaspoon ground thyme
   Few grains black pepper

1. Combine bread cubes and raisins in a large bowl.
2. Sauté onion and celery in butter. Mix in orange peel and seasonings. Add to bread mixture and toss until well mixed.
3. Spoon lightly into birds.

Stuffing for three 2-pound ducks

Sweet-Sour Beans in Tomato Shells

⅓ cup cider vinegar
2½ tablespoons dark brown
   sugar
½ teaspoon salt
1 can (16 ounces)
   diagonally sliced
   green beans, drained
1 tablespoon finely
   chopped onion
6 tomato shells, chilled
1 tablespoon basil,
   crushed

1. Pour a mixture of the vinegar, brown sugar, and salt over the beans and onion in a bowl; toss lightly. Set in refrigerator to marinate 1 hour, tossing occasionally.
2. Sprinkle the inside of each tomato shell with salt and crushed basil. Spoon beans equally into tomato shells. Garnish with crisp **bacon curls.**

6 servings

Zucchini Bread

3 eggs
2 cups sugar
1 cup salad oil
2 cups grated pared
   zucchini
1 tablespoon vanilla extract
3 cups sifted all-purpose
   flour
1 teaspoon baking soda
½ teaspoon baking powder
1 teaspoon salt
1 tablespoon cinnamon
½ cup chopped walnuts
½ cup snipped dates

1. Beat eggs well; add sugar, oil, zucchini, and vanilla extract and mix well.
2. Sift flour, baking soda, baking powder, salt, and cinnamon together. Add dry ingredients, nuts, and dates to egg mixture; mix well.
3. Divide batter in 2 greased and floured 9×5×3-inch loaf pans.
4. Bake at 325°F 1 hour.

2 loaves bread

INDEX